86t

D0636816

CHARLES OF ORLEANS

By the Same Author

BIOGRAPHY
Héloïse

TRANSLATIONS
Of Colette
Creatures Great and Small
My Mother's House *and* Sido
The Vagabond
Break of Day

Of Maurice Goudeket
Close to Colette

Of Jules Supervielle
Stories in 'Selected Writings'

CHARLES OF ORLEANS

Prince and Poet

Enid McLeod

1969
CHATTO & WINDUS
LONDON

PUBLISHED BY
CHATTO & WINDUS LTD
40 WILLIAM IV STREET
LONDON W.C.2

*

CLARKE, IRWIN & CO. LTD
TORONTO

SBN 7011 1315 4

PRINTED IN GREAT BRITAIN BY
R. & R. CLARK LIMITED
EDINBURGH

Contents

Introduction   *page* vii
Note on the Poetry   xi
Note on Coinage   xiv
Note on Primary Sources   xvi

PART ONE

Prologue   1389   3
Chapter I   1390–1394   10
Chapter II   1395–1407   16
Chapter III   November 23, 1407–December 8, 1408   33
Chapter IV   January 1409–December 1410   51
Chapter V   January 1411–November 1412   67
Chapter VI   Winter 1413–Winter 1415   89

PART TWO

Chapter VII   January 1415–November 1415   113
Chapter VIII December 1415–August 1422   134
Chapter IX   1422–1429   159
Chapter X   1430–1432   177
Chapter XI   1432–1436   186
Chapter XII   1436–1440   218

PART THREE

Chapter XIII 1440–1444   247
Chapter XIV   1444–1449   271
Chapter XV   1450–1460   291
Chapter XVI   1453–1465   324
Epilogue   345
Appendix I   347
Appendix II   351
Appendix III   354
Notes   358
Bibliography   391
Index   399

Illustrations

1 Honoré Bonet presents a copy of his poem *L'Apparicion de maistre Jehan de Meun* to Valentina. Bibliothèque Nationale *Mss. fr.* 811, fol. IV   *facing page* 12

2 (a) Charles of Orleans and his two younger brothers receiving instruction. From a manuscript of Sallust's *Jugurtha*, Bibliothèque Nationale *Mss. lat.* 5747, fol. 1

2 (b) The first known signature of Charles of Orleans, on a treaty with the Duke of Brittany dated 1408. Bibliothèque Nationale *Mss. fr. nouv. acq.* 6525

2 (c) A signature on a document of 1438, for comparison. British Museum *Add. Ch.* 12003

2 (d) A *chantepleure*. Bibliothèque Nationale *Mss. fr.* 25528, fol. 1   44

3 A bust of Louis of Orleans, from a tomb in the Musée Calvet, Avignon   76

4 John the Fearless, Duke of Burgundy, by an unknown painter of the French school, in the Musée de Besançon   108

5 The Bastard of Orleans, Count of Dunois, a statue in the castle of Châteaudun   172

6 Philip the Good, portrait by R. Van der Weyden, at Bruges   204

7 Isabella Duchess of Burgundy, a portrait of the Flemish School, in the Louvre   300

8 The *Lit de Justice* trying the Duke of Alençon at Vendôme in 1458. Illustration by Jean Fouquet in a manuscript of Boccaccio's *De Casibus* etc. at Munich   332

Charles of Orleans' coat of arms on the cover is reproduced from Mss. lat. 458, fol. 249, in the Bibliothèque Nationale, by kind permission of M. Marcel Thomas, Conservateur en Chef of the Cabinet des Manuscrits.

Introduction

POSTERITY has been strangely neglectful of Charles of Orleans. As a youth he played a far more important part in the political and military life of his country than fell to the lot of most princes still in their teens; a part as much inspired by his desire for the good of the realm as by his wish to avenge the murder of his father. And as a mature man he strove with single-minded devotion to make a peace with England that should allow France to regain her long-lost prosperity, and free his fellow-countrymen from the miseries of the Hundred Years War. The chroniclers of his own days were well aware of these actions and gave him due credit for them. Despite this, nearly all later French historians—and English ones too—have passed over him in silence, or at best mention him merely as one among the group of princes who were his allies. It almost seems as if their knowledge that he was also a poet inclines them not to take his other capacities seriously.

One slight possible reason for this neglect, or unawareness, of Charles as an important figure is that we have no idea what he looked like. For, unlike his chief enemy John the Fearless, Duke of Burgundy, and his friend, John's son Philip the Good, whose faces are so familiar from the many representations of them, Charles never had his portrait painted.* This omission, in the case of one so close to the throne, and in an age when portraiture, in France, England and Italy, was beginning to be a notable art, was typical of him; for unlike his Burgundian cousins he was not given to the sumptuous adornment of his castles with works of art, or to any form of self-glorification. And as far as we know, he took no interest in painting or any plastic art other than that which was concerned with the writing and illuminating of beautiful manuscripts.

But although his aspect has not been recorded, he left behind a speaking likeness of his essential self in poems that clothe his thoughts and moods in such direct and simple words that, unlike the work of

* A well-known tapestry in the Musée des Arts Décoratifs, depicting a knight and lady in fourteenth-century costume, is widely supposed to represent Charles and his third wife Mary of Cleves. But there are no gounds for this supposition.

some of his contemporaries, they can be read to-day with no effort and bring him before us in his habit as he lived; poems moreover that most modern critics, French and English, now agree have few rivals in French literature for grace, harmony and felicity of expression.

It is therefore all the more strange that, until comparatively recent times, posterity should also have neglected Charles of Orleans as a poet. The fact that during his lifetime his poetry was known and appreciated only by a restricted circle is understandable enough, at a time when the art of printing had not yet been invented and the manuscripts of his work were few in number, since he wrote chiefly for his own pleasure and that of his friends and took no pains to obtain a wider audience. But that neither his own son, Louis XII, nor his great-nephew, François I, seems to have been aware of his quality or taken any steps to make known that considerable body of more than six hundred poems, seems incredible; especially as François I charged Clément Marot with the task of publishing the poems of Villon who, as a poet, for all that his range of subject and vocabulary were wider than those of Charles, was not necessarily a greater poet.

The inability of a man's own family to recognise his gifts is perhaps no uncommon thing. More difficult to understand is the fact that, except for one or two lesser poets at the beginning of the fifteenth century who plagiarised his work, Charles of Orleans had to wait for three centuries after his death before the literary world of France began to be aware that in him they had one of the rarest poets of the Middle Ages. The first to draw their attention to this was the Abbé Sallier who, in 1740, published in the *Mémoires de l'Académie Royale des Inscriptions et Belles-Lettres*, some of the poems which he had discovered in one of the manuscripts of them in the Bibliothèque du Roi. But it was not until the nineteenth century that Charles of Orleans and his work became a subject for serious study. Various editions of the poems then appeared (for the titles of which, as of all other books mentioned here, see Bibliography), not always complete and based on different manuscripts. These were all preceded by short historical introductions which, although they often contained inaccurate statements, did at last do something to restore Charles to his rightful place as prince and poet. This place was further stressed by Champollion-Figeac in his *Louis et Charles, ducs d'Orléans, leur influence sur les arts, la littérature et l'esprit de leur siècle*. The culmination of these studies was reached over a period of twelve years:

first when, in 1911, Pierre Champion published his *Vie de Charles d'Orléans*, a volume now rather old-fashioned and made unnecessarily long by repetitions, but invaluable to subsequent scholars for its unearthing of the contemporary documents on the life and times of his subject. And secondly when, in 1923 and 1924, he followed this with his edition of the poems, based on the duke's own manuscript of them, which Champion had been the first to identify; an edition which remains the standard one.

In France these two major contributions, together with a few monographs by Champion on different aspects of Charles' interests, seem to have put an end for the time being to further work on the poet and his verse, except for one small but excellent study by Jacques Charpier and some research on the manuscripts (see Appendix I). As a result, although selections from the poetry (nearly always the same) continue to appear in anthologies, and although the poet has his fervent admirers in his own country, his life and work in general remain largely unknown, especially as Champion's biography has long been out of print.

In England also the poems of Charles were virtually ignored for the first four centuries after his death, in spite of the fact that a superb manuscript of them was made for Henry VII in 1500. This large volume, on vellum, which is now in the British Museum (Reg.16.F.ii), is chiefly known for one of its beautiful illustrations, frequently reproduced, depicting Charles writing in the Tower of London, and being greeted as he leaves it. There is no evidence as to whether the king or anyone else ever looked at the text, and it was not until the nineteenth century that any critic was aware of the author. Then, the attention of Robert Louis Stevenson was drawn to him by one of the French nineteenth-century editions of the poems, and as early as 1882 Stevenson devoted one of his *Familiar Studies of Men and Books* to the life and work of Charles, of whom as a man he obviously had no great opinion but of whose poetry he says some perceptive things. Hilaire Belloc, too, in his *Avril* (1904) praised him as the first representative of what he calls the 'long glory' of the French poets of the Renaissance. Since then, although there have been occasional translations of some of the poems and some academic studies on different aspects of the poetry (see Appendix II), little has been written about Charles. A few monographs, chiefly on the poetry, have recently appeared in Italy and America. A romantic life by

N. L. Goodrich came out in America in 1963. But no biography of the poet has yet been published in this country.

In attempting to fill that gap it has not been in any way my aim to study the poetry critically, either in itself or in relation to the work of the other poets of the time. I have used it rather to help portray the character of its author and to illuminate his life. To that end I have made my own assumptions both as to the periods of his life when the poems were written, and as to the identity, or identities, of the women to whom the love poems were addressed. These assumptions are in part in agreement with the views of Champion, but not with those of some later English critics, whose theories and methods are discussed in Appendix II. These are questions that will admit of no definitive answers unless more evidence comes to light than we at present possess. Charles himself has afforded no help with either, partly by his decision, in the last decade of his life, to have his poems copied in his personal manuscript, grouped according to their form–*ballades*, *rondeaux*, *chansons* etc.–rather than chronologically; and partly by his discretion in refraining from naming the women who were the inspiration of some of them. Much therefore must depend on internal evidence, and on a full knowledge of the life of this most human prince, which it has been my main aim to provide.

I should like here to express my warm thanks to Alethea Hayter, who first suggested to me that the life of Charles of Orleans might be a subject well worth studying by someone who, like myself, is interested in the historic links between France and England, and to Charles and Enid de Winton for their hospitality during my researches in Paris, and other kindnesses. But most of all to Ethel Whitehorn, whose unflagging interest and constant encouragement have sustained me through six years of research.

Autumn, 1968   E. McL.

Note on the Poetry

SINCE lyric poetry loses everything in a prose translation, and as I am not capable of a poetic one, I have kept the poems quoted in their original tongue and have not modernised the old French, as to do so sometimes destroys a rhyme.

However, the vocabulary of Charles of Orleans contains so few obsolete words that anyone with a moderate knowledge of French should experience no difficulty in understanding his poetry. To assist this understanding I give below a short glossary (covering only the poems quoted) which includes not only the obsolete words but some that are still current but unusual, or which possessed an ancient meaning now dropped. I have also added to the list one or two words where the slight difference of the old spelling may at first be puzzling. In all cases I have given the English translation, and wherever possible the modern French spelling, or form.

	ENGLISH TRANSLATION	MODERN FRENCH FORM
Aucunement	sometimes	
(Non aucunement)	never	
Au derrain	in the end, finally	
Au par aler, or aller	previously	auparavant
Bobo	red blotches (now more usually sore places)	bobo
Bouter	to put, drive out	
S'y bouter	to put one's mind to	
Chiere, or chierre	cheer, good cheer	chère
(belle chiere, or	welcome, kind welcome	bonne chère
a lye chiere)	joyful reception	chère lie
Contre (as musical term)	counter-tenor	
Courage	heart, will, desire	
Cuider	to think	cuider

Destourber	to dissuade or prevent	détourner
Dont	whence	d'où
Embres, enpres	close to	auprès de
Estrener	to give a present, a New Year's gift	étrenner
Faindre	to betray, to feign	feindre
Fauldre	to fail when needed	
Gent	(1) people, or the race (2) gentle, tender	gent (rare) gent
Grever	to annoy or encumber	grever
Lie, lye	gay, joyful	lie, but only in faire chère lie
Liesse, lyesse	gaiety, joy	liesse
Mie	not at all	mie (but rare)
Mirlifiques	trifles, or (ironically) marvels	
Montjoye	a great quantity	mont-joie, a cairn or heap of stones
Musser	to hide	
Nonchaloir	pleasant indifference, not caring, happy resignation	nonchaloir
Non pour tant	nevertheless	pourtant
Oberliques	trifles, trinkets	
Orroye	would hear	archaic tense of modern ouir
Ort	dirty	
Ouil	yes	oui
Pais (not to be confused with paix)	country	pays

Per	companion	
(Sans per)	without a companion	sans pair
	peerless	
Peresse	laziness	paresse
Pieça	long ago	
Quoy	tranquil	coi
Quéquerir	to seek (a variant of quérir)	quérir
Quitaine	a game much played at Orléans	
Ramenter	to recall	
Renc	rank	rang
Souloir	to be accustomed	souloir (archaic)
Sus et jus	high and low	
Voye	manner, means	voie

A minor obstacle may be words which in old French had an extra letter, now dropped, or sometimes replaced by a circumflex accent. Examples are:

The 'i' between 'a' and 'g' in langaige, menaige, hommaige, davantaige etc.
The 's' in beste (now bête).
The 'l' in mieulx, vieulx, veult, cieulx, maulx etc.
The 'e' in veoir.
The 'a' in paeur.
Forms like amer for aimer, cueur for cœur, cuevrir for couvrir, dueil for deuil, vueille for veuille occur so often that one quickly gets used to them.

The reader is advised in any case to read the poems aloud to himself, when words that may have seemed incomprehensible, e.g. scet for sait, soussi for souci, serchier for chercher, pascience for patience, jaulier for geôlier, face for fasse, quickly become clear.

Note on Coinage

THE documents referred to in this book mention a variety of coins: *livres, écus d'or, francs, saluts* (sometimes spelt *saluz*), *marcs, sols* and *deniers*, all of which were current in France in the time of Charles of Orleans. Any attempt to establish with exactitude their relative values is so complex that it has baffled even experts, partly because their equivalences were not always constant and partly because the values of the coins themselves varied with the political situation. I have therefore made no attempt to enter this dangerous field, but have followed the example of most writers on the period, and let the names of coins given in the documents mentioned stand without comment.

However, one or two remarks may be of interest; and in spite of what has been said above, there are one or two indications of relative value which may be helpful.

1. The *livre*. There were two kinds of *livre*: the *livre parisis* (of Paris) and the *livre tournois* (minted at Tours). The former was a coin of higher value, but the latter was the more widely used and is in fact the one generally referred to in the documents I have quoted. The *livre* contained 20 *sols* and 240 *deniers*, and this parallelism with English pounds, shillings and pence, and the use of £. s. d. as signs for them in both languages, may occasionally confuse the English reader. In spite of this resemblance, from the fourteenth century onwards there was no correspondence between the two systems in metallic pound weight. But in later times the *livre* came gradually to approximate more to the English pound. The *livre* with its *sols* and *deniers* was the main system of account in France from the time of Charlemagne up to the Revolution.

2. The *écu*. There were both silver and gold *écus*, so called because they were engraved on one side with a shield. The silver *écu* was a coin in wide use in France over a considerable period, so much so that "avoir des écus" is still a current phrase for having plenty of money. (The complexity of the subject of value is illustrated by the fact that, according to both Littré and Larousse, there were silver *écus* worth three *livres* and others worth six.)

However, it is the *écu d'or* which figures so largely in the history of Charles of Orleans. And some idea of its value, at least at one stage, is given by a document in the *Chambre des Comptes* of Blois (on which see my *Notes, Primary Sources* page 358), which says that a payment of 70 *livres* 15 *sols tournois* was to be made for a black horse which had been bought for 70 *écus d'or* (Laborde 6222). For general purposes, then, we may assume that these coins were *sometimes* interchangeable.

3. The *franc*. One modern historian (R. Vaughan, *Philip the Bold*, p. 5, note 1 and p. 18, note 4) says that the gold *franc*, which had been introduced by King John the Good, was a coin of the same value as the *livre tournois*, and certainly in more modern times the *livre* and the gold *franc* were equivalent in value.

4. The *salut d'or*. This coin was introduced by Charles VI, and owed its name to the fact that on one side it was engraved with the Angel of the Annunciation. The only covering of its value which I have been able to discover is in another document of the *Chambre des Comptes* of Blois (*Add. Ch.* 3251) which states that in August 1433 the *saluʒ* was worth 30 *sols* (i.e. approximately 1½ *livres*.)

Even more difficult than the problem of establishing the relative values of fifteenth century coins is that of equating them with any modern currency, a task made impossible by suppressions and fluctuations over the past five hundred years. One can therefore only consider the sums mentioned in relation to their own period. Whether any given amount was large or not can best be determined by comparing it with other current costs of the time. Thus, the expenses of Charles' Court at Blois for the year 1448, covering the wages and clothes of some 200 staff, a large number of them senior officials, with the food of the whole household and many visitors, including all the costs of the stables, hunting equipment, not to mention the expenses of Charles himself and his duchess, with the upkeep of the furnishings and fabric of the castle, amounted to 22,974 *livres* 9 *sols*, 5 *deniers* (Laborde 6664). As a good many of such charges would have continued during his captivity, it is obvious that the debt to the English of 210,000 *écus d'or*, which Charles of Orleans incurred in his youth, was indeed heavy enough to cripple him financially throughout the greater part of his life, and that if his fellow prisoners had not helped to pay his ransom of 240,000 *écus d'or* he would have died a prisoner in England.

Note on Primary Sources

THE two main contemporary sources for the life of Charles of Orleans
are the narratives of the chroniclers in which fifteenth-century France
was so rich, and the documents in the *Chambre des Comptes* at Blois
(on which see my *Notes, Primary Sources* page 358.) The names and
pseudonyms of the chief chroniclers, which occur frequently in my
text, are, in roughly chronological order: Jean Froissart (for the
Prologue only); Enguerrand de Monstrelet; Le Religieux de Saint-
Denis; Jean Juvenal des Ursins; Guillaume Cousinot; Un Bourgeois de
Paris; Pierre de Fenin; Guillaume Gruel; Jean Le Fèvre de Saint-
Remy; Jean de Wavrin; Jean Maupoint; Mathieu d'Escouchy; Olivier
de la Marche, and Georges Chastellain.

Some of these were present at the events they record; some copied
their narratives, or parts of them, from those of others; some omit
details that others give; and occasionally they contradict each other.
I have taken from each those parts of their chronicles that, added
together, make the most consistent narrative, not pointing out all their
contradictions because to do so would be tedious, but occasionally
giving a particular reference to one or other in my Notes, as a rule
under the names of the chronicler rather the title of his work. The full
titles of their chronicles, all of which are published, are given in the
Bibliography.

As the Notes also contain references to a considerable number of
other contemporary documents which I have used, either published or
in manuscript, I have in general refrained, in order to avoid too great a
proliferation of numbers in the text, from giving references there to
the modern sources on which I have drawn for, e.g. the biographies of
secondary personages. The titles of all these are given in the Bibliography. I have not however listed in the Bibliography the general
histories of the period, both French and English, which I have consulted, nor such things as general biographies.

Only those persons mentioned in the book are included in the following genealogical tables

THE ROYAL HOUSE OF VALOIS

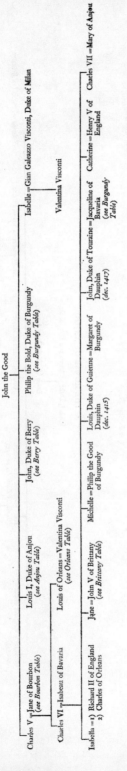
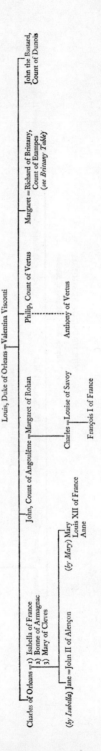

THE HOUSE OF ORLEANS

THE HOUSE OF BURGUNDY

Philip the Bold ⊤ Margaret of Flanders

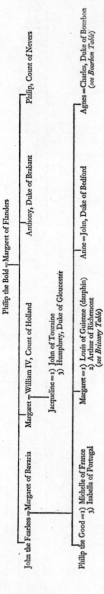

John the Fearless = Margaret of Bavaria   Margaret ⊤ William IV, Count of Holland   Anthony, Duke of Brabant   Philip, Count of Nevers

Jacqueline = 1) John of Touraine
         3) Humphrey, Duke of Gloucester

Philip the Good = 1) Michelle of France
          3) Isabella of Portugal

Margaret = 1) Louis of Guienne (dauphin)
        2) Arthur of Richemont
        (see Brittany Table)

Anne = John, Duke of Bedford

Agnes = Charles, Duke of Bourbon
       (see Bourbon Table)

THE HOUSE OF ANJOU

Louis I, Duke of Anjou and King of Sicily

Louis II ⊤ Yolanda of Aragon

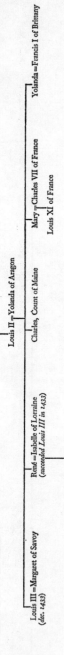

Louis III = Margaret of Savoy
(dec. 1434)

René = Isabelle of Lorraine
(succeeded Louis III in 1434)

Charles, Count of Maine

Mary ⊤ Charles VII of France

Yolanda = Francis I of Brittany

James of Lorraine

Louis XI of France

THE HOUSE OF BERRY

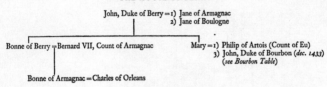

John, Duke of Berry = 1) Jane of Armagnac
2) Jane of Boulogne

Bonne of Berry = Bernard VII, Count of Armagnac

Mary = 1) Philip of Artois (Count of Eu)
3) John, Duke of Bourbon (*dec. 1433*)
(*see Bourbon Table*)

Bonne of Armagnac = Charles of Orleans

THE HOUSE OF BOURBON

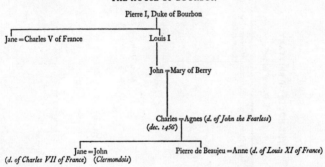

Pierre I, Duke of Bourbon

Jane = Charles V of France

Louis I

John = Mary of Berry

Charles = Agnes (*d. of John the Fearless*)
(*dec. 1456*)

Jane = John
(*d. of Charles VII of France*) (*Clermondois*)

Pierre de Beaujeu = Anne (*d. of Louis XI of France*)

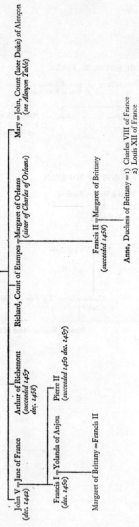

THE HOUSE OF BRITTANY

John IV, Duke of Brittany

John V = Jane of France
(dec. 1442)

Arthur of Richemont
(succeeded 1457
dec. 1458)

Richard, Count of Etampes = Margaret of Orleans
(sister of Charles of Orleans)

Mary = John, Count (later Duke) of Alençon
(see Alençon Table)

Francis I = Yolanda of Anjou
(dec. 1450)

Pierre II
(succeeded 1450 dec. 1457)

Francis II = Margaret of Brittany
(succeeded 1458)

Margaret of Brittany = Francis II

Anne, Duchess of Brittany = 1) Charles VIII of France
2) Louis XII of France

THE HOUSE OF ALENÇON

John, Duke of Alençon = Mary of Brittany (sister of John V of Brittany)

John II = Jane of Orleans (d. of Charles of Orleans)

PART ONE

PROLOGUE
1389

O N the morning of Sunday, August 22nd, 1389, the people of
Paris turned out in dense throngs to watch what promised to be
a procession of rare splendour. They realised that they themselves,
through the heavy taxes imposed on them, were paying much of the
cost of it, as they did for all such occasions. But though in the past they
had sometimes rebelled against similar extravagances, this time they did
not. They knew that their twenty-one-year-old king, Charles VI, of
whom they were fond, had been preparing the pageant for months past
and set great store by it. And they hoped that, by putting their grievances aside for the moment and rejoicing with him, they might incline
him thereafter to ease the burdens that bore so heavily on them.

The purpose of this particular procession was to celebrate the
solemn entry into her capital of the queen, Isabeau, and her coronation
in Notre-Dame. It might have seemed rather late in the day for such
events, for it was now four years since Isabeau, then a young princess
of thirteen or fourteen, had been brought from the home of her father,
Duke Stephen of Bavaria, to marry Charles. Since then she had already
borne him two children, both of whom died in infancy. During those
four years she had in fact frequently visited Paris, although she had
never been formally welcomed by its citizens. Apart from these things,
the present was hardly an ideal moment for her to undergo the rigours
of a long-drawn-out state occasion, for she was within three months of
the birth of her third child, one who this time was destined to live, at
least long enough to play a part in history in general and this history
in particular.

In spite of her condition her husband was anxious not to defer the
festivities; for although they were primarily to honour his queen, he
intended them also as a celebration of the marriage, which had taken
place in his presence five days previously at Melun, of his younger
brother Louis, Duke of Touraine and Count of Valois and Beaumont,
to Valentina Visconti, daughter of Gian Galeazzo, Lord of Pavia and
Duke of Milan. The king was devoted to his brother Louis. Both,
according to the writer Christine de Pisan, who knew them well,
were striking-looking princes,[1] and both were high-spirited, recklessly

3

extravagant, generous and pleasure-loving. The king in fact was little else, for although he had a naturally sweet and gentle nature, he had also a restless excitability that made him constantly crave for change and new enjoyments at no matter what cost to his realm and people – and the cost proved great. Louis was a more complex character. He loved games of all kinds, chess, dice and tennis too; but as he was a great gambler, he played them all for high stakes and as a result was often in debt for huge sums. At the same time he was cultivated, taking pleasure in his library and delighting in the society of poets and musicians. He had a devout side to his nature too, and was charitable not only to the church but to the poor and the sick. Soon after his marriage he began to develop into an ambitious politician; but at the time of the procession he was only seventeen.

His Italian bride, Valentina, was two years older than Louis and had spent all her life hitherto in her father's castle at Pavia. His court there was one of the most brilliant in Italy for Gian Galeazzo, though a ruthless and ambitious ruler, had also a genuine love of the arts and literature, and had built up a magnificent library where Valentina had been able to acquire a taste for reading. But although she was her father's only daughter there is no evidence that she took much part in the life of his court. Her mother, the French princess Isabelle, sister of Charles V and thus aunt to Charles VI and Louis, had died when Valentina was not more than two and her father had soon married again. The child was therefore brought up by her grandmother, Blanche of Savoy, an intelligent and gentle old lady. And it seems probable that it was her influence, as well as the girl's own nature, that made of her the modest and patient princess she later showed herself to be.

As Gian Galeazzo was not only a powerful prince but a man of great wealth, his only daughter was obviously a most desirable match for the young Duke of Touraine, supplementing the king's German alliance by an Italian one. Valentina brought Louis a large dowry, the overlordship of the town and county of Asti in Lombardy, and also the title of Count of Vertus, near Châlons-sur-Marne, which her French mother had received for Gian Galeazzo as part of her own marriage-portion. For Valentina, too, the choice of Louis had everything to commend it. Like any young princess of the time she might have been handed over to the highest bidder, whether he was a man old enough to be her grandfather or a child not yet out of the nursery. It was, therefore, a rare stroke of luck when the lot fell on a youth only a year or two her junior, and one of the most elegant and eligible princes in Europe. Moreover, this union was not exactly like a foreign alliance, since she was half French herself, and a first cousin of her bridegroom, whose tongue she already spoke.

On her journey across France that summer she had been given a royal reception at every town where she stopped, so that she could not have felt other than welcome. There is no record of her arrival at the French court, but from the affection which we know they later felt for her, she clearly pleased both Louis and the king. It would indeed have taken someone of ill-will not to like her, for she was noble, generous-minded and compassionate, hating injustice and deeply loyal: 'Loyauté passe tout' was one of her chosen devices. There is no portrait of her but a contemporary poet, Eustache Deschamps, who praised her for those qualities, says also that she 'gent corp a, juene, fresche, joly'.[2] What Isabeau's reaction was to this sister-in-law of her own age is less certain, for there was an awkward family situation between them. Isabeau was half a Visconti herself, through her mother; and Gian Galeazzo had had her mother's father, her own grandfather Bernabo, then Duke of Milan and his uncle, thrown into prison and some say murdered there, in order to get the title for himself. Both Valentina and Isabeau were of course aware of this story, Isabeau particularly so, for she too had a great sense of loyalty, especially to the paternal side of her family, the Wittelsbachs. Her brother, Louis of Bavaria, came to France with her and remained always her constant companion there, a situation that did nothing to increase her popularity with her new subjects, whose favour she herself never made much effort to win.

However, there is no reason to suppose that any latent hostility in her to Valentina clouded the atmosphere that summer morning, when the two young royal couples were preparing for the week of festivities and revelries that that day's procession was to inaugurate. Not all the members of the royal family who took part in it were as young and pleasure-loving as the king and his brother. Three of their uncles accompanied them. The oldest and by far the noblest and kindest was Louis II, Duke of Bourbon, brother of Charles' and Louis' mother Jane of Bourbon, wife of Charles V. Like many a prince, and king too, of those days, he was nicknamed 'the Good', but in his case the sobriquet was deserved. He had helped to bring up Charles and Louis after the death of their father and he remained one of their staunchest supporters, particularly of Louis and his family, until the end of his life.

5

Very different were their father's brothers, the Dukes of Berry and Burgundy who, both by virtue of the great apanages they held, and in their wealth and the authority they wielded, were richer and more powerful than the king himself.

John Duke of Berry was the elder of the two, being then forty-nine. His main characteristic was his devouring passion for works of art and beautiful objects of all kinds, one of his most famous possessions being that exquisite manuscript known as *Les Très Riches Heures du Duc de Berry*, which the Limbourg brothers had illuminated and adorned with delicate illustrations for him. He was always sending to the orient for precious stones, which he loved. He had a choice collection of religious relics too, including one of the hands of St. Thomas, the very one, it was said, that had touched Christ's wounds. Although kindly enough by nature, his lust for possessions was such that he allowed his subjects in Languedoc to be cruelly oppressed in order to obtain the money to gratify it. And although also by nature pacific, he was ambitious enough not to like being left out when positions of importance were being distributed, and so played a considerable part in politics almost in spite of himself. At the time of the procession, however, his mind was not on any of these things but on his twelve-year-old second wife Jane of Boulogne, whom he had only just married and of whom he was deeply enamoured.

Philip Duke of Burgundy was two years younger than his brother of Berry, and the first of that succession of four dukes who made of Burgundy in the fifteenth century one of those 'almost kingly dukedoms', as Shakespeare calls them. Like all his line, he too was a great patron of the arts and himself a collector and lover of beautiful things. But he loved politics and power still more. His nickname 'the Bold' was given him not for valour, though he was courageous enough, but because of his arrogant and self-assertive ways. In the intrigues in which before long he involved the kingdom he was closely abetted by his wife Margaret. To her he owed the lordships of Flanders, Artois and other territories on the north-eastern borders of France, which she had brought him at her marriage and which made him such a dangerous rival to the French king. But power only bred in both of them a desire for more.

All these, with the exception of the king himself, took part in the procession that formed up early that morning outside the Church of Saint-Denis, where the route was lined by twelve hundred of the chief burgesses of the city of Paris, all clad alike in rich gowns of green and crimson silk. Queen Isabeau, the chief figure in the procession, travelled in a sumptuously decorated litter, with the Dukes of Berry, Burgundy, Touraine and Bourbon riding on either side; but Valentina of Touraine and Jane of Berry rode on richly caparisoned palfreys. The king was not with them because his excitable mood had put it into his head that it would be more amusing to disguise himself and join the crowd gathered to watch the pageants that were to enliven the route; an escapade he thoroughly enjoyed, although it led to his being soundly belaboured about the shoulders by the officials, armed with cudgels, whose rôle it was to keep order and who did not recognise him.

The splendours began as soon as the procession passed the first gate of Saint-Denis and entered the narrow streets of Paris, where all the houses were hung with tapestries and rich stuffs. The king himself had devised the spectacle at that gate, which consisted of a 'sky', representing heaven, stretched above it full of stars, sheltering children dressed as angels, surrounding an image of the Virgin with the Holy Child, and singing. Further on another 'heaven' had the Trinity inside it, and as the queen passed under it two angels came down holding a crown of gold and jewels which they placed on her head with a suitable message. Elaborate pageants were enacted on stages erected all along the route. The queen had to stay and watch all these little dramas so it was getting late when, crossing the new stone bridge of Saint-Michel (now the Pont Notre-Dame) she witnessed the most staggering display of all: an acrobat appeared through a slit in a gold-starred blue silk 'sky' and walked slowly down on a rope slung between the highest tower of Notre-Dame and the tallest house on the bridge, carrying two lighted candles in his hands and singing as he went. When at last she entered the cathedral the Bishop of Paris placed a still richer crown on her head, receiving the angels' offering in return. From there it was but a short step to the old royal palace of Saint Louis on the Île de la Cité, only used by the Valois on official occasions, where the king was waiting to greet them all before they retired to their rooms.

The following morning the queen was anointed at a High Mass in Notre-Dame, after which the king gave a great banquet served on the huge marble table in the palace, and his party then repaired to the favourite royal residence known as the Hôtel de Saint-Pol.[3] This great rambling dwelling covered a vast stretch of land between the present

Quai des Célestins and the Boulevard Saint-Antoine. It was made up of a number of smaller houses which had previously stood on the site and which Charles V had bought up, with their surrounding gardens, and then added to and enclosed. It thus consisted of innumerable rooms, great and small, with chapels, courtyards, galleries and gardens full of fruit and flowers–one big enough to hold a cherry-orchard–an immense vine-arbour, fountains and even a small zoo where lions were kept. There were stables too, and–by no means so uncommon then as one might suppose–bath-houses fed by the water of the Seine. Only the names of some of the streets in that now-sordid quarter–the Rue de la Cerisaie, the Rue du Beautreillis and the Rue des Lions – carry still an echo of the gardens of that vanished palace, but in those days it was so vast that there was room in it to lodge not only the king and queen and their households, but Louis and Valentina and their followers and many other courtiers too.

The main municipal ceremony of the week took place the next day. At twelve that morning a deputation of the burgesses of Paris, all dressed alike, arrived at the Hôtel de Saint-Pol, bringing with them costly offerings of gold and silver plate, to the value of more than thirty thousand gold crowns, as offerings for the king, queen and Valentina. They were carried through the streets on litters so that the people might see them. The king thanked his people politely though briefly, but seems to have shown no special awareness of what it must have cost them to honour him in this way. Yet he could hardly have forgotten how, at his own coronation seven years before, they had had to pay so much for the festivities that they had revolted. But their insurrection had been harshly repressed and the king, though affable by nature, never learnt either sense or consideration.

If now they paid up once again, and this time without grumbling, it was because they hoped that the young queen would be sufficiently touched by their welcome to use her influence, once the child she was carrying was born, to have at least some of their taxes remitted or reduced. They did not then know how little her people were ever to mean to her, and that once again their hopes were doomed to disappointment. As soon as the feasting was over and the king and queen with all their followers had left Paris for the joustings that were to terminate the week's ceremonies, the salt tax was increased by royal decree, and heralds announced that the use of certain silver coins of low value, that had been current since the time of Charles V, was

8

henceforth prohibited under pain of death. The result of this was that, for a short time, the poorest people, who had no other coins, found themselves unable to buy even the food they needed. And the birth, in the following November, of the Princess Isabelle, did nothing to alleviate their misery.

CHAPTER ONE
1390–1394

DURING the five years that followed that week of ceremonies and revelries, many of the threats that then lay hidden beneath its glittering surface emerged and darkened the scene. The king had continued on his headstrong and extravagant way, heedless of the needs and miseries of his people and taking little thought for the government, which he was content to leave in the hands of his Council. As he had been only a boy of twelve when he succeeded to the throne in 1380, the royal authority was then divided among the royal dukes, his uncles. But by the time he was eighteen Charles, resenting their control, had informed them that he intended in future to govern without their help. In their stead he appointed as his main councillors several able and loyal men who had served his father before him. As they were not of noble birth, although of good family, the dukes contemptuously called them the Marmosets; and Burgundy and Berry especially were their sworn enemies. For all that, the dukes had to bow to the king's decree as long as the Marmosets ruled with the royal authority.

Unfortunately as time went on that authority gradually diminished, as the king's nervous agitation and excitability increased. The climax came one day in August 1392 when the king was journeying to Brittany, accompanied by his brother Louis and a band of armed followers. On their way the company halted in a wood near Le Mans to enjoy the shade, for it was an exceptionally hot and sultry day. Suddenly a man in rags came up to the king, as he sat on his horse, and warned him to go no further, telling him that he had been betrayed. At the same moment one of the king's men-at-arms let his sword fall with a clatter. At the sound of these two things the king's wits, already affected by the brooding atmosphere, gave way completely and, in a mood of furious madness, he drew his sword, slew four of his followers standing by, and then galloped over the countryside until at last he was found, at nightfall, lying under a tree unconscious.

That fatal day may be said to have marked the beginning of one of the most wretched epochs in the history of France. The king's illness, in the light of modern knowledge, was clearly a manic-depressive psychosis of an extreme kind. When the depressive phase was on him—

and it sometimes lasted for months—he would, says Le Religieux,[1] refuse to eat or sleep, to change his shirt or let himself be washed and shaved, and it sometimes took as many as ten men to control him. Although lucid intervals, when he appeared normal again, were fairly frequent, it was obvious that his judgment was impaired, as he changed his mind with bewildering frequency and could always be persuaded to agree with the most dominating of those about him. His natural characteristics were then exaggerated, especially his reckless generosity when he would give away vast sums from the royal treasury, to the despair of those responsible for his exchequer. But because those lucid intervals did occur, no suggestion that he should be deposed was ever made. It was, however, plain that some other authority must take charge when the king was, as the contemporary chroniclers discreetly put it, 'absent'. And so began that struggle for power which was to plunge the country into a civil war that dragged on for half a century and made her fall an easy prey to her English foes.

The first to suffer were the Marmosets. Philip of Burgundy, who saw in his nephew's madness the chance to regain the power that he had long sought, supported by John of Berry, had them deprived of office, arrested and thrown into prison. But Burgundy had a more powerful rival than any of the Marmosets and that was the king's young brother Louis. Although since his marriage he had remained the king's constant companion in pleasure-seeking, and seems to have been universally regarded as a light-weight young man, he had also employed some of his time in increasing his wealth and possessions and building up his own position, in order to put himself on an equality with his powerful uncles, and with other political aims in view.

He was already a considerable landowner in Paris. In 1388, while he was still a bachelor, the king had given him the Hôtel de Behaigne, or Bohème,[2] a great house near the Louvre, so called because it had at one time belonged to a King of Bohemia, that he might have a fitting establishment of his own, just as the Duke of Burgundy had his great Hôtel d'Artois, and Berry his Hôtel de Nesles. Four years later Louis was even richer than they in town houses, for in 1392 the king gave him the Hôtel d'Orléans too, a house in the street of Saint-André-des-Arts. As well as these he had several lesser houses, some with splendid gardens.

But it was chiefly in the provinces, and especially in Touraine and the Île-de-France, that Louis was at that time anxious to extend his possessions and power. To this end in 1391 he bought the counties of Blois and Dunois, with all their castles, from their then owner Guy of Châtillon, mainly so that they might form a rich patrimony for him to leave to a son, Louis, to whom his wife Valentina had just then given birth. This son did not in fact live long enough to inherit it; but Blois in due course fell to another son, Charles, not then born, to whom it was to mean much, and Dunois to another. In 1392 the king gave his brother not only the fortresses of Pierrefonds and La Ferté Milon, but the counties of Angoulême and Périgord also.

More important still, in June of that year, just before the king's first attack of madness, Louis persuaded his brother to give him the Duchy of Orleans as an apanage in perpetuity, in exchange for that of Touraine,[3] as it was a much richer duchy and he was in constant need of money for his endless purchases of fine clothes, jewels, tapestries and rich furnishings for his houses, books and works of art, not to mention the handsome presents that he gave with lavish munificence on all occasions—an almost unbelievable expenditure recorded in the elaborate orders and receipts of his *Chambre des Comptes*, which he had set up on the plan of those established by the king and the Duke of Burgundy, and of which, fortunately, several thousand documents remain.[4] The people of Orleans were not particularly pleased at being thus handed over to this new, ambitious and spendthrift overlord, and begged the king not to detach their lands from the royal domain, of which they had formed a part. But the king refused their request, telling them through his chancellor that the duke was "endowed with a penetrating glance, rare eloquence and extreme affability, while his elegance and grace of person denoted an illustrious prince".[5] Whether or not the idea of Louis' penetrating glance and other attributes won them over we do not know, but they had to accept him as their duke and so he remained.

These increases in territory, wealth and titles of course made the young duke—still only twenty—a much more formidable rival to his uncles than formerly, and emboldened him to stand up to them and claim what he considered to be his right, as the king's nearest relative, to govern in his brother's stead whenever that was necessary. He had in fact persuaded the king to promise him that he should. But the Dukes of Burgundy and Berry, remembering how they had ruled when Charles and Louis were both boys, deeply resented this and a relentless struggle for domination now began between Louis and his uncles, but

1 Honoré Bonet presents a copy of his poem to Valentina

chiefly with Philip of Burgundy. It was, however, some time before the struggle became an open clash. At first it was a question of quiet intrigue and a certain jockeying for place, as when the Duchess of Burgundy established herself as the queen's closest adviser, suffering no one else to approach her without her consent, since the king's illness naturally increased the power and influence of the queen.

In any case, in those early stages of the king's malady, the need for some other authority to govern was still only intermittent. The king had in fact recovered from his first attack fairly soon, though it was hardly a recovery that gave anyone much hope of stability and good government. Rather was it marked by an increase in that frantic craving for pleasure and entertainments that, so some allege, often ended in debauch. One of the most tragically memorable of these occasions was a ball that took place in January 1393. The king and some of his wilder companions attended this disguised as savages, in skin-tight garments to which fur and feathers had been stuck with pitch. In order to see them better Louis of Orleans seized a torch from an attendant. Drops of resin from it fell on one of them and he flared up like a human torch. Crowded together as they were, the flames leapt from one savage to another until all were ablaze. The valiant young Jane of Berry flung the train of her gown over the one nearest to her, who happened to be the king, and put the flames out, so he was saved, though four of his companions were burnt to death.

When the people of Paris heard what had happened they began to murmur, thinking it a judgment on the court for their frivolous and dissolute ways. Although he had only been the involuntary cause of the tragedy, Louis of Orleans took the blame for it on himself and in expiation built a chapel in his favourite convent of the Celestines, adjoining the Hôtel Saint-Pol; and he and Valentina both made a vow that they would be buried there.

As far as is known, Valentina herself was not present on that terrible occasion, perhaps because she was at that time again with child. Her life during those first years of her marriage can hardly have been very enjoyable, for while her young husband was occupied with all the activities and pleasures that filled his days, she was enduring that monotonous cycle of child-birth and child-death that was the ordinary lot of even the most pampered women at that time. The lying-in of a great lady was conducted with a solemn ritual of costly preparation and almost excessive care. But when all this had been carried out, as often as not the child thus brought into the world died at birth or only survived a very short time; presumably either because the medical skill then available was not great enough to bring it through the first hazardous months of life, or because the hygienic conditions, even in a noble household, were inadequate for the care of a new-born child. And so, of the first three sons whom Valentina bore, the first, in 1390, died within a few weeks, the second, Louis, only survived four years, until 1395, while the one who was born after the tragic ball died in that same year.

Perhaps also the febrile atmosphere in which Valentina was then condemned to live had a deleterious effect on her naturally quiet and sensitive spirit, that communicated itself to her frail children. For she can hardly have been happy or at ease in that court whose irresponsible pleasures were so foreign to her nature. Then, too, she had had the sorrow of learning, only two years after her marriage, that Louis had already been unfaithful to her. She had tackled that first occasion with considerable spirit and put a stop to the affair. But Louis was so naturally fond of women and so attractive to them that she must have feared the situation would repeat itself, as indeed later it notoriously did. Such things never affected her own unswerving devotion to her husband who, for his part, remained fond of her if not faithful to her; but they could not but have given her pain.

Another factor that contributed to the tensions of her life at this time when she lost her third child, was that the king's illness was bringing her into painful prominence at court, and that certainly through no wish of her own, as she never showed any desire to play a part in public life. It so happened that, when the attacks of madness seized the king, he turned violently against Queen Isabeau and did not even recognise her, although in his lucid intervals he was still deeply and indeed passionately attached to her. The only person whom he did recognise and could bear to have about him at those times was his sister-in-law Valentina, whose gentle presence alone had power to soothe and calm him. Perhaps it was that he was dimly aware that, of all the self-seeking and cold-hearted nobles and courtiers who surrounded him, Valentina was one of the few who was truly pitiful and grieved for him, sincere and loyal as she was. But innocent as was his need of her, it could hardly have failed to rouse Isabeau's jealousy that Valentina should be preferred before her. Equally, the Duke and Duchess of Burgundy were filled with apprehension lest Valentina's obvious influence over the king should strengthen that of her husband and enable him to obtain the powers and privileges from which they were so anxious to exclude him.

So matters stood when on November 24th, 1394, at ten in the evening, at the Hôtel Saint-Pol, Valentina gave birth to yet another child.[6] Once again the baby was a boy. The king at that moment happened to be in his right mind, and he not only agreed to stand godfather to the baby, who was christened Charles after him, but himself held him at the font. Charles was the first of Valentina's children to receive this honour. Great though it was, it can hardly then in all the circumstances have seemed a very happy augury; and indeed the child was to experience little good fortune in his life, as far as most of the outward events of it went. Yet for all that, looked at in the longer light of history, gifts unsuspected by those gathered round that font were in store for him. For one thing he was the first of Valentina's children to have a strong hold on life, strong enough to enable him to live through one of the worst half-centuries in his country's history, and to play a part in releasing her from the fetters of the war that was so largely responsible for her wretched state. Never a ruler himself, he was to give France one of her best kings. And finally, apart from all such mundane matters, he was destined to become that rare thing in any period, a prince who was also a true poet and whose most individual voice can still evoke the pains and pleasures of his existence over five hundred years ago.

CHAPTER TWO

1395–1407

THE story of a child's life in those far-off days, even of a young prince's, can as a rule only be told, in its main lines at least, in terms of what was happening to his parents, and particularly at first to his mother. During the first two years of Charles' existence the atmosphere surrounding him must have been agitated, for Valentina's circumstances grew daily more uneasy. The jealousy of which she had already for the past year or two been the object was now turning into a more sinister feeling against her. Since the physicians had proved unable to cure the king of his malady, Louis' enemies began to attribute Valentina's ability to soothe the patient to some kind of witchcraft, designed to get him in her power in order to further her husband's ambitions. This atmosphere of distrust and suspicion soon spread to the people of Paris, who in any case were becoming none too well disposed to Louis, since he was using his power to impose even heavier taxes on them than the king had done, to pay for his pleasures and possessions.

Matters finally reached such a pitch that it was decided to exile Valentina from Paris. To banish the king's own sister-in-law, who was also a foreign princess, from the capital and all her husband's houses there, was such a grave step that only the highest authority could have decreed it; so it is generally thought that the queen was responsible, although there is no proof that she was. Louis appears to have accepted the sentence without question. It may be that he thought it would be safer for Valentina as well as more politic for himself if she were to leave Paris; but it is surprising that, as far as is known, he made no attempt to refute the charges on which the decision to banish her was based. In their chronicles Le Religieux and Juvenal des Ursins make it clear that they did not believe the accusations against her.[1] Apart from them only two people are on record as having spoken out as champions of the slandered duchess.

One of these was Honoré Bonet, prior of a monastery at Salon in Provence, who had undertaken a few official missions and was thus in touch with worldly events. In 1398 he wrote a curious long poem called *L'Apparicion de maistre Jehan de Meun*, and addressed it to

16

Louis of Orleans in the hope that he would undertake to reform the abuses and injustices of the time, which were the subject of the poem. He had a second copy made especially for Valentina and sent it to her with a touchingly simple and sincere dedication, begging her to use her influence with her husband to that end, and humbly hoping she would accept the modest gift: "Si vous suppli très humblement que de petite personne vueilliez prendre en gré le petit présent". He had her copy illustrated with two delightful miniatures showing him offering it to her; and in one of them there is between them a scroll on which are inscribed, as though to make it quite clear that Valentina is the subject of them, the lines with which the poem ends–lines unconnected with the subject of it, describing how the chaste Susannah was baselessly defamed and wrongly condemned, but in the end loyalty– the word so constantly associated with Valentina–triumphed. "Très haulte dame, entendés ma chançon", he ends.[2]

Valentina's other champion was the much better-known writer Eustache Deschamps, who was in fact one of the major poets of the time. Then a man of fifty, he had always held offices at court and was on easy terms with all the nobles; but since 1392 he had been attached to the household of Louis of Orleans in various capacities. There he had learnt to venerate Valentina, his 'très chière et redoubtée dame' as he calls her; and he courageously chose this moment, so humiliating for her, to address to her one of his most beautiful *ballades*.[3] Although he does not expressly refer in it to the charges against her, he makes it abundantly clear what he thinks of them by his warm praise of her who 'A bon droit doit de tous être louée' for her honour, her good renown, her gentle bearing and her humility, always worthy of her high lineage. Wherever she goes she remains beyond reproach. The whole poem breathes a deep indignation on behalf of her of whom, he says, skilfully repeating one of her favourite devices, 'a bon droit', at the end of each stanza, it can rightly be said that there never was a more loyal heart.

Valentina herself was both angered and deeply hurt by the false accusations levelled against her; but with her customary patience and dignity she made no attempt to defend herself and accepted the sentence of banishment from Paris. Apart from her pity for the king, there was indeed little to make her want to stay in that capital so full of intrigue, suspicion and dislike as far as she was concerned; but that made it no easier to be the victim of it. The only circumstance that spared her the outward humiliation of having been sent away—a sort of negative re-buttal of the charges against her—was that when she departed, in April 1396, she went in splendid state; and it was given out that she was merely going to visit one of her husband's castles, Asnières, in the county of Beaumont, that she had never yet seen. But this pretence cannot long have taken anyone in, for in fact she never did return to Paris until the year before her death.

Valentina of course took with her her one surviving son, Charles, then seventeen months old. Harsh though the sentence of banishment against her seems, it at least enabled her to bring him up away from the crowded city; and this was perhaps the reason why he was the first of her children to survive the then perilous years of childhood, as did also the brothers he was to have. Much in the character he developed later bespeaks a quiet country boyhood too: his gentle, reflective temperament, his patience and his serene, philosophical acceptance of his destiny. Even more clearly does it reveal the influence of his mother who was now, as far as his upbringing was concerned, very much his sole parent, just as he was the main object of her care.

Much documentary evidence of that care on the material side still exists. In March, in preparation for the April journey, the baby was provided with a long surcoat of green damask furred with squirrels' bellies at neck and wrists, a tunic of fine vermilion cloth similarly furred, two caps of the same cloth, two pairs of woollen hose and two little doublets of Rheims linen.[4] His father had taken some hand in all this too, and had ordered the king's shoemaker to make eighteen pairs of leather shoes for his son.[5] Every month during the following summer more garments were ordered, though as the weather grew warmer satin and damask took the place of woollen cloth for tunics, hose and caps. Vermilion, 'English green' or black were the colours used; and many of the garments were embroidered with his father's emblems of genista flowers, trees or climbing wolves. Charles was still under two when a long cloak of vermilion cloth was made for him, with a cross-bow embroidered on the left side, trimmed with fur for which a hundred and sixty-two skins were needed.[6]

It all sounds rather an overpowering wardrobe for a child of under two. But it must be remembered that in the Middle Ages children always wore small replicas of grown-up styles, and it would be normal even for so young a prince to be as richly clad as the father of whom he looked like a tiny copy. One wonders too how a child could have had time to wear so many clothes before he grew out of them, but so extravagant were the Orleans' ways that no doubt a garment that had been worn a few times was considered no longer fit to use.

Care was taken not only for Charles' wardrobe but for his health when he first went with his mother to live in the country. In July 1396, when they had only been at Asnières three or four months, Louis sent two doctors, accompanied by an apothecary, a clerk and three valets all on horseback, with an eighth horse for the baggage, to visit the duchess and 'our very dear and beloved son Charles', who were indisposed.[7] This little visit, quite in the lavish Orleans style, lasted eight days. It is not known what caused Charles' indisposition, but it was probably a mere childish complaint with no lasting effect, for he appears to have enjoyed good health thereafter. Valentina's, no doubt, had something to do with the fact that, later that month, she gave birth to another son, Philip, who was to become Count of Vertus and to whom, in spite of the tensions between the two families, Philip of Burgundy stood godfather. Philip also came safely through the risky years of infancy and was to live to become the devoted adherent of his elder brother. There is an indication that they were good playmates in childhood too, enjoying the pleasures of outdoor life together, for in 1403 their boots and shoes were ordered to be 'felted and roughed'.[8]

Although Valentina and Charles were still at Asnières when Philip was born, she and her children were by no means confined to one place during the eleven years of her exile. They moved constantly and freely from one to the other of the many castles that Louis never ceased to acquire, so that as a child Charles became familiar with all the great estates, one day to be his. Fortresses like Pierrefonds do not seem to have attracted Valentina, although she went at least once to Coucy; but she passed many months at Villers-Cotterêts in the midst of its beautiful forest, and after 1400, when the king gave his brother Château-Thierry,[9] in what is now the Aisne, she and her family spent much time there.

But of all places she seems to have preferred some of the residences in the lovely valley of the Loire: Châteauneuf, which Louis had restored after it had been destroyed by the English, and the nearby castle of Montils where she added, at her own expense, four rooms, each with a fireplace, between the walls of the great hall and the wall of the fortress, in an attempt no doubt to make it a smaller and cosier place to live in.[10] Yet only once is there a mention of her at Blois, which later was to become the favourite residence of Charles. It was the real headquarters of the duchy, where the principal officers of Louis' household lived, charged with the maintenance and administration of his great possessions; and as Valentina was far from being a managing duchess, she probably preferred the quieter castles where she could pursue her own interests and watch over her children in peace.

In whichever of these Valentina and her children happened to be, their life was one of princely state, a state vividly evoked by the records of expenditure in the documents of the *Chambre des Comptes*. Louis himself would of course have paid for the maintenance of the houses his family inhabited and perhaps the wages of the large number of officials and retainers that Valentina, like any other royal duchess, naturally had: her chamberlain, the steward of her household, the knights and esquires who were responsible for supervising every department of the domestic economy, the ladies-in-waiting, serving-women of all degrees and pages. Attached to Valentina's household too, though possibly not resident, were her confessor, a physician called Pierre de Vaulx,[11] and a surgeon. But no doubt the day-to-day cost of feeding and clothing this large establishment, the ritual gifts to all of them on New Year's Day according to their rank—rich jewels for the senior staff and necessaries for the humbler members—and certainly all her personal expenditure was met by Valentina herself.

For this she had plenty of money, for not only did Louis give her a monthly allowance of two hundred gold francs,[12] but as soon as she left Paris in 1396 the king ordered that she was to be paid 6000 gold francs annually for the expenses of her wardrobe, her household plate and her stables, which had hitherto been met out of the king's and queen's own allowance for similar purposes.[13] (Much light, incidentally, is thrown on the corruption of the times by the fact that this money was ordered to be paid out of the subsidies for the wars!) With these considerable sums at her disposal Valentina was able to dress richly, to buy luxurious objects and to enjoy one of her chief pleasures, riding and hawking. Some of the heaviest items of expenditure were obviously connected with her stables. There were her saddles, for instance, sumptuous objects, padded, embroidered and adorned with silk fringe and gold ribbon; and she obviously rode hard for she needed a new one every three years. And the bells and hoods for her falcons, which came from Italy.[14]

A considerable part of her household was devoted to the care of Charles. Even while Valentina still lived in Paris he had his own chambermaids, and in January 1396, just before the move, there is an order for five pairs of high boots for them, stiffened with felt, obviously for use in the country.[15] There he and Philip had a governess called Jeanne d'Herville or d'Ierville, who was obviously a person of some consequence as she is described as the lady of Maucouvent; a nurse whose name is not recorded; and a nursery-maid called Jeanne la Brune, whose office went by the pleasing name of cradle-rocker.[16] These people, even the cradle-rocker, remained in Valentina's service for many years, for at last the nursery had ceased to be merely a temporary resting-place between the cradle and the grave. After Philip, at the turn of the year 1399–1400, Valentina bore yet another son, John, who also survived. In 1401 she had a daughter, born at Coucy, who died, but in 1406 she was followed by another, Margaret, who lived. So the cradle-rocker was rarely idle and the nursery remained an important part of the household long after Charles had left it for the schoolroom.

This soon took place, for the education of a prince began early in those days. Charles was only four when he had a schoolmaster, Nicolas Garbet, who was both a master of arts and a bachelor of theology, and acted as secretary to Louis on occasion.[17] Philip, too, could obviously read at the age of four-and-a-half, for in February 1401 Valentina ordered a craftsman of Paris to illumine in gold, azure and vermilion, and bind in vermilion Cordovan leather, two little books for 'Monseigneur d'Angoulesme'—the title Charles bore in infancy—and 'Monseigneur Philippe d'Orléans'.[18] Two years later she bought a special psalter for them too.[19] By 1404, when Philip had joined Charles in the schoolroom, Garbet was master to both of them[20] and from him they would of course have received the ordinary education of a young noble at that time, which included instruction in Latin grammar and a study of such classical authors as were then known, as well as of the writers of their own epoch. In one of his *ballades* Charles says that he knew the seven liberal arts: grammar, logic and rhetoric, arithmetic, geometry, music and astronomy. Another accomplishment which he certainly acquired in youth was his fine handwriting; he had from boyhood a beautiful signature, that varied little from youth to age. It must have been a pleasure to teach him since, as he said later, in his 'jeunesse fleurie' he was 'de vif entendement'.*

* See page 317 below.

This regular education continued throughout the whole of Charles' boyhood under his mother's care, for, at some moment after John had joined his two elder brothers in that studious schoolroom, a charming picture of it is evoked in an illustration in one of the books out of which Garbet taught them. This was Sallust's *Jugurtha*,[21] which their master had himself transcribed for their use. At the top of the first leaf there is a miniature showing a man, wearing a crown, instructing three little boys standing in a row before him, dressed in long surcoats and with wreaths of leaves on their heads. As they have nothing to do with the text, they were presumably intended to represent Charles and his brothers. This manuscript, a large quarto of forty-six leaves, was obviously precious to Charles, for he kept it all his life and later himself wrote his name in it—a beautiful 'Karolus' in red.

In addition to this formal instruction Charles had early opportunities to acquire his life-long love of books from those belonging both to his father and his mother. The formation of libraries was one of the more admirable habits of the members of the house of Valois. The splendid one that Louis' father, Charles V, built up in the Louvre, later formed the nucleus of what to-day is the Bibliothèque Nationale. His son inherited this interest from him; and though it might be thought that so active and worldly a prince would have little time for reading, and that he acquired books chiefly as the luxurious objects they then were, his household accounts prove that this was not so, for there are continual payments to translators for particular texts, which surely indicate a desire to read what he otherwise could not have done.

His library was a large one for the time and contained works by a great many of the classical writers then known: among them Aristotle, Ovid, Horace, Lucan, Cicero and Virgil. There were theological works too: St. Augustine's *City of God*, the *Homilies* of St. Gregory and the *Lamentations* of St. Bernard. That favourite book of the Middle Ages, Boethius' *Consolations of Philosophy*, of course had a place, and scholars were always at work on a translation of the Bible into French that Louis had commissioned. In 1397 Gilles Malet, who had inventoried the library of Charles V a quarter of a century earlier, installed Louis' books for him in one of his smaller Parisian houses, near the Hôtel Saint-Pol.[22] And as, later on, Louis also gave him a post in his castle at Asnières, where he became a favourite with Valentina too, no one could have been better able to take down to the country from time to time some of the volumes more suitable for Charles: the chronicles of the history of France, for instance, Froissart's *Dit Royal* and the *Golden Legend*.

If any of Louis' books were considered too precious to be put in the hands of a child, there were some in his mother's collection for Charles to enjoy. Some of her own books would certainly have been above his head at that time: for example, Christine de Pisan's *Description de la Prudhomie de l'Ome*, which that remarkable woman writer had dedicated to her. But Valentina also possessed stories of Troy and of King Arthur, with other romances like *Percival le Gallois* and another, now forgotten, called *Giron le Courtois*, which must have been a favourite with the children, for it got so much read that its leaves fell apart and it had to be rebound in good vermilion leather. Another of Valentina's volumes that would have appealed to any imaginative child was Sir John Mandeville's *Travels*, a book of which she was so fond since girlhood that she had brought her copy with her from Italy when she left to get married.²³

Besides all this general reading at Charles' disposal, there were books with a particular appeal to the poet that he was destined to be. Chief among these must certainly have been *Le Roman de la Rose*, for its influence is clear in the first long poem that he himself wrote as a young man, although strangely enough it does not figure in the later inventories of either his father's or his own books. However, Valentina possessed an illustrated copy of the poem and also a book by Christine de Pisan on it. A volume of poems that certainly was in Louis' library was a small one called *Les Cent Ballades*, and this may well have held a particular interest for Charles, since his father had himself contributed one not very good poem to it, and others were by his chamberlain, Jean de Garencières, and another friend, Marshal Boucicaut. Circulating at least in manuscript there must also have been the poems of Valentina's champion, Eustache Deschamps; and no doubt too his *Art de Dicter*, a long treatise on the poetic art that Deschamps had written in 1392, analysing in detail all the complicated measures then in vogue, beginning with the *ballade* and the *rondeau* that Charles himself later particularly favoured and used with rare skill and elegance. Although Charles nowhere mentions Deschamps, it is impossible that he should not have been influenced in some ways by this gifted man, who was not only one of the chief poets of the time but a gay and delightful companion, held in affectionate regard by Valentina, of whose household he was a frequent member. He had that gift, which Petrarch was the first to make use of in European poetry and that Charles later developed, of being able to make every sort of simple domestic occasion, passing mood and even the private jokes of the household, subjects for spontaneous, fresh and charming lyrics, such as one in which he asked Louis's permission to wear his hat indoors in winter.[24]

With poetry so much in the air it would not have been surprising if Charles himself should have tried his hand at it, even as a very young child. And there are considerable grounds for supposing that he may indeed have written a poem called *Le Livre contre tout péché*, inscribed on one of the blank leaves of a manuscript of Sallust's *Catalina*, one of the books from which Nicolas Garbet taught him and his brothers—a manuscript which contains a good deal of extraneous matter.[25] The subject of the poem is the seven deadly sins—just the kind of theme that a schoolmaster who was also a chaplain would have set a young pupil in those days. It reflects the writers Charles was then studying—particularly the twelfth-century theologian Alain de Lille—and is a naïve composition, not without charm, obviously written by one not well acquainted with the vices he has been set to condemn and rather short of an adequate vocabulary for the task. But he plods through them all:

> Puisque j'ai parlé d'orgueil,
> Maintenant parler je vueil
> D'un tres deshonneste peché
> Qui avarice est appellé.

Lust, too, he describes as 'deshonneste', a favourite adjective. Only when he comes to laziness, 'peresse', is there a personal ring. It is a sin unbecoming even in a young child, he solemnly states, and one can almost hear Garbet lecturing him. The last stanza contains the statement that this little book

> Je, nommé: d'Orleans
> Fiz quand j'eus accompli. x. ans.

He thanks God and the Virgin for helping him to compose it, and begs any who may read it to forgive him for any shortcomings in it:

> Car je n'estoie pas si saige
> Pour ce qu'estois jeune d'age,
> Quand je peusse faire traitté
> Qui fust de grant moralité.

The blank in the name has given rise to the supposition that someone other than Charles, and most probably his brother John, was the
author, partly on the ground that the solemn tone of the poem suits
what we know of John's nature later in life better than it suits Charles,
and also because John is known to have written another moral childish
poem.[26] Further, there is textual evidence in the additional matter in the
volume of which the *Catalina* manuscript forms a part, that it was later
used for teaching John by his own schoolmaster, Eudes, or Oudart,
de Fouilloy. What makes this hypothesis unlikely if not impossible is
that, by the time John was ten, in 1409 or 1410, he was invariably
known as John of Angoulême and not Orleans.[27] As for the tone of
the poem, is it in fact so solemn? Those four lines about the inadequacy of his youth to treat of 'grant moralité' suggest rather that
demure humour characteristic of Charles' later poetry. There seems
therefore no good reason why we should not consider this youthful
effort as the first poem by Charles of Orleans that we have, and explain
the blank by supposing that the scribe either deliberately left it, or
created it by erasure, so that the youthful author could fill in his own
name; though why he never did so remains a puzzle.

Other pleasures besides reading and writing were enjoyed in those
country dwellings where Charles spent his boyhood. One of these was
music. On Valentina's staff there was a young woman always referred
to as 'the little harpist', and the duchess herself played the harp too, so
much so that her instrument was always needing re-stringing.[28] Then,
as in every princely household, there would have been minstrels. By
way of outdoor sports there were of course hawking and hunting, and
with a mother so fond of these no doubt Charles followed her in the field.

But more in accord with his own tastes and temperament were the
indoor games like chess, merels—a sort of very elaborate noughts and
crosses—and tables, a type of backgammon or *trictrac*, which we know
Valentina played with her ladies. With all these pleasures it is clear
that Charles had a happy childhood during which, as he himself said
later in his first long poem,* written in early manhood, he knew
'neither care nor melancholy', in the company of his brothers and his
mother.

While Valentina and her children lived thus peacefully in the
country, Louis was pursuing his ambitious plans for extending his
territorial possessions and thus increasing his political power. He made

* See pages 106 and 318 below.

several attempts of this kind in Italy, through his claim to the lordship of Asti that was part of Valentina's dowry. In 1400 he had adroitly bought, from the widow of its former owner, Enguerrand de Coucy, the great barony of Coucy in Vermandois,[29] one of the four chief baronies of France, its magnificent castle, with its huge cylindrical keep,* then the greatest tower in Europe, set on a promontory overlooking lakes and forests, from which he was in a position to threaten his uncle of Burgundy's provinces. This acquisition was so important to him that thereafter he always added the proud title of its former owners, 'Lord of Coucy' to those by which he was habitually known, as did his son Charles after him. Two years later he bought the Duchy of Lorraine too, to strengthen the eastern frontiers of his lands still further, and to divide Burgundy's northern territories of Artois, Picardy and Flanders from his Duchy of Burgundy and his county of the same name.

In all these acquisitions he was helped by the lavish allowances which the king never could refuse him, in return for various rather vaguely described services, or losses and damages said to have been incurred in the course of them. There is at one time a reference to an annual pension of no less than 100,000 gold francs, and later to another of 12,000 a year—tremendous advances on those he had received at the time of his marriage.[30] In accepting this money Louis was of course helping to deplete the royal treasury to an almost desperate point, just as his fellow nobles likewise did. But in spending much of it in acquiring territory, it is just possible that part of his intention, as the king's closest relative, was to increase the royal domain and strengthen the power of the crown in opposition to the increasingly independent and wealthy position of Philip the Bold.

In the midst of his political preoccupations Louis did not forget his wife and family and frequently went to see them and sent them gifts. When he appeared among them the sumptuous raiment and jewels that he habitually wore must have made him seem like some brilliant exotic bird in those quiet green landscapes of the Île-de-France and the Loire. His retinue of esquires and pages added to the impression of splendour, for Louis was constantly ordering for them new liveries of rich stuffs in his favourite colours, of which green was the chief. The tale of his purchases for his wardrobe and theirs is too long to tell, but the fact

* The great keep of Coucy was deliberately destroyed at the end of the First World War.

that on one occasion he had all his esquires dressed in white taffeta for a joust, gives some idea of the extravagance of them.[31] The jewels that he had made both for himself and to give as New Year's gifts to the royal family and his fellow princes were often fantastically rich and complicated.

But the presents that he chose for Valentina seem to show thought both for her simpler tastes and for her comfort. On one occasion for instance, he gave her an unusually simple-sounding ring of gold enamelled with her initials, V. V., and set with a single diamond. On her first leaving for the country he had given her a round gold necklace, enamelled with a design of little pods of genista flowers—one of his emblems—in red and white, with a jewelled clasp. A more useful gift that he had specially made for Valentina at that time was something that was certainly most unusual in those days of plain wooden litters, that were little better than farm-carts: a four-wheeled *char branlant*, in other words a sprung chariot, painted green with her arms and the letter 'V' everywhere, that must have done a great deal to render her country journeys along the rough tracks of those days bearable.[32]

There is more serious evidence of his care for his family in the wills that he made. In 1399 an epidemic broke out in Paris and one of Louis' first thoughts seems to have been to make a will in their favour. Only a part of this document survives. It was superseded by another, longer and apparently complete, which he made in October 1403, while he was staying with Valentina and the children at Châteauneuf-sur-Loire, before leaving for one of his Italian expeditions.[33] In this he left, of course, all his main territories—the Duchy of Orleans, the Counties of Valois, Blois, Dunois and Beaumont, the Barony of Coucy, the Duchy of Lorraine and the County of Asti in Lombardy—to Charles. To Philip went the County of Vertus and other lands in Champagne, and to John the Counties of Angoulême and Périgord. Valentina was to have the equivalent of her own dowry, and the castle of Château-Thierry, of which she seems to have become particularly fond, with the town and its surrounding lands.

There is a significant phrase in the section of the will concerning the bequest to Valentina. Louis says that he makes it "in recognition of the goodness that I have found in Valentina my wife and companion." This has such an unusually personal ring in an otherwise formal document that it is tempting to wonder whether it does not perhaps refer to something that occurred just at that time, and in which Valentina had shown her usual goodness of heart and nobility of character in a very marked way. The precise date of this event is not known, but at some moment in 1403 or 1404 Louis brought home, for Valentina to bring up, a son he had had by a certain Mariette d'Enghien, the wife of Albert of Cany, one of his own officers, and reputedly a very attractive lady.

Although it was customary at the time for a nobleman to recognise his bastards and have them brought up with his own family, it can hardly have been other than a sorrow for Valentina to learn of this baby's birth, and a shock to be asked to take charge of it. But with her accustomed generosity of mind and largeness of heart she not only welcomed the child but quickly learnt to perceive the quality of the sturdy little boy he became, to regret that he was not her own and to love him as if he were. 'I have been robbed of him' was the charming way she put it, according to Juvenal des Ursins.[34] Later, this trust and love of hers were amply repaid, not to Valentina herself but to her own son Charles. For the boy was to become John Count of Dunois, better known as the Bastard of Orleans, who was not only one of the most famous military commanders of his time and the loyal friend and comrade in arms of Joan of Arc, but remained the staunchest of all Charles' supporters, serving him with unswerving devotion throughout all his reverses of fortune.

More important at that time than the birth of a bastard were Louis' plans for marrying his legitimate heir, Charles, since these were inevitably tied up with his political schemes. Charles was only three-and-a-half when his father, who was then occupied in strengthening his German alliances, conceived the idea of marrying him to Elizabeth of Goerlitz, niece of Wenceslas King of Bohemia.[35] He sent Eustache Deschamps, the poet, on a mission to Bohemia to sound the king and shortly afterwards, when Wenceslas came to France on other business, Louis arranged that Valentina should take her little son to Épernay to meet him. Louis made tremendous preparations for the meeting. Charles and his baby brother Philip, who went too, both wore cloaks and capes of green cloth trimmed with green velvet; while their governess and the cradle-rocker, and the seven ladies in Valentina's suite, were all attired in new robes of green cloth, those of the ladies lavishly trimmed with ermine. Louis himself and seven of his pages were all in black at this time, he in velvet and they in felt jackets.[36] After all that, the project came to nothing.

The question of a possible marriage for Charles then lay dormant for six years; but in 1404, when he was ten, his father, abandoning the idea of a foreign alliance, decided to marry him to his cousin Isabelle, eldest daughter of Charles VI, the child to whom Queen Isabeau had given birth soon after the coronation procession in 1389. This poor little princess had lived through a tragic time since then. At the age of seven she had gone to England, as the bride of Richard II. He had conceived a tender affection for the child who was too young to be made a wife, and she was happy with him. But when that brief happiness was brutally ended by Richard's murder four years later, the young queen had had to endure a time of loneliness and grief among virtual strangers before, after much negotiation, she was brought back to her father's court to become again that sad thing, a marketable princess. To marry her to Charles was not, on the face of it, a very enterprising idea and one wonders why Louis was so set on it as he obviously was; for he got his brother the king to agree to the proposal two years before the marriage was solemnised.[37] Isabelle was Louis' god-daughter and he had taken her treatment in England so much to heart that he had broken with Henry IV, who was formerly very much his friend.

But a more cogent reason than pity must be sought, and a very understandable one would have been a wish to counter the increasing Burgundian influence at court. In that same year, 1404, Louis' uncle Philip the Bold had died and been succeeded by his eldest son, John the Fearless. John was a very different character from his father, a difference that shows in their portraits. For whereas in the paintings and statues of Philip there is a certain avuncular good humour, and even a twinkle in his shrewd and crafty glance, John's grimly pursed lips and the shifty, downward look of his close-set eyes plainly reveal the cold calculation and pitiless cruelty that so many of his deeds betray, and that even staunch Burgundian chroniclers like Olivier de la Marche and Le Fèvre de Saint-Remy[38] do not attempt to justify. John had won his sobriquet of 'the Fearless' in the battle against the Turks at Nicopolis; but if he was not afraid of the enemy, neither did he fear God or the devil; and he was equally contemptuous of his fellow men. He had inherited to the full his father's ambitions and was first and foremost determined to keep his cousin Louis in check. By way of increasing his own and his family's influence at court, as soon as he had succeeded his father he obtained the royal consent to the marriage of his daughter Margaret to the seven-year-old dauphin, Louis, generally known as the

Duke of Guienne, or sometimes Aquitaine, while on the same day his only son Philip was affianced to another of the king's daughters, Michèle. It therefore seems not unlikely that it was in order to counter these moves that Louis of Orleans, that same summer, obtained the consent of the king's Council—a meeting of the Council at which John of Burgundy was not present—to the betrothal of the Princess Isabelle to his son Charles of Angoulême, as he was then still often called, even though the marriage was not to take place until two years later.

During that interval the situation between Louis and his cousin worsened greatly. Freed from the restraining hand of the old duke, Philip, Queen Isabeau acquired much more power in the government and sided more and more openly with Louis against John, whom she had never liked.[39] The wretched king was left more and more to himself in his fits of madness, and Louis aroused the wrath and enmity of the people of Paris by his excessive taxation in the king's name, and of the University and some of the ecclesiastics by his high-handed ways and selfish pursuit of his pleasures, in which the queen was only too ready to join him. John of Burgundy astutely turned this state of things to his own advantage by representing himself to all those with grievances as their champion against Louis, whom he accused of responsibility for the prevailing maladministration and abuses of justice. By these means he secured in particular the almost fanatical devotion of the Parisians, whose favour he lost no opportunity of cultivating. Thus the rivalry between the two cousins began to assume the dangerous look of civil strife.

Such was the state of feeling when, on June 29th, 1406, the marriage of Charles and Isabelle eventually took place at Compiègne. The occasion was one of twofold importance, for it had been decided that at the same ceremony the king's second son, John, Duke of Touraine, who was a year younger than the dauphin, should be married to Jacqueline of Bavaria, daughter of Margaret, Countess of Hainault and Holland, who was a sister of John the Fearless. This marriage meant a further strengthening of Burgundian power since, if the present dauphin died before succeeding, there would still be another chance for a member of that family to become one day Queen of France. Queen Isabeau was of course present for this double wedding of her eldest daughter and younger son, but there is no mention of the king, so presumably he was absent then in both senses of the term. The ceremony was one of great splendour as the queen had come with much pomp. Even so she was outdone by the Burgundians, for the equipage of the Countess of Hainault surpassed the royal magnificence. Very much to the fore also was John the Fearless, who seized the opportunity of the festivities after the wedding to stage one of those fulsome, public protestations of undying love and friendship for Louis that he was in the habit of making whenever the opportunity offered, as his hatred for his cousin grew more and more bitter.

Louis himself had done his magnificent best to vie with the Burgundian splendours. The ever-generous king, who had already given his nephew and godson Charles a pension of 12,000 gold francs even before his betrothal, and made him a further handsome money present on the eve of his marriage,[40] had also given Louis 15,000 gold francs ten days before the ceremony to help him with the heavy expenses of his son's wedding. Even so, Louis had had to have some of his gold and jewelled treasures melted down to pay for the 714 pearls with which his own black damask doublet and his surcoats of crimson and tawny velvet were embroidered. There is no record of what the young bridegroom wore although, as he had had for some years previously his own tailor, who was always making him garments of 'bronze-green, gay-green and vermilion' no doubt he too was sumptuously attired.

But it is difficult to believe that Charles can have felt very happy that day. Isabelle, who was then sixteen, made no secret of the fact that this marriage held no attractions at all for her. To become the bride of an English king had appealed to her vanity even as a child. On her marriage contract she was still described as 'Daughter of France, Queen of England'.[41] To give up that glorious title to marry a mere cousin four years her junior was a great come-down. The fact that, on the occasion of his marriage, Charles' father had transferred to him his own Valois title, which the king had just raised from a county to a dukedom,[42] could not have seemed much compensation to her. So she wept openly during the ceremony, painful and humiliating behaviour for her bridegroom to bear. Moreover, apart from his resplendent father, Charles was evidently very much alone on this important occasion in his life, surrounded by so many great personages virtually unknown to him, for there is no mention of his mother's presence there. At some unrecorded date during that year she gave birth to a daughter, Margaret, so perhaps that had something to do with her absence. The only person who there is some reason to think may have come from Château-Thierry to give him moral support was his tutor

Nicolas Garbet; for on the fly-leaf of that manuscript of Sallust's *Catalina*,[43] Garbet wrote a little poem about the marriage which gives the impression that he was there.

When the ceremonies were over Louis sent the young couple back to join Valentina at Château-Thierry, where Isabelle took her place rather as one of the children than as the wife of Charles. Although her father had given her a dowry of 300,000 francs and Louis had promised her an income of 6000 pounds and given her the castellany of Crécy-en-Brie,[44] there could be no question yet of a separate establishment for two such children. So the knowledge that he was now Duke of Valois, with a wife and considerable means of his own, made no difference in Charles' life for the time being, and he was able to resume the quiet pleasures of boyhood for nearly a year and a half before the blow fell that put an end to them for ever.

November 23, 1407–December 8, 1408

O N the evening of Wednesday, November 23rd, 1407, the day
before Charles' thirteenth birthday, his father Louis went to dine
with the queen at the Hôtel Barbette, a house which covered a large
stretch of land in the quarter now known as the Marais, and which she
used occasionally as a private retreat for herself. Louis of Orleans, her
close companion, visited her there upon occasion; and there were not
wanting those who suspected that they were lovers. But there is no
proof of this; and whatever the truth may have been, any visits that he
paid her during that November could only have been inspired by a
purely friendly wish first to encourage and then to console her. For
Isabeau had taken up her residence at the Hôtel Barbette on that occasion in order to lie in for the twelfth time. The child, a boy, had been
born on November 11th, but died the same day; and his loss seems to
have caused her particular grief.

On the evening in question Louis had not been long with the queen
when, at about eight o'clock, one of the king's servants arrived to tell
him that the king wanted to see him urgently. Louis, always devoted
to his brother, set out at once for the Hôtel Saint-Pol, riding his mule and
accompanied by a mere handful of retainers, some mounted and some
on foot carrying torches. As the little cavalcade turned into the street
then called the Vieille Rue du Temple and came abreast of a house
known as the House of the Image, a band of men rushed out of it, armed
with swords, axes and wooden clubs and fell upon Louis. Hacking off
his left hand that held the reins, they dragged him from his mule into
the mud and there inflicted on him such terrible wounds that he died
at once. At the noise of the attack the horses of his mounted retainers
bolted with their riders; of those on foot one, a young German page,
was killed trying to protect his master while another, grievously
wounded, took refuge in a house in the near-by Rue des Rosiers. By
the time the mounted retainers managed to check their horses and
return to the scene they found their master beyond help; and as the
murderers threatened them too, they made off as fast as they could to
spread the alarm. The assassins, meanwhile, set fire to the house in
which they had lain in wait and then, leaving one torch burning on the

cobblestones beside the body, mounted their horses and galloped off through the narrow streets in the direction of the Porte Saint-Denis, leaving in all who heard them thunder past an uneasy sense that something terrible had happened.

The news of this appalling murder spread quickly. Alerted by his servants, some of Louis' friends and allies were soon on the scene. Together they gathered up the battered body, the hand and the spilt brains, and carried them into a house belonging to the Marshal de Rieux, immediately opposite the House of the Image. An esquire was sent to fetch Guillaume de Tignonville, the Provost of Paris and, as such, head of the police. Accompanied by some of his officers he went at once to the house of the marshal and there, he says in his report, saw Louis' body, dressed in black damask, lying on a table and bleeding from two enormous wounds that had split not only his head from ear to ear, but his face across the forehead completely open.

As soon as he had noted these hideous details, Guillaume de Tignonville sent messengers to tell the princes of the blood, Bourbon, Anjou, Berry and Burgundy, and the other members of the Council, what had happened and ask for instructions. They summoned him to meet them without delay at the Hôtel d'Anjou and there ordered him, first, to have all the gates of Paris closed, and then to have Louis' body put in a lead coffin and taken for that night to the nearby convent of the Blancs-Manteaux. That done he was to begin enquiries that same night to try and discover the authors of this terrible deed.

The report[1] of that questioning, which began so few hours after the crime and went on late into the night in that blood-stained street and all next day at the Châtelet, has such a breathless actuality that it is as if one were present at a murder trial of today. But all that could be elicited from the men and women in the neighbouring houses, mostly humble artisans and tradesfolk whose evidence, quoted verbatim, brings them vividly alive, was that a week or so before the murder, they had seen a number of horses taken into the house, while about a dozen men, none of whom they knew, had come and gone there, but kept much to themselves and let no one in. So the only useful information obtained was that this murder had clearly been premeditated and most carefully and ruthlessly planned by men who were obviously well-informed as to Louis' movements.

The next morning, while the questioning was still continuing, the princes and other members of the Council assembled at the Blancs-

Manteaux; but the king was not there, not being well enough to attend the funeral of his beloved brother. There they all looked their last at the mangled body of him who, as Nicolas de Baye, the Clerk of the *Parlement*, says in words that reveal how difficult it must have been for them to realise it, "at about eight o'clock yesterday evening was the Duke of Orleans and many other lands, and now is ashes and putrefaction."[2] A great cortège, the royal dukes holding the corners of the rich cloth that covered the coffin borne by Louis' esquires, and all loudly lamenting, John of Burgundy more loudly than any, the death of the brilliant young prince so brutally struck down, followed the body to the convent of the Celestines, to which Louis had been a generous benefactor and where in his will he had asked to be buried, in the chapel which he himself had founded. When this ceremony was over, all dispersed to their houses, to wait until the provost was ready to submit his report to them.

This he did on the morning of the next day, Friday the 26th, when the Council met in the Hôtel Saint-Pol. Although he was not yet able to inform them who the murderers were, it seems that he had begun to have his suspicions, for he followed up his report by asking permission to search the houses of the nobles, the princes of the blood among them. This request, which might have been resented on a less grave occasion, was readily granted by all present—except one. Neither agreeing nor dissenting, the Duke of Burgundy rose from his place and asked his uncle of Berry and his cousin the Duke of Anjou to withdraw with him. Alone with them, he bluntly announced that the murder had been done at his order. Knowing that all the assassins were harboured in his Hôtel d'Artois,* he realised that the proposed search with its accompanying questioning might easily reveal the truth. Better then to admit it straightaway. In any case he neither felt nor expressed the slightest remorse for his deed; he was confident that his own position and power would save him from any serious consequences; and he cared less than nothing for what his fellow princes would think of him because of it.

Berry and Anjou were so stunned by this revelation that they let him go. Unable to find words or to face the Council again that day, they summoned it to meet the next morning, this time at Berry's great house, the Hôtel de Nesles. It was typical of Burgundy's arrogant

* The tower of Burgundy's Hôtel d'Artois, which stood in the angle of the present Rue Étienne Marcel and the Boulevard Sébastopol, is still there.

effrontery that he turned up for this meeting with the rest. But Berry refused him entrance, on the ground that his case was to be discussed. At that, perhaps at last seeing that he might be in danger, he took horse and, ordering the assassins at his Hôtel d'Artois to accompany him, set off at once for his own territories.

It is not difficult to imagine the consternation of the Council when Berry and Anjou told them of Burgundy's confession. The greater number of them were friends and partisans of Louis and were still grief-stricken at his death. On top of that to learn that it was one of themselves who had cold-bloodedly done this terrible deed came as an appalling shock. Familiar though they were with Burgundy's dislike of his cousin and his constant quarrels with him, the idea that he might go so far as to murder him never seems to have occurred to them, especially as the quarrels were always patched up. Indeed, one of them had taken place only a day or two before the murder and, after Berry and others had intervened, Burgundy had even carried his hypo-critical treachery so far as to invite the unsuspecting Louis to dine with him on the following Sunday, when he knew he would be dead. The realisation that, at that very moment, Burgundy's hired assassins were already lying in wait for Louis and that he had, as they soon learned, bribed one of the king's servants to summon him to his death, must have seemed almost impossible to take in. And then, too, there was the memory of Burgundy's heartless duplicity at the funeral, when he had lamented with the rest. It was no wonder that, when they recovered from the shock of that revelation, some of Louis' followers wanted to ride immediately in pursuit of Burgundy with the aim of killing him on the spot. But the Duke of Anjou restrained them.

Looking back on the events of that day in the light of subsequent history, it is clear that both the Duke of Berry, in refusing Burgundy entry into the Council chamber where he would have been at the mercy of his peers, and allowing him to depart into his own country, and the Duke of Anjou in preventing summary justice, made a fatal mistake. Their hesitations were more than understandable, for they were in a situation that was delicate and difficult. John the Fearless was the doyen of the princes of the blood; he was easily the richest and most powerful of them, with many allies and the means of raising an army greater than any of his opponents could muster; he was the father-in-law of the dauphin; and by posing as their champion against Louis, he had won the almost fanatical devotion of the people of Paris.

To have taken instant and possibly violent action against him would therefore have been a very grave step, involving perhaps some risk. But at least it could have been explained and to some extent justified as retribution against a self-confessed murderer; and that would have made revenge difficult to organise. As things were to turn out, swift action would probably have saved France many disastrous years. For it is fair to say that it was because of the mistakes and hesitations of that fatal day, which gave Burgundy time, in the security of his own territories, to prepare what he was brazenly to call a justification for his deed, to surround himself with allies and organise resistance, that France was soon afterwards plunged into the horrors of a civil war that reduced the country to as wretched a state as at any time in her history, and made her for so many years a prey to her English enemies.

More resolution on the part of the Council that day might also have saved Valentina much cruel frustration, though it could not have lessened her grief; and spared her son Charles many years of bitter strife. So taken up were the chroniclers with recording the events in Paris that none of them mentions how or when the news of her husband's murder was conveyed to Valentina. The only document in the Orleans archives relating to that time conjures up a poignant scene, for it records a payment to one of Louis' servants who, after the murder, took his favourite dog, Doucet, back to Valentina;[3] but it can hardly have been so humble a messenger who was charged with bearing the news of their loss to Louis' widow and children. They were at Château-Thierry, some sixty miles from Paris, when the tragedy happened, so it would have taken a fast horseman six or seven hours to reach them, even if anyone had thought of sending one in the confusion of that night. As the funeral took place the next morning it seems not unlikely that her husband was buried before Valentina even knew of his death; and that Charles had been able to enjoy his thirteenth birthday in the company of his mother, his brothers and his young wife, unaware of the doom that was about to end their quiet and carefree life together.

If that were so, the shock of the news when it came must have been all the more fearful. Indeed Valentina's grief at the loss of the husband to whom she had remained steadfastly loyal for eighteen years was so overwhelming, and her bitter anger against his murderer so violent and relentless, that it is not too much to say that in the end they were her death-blow.

The effect on Charles is less easy to gauge. Towards the end of his life, comparing it with later sufferings, he was to say: "As for the death of the late lord my father (whom God pardon), I was then a young child and did not know how to suffer grief." * This was probably a true enough statement, since it is in any case difficult for a child to comprehend death, especially a death he has not seen, and an unnatural one at that. Then, too, Louis had never been an intimate part of his son's life or an abiding influence in it. He was more like some dazzling godfather who suddenly appeared bringing gifts, or occasionally turning the household upside down, as when he took the boy off to Compiègne to be married. The memory of that marriage could also only have made the present situation still more difficult for Charles to understand, for it must have seemed incomprehensible to him that the uncle who had then made so much of his father, protesting his loyalty and undying love for him, should now have murdered him.

If these things were at first almost impossible for him to grasp, it was at any rate quickly borne in on him in a very practical way that, as a result of what had happened, his own position had suddenly and completely changed. His mother's first thought seems to have been to secure as far as possible the safety of Charles. This was an essential precaution, for though it was perhaps chiefly Burgundy's deep personal hatred of his cousin that had caused him to murder him, it was also his enmity for him as head of the House of Orleans, an enmity that would now embrace Charles as his father's successor. On December 6th, therefore, Valentina appointed Sauvage de Villiers,[4] a faithful friend of the family, as counsellor and chamberlain to Charles, and sent the boy in his care to Blois, the headquarters of the duchy. There, a still older and more valued friend, Pierre de Mornay, the governor of Orleans, (always known as Gauluet, even in official documents, from his property called Les Gaules), would be, she knew, well able to guide the young duke, as he had long served his father. Charles' brother, the eleven-year-old Philip, Count of Vertus, went with him, and although there is no mention of them, presumably the little bastard John and the one-year-old Margaret were in the party too, together with their servants and various lords to guard them. They made part of the journey by boat down the Loire and when on December 10th they reached Jargeau, the citizens of Orleans came there to acclaim their young lord and bring him a gift of twelve fat capons, twelve pheasants and twelve

* See page 333 below.

dozen partridges and larks, as well as two barrels of the red and white wine of the country.[5] It was an offering that his father, who was a considerable gourmet and enjoyed things like lampreys and truffles, would much have appreciated; but it was hardly an exciting present for a child who had never had to give a moment's thought to where his food came from, and had not even his young wife with him to help him enjoy it and keep him company.

For Valentina had kept with her not only her youngest son, John, but her daughter-in-law, Isabelle. This separation of Charles and Isabelle seems odd on the face of it; but the reason for it may have been that Valentina thought the presence of this young daughter of the king would be of help to her in the next ordeal that lay before her. There was only one thing in the world that she now wanted: justice against the man who had taken her husband's life. Although the murderer was self-confessed and his guilt plain, it was none the less necessary to present her case against him convincingly. Fortunately she had a most able counsellor to help her. This was Guillaume Cousinot,[6] the chancellor of the duchy, who was to prove not only a staunch supporter of Valentina, but in the years to come the most faithful guardian of the interests of Charles and of his brother John too. By the end of the first week of December all was ready for Valentina's departure for Paris. No ban on her presence there could have kept her away now.

Her cortège entered the city she had left so many years before on Saturday December 10th, the day when Charles was being received by his subjects at Jargeau. It was one of the saddest and most solemn processions that the city had ever witnessed. Valentina herself, with Isabelle and all her ladies, were of course in mourning, while the litter in which she travelled and the four white horses that drew it were all draped in black. A great retinue of Louis' esquires and other members of his household followed them, in black too. To add to the desolation of the occasion the weather was bitterly cold, for winter had begun very early that year, some said on the night of the murder. The only warming touch for Valentina on that cold, sad journey was the welcome she received from her husband's friends and allies, who were awaiting her outside the gates of Paris. Attended by them she drove straight to the Hôtel Saint-Pol and was admitted at once to the presence of the king, whom she had not seen for eleven years, and who was momentarily in his right mind. When he beheld the young duchess whose presence had once meant so much to him he wept and embraced her; and having heard her piteous complaint, he promised to do whatever his Council advised.

The Council duly met to hear her case five days later. The meeting took place at the Hôtel Saint-Pol in the presence of the king. It was the handsome Count of Alençon, then a young man of twenty-two, who led in Valentina, accompanied by the king's young daughter, by her own small son John and by many members of her husband's household. With them was also Guillaume Cousinot, and after Valentina herself had begged the king for justice, her case, based on the eloquent circumstances of the murder, was set forth by one of the king's own advocates in the *Parlement*, prompted word after word by Cousinot. If Valentina had hoped that this pleading would provoke an instant decision to bring Burgundy to trial forthwith and a plan of how to do it, she was doomed to disappointment. When it had ended the Archbishop of Sens, as Chancellor of the Kingdom, merely stated in vague and general terms that good and speedy justice would be done, whereupon there was nothing for her and her advisers to do but to withdraw while the Council deliberated.

Alas for her hopes, fear and expediency again won the day and appeasement was the craven course on which they decided. A mission was to be sent to John the Fearless, then in Amiens, to try and persuade him to ask forgiveness for his crime and to make peace for the good of the realm. The king asked Berry and Bourbon to undertake this ignoble task. Berry, always rather weak and pacifically inclined, accepted, but Bourbon declined to go, saying, according to Le Religieux, that never again could he bear to look on the face of 'the author of so black a treachery.'[7] Very likely, too, his noble spirit revolted at the nature of the mission. In place of him the Duke of Anjou was asked. He was at that time a man of thirty, not of great authority, and always too obsessed by his dream of becoming the ruling King of Sicily, a title to which he had inherited a legitimate claim from his father and by which he was invariably known, to pay much attention to his French dukedom and affairs; but, although reluctant as ever, he did agree to go.

These two not very forceful ambassadors proved no match for Burgundy. He had been quite subtle enough to realise that the failure to take earlier action against him showed the wavering weakness of his peers and the strength of his own position. So when the peace mission arrived they found him in company with certain doctors in theology who had already prepared a lengthy so-called defence of his crime. He therefore insolently informed Berry and Anjou that he had done nothing for which he need ask pardon – in fact he should rather be thanked for what he had done – and that he intended soon to come to Paris to make this defence in public. Berry and Anjou told him that the king forbade him to come, but he merely repeated his intention. Although they stayed some time in Amiens they entirely failed to weaken his arrogant and contemptuous assurance. There was therefore nothing for it but for them to return ignominiously to Paris to report their failure.

While they were gone Valentina had had to possess her soul in patience as best she might. The terms of their mission, which must certainly have been communicated to her, could only have been a bitter disappointment, so far short did they fall of the promised justice. Yet she must await the outcome of it and continue to hope that, if it failed, some stronger action might be adopted. It was a time when nature itself seemed to be in a state of suspense, for the numbing cold of that winter, one of the worst that anyone could remember, continued relentlessly. Snow fell endlessly. In Paris life had almost come to a standstill. The Seine was frozen so hard that the citizens used it as a highway. Nicolas de Baye, the Clerk of the *Parlement*, says in his *Journal* that he was unable to do his work because, in spite of having a brazier behind his chair, the ink froze on his pen at every third word, and sometimes in the ink-horn too.[8] When at last the thaw came, huge blocks of ice floating down the Seine destroyed the bridges with the houses on them, and the swollen river flowed so swiftly and dangerously that no boat dared cross it.

On January 4th during that dreary wait Valentina did homage to the king, on behalf of herself and the children, for her late husband's lands: that is to say for those that she still retained. For however dilatory the Council might be over her claim for justice, they acted briskly enough when they were merely the mouthpiece of the members of the king's *Chambre des Comptes*; and these officials never let slip an opportunity of getting back into the royal domain and the royal coffers the gifts by which the king, in his limitless prodigality, so dangerously impoverished them.* In their eyes the assassination of Louis of Orleans seems

---

* Le Religieux, I, 609, says that, when recording a gift they considered excessive, these officials would sometimes scribble in the margin of their registers: "He has had too much", or "To be recovered".

to have been an ideal opportunity of this kind and no fine feelings prevented them from pouncing on it even while he was being buried. For the royal decision to take back a considerable number of Louis' estates – Château-Thierry and Crécy-en-Brie among them – is recorded in a document prepared in those last days of November 1407.[9] But it is the voice of the officials rather than the king's own voice that speaks in it to justify this action by saying that Louis, by his daily requests, had obtained more apanages than his late father Charles V had ordained as proper; and excusing the withdrawal of them because of the great number of children the king already had, 'and by the grace of God is disposed to have'. The Council ratified this decision on December 12th.

It was an extraordinary choice of properties which these zealous officials had taken on themselves to withdraw. One of them, Crécy-en-Brie, had been given by Louis to the king's daughter Isabelle on her marriage for her own possession, so that they were hardly in a position to deprive her of it. As for Château-Thierry, it looks very much as if none of them had thought of reading Louis' will before this hasty act was passed, otherwise surely even they would have hesitated before taking back into the royal domain the one property that Louis had bequeathed to Valentina and which, incidentally, the king had given his brother 'in perpetuity'.[10] There is nothing to tell us what Valentina thought of being thus debarred from the castle that Louis had intended as her future home. But one can imagine that any regret for the loss of what had hitherto been one of her favourite residences was numbed by the fact that it had been the place where she first heard of her husband's murder. Then, too, there could now be no question for her of retiring to a quiet life as a dowager. Her presence was necessary at Blois where many heavy tasks awaited her. So perhaps after all the main effect of the withdrawal of those lands was the loss of revenue it entailed, a loss which in her new circumstances was serious enough.

Any hopes that Valentina may have had that the Council were going to get the better of Burgundy were crushed by the news that he was planning to arrive in Paris on February 28th. This news caused her much distress and she immediately left. It was understandable that she could not bear to look on the unrepentant face of her husband's murderer. But apart from that she had already seen and heard enough to realise that any fears she may previously have had of him were amply justified. If his peers had not yet fully realised the danger he constituted to them and the kingdom, she saw clearly enough that, as long as he remained unchastised for his deed, the security of the House of Orleans and all its lands was threatened. As soon as she reached Blois, therefore, she set to work to strengthen the defences of both the castle and the town, provisioning both as for a siege, calling up Louis' men-at-arms and archers and setting guards at the gates 'as if her enemies had been in the neighbourhood'.[11]

In addition to these warlike preparations she had to assume the burden of the administration of the great household and all its estates. In Louis' will he had asked that all his debts should be paid 'to the last penny', and steps taken to find out who his creditors were. This request naturally imposed not only much labour on Valentina but many sacrifices to find the money necessary for the payments. To discharge this duty she had to sell a great many of the family jewels and treasures. One such transaction took place that April, when she sold a fine long ruby, set in a gold ring, to the Duke of Berry—a splendid enough stone for it afterwards to be known as 'the ruby of Berry'.[12] In July Denis Mariète, who had been auditor of Louis' accounts, handed more of his late master's jewels and plate over to Valentina. A receipt from a pewterer of Paris for certain pewter vessels he had supplied for her use seems to suggest that she had put an end to the old sumptuous life and was beginning a more simple existence. And in August she sold to the dauphin, for 10,000 gold francs, one of her houses in Paris, situated near the castle of Bastille.

In the documents recording all these details she is always described as "Valentina, Duchess of Orleans, Countess of Blois and of Beaumont and Lady of Coucy, having the guardianship and government of our very dear and very beloved eldest son, Charles, Duke of the aforesaid Duchy of Orleans and of Valois, and of our other children." So it is obvious that in all these day-to-day internal and domestic matters she was continuing to see to everything herself and treating Charles merely as one of the children. This was reasonable enough since he was legally still a minor.

But when anything concerned the duchy in its external relations, especially something likely to be of lasting effect, Valentina duly brought Charles into it. Thus when in May she renewed a treaty of alliance that Louis had made with their nephew John V, Duke of Brittany, then a young man of eighteen or nineteen who had written to say he would like to continue 'love and alliance' with his 'fair aunt of Orleans and fair brother her son', it was Charles who signed the treaty—a beautiful signature, the first of his that we have—promising to keep the engagement made by his greatly revered lady and mother.[13] The re-affirmation of this alliance was, incidentally, a keen stroke of policy, for the Duchy of Brittany was an even more independent principality than that of Burgundy. John V's father had been very pro-English, barely recognising and constantly flouting the authority of Charles VI, and his son John was equally his own master. Because of this Burgundy strove on many occasions to win the young duke to his side; but Brittany, though later he was not always to be depended on, preferred to retain his alliance with his cousin of Orleans and had even had the courage, only two months previously in Paris, to show openly what seemed like disgust with the powerful duke.

John the Fearless had fulfilled his threat to go to Paris at the end of February to have his so-called defence heard. Although the queen and the princes were reluctant to grant him this privilege, he had arrived with so many allies and armed followers, all of whom he had lodged in his vast Hôtel d'Artois, that they feared to refuse and accordingly agreed that the ceremony should take place in the great hall of Saint-Pol on March 8th. As he rode there that morning Burgundy saluted the people who thronged their doors and windows to acclaim him and wish him success. The great hall was packed with members of the University, the *Parlement* and other officials and citizens, as well, of course, as the princes with two notable exceptions: the kindly old Duke of Bourbon and his son the Count of Clermont. Among the princes was the young Duke of Brittany, and when Burgundy finally arrived, the last to enter, and was shown to a place between Berry and Brittany, 'the said Duke of Brittany was not at all pleased', as even one of Burgundy's own officials records.[14]

The eleven-year-old dauphin presided over the session as the king, though not actually in one of his bad periods, was not well enough to do so. One wonders indeed how even those in their right minds and full health could have sat through the monstrous 'defence' which Jean Petit, the master in theology whom Burgundy had charged to prepare it, poured out for four hours without a pause.[15] This diatribe was nothing more or less than a vilification, outrageous to the point of absurdity, of Louis of Orleans, in the course of which every petty charge, every scrap of rumour that had ever been uttered, was scraped together to prove him not only a man of insatiable ambition and endless

2 (a) Charles and his two younger brothers receiving instruction

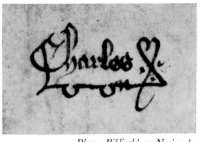

2 (b) The first known signature of Charles of Orleans, on a treaty with the Duke of Brittany dated 1408

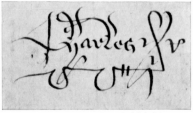

2 (c) A signature on a document of 1438, for comparison

2 (d) A *chantepleure*

intrigue, continually plotting the assassination of his brother by poison, fire or witchcraft, but in his private life given to all the vices: a gambler, an idolater, a tyrant, a seducer of women, using magic spells to that end. All this was grotesquely interlarded with Latin texts drawn from Holy Writ and the Fathers, and copious 'instances' in the manner of the time, its one object being to 'prove' that in ridding the world of 'the criminal of Orleans' Burgundy had performed a virtuous act and would have been guilty of a grave sin if he had left it undone. So fantastic a justification left the queen and the princes stunned, as well it might. But once again this example of Burgundy's blatant and cynical arrogance, combined with the evidence of his armed might and popular support, deprived the princes of any power to stand up to him.

The queen alone took some action, if it was only flight. Like Valentina, she seems to have been quick to feel the latent threat of further violence in John's attitude and so, immediately after that extraordinary session, she left for the castle at Melun, taking the dauphin and his wife with her, and accompanied by Anjou, Berry, Brittany, the Constable, Charles of Albret, her brother Louis of Bavaria and other nobles. There, like Valentina again, she had the citadel repaired and provisioned and the gates closed at night. But it was not John's idea at that time to provoke an open conflict. His main intent was still only to weaken the power of the hated house of Orleans and for that he had wilier means than force at his disposal. He sought a private audience with the king, who had remained in Paris, and with instinctive cunning found just the right way to touch the easy emotions of his poor vacillating mind. He quickly convinced him that Louis had really plotted his death and then begged his forgiveness for having killed his would-be assassin. At that the king, "in the weakness of his malady forgave so horrible a murder benignly and gently",[16] whereupon Burgundy persuaded him to sign and seal on the spot a letter stating that he had "put out of his heart all his displeasure and reinstated his cousin of Burgundy in his particular love, as in the past".[17] Armed with this valuable document, John persuaded the king to remove Louis' friend and nominee Guillaume de Tignonville from his post of Provost of Paris, and to appoint instead one of his own creatures, Pierre des Essarts.[18] This done, he left for his own country.

It is not difficult to imagine the effect on Valentina's loyal heart when she heard what a foul picture of her husband's character and conduct had been publicly painted in Paris. His memory had been slandered before the whole world, and not a word said in his defence. Hitherto she had merely asked for justice and been content to rely on the king and his Council for the form that this should take. But now her whole being craved for vengeance and in her solitude she began to work out in all its details the kind of punishment that alone would fit Burgundy's crimes, not only the crime of murder but this latest infamous slandering of the dead. But how and when could such a plea be put forward? It is doubtful whether she then knew of the king's shameful forgiveness of Burgundy, which was enough to make her lose heart altogether; but although she was not yet daunted, it was clear that she could hope for little from her allies; and on whom else could she rely? In this cruel uncertainty the summer wore on.

It was the queen who put an end to this period of suspense. Although in the past she had been far from friendly to Valentina, now it was she who stretched out a hand to her sister-in-law. John of Burgundy was their common enemy; and, like Valentina, Isabeau had had to endure months of suspense, bred of uncertainty concerning Burgundy's intentions and the attitude of the Parisians that had kept her and the court all that summer at Melun. This stalemate had to be broken some time, for both of them. Accordingly the queen invited her sister-in-law to go to Paris again and plead her case there anew; and she herself returned there on August 26th, making a state entry with the little dauphin, riding a white horse, accompanied by the princes of the fleur-de-lis, as the chroniclers call them, and followed by some thousands of men-at-arms. The fickle Parisians, who by then had not seen their favourite Burgundy for some months, seem to have been impressed by this spectacle and its show of force, and gave the royal family a warm welcome as they passed through the streets on the way to the Louvre, where the queen took up her residence.

That invitation to Valentina was enough to make hope spring up afresh, even in a heart as weary as hers must then have been, and she set off without delay. So, on August 28th, once again the duchess's solemn cortège with its mourning figures and black-draped horses and litters entered the city as they had done nine months previously. Once again Valentina brought with her her daughter-in-law Isabelle. But this time she had planned that Charles, too, should be present to hear Jean Petit's accusation answered, and to support her plea for vengeance against his father's murderer.

Accordingly, as soon as the date of September 11th was fixed for the hearing, she sent for him, her secretary having already provided him with money for his journey—a sum for which we still have the receipt that he gave to the secreatry of the '*parlement* of Blois'.[19] It was September 9th when he arrived in Paris, a city that he had not seen since he left it as a child of two. He was attended by a good many followers but came himself 'in very modest state',[20] dressed in black, a colour that he was to wear for many years. His great-uncle of Berry and other lords met him at the Porte Saint-Antoine and conducted him to the queen and the dauphin. The queen he had already seen at the time of his wedding at Compiègne, but this was probably the first time he had met the young Duke of Guienne, heir to the throne and two or three years his junior, of whom he was to see much in the years to come. When he had recommended his person and his mission to the queen, Charles went to join his mother and his wife in the Hôtel de Behaigne, that house that the king had given his brother Louis long ago in the happy days of their youth, so that he might be close to him when he was in his palace of the Louvre.

It was in the great hall of that palace that the audience was held this time. It was packed with all those who had heard Burgundy's defence six months earlier. As Burgundy himself was not there, the old Duke of Bourbon came this time with the other senior princes. With them were several other nobles who later became staunch allies of Charles of Orleans, chief among them the Counts of Alençon, Eu and Vendôme. But once again the king was 'absent'. Besides Charles and Isabelle, Valentina had with her Guillaume Cousinot, the chancellor of her duchy; but this time the man who spoke first for her was Serisi, or Cerisy, the Benedictine Abbot of Saint-Fiacre. He replied point by point to the monstrous accusations of Jean Petit, demolishing each in a speech which was as long as Petit's[21] had been but must have been much easier to listen to, so human and dramatic was it, at times painfully so, as when he imagined the dead Louis calling to the king: "O my lord, my brother, see how I have received death for you. It was for the great love that was between us. . . . Look on my wounds and at my body, battered, trampled, and abandoned in the mud. . . . Look on my broken arms and my brains strewn far from my head". If Charles had not been able to feel real grief on first hearing of the death of his father, neither he nor the rest of the audience could have forborne a shudder of horror at this grisly evocation of the manner of it. The abbot got in some shrewd thrusts as well, pointing out for instance what a danger to the kingdom it was to let someone like the Duke of Burgundy flout the royal authority as he had done. He spoke so eloquently, says Juvenal des Ursins, that all present agreed that "never would so great a fault have been committed in France if justice were not done, and clearly the Duke of Burgundy had forfeited his life and possessions".[22]

As soon as the abbot had finished, Cousinot rose and set forth in full detail the vengeance that Valentina now claimed against the duke.[23] She wanted him brought to Paris and forced to confess his fault and ask pardon for it both at the Louvre, Saint-Pol, and on the site of the crime, where he was to kiss the earth. He must erect great stone crosses there; and on the site of the house where the murderers had lain in wait a religious house must be built, where a chapter of canons would say daily masses for Louis' soul. Chapels must be built elsewhere too, including Jerusalem and Rome, where such masses would also be said. While all this was being done the duke was to be kept in prison, and when the work was completed he should be exiled abroad, if not for life at least for thirty years. Finally, in his public confession, he was to say that he had had the murder committed out of hate, envy and covetousness, and not for any of the other reasons he had afterwards alleged. These were of course wildly exaggerated demands which, after all the rebuffs and disillusionments she had suffered, Valentina could hardly have hoped would be granted, let alone enforced against so powerful a man. But there is something pathetic about their very wildness, as evidence of the agony of mind that those long months of frustration had bred in her, and perhaps too, in that religious age, of genuine fears for her husband's soul. She had now been pushed almost to the limit of her endurance and it was to need little more to drive her beyond it.

That little was not long in coming, although immediately after this session things looked momentarily brighter for her. The king, well again, revoked the letters of pardon he had given Burgundy and gave Valentina a document to prove it.[24] He also sent ambassadors to Burgundy telling him that he intended to take proceedings against him. And the princes agreed that, if he continued to flout the king's commands, they would take up arms to subdue him. Encouraged by these declarations, Valentina returned to Blois with Isabelle and Charles who, before leaving Paris, did homage to the king for his lands and for the help the king had promised him.

But sending ambassadors to Burgundy was one thing and getting hold of him was another. Ever since July he had been fighting a domestic war against the citizens of his own town of Liège. On September 23rd he crushed them by a resounding victory. Although it was not an important war, this victory acted like a cold douche on the flickering ardour of his opponents in Paris, many of whom "began to lower their heads and to be of the opposite opinion, seeing the constancy, the boldness and the power of that duke. . . and the decisions that had previously been taken against him were set at nought and broken."[25] The resolution of Valentina's allies was still further shaken by the news that Burgundy, insolently disregarding all the king's commands, was now marching on Paris. Once again the queen showed herself more valiant than the princes. She appealed to the people for funds to defend the city and oppose him with arms; but the news that had scared the nobles had encouraged the people and they refused the queen's request. So after pleading with them to remain loyal to her and the king, the royal family and all the princes—Anjou, Berry, Brittany, Bourbon, Clermont, and Alençon—left Paris once again, this time for Tours, early in November.

So once again, and for the last time, Valentina had lost; for now even her valiant spirit was broken and with it her bodily strength gave way too. When the royal family, who had embarked on the Loire at Gien, stopped at Orleans, she was too ill to receive them and it was the faithful Gauluet who lodged them in her castle there. And when their barges continued downstream to Tours, they passed Blois without stopping. On December 4th a doctor called Jean Lelièvre was summoned from Paris,[26] but he arrived too late, for Valentina died that same day. No one has recorded what disease it was, if any, that ended the life of this young woman of thirty-seven or eight. But when one remembers the sufferings and trials that she had had to endure in those last twelve months, one is inclined to believe those of her contemporaries who said that the bitterness of her grief and her despair had brought on an incurable langour from which she died. On her deathbed she wept with sorrow at having to leave her own four young children and also Louis' little illegitimate son, of whom she is reputed to have said, perhaps divining the warrior he was to become, that of them all he seemed the likeliest to avenge his father.[27]

After her death her heart was taken to Paris, to join her husband's body in his chapel at the Celestines; but her own body was buried in the church of the Cordeliers at Blois. On the walls of the chapel where the tomb was, and on the walls of the choir of the church too, was inscribed that device—"Nil mihi praeterea, praeterea nihil mihi"—which she had adopted since her widowhood and which so well expressed the hopelessness of her despair. A true daughter of her age, she had chosen an emblem for her sorrow too, a *chantepleure*, a kind of watering-can shedding great tears. But it is the device in its laconic French version: "Rien ne m'est plus, plus ne m'est rien", by which her memory has been kept alive in France for the past five hundred years and more.[28]

When John of Burgundy heard the news of her death, he was overjoyed because, says Monstrelet, that duchess had opposed him with such zeal and such diligence.[29] Now there was only a boy of fourteen to continue the struggle, a puny adversary whom he thought he could quickly overcome once for all. But in that he was to find himself mistaken.

WITH the death of Valentina so many burdens fell on the un-accustomed shoulders of the young Charles that there was little leisure in which to mourn the loss of the mother who had until then been the lodestar of his days. Life went relentlessly on and he had to adjust himself without any pause to the rigours and responsibilities of his great estate. Fortunately he was surrounded by faithful counsellors and servitors of all ranks to guide him in his decisions and to carry out all the tasks that had to be performed: men who had served his father before him, like Cousinot, Gauluet and Denis Mariète, and one or two new ones whom he appears to have appointed himself, among them Pierre Renier, who was to remain his treasurer-general for years to come. But before he could undertake the responsibility for the affairs of his dukedom, his own authority had to be established; and as he had now attained the age of fourteen which, by a decree of his grand-father Charles V,[1] was that at which royal persons came of age, he was now able to take over the governance of all those lands his father had left him and, in addition to his own title of Duke of Valois, assume those of Duke of Orleans, Count of Blois and Beaumont and Lord of Coucy.

Glorious titles indeed they had been for Louis, who had so lightly borne them; but for his son this great inheritance brought at first little but obligations. One of the first necessities was to realise the extent of the rich personal possessions, as opposed to the lands and cities and castles, of which he had suddenly become the owner. To this end, the officers responsible began to list Valentina's treasures on the very day of her death. The list of these still exists[2] and not only conjures up a picture of the splendour of the daily life in the house of a prince of the fleur-de-lis, but evokes poignantly the personal existence of the dead duchess. For alongside all the tapestries, the gold and silver plate, and the fabulous jewels for great occasions—crowns, necklaces and belts of gold—there are the small personal belongings of Valentina: nine chemises from Lombardy, two pairs of galoshes covered with vermilion cloth 'for getting up at night', two boxes of soap, a gold fork with her arms on it with one prong broken and, most touching of all, the "gold ring, with the square ruby, with which Madame was married."

There were her precious books, too, which she had left to Charles and which, with all his other books, seem to have been dearer to him than any of the more obvious riches; for it was only in one of the most desperate moments in his later life that he decided that he must, at last, part with his library, whereas he constantly disposed of the treasures of gold and silver and precious stones, as his father had before him, but out of a much grimmer necessity. But this after all was the normal practice at that time, when the purchase of gold, silver and jewels was the recognised way of investing one's liquid assets, and to realise them when need arose does not seem to have caused any particular distress because the objects happened to be works of art.

In these sad tasks that death imposes, Charles had, besides his excellent staff, the company of his second brother Philip, and his wife Isabelle. We know none of the intimate, and at that time few of the factual, details of Philip's life, but it is clear that he must have been devoted to his elder brother for, shadowy though he may be, he appears constantly by his side in all crises and seems only to have lived to serve him, in great things and small. So now there is a particular mention of his presence—perhaps as a witness?—on an occasion when Charles removed the round clasp, which had a great square ruby, five large pearls, three big diamonds and other stones in it, from a necklace of twisted gold, itself set with fourteen great rubies and sixty-three pearls.[3] As for Isabelle, though none of these documents mentions her, she was certainly there too, for now that Charles was considered to have reached man's estate, the marriage between them had been consummated, as a sad later event reveals. And we know that they were certainly much in each other's company during that year.

All these more or less domestic preoccupations were, however, but a prelude to the one overwhelming obligation that filled Charles' mind: the avenging of his father's death. Valentina had not, as far as we know, laid any express command on him to that end; but to one of his princely nature this was hardly necessary. To avenge his father was a clear duty from which, Hamlet-like, he never swerved. But since, like Hamlet also, he was naturally given more to meditation than to action and, though courageous enough, was not primarily a man of war, he tended to rely on others to help him achieve his end, at the beginning at any rate. That he should have done so while he was still only an inexperienced boy was natural enough. And fortunately he had no lack of allies to help him, for all the princes and other nobles who had supported Valentina, even though not very actively, remained true to his cause. But although still loyal, they were also still as lacking in initiative as they had previously shown themselves and seemed content to wait upon events to resolve a situation that could not but cause a general sense of uneasiness in the kingdom; a feeling of which even Burgundy himself was apparently aware.

For it seems to have been he who took the first step to break the deadlock; a step that revealed his confident assumption that he could make short work of Charles. Some time after Christmas Burgundy's relative and ally, the powerful and influential Count of Hainault (whose daughter had been married to the dauphin's younger brother John on the day that Charles had married Isabelle) went to Tours, presumably on Burgundy's behalf, to urge the king to try and make peace between him and his young cousin Charles. The king, always for peace at any price, naturally agreed and it was decided that an assembly to that end should be held in the Cathedral of Chartres on March 9th, 1409 – a year and a day after the assembly when Jean Petit defended the duke; and Charles and his two brothers were summoned to attend it.

Whether or not they were aware of the ordeal that awaited them there, the occasion could not have been other than awe-inspiring, if only from its setting in that great cathedral. A high platform had been erected there and on it sat the king with the queen, the dauphin and the princes. Charles and his brother took their places behind them. Also present were the Constable, Charles of Albret, the Chancellor and Marshals of France, the members of the *Parlement* and many citizens. Burgundy was attended by six hundred of his followers, but Charles and his brothers had only fifty attendants. The proceedings began with a brief speech by a spokesman of Burgundy's, who simply stated that the duke, having heard that the king was displeased at what had been done by his orders, for the good of the king and the realm, to the person of his brother, my lord of Orleans, was himself greatly distressed. He therefore humbly begged the king to banish this displeasure from his heart and to confer on him again his favour and friendship. Burgundy then added that he had himself dictated this speech, and fervently begged the king to consider his request. That was all. There was no word of remorse, no request for pardon. The effrontery of it was almost sublime. It was in fact merely a repetition of what he had said to the king in private audience after the session of the previous March. And just as the bemused king had then without hesitation meekly forgiven him, so now once again, almost as though he were repeating a rehearsed speech, he replied that he granted the request of his 'fair cousin' for the good of the kingdom, for love of the queen and the other princes of the blood, and for the faithfulness and good service that he expected of Burgundy.

To Charles, who could not but have remembered that occasion only six months before in the great hall of the Louvre, when at the end of Abbot Cerisy's speech the whole assembly had condemned Burgundy and promised justice, this interchange must have seemed a nightmare betrayal. But he was given no chance to say a word of protest. The king immediately ordered him and his brothers to approach, whereupon the spokesman repeated Burgundy's words to them and added: "My lord of Orleans, and you my lords his brothers, here is my lord of Burgundy who begs you to banish from your hearts all the anger and resentment you have conceived against him, to be henceforth his good friends and to forgive all the past".4 Then Burgundy himself, who had so far ignored them, deigned to address them, and said: "My very dear cousins, I beseech you to do so". To this the three children answered never a word. At that the queen, the dauphin and all the lords approached them, begging them to accord to the Duke of Burgundy what he was asking so humbly; and finally the king said to them: "My very dear son and you my very dear nephews, approve and accept what we have done and what has been put before you, and forgive him everything".

It is difficult to imagine a more agonising situation for the three children to find themselves in, and especially for Charles on whom the main responsibility of replying lay. In her public pleadings their mother had always had eloquent counsellors to speak for her, but they stood alone face to face with their frightening cousin of Burgundy, as she had never been. "The Orleans children", says Monstrelet, "had been very strictly brought up and taught", so they were accustomed to obey their elders without question. And now here they were in the presence of their sovereign lord and his family, with his whole court and Council, all waiting in silence for their expected acquiescence. They were caught in a trap. What would happen if they refused the king's request? Such a thing was almost unthinkable, especially in view of the silence of the allies, who were the only friends they had.

One can only hope that those allies managed somehow to convey to Charles that what was being asked of him was merely lip-service, a mechanical formula which they, at least, had no intention of regarding as binding and would not expect him to either. Although such a revelation of cynical perfidy on the part of his elders could not but have been a shock to an honest and innocent boy, it would at least have helped Charles to pronounce those words that must have stuck in his throat, so much did all his subsequent conduct belie them. "My very dear lord" he said, "I obey your order, I consent, I approve all that you have done and I forgive him everything." The king then charged both sides never to quarrel again about this affair and to forgive everyone concerned except those who had actually assassinated his brother—a convenient conscience-saving formula which never led to the punishment of those assassins. The princes in turn swore to this on the Cross of Our Lord and the holy gospels. As a proof of his desire for unity Burgundy promised one of his many daughters to the little Philip of Vertus—a promise that, as the boy grew older, he managed to evade. The two rival dukes exchanged a formal kiss of peace after which Burgundy, having obtained all he wanted, mounted his horse and left the town with his followers, not waiting even to eat and drink.

So was concluded that strange mockery known as the Peace of Chartres. It is a significant commentary on the depths to which moral and ethical standards had sunk in that dissolute court, in an allegedly religious age, that all the parties to that treaty should so cynically and blatantly have regarded the most solemn of oaths sworn in so sacred a place as of no force whatever. The only person who may have been deluded into thinking it meant something was the poor, weak-minded king. And the only person who ever thereafter pretended, for his own purposes, to regard it as binding, was John the Fearless, although of course he too realised what a mockery the whole thing had been.

The general attitude of the assembly after the ceremony was aptly summed up by a jester in Burgundy's service, who used his fool's licence to declare openly, in one of those elaborate plays on words dear to the members of his profession, that this was a 'paix fourrée', a plastered-over peace—in other words a hollow sham.* Nicolas de Baye,

* The play on words is twofold. The word *paix*, in addition to 'peace' also means a 'pax' or osculatory, a kind of tablet with a representation of

the clerk of the *Parlement*, echoed the same belief when, in the margin of his official report of the day's doings, he scribbled: "Pax, pax, inquit propheta, et non est pax".[5] When the story of it got around not only the Orleans children, says the chronicler Perceval de Cagny, but "the greater part of the knights and esquires and the good people of Paris were not at all easy in their consciences".[6] And Monstrelet adds that many lords murmured in secret that "henceforward one might murder nobles with impunity since one was let off without reparation".[7]

The only immediate result of this farcical peace was that the king and queen with their court felt able to return to Paris; and their subjects there, who had deplored their long absence, welcomed them joyfully, perhaps deluding themselves that all might now be well. As no particular events arose during that summer to bring the hidden discord to the surface, an uneasy truce prevailed. Charles had returned to Blois from Chartres and, while waiting for some turn of events that would enable him to forswear the infamous oath he had been forced to pronounce, he spent most of his time with his wife Isabelle. Her company could not but have been a consolation to him after the humiliation he had been made to endure, at a time of otherwise lonely suspense.

They were drawn together then too by the fact that Isabelle was expecting a child at the end of the summer. While waiting for that they travelled about their duchy and were everywhere welcomed by their subjects. In the late summer they were buying horses and hunting equipment, no doubt hoping that they might enjoy some days of pleasant sport, once the young duchess had recovered from her child-bearing, for which the usual sumptuous preparations were then being made. But this hope was not to be realised for on September 13th, after giving birth to a girl, Isabelle died at Blois, still only nineteen. Her death filled Charles with grief for there is no doubt that she had come to mean much to him. Even thirty-seven years afterwards, when he had been twice re-married, she remained so precious a memory that he had her anniversary – that of 'the most excellent and most generous lady', says the abbey cartulary,[8] underlining the words 'most generous' – celebrated in the abbey church of Saint-Laumer, where she was buried.

---

the crucifixion or some other holy image, which the priest and congregation kissed during the Mass. The verb *fourrer*, in addition to its simple meaning of 'to cover or wrap round' is used in the sense of coating, plating or plastering over something to make it look better than it is, e.g. to silver or gild an osculatory of cheap metal.

So now, with father, mother and wife all gone in less than two years, he was more than ever alone, with for youthful company only three little boys all under twelve, and two baby girls, his three-year-old sister Margaret and the baby, Jane, of which he had become the four-teen-year-old father.

But once again there was little time for him to dwell on his private sorrows, for less than a month after the death of Isabelle discord broke out afresh; and once again it was a brutal act of Burgundy's that provoked it. During that summer he had been virtually a dictator since, probably at his persuasion, Charles and his allies were barred from the Council, leaving Burgundy a free hand there. But he had used his power to no good end for, although the Parisians continued to trust him, he did nothing to improve the general maladministration from which they suffered. There have been few periods in France's history when such corruption prevailed. The intermittent madness of the king and his reckless generosity created a situation from which even the best of the nobles seemed unable to resist profiting, with the result that they all grew richer and more powerful while the royal coffers became more and more depleted, to the point where the king himself often lived in a state of poverty. With the example of the nobles before them, lesser men often indulged in corruption and graft, with inevitable results on the administration of justice. For want of some strong central measures of reform, each man continued to blame everyone else for the disastrous situation from which all suffered, suspicion was rife and none was safe from the accusations of his neighbours. Among those who were especially suspect, often with good reason, were court officials who were close to the king and thus had exceptional opportunities of enriching themselves at the expense of the royal treasury.

One of the most important of these was Jean de Montagu, a man of good but not noble birth who had been a considerable figure at court since the time of Charles V. He and his two brothers had all by their abilities secured high positions. One of them had become Bishop of Poitiers and Paris and the other had been made, first, Chancellor of France and then Archbishop of Sens. Jean's ambitions were more worldly. High office at court and the acquisition of rich possessions were his goal. Faithful service of Charles VI from the time of his accession secured him the former, and he had become Grand Master of the household, a position of immense power and influence. Through his offices he had gradually acquired great wealth, not only from the remunerations for them but because the king, who so greatly relied on him, constantly showered gifts of money and presents on him until he became one of the richest men in the kingdom.

All these things had made him a person of considerable importance in the state; but this had not tempted him to play any part in politics during the recent quarrels and he had managed to remain on good terms both with Louis of Orleans and his allies and also, as far as he knew, with John of Burgundy, although he was closer to the former. However, wealth and influence like his were enough to make Burgundy want him out of the way, and also to make him a convenient scapegoat in the prevailing climate of suspicion. So it was that on October 7th Pierre des Essarts, whom Burgundy had appointed Provost of Paris the year before, arrested Montagu, imprisoned him in the Châtelet and there charged him with a variety of crimes, among them that of abetting Louis of Orleans in exerting an evil influence on the king. Whether there was any truth in any of them cannot now be known, as no evidence was produced and there was no trial. The wretched elderly man—he was nearly sixty—was tortured until, unable to bear the pain any longer, he finally made a confession.

All this time Burgundy had kept out of the way, but it was universally taken for granted that des Essarts was acting on his instructions, and it was not long before, as was his wont, he openly admitted his responsibility for the affair. For one thing the accusation of having been in league with Louis of Orleans could have come from no one else. It was noticeable, too, that a great many lords were sent from Burgundy, Flanders and Artois to witness the final stages of this cruel drama. As soon as he had signed his confession, only ten days after his arrest, Montagu was taken to the place of execution. Before he died he told the spectators that he had only confessed under torture, showing them his dislocated hands and broken body to prove it. Then his head was cut off and set on a lance in the Halles; and his body was hung up by the armpits on the huge and terrible gibbet of Montfaucon,* where it remained for three years.

* This huge gibbet stood at the angle of the modern Quai de Jemmapes and the Rue de Lagrange aux Belles. It consisted of sixteen stone pillars over thirty feet high, joined by wooden cross-beams on which not only living people were hanged, but the bodies of those executed by different means elsewhere were hung up in sacks until they rotted and fell into the ditch below.

This shocking deed horrified both the court and the Orleanists. Among the latter it was as usual the tender-hearted old Duke of Bourbon who was most genuinely grieved; he and his son the Count of Clermont had left Paris before the execution, 'full of indignation'.[9] Berry's sorrow was alleviated by the receipt of some of Montagu's jewels. But the main effect of this tragedy was that it acted as a kind of spring to release the princes from the paralysis that the Peace of Chartres had imposed on them; and this fresh proof of Burgundy's continuing determination to oust from power anyone friendly to themselves galvanised them at last into action.

The first to move was Charles, and the speed with which he acted is enough to indicate his relief that the period of waiting was apparently over and his hope that now perhaps something was going to be done. His deeds at that time reveal too how far he had developed in the last half-year from the passive boy he had been at Chartres. Not only did he immediately begin to collect troops and send a stream of messengers to all his allies, keeping the queen informed of all he was doing, but on October 24th, only a week after Montagu's execution, he and his brothers signed a military agreement with Count Bernard of Armagnac,[10] promising to serve him against all but the king, the queen and the Duke of Guienne (the usual formula in such feudal alliances). This was an act of far-reaching importance, for by it Charles not only immeasurably strengthened the cause of himself and his allies for the immediate future, but helped to bind the powerful Bernard still more firmly to the royal house, thus counterbalancing with his Armagnac force the weight of the Burgundian support of England in the later conflicts of the Hundred Years' War.

The Counts of Armagnac, whose fief covered a great stretch of land between the Garonne and the Adour, were already staunch supporters of the French kings, so greatly had they resented the English rule in Aquitaine which had made them vassals of England. Charles VI had appointed Count Bernard his lieutenant-general for Languedoc; and he was closely connected with the Duke of Berry whose first wife, Jane of Armagnac, had been an aunt of his, and one of whose daughters, Bonne of Berry, he had himself married. He had been on good terms with Louis of Orleans too; but it was not until Charles thus drew him in that he became an active supporter of the Orleans cause and certainly the most redoubtable of all Charles' allies. Bernard was at that time in his late forties, a man who combined some of the cultivated tastes of his father-in-law, Berry, with military skill and great courage and dash. As a soldier he had a reputation for ruthlessness and even ferocity, and as the leader of his fierce Gascon troops he was powerful enough to give even Burgundy pause.

He, meanwhile, was busy trying to pacify the king who, making one of his periodic recoveries not long after the execution of Jean de Montagu, was outraged at learning what had happened to his trusted servant of so many years' standing, the more so because, while he was momentarily 'absent', he had been made to sign a document justifying what had been done. Hearing, too, of the warlike preparations of the allies, he summoned all the nobles to Paris that Christmas to attend a great dinner. Charles of Orleans, with Brittany, Armagnac and others of his following thought it better not to accept an invitation to a function where Burgundy was sure to be, so they did not attend. No doubt Burgundy was pleased by their absence, for it not only gave him a chance to poison the king's mind about Montagu, uncontradicted, but to persuade him and the queen to entrust him with the care and education of the twelve-year-old dauphin, his son-in-law. This position he had long coveted because of its great potential influence, in view of the fact that the dauphin would obviously have more and more to act for his father in the years to come.

With his favour at court thus restored he awaited whatever developments Charles and his allies were planning. For some months during the winter of 1410 it looked as though he had nothing to fear from them, for although they met on several occasions it was only to cement their alliances formally, or to discuss policy. These discussions sometimes revealed differences of opinion as to what should be the declared aim of their eventual action. Although all were agreed that this should be to obtain revenge against Burgundy, there were two views as to the best method of seeking this. Some, of whom we may be sure Charles was one, felt that he should now declare and make war to the death against his cousin, with their help. But others thought that they should rather continue to press the king to give Charles justice by avenging his brother. Finally, on April 15th at Gien-sur-Loire, the Dukes of Berry, Brittany and Orleans, and the Counts of Alençon, Clermont and Armagnac, all signed an alliance against Burgundy.[11]

Another matter of great personal importance for Charles was also settled at that meeting. In order to strengthen his recent alliance with Bernard of Armagnac, it was decided that he should marry the eleven-year-old Bonne, third daughter of the count and his wife Bonne. The old Duke of Berry seems to have taken a particular interest in this betrothal of his grand-daughter, and it was his Chancellor, the Archbishop of Bourges, who read to the princes assembled at Gien that April the contract of marriage,[12] a document exemplary in its businesslike brevity, clarity and common sense, and worth quoting as an example of how such things were done at that time. The Lord of Armagnac agreed to give Charles, as a dowry for his daughter, the sum of 100,000 francs, about a third of it at the time of the marriage and the rest by annual instalments, this sum, or what remained of it, to be repaid if Bonne died leaving no children. If on the other hand Charles died before Bonne, she was to receive a dowry of 6000 francs, drawn from Charles' lands. Their heirs male were to succeed to all their father's lordships that were not royal apanages, except for what ought to go to Charles' daughter Jane. For the marriage itself, the Lord of Armagnac agreed to clothe his daughter 'well and honourably according to her rank', and to send her at his expense on the fifteenth of August next to Riom, one of Berry's castles, to be handed over to Charles or his messengers. Charles, on his side, was to 'enjewel' her according to her rank.

When all this had been concluded the princes dispersed to their own homes for the time being. Charles took the Duke of Brittany back to Blois with him for a few days and during his visit he gave to his youthful ally one of his treasures, a splendid illuminated Book of Hours written in gold and azure, bound in black velvet adorned with rubies, sapphires and pearls and embroidered with leaves in gold thread.[13] Various other people, the Constable Charles of Albret among them, received gifts from his treasury at that time too. But the most sumptuous Charles sent to Bonne of Armagnac and her mother: to his future bride an image of Our Lady, in gold, in the form of a *pax* or *osculatorium*, and to her mother a Book of Hours 'quite new', its covers of massive gold enamelled with figures and flowers, in a box of vermilion satin, the whole enclosed in a case of gilded leather. In May he arranged a betrothal between his daughter Jane, now a baby of eight months, and the six-year-old son of his ally John, Count of Alençon,[14] who was himself married to a sister of Brittany's: a betrothal that thirteen years later resulted in marriage, and a happy one too.

All these things seem to suggest that Charles was now taking a certain pleasure in his princely position and the munificence that it enabled him to show, that liberality which he later urged as a quality that made nobility more noble:

> . . . qu'il soit plain de largesse,
> Car c'est chose qui avance noblesse.

He was clearly feeling himself more on equal terms with his allies, especially the younger ones; and above all happier because of the prospect of the new marriage that awaited him, this time with a girl younger than himself, even though she was as yet probably unknown to him.

The marriage of Charles and Bonne took place on August 15th but where and how we do not know. No document records whether he went to meet her at Riom, or sent some of his officers to bring her to Blois. We do not even know whether or not she went to live with him at Blois in those first years when she was still a child. The probability is that she did not, as neither the chroniclers nor the archives ever mention her, even on occasions when the other feminine members of the household, Charles' sister Margaret and his daughter Jane, are in question. And there is neither portrait nor description to tell us what manner of girl she was. From poems that Charles wrote to her very much later it is clear that she gradually came to mean much to him, and that she deserved his devotion. But in those first years of their married life they had little chance of any settled happiness together.

Two days after their marriage the old Duke Louis of Bourbon died. This upright man had for some time past been longing to retire from the world, whose cruelties always weighed so heavily on his tender heart, and to end his days in a monastery of Celestines which he had founded at Vichy. But his affection and sense of responsibility for his great-nephews the Orleans children, of whose father he had been so fond, always held him back so that he was still in the world when, at the age of seventy-three, death overtook him. He was succeeded by his son John, Count of Clermont, then aged twenty-nine or thirty. In his youth, and indeed until fairly recently, the count had been on good terms with John of Burgundy and his father Duke Philip before him, partly because in his infancy he had been married to one of John's sisters. But after she died in 1399 he had in 1400 contracted a more comfortable marriage with Mary, a daughter of the Duke of Berry, and thereafter, outraged by Burgundy's murder first of Louis and then of Montagu, he had gradually broken with the house of Burgundy and, like his father, warmly espoused the Orleans cause. After he had succeeded to the dukedom he became one of Charles' most loyal supporters; and Charles was bound to him, and his family after him, by a deep affection that lasted all his life.

An incident that arose out of Bourbon's death revealed to the allies that Burgundy, although he already controlled both the king and the dauphin and dominated the Council, was still seizing every chance to increase his grip on the court and the country. The old Duke of Bourbon had for many years been the Great Chamberlain of France and it would have been normal for this important office to pass to his heir. But before this could happen, in September, Burgundy obtained it from the king for his own brother Philip, Count of Nevers.[15] This comparatively small matter seems to have provided the final prick of the goad that at last prodded the allies into taking the action that the daily worsening state of the kingdom had now made imperative. This was now such that it no longer seemed possible for the allies to take up arms solely to seek revenge for the murder of Louis of Orleans. They must fight to put an end to this state of things and to restore law and order.

This, at any rate, was the view of the Duke of Berry. His opinion may well have been coloured by his displeasure at finding himself excluded from the Council and from any control over the dauphin, but since he was now the only remaining representative of the older generation of the princes of the fleur-de-lis he was able to impose it on the allies when they met again at Gien. Accordingly, on September 2nd, they sent a manifesto to the king, telling him of their humble desire to restore him to his rightful position and power and give good government and justice once again to his people, and asking him to help them achieve this aim. A similar declaration was sent to the prelates,[16] and finally one to the *Parlement*.[17] This last document paints an appalling picture of the state of the realm, of the king's abject poverty and powerlessness, and of the crimes and sins daily committed. These they attribute to the fact that God was blasphemed everywhere, even by churchmen and children; and they end the document with a prayer that God 'in his compassion may have pity and mercy upon us and make us see our faults and pride and wickedness".

This done, without waiting for replies the allies began to assemble their troops. No doubt Charles was disappointed that the seeking of revenge, which could not but be to him the most important objective, had been swallowed up, for the time being at any rate, in the wider aim.

But if he and his allies were victorious, vengeance might automatically follow. Meanwhile, after such a long period of inaction, the prospect of taking up arms at last could only have brought relief and excitement. Already in August he had begun to prepare, by ordering from an armourer near the Bastille in Paris a harness, or complete set of armour for a knight and his horse, for himself and another for his brother Philip.[18] Then early in September he began raising money for his military expenses. To this end two of his principal officials, one being Denis Mariète, his auditor of accounts, were ordered to sell or pledge for the best terms they could obtain some of the seemingly limitless Orleans jewels of gold and precious stones, among other things a ship of gold, which was of such value that its parts were to be sold piecemeal.[19]

Charles needed all the money he could get, for he not only had to pay his own troops but to help with the cost of those supplied by allies like the Duke of Brittany or the Count of Armagnac, who were fighting more in his cause than their own. A special appeal had been made to Brittany[20] because the king had earlier expressly forbidden him to help the allies. He disregarded this and sent a strong contingent of Bretons under the command of his young brother, Arthur Count of Richemont, a universal favourite only a year older than Charles, who had first been brought up at the court of Philip the Bold of Burgundy and, after he died in 1404, at the Duke of Berry's court, where he became a friend of the dauphin. Armagnac came himself with an army of his fierce Gascons. In addition to these some troops arrived from Lombardy to fight for Charles as Lord of Asti. Altogether the allies managed to assemble over 20,000 fighting men, a considerable army for that time. The most redoubtable of them were the Gascons, whose distinguishing badge of a white scarf or band, worn over the left shoulder, was soon adopted by the allies, nobles and ordinary soldiers alike, while their name of Armagnacs, because of the dread they inspired, gradually became used by all their opponents to denote the whole body of the allied army.*

* The princes of the Orleanist party were not at all pleased that this name should have been adopted, since the Count of Armagnac was merely an ally who had joined them at the request of the young Duke of Orleans. Juvenal des Ursins always refers to the Orleanist party "called Armagnac" and Pierre de Fenin, p. 578, says that in the party opposed to the Duke of Burgundy there were "many great lords beyond comparison greater than the Count of Armagnac" who, when their forces were called

The only notice the king had taken of their manifesto was to order them to disarm, but this they refused to do until he consented to hear them, and accordingly in October they marched on Paris. They reached the city unopposed and encamped all round the western outskirts. Only then does Burgundy seem to have realised that they were now in earnest, whereupon he summoned his own allies, his brothers the Duke of Brabant and the Count of Nevers, with the Count of Savoy and others, to come to his aid, and assembled forces from his own territories. Greatly alarmed at finding themselves hemmed in between the opposing armies, the Parisians put troops on guard at their own expense, to protect themselves and their city from the pillaging soldiers of both sides. It really looked now as if the long-feared civil war was about to break out, and the whole populace waited in dread for the hostilities to begin. According to the chroniclers, even Nature herself seemed to presage the danger that threatened for, as is the way with chroniclers in all ages at such times of tension, they were on the lookout for signs and wonders, and record how at that time unwonted numbers of birds appeared in the air—storks and herons, magpies and crows and smaller birds too—who attacked each other so fiercely that great numbers of them were picked up dead. It was enough to make the superstitious—and who then was not?—quake with apprehension.

This tension was suddenly relaxed in a quite unexpected way by the Duke of Burgundy. Whether or not he was taken aback by the size of the forces the allies had mustered, and was not sure of being able to combat them successfully, even with the help of the troops that the king himself had summoned to his aid, he himself was obviously not anxious to fight at this time. He therefore offered terms. He would renounce his annual pension from the royal treasury and in future serve the king for nothing. He would return to his own territory immediately, provided the Orleanists did the same. Pierre des Essarts should be removed from his post as Provost of Paris and a successor appointed by the king. And Berry should in future have equal authority with him both in the royal Council and over the dauphin.

As these offers promised an alleviation of at least some of the abuses against which the allies were protesting, and as winter was coming on, when it would be difficult to maintain the armies in the field, they found

Armagnac, "were greatly angered, yet they could never change it and as long as the war lasted they had no other name". This name, as we know, is still in use to-day.

it difficult not to accept them, even though the terms by no means guaranteed the radical reforms they were pursuing. However, a door to future action was left open by a clause to the effect that hostilities would not be renewed until Easter 1412. This curious half-baked peace, known as the Peace of Paris, was signed on November 2nd, 1410.[21] On the 8th the princes and their allies returned to their own homes, followed by the curses of the populace, for the troops in dispersing wrought their usual havoc, 'eating the poor' as Monstrelet dramatically put it.[22] They especially dreaded the Gascons, who had a terrifying habit of making their horses suddenly rear and wheel about as they galloped through the narrow streets.

The meagre results of this abortive rising may have given the Duke of Berry personally a certain satisfaction, but they could not have been other than disappointing to Charles. After all his preparations it was a sad anti-climax to be defrauded of fighting and to have to return tamely home. He returned poorer than he went too, for many of his possessions, which he had placed for safety in his Hôtel de Behaigne in Paris, had been pillaged by the Burgundian troops and were never recovered.[23] Then again, Berry's decision to omit their desire of revenge in their petition to the king had been galling enough; but the agreement not to resume hostilities until Easter 1412 was even worse, as it meant that, if this promise was kept, Charles could not hope to avenge his father for another eighteen months, by which time it would be four and a half years since he had been murdered. Already the third anniversary of that dreadful event was at hand, an anniversary whose tragic memories must each year have cast a gloom on his own anniversary the following day. Decidedly he had been born under an unlucky star, and with each year that passed it was in November that his fortunes always seemed to be reduced to their lowest ebb. But even so his courage was not daunted, nor his determination dimmed. He was now sixteen. Already in the year that was ending he had managed to strengthen his cause with new alliances. In the one that lay ahead he was to cast off the restraint of his great-uncle Berry's caution, to take an independent line and plead his own cause directly with the king.

DURING that winter and the following spring Charles and his brother Philip were busy improving the defences of their castles of Coucy, Chauny and Valois,[1] and selling everything they could possibly dispose of, down to a birdcage "with a goldfinch in it"[2] and broken mirrors, in order to pay their troops. These warlike preparations came to the ears of Burgundy who, though apparently still not anxious to confront the allies in the field, strove to stir up feeling against them by painting their intentions against the royal family and the people of Paris in the most lurid terms. Meanwhile Charles, though clearly realising that he would achieve nothing unless he were strong enough to defend his cause by force of arms, was by nature far more disposed to try and gain his ends by legitimate and pacific means rather than by warfare.

Therefore his first step, when spring came, was to send ambassadors to the king to beg him once again to punish his father's murderer, and to point out how Burgundy had managed to oust all Louis' adherents from the government. The king's only reaction to this embassy was to ask the Duke of Berry to try and make peace between Charles and Burgundy. In reply to this attempt Burgundy merely said that it was not his fault if the promise to forgive and forget was not being kept. But Charles was not now to be fobbed off and silenced in this way. Since the king had ignored his ambassadors, he determined to appeal to him once again, but this time in writing.

The letter[3] that he sent in the last days of May was very short, but affords valuable evidence of what he was like at that time. There is something so youthful and inexperienced in its mixture of outspokenness and deference, and in the many repetitions that reveal so clearly his desperate anxiety to make the king understand and help him without doubting his loyalty and obedience, that there is every reason to believe he wrote it himself. If that is so, we hear in it for the first time his authentic voice. He goes straight to the point at the outset, offering to lay down his arms if the king will proceed against the traitors who haunt his court, all of whom he names, and especially two, both pensioners of the Duke of Burgundy, whom he alleges were guilty of what he calls "the enormous and cruel death of my lord my father." "If you will do these things," he goes on, "I will, with God's help, so answer you and lay before you so openly my purposes and plans that God and you and the whole world will perforce be satisfied with them. And for the love of God, very redoubted lord, do not fail in this! For as I clearly see, the requests and supplications that I have at other times made in formally seeking justice will always be thwarted. For that reason, my very redoubted lord, do not fail me; for I am only asking what is just and reasonable, as you and all others can clearly see. My very redoubted lord, may it please you to send for me and lay your good pleasure on me and, God willing, I will accomplish it." Charles strove to strengthen this plea by appealing at the same time to such friends as he had on the Council to help him persuade the king to do what he asked. But it was all of no avail; in spite of its obvious sincerity his letter fell on deaf ears. The bemused monarch, apparently unable even to realise the baseness of such an act, merely sent a copy of it to Burgundy, who of course said that the accusations in it were not true, and immediately set about assembling his forces.

Although his first approach to the king had produced no result, Charles did not lose hope. Nor did he abandon his determination to seek justice by legitimate means if at all possible, and that meant with his sovereign's approval. If the king would not grant him an audience then he must try to put his case in writing as clearly and persuasively as possible. The essential thing was to catch the conscience of the king. And this time he would send copies of his letter not only to the members of the Council but to all the main towns of France, even those in Burgundy's own territories, so that everyone, including the Parisians who continued to curse him as a troublemaker, might learn the true situation as he saw it.

He despatched this second letter, a huge document some three feet square,[4] from Jargeau near Orleans on July 14th. He says at the beginning of it that it was the result of joint deliberations between himself and his brothers Philip and John, but he clearly wrote it himself. It is much longer than the previous one—too long indeed to reproduce—and not without a good deal of repetition, arising, one feels, from the intensity of his wish to convince. But it is written with a command of language, and a power of exposition that is quite unlike the stilted formal style of the time and clearly foreshadows the man of letters he was to become. More than the style, though, it is the substance that is of particular interest, revealing as it does his own attitude of mind.

He opens with a subtle and courtier-like approach. He and his brothers, he says, know that the "piteous and inhuman death" of the king's only brother is so deeply rooted in his heart and memory that he will never forget it. Nevertheless "the office of pity, the rights of blood, and the duties of nature" force them to remind him of it. Charles then relates the whole story of the murder in all its details; but he does it with such a burning intensity of imagination that the familiar tale takes on new and horrid life. He analyses Burgundy's motives for the deed with rare perception for so youthful a mind. But it is when he lists all the reasons which made this crime so peculiarly appalling – the fact that Burgundy was bound to his kinsman by oaths, his duplicity in the planning of the murder and hypocritical behaviour after it, and his subsequent insolent refusal to admit any guilt for it – that Charles reveals himself most clearly. He speaks with the repugnance, indeed loathing, of a noble nature that can barely comprehend how such conduct, against all principles of honour and decency, could be possible. Yet he is not only concerned with the personal aspects of the tale; he has already enough political wisdom to see, and point out to the king, the danger to the State of allowing such a deed to go unpunished. "Briefly, it has revealed and brought into this realm methods whereby all crimes and all evil-doing may be committed indifferently, without any punishment or correction ensuing." That is why his allies, Berry, Bourbon, Alençon, Clermont and Armagnac have joined him in trying to bring this home to the king. Charles ends this most eloquent letter by reminding Charles VI of all the broken promises made to his mother, Valentina, and imploring him to allow her son to obtain retribution for the death and wounded honour of his father from the murderer whom he must clearly see is "a liar, evil, false, treacherous, cruel and disloyal". Even a man of the lowest estate in the kingdom would do likewise, in a like situation. And if he and his brothers do not, they will risk being thought unworthy of their father's name, and even held not to be his sons.

One wonders how anyone could have read this passionate appeal from a youth who, as he assures the king "has always been, is and will be, honest, without reproach and speaking truth", and not be convinced by it. It did in fact convince many of the king's advisers when the letter was read aloud at a very fully attended meeting of the Council and *Parlement*.[5] But once again the fatal dominance of Burgundy prevailed, even at a distance. He had not troubled to attend the meeting himself, but a copy of Charles' letter had been sent to him and he merely replied that he took his stand on the Treaty of Chartres. His appeal to the peace-at-any-price policy of that hollow document prevailed in the end, after a very long debate, even with Charles' supporters; and echoes of it ring clearly through the rambling, inconclusive letter that was then drawn up and sent to Charles and his brothers in the name of the king.[6]

He had never, he was made to say in it, refused them reason and justice; the delays had all been due to treaties imposed for the sake of peace by "the greatest of our blood and lineage", as they must know. Even at that moment, with the consent of both sides, the queen, with the Dukes of Berry and Brittany, were striving to reach a good agreement between the parties. He was surprised that Charles should have written to him while this was going on. All the same, if it should chance that "God should not wish" that their efforts should succeed, the king offered to do such justice that neither Charles nor anyone else could complain that it had not been done. In conclusion the king stressed his displeasure that Charles and his party should have assembled such forces that the poor people were ruined and the kingdom destroyed. There must be no more of that.

This depressing letter, dated July 20th, must have been sent to Charles at Jargeau by very fast messenger, for by the 24th he had already taken his next step. It was clear now that it was useless to try to enlist the king's support. If Louis of Orleans were to be avenged, his son must do it himself. So on the 24th Charles despatched a herald to Burgundy, bearing a letter from himself and his two brothers, to apprise him of their intentions. There is in fact reason to suppose that, even before the king's answer came, realising that there was nothing to be hoped for from it, the brothers had begun drafting this letter, for a version dated July 18th exists.[7] The final missive was brief but to the point. The superscription, in their three names, was addressed "to you, John, who call yourself Duke of Burgundy". In view of the youth of the writers there is something pathetic about that taunt, and in the obvious awareness of their comparative powerlessness that underlies the vague threat with which the note ends. Because of "the great treason and cruelty" committed by him against their lord and father, his own first cousin, "we are writing to let you know", they say, "that from this time forth we are going to harm you with all our power, and against you and the disloyalty and treason you have committed we call to our aid God and all the honest men of this world".

Burgundy, usually so quick to respond to threats, showed his contempt for this one by deferring his reply for nearly a month. But on August 13th he sent Charles a brief and insolent note by the hand of an armed officer, stating in violent terms that he had been forced by his conscience to kill Louis because of his foul treason. "And since you and your brothers", he continued, "are following in the footsteps of your perfidious father, and wish to attain the same ends as he, we have received your letters of defiance with the keenest joy. As for their contents, we declare that you have lied, like infamous impostors and detestable traitors."[8] And he repeats the taunt of "who call yourself" to the three brothers in turn. It is typical of Charles' always chivalrous behaviour–he and his brothers all had princely manners, remarks the chronicler Pierre de Fenin[9]–that in spite of the nature of the answer he had brought, and his own distress on receiving it, he entertained the messenger well.

After this interchange there was nothing for it but war, and all the evidence goes to show that Charles was among the first, if not the first, of the allies to realise it. He was obviously now the leader of his faction, and all his actions that summer reveal how fully he assumed responsibility for it. Already in May he had despatched forces to defend Angoulême and begun sending messengers to Lorraine, Champagne, Auvergne and the Bourbonnais to summon knights and esquires. In May too there is a reference to Welsh troops to serve in his army "beyond the Seine".[10] But now the need for help and support was graver still, and a document in the Orleans archives[11] evokes in a vivid way the intense activity that went, that August, into appealing for it. It refers to a ream of paper to be used for "long, closed letters, sent to all those of the lineage of the said lord and to the noble officers and principal servitors of the king and of this realm and outside this realm". These letters were written at Yèvre-le-Châtel, one of Charles' castles near Pithiviers, and there were so many that on them "were employed all the clerks of the secretaries and three clerks who had been brought from Orleans."

Charles not only had to pay the wages of all the soldiers he collected–and some of the knights had to be provided with both armour and horses[12]–but on him as leader fell also the duty of paying the expenses of his principal allies.[13] It was no wonder, then, that in September he was again forced to sell a long list of jewels and plate, all the items in which are minutely described.[14] His dealings with these money matters reveal him as having become both a careful and conscientious administrator, and also as being fully aware of the dangers of his situation; for by a document of August 29th[15] he authorised those responsible for his finances to accept as final the signature of Pierre Sauvage, his secretary and manager of his accounts, and stated that he was doing this in case he himself died before he had made his own personal inspection of the said accounts.

In addition to all the military preparations that August, Charles had his responsibilities as the head of his youthful family. On the 28th he ordered one of his officers, Macé le Borgne, to go to Blois and convey to Châteauneuf-sur-Loire his young brother John, together with their sister Margaret, and his own baby daughter Jane, apparently to avoid some epidemic.[16] Later, on September 22nd, a payment was made to Jean Malescot, citizen of Orleans, for the expenses of himself and twelve companions, who went mounted and armed from Baugency to Blois, to accompany the little Count of Angoulême; so Charles was apparently moving his young brother constantly about, perhaps in fear for his safety.

Finally, all was ready for the army to march. Composed though it was of elements from all over France and from outside France too, Charles had seen to it that some sort of unity was given to it by the thousands of escutcheons and banners that he had had painted with his device of a nettle.[17] With the help of his oldest captains, he drew up his battle array. He himself commanded the main body, the *grosse bataille*, his father-in-law Armagnac led the advance-guard, the Count of Alençon the rear-guard and the other princes the flanks. In this formation they began their march not in the direction of Burgundy's territories, but towards Paris, whither Bourbon and Philip of Vertus had proceeded separately. For they still entertained some hope that, at the sight of so large and determined an army, the king and the Council might think it better to receive them peacefully and grant their demands rather than let matters come to bloodshed.

It seems to have taken Burgundy some time to realise that the letter of 'the Orleans children' was no empty threat, and so it was only belatedly that he himself began to collect troops. Although his own family, by blood or marriage, were always loyal to him, and his subjects of course fought for him, he never seems to have had at his disposal either so many allies or such forces as Charles was able to command.

So much so that on this occasion he went so far as to appeal to Henry IV of England, who agreed to send him a contingent of English soldiers under the Earl of Arundel. To ask help of a foreign power, even against one's own countrymen, was not necessarily considered treacherous or reprehensible in those days, when the sentiment of nationalism was not yet born and ties of blood among the rulers and princes of Europe were often close. So Burgundy's action seems to have been calmly enough accepted by the court and the Council, where Arundel was later received as an honoured guest.

Apart from actual troops, Burgundy's stoutest supporters were still the people of Paris, especially the butchers, who were not only the toughest but the most privileged of all the workers. To make sure of their loyalty, in September Burgundy had had his old adherent, Pierre des Essarts, reappointed as Provost of Paris, thus breaking one of the clauses of the treaty of the previous November, by which he had been dismissed from his post after the execution of Jean de Montagu. From this reappointment, as a marginal note by Nicolas de Baye in the register of the Council recording it remarks, "infinite injuries and evils arose".[18]

Another of Burgundy's allies, Count Waleran de Saint-Pol, of the house of Luxembourg, was made Captain of Paris. Divining with a sort of prophetic instinct that Parisian liking for headgear as a symbol of rebellion (which in the Revolution led them to adopt a bonnet of Phrygian style), he issued to all who asked a blue cap adorned with Burgundy's device of a Saint Andrew's cross with a capital J in the middle of it, to mark them as his supporters, and a fleur-de-lis with the motto 'Vive le Roy' to give them the illusion that they were the king's men. Whether or not it was because the butchers then felt themselves to be the leaders of what now looked like a compact citizen army, they suddenly assumed surprising power. It happened at that time that the king, who had recently been as normal as he ever was, had another of his attacks of madness. He was in his palace of Saint-Pol when this occurred, while the queen was at Corbeil with the Duke of Berry, whom the Parisians always disliked. Fearing that the queen in this crisis might entrust Berry with the government, the butchers, through one of their leaders, Thomas Legois, asked the dauphin to rule in his father's stead. As he was now fourteen, and thus of age, this was constitutionally possible, and the dauphin agreed.

It is difficult not to suspect that Burgundy was somehow behind this initiative of the butchers, which so aptly suited his purposes. But even if it was they who spontaneously put the dauphin in power, there is little doubt that it was Waleran de Saint-Pol (representing Burgundy, who had not yet reached Paris) who induced them to act in the way the duke desired. On October 3rd royal letters[19] were sent throughout France declaring the Duke of Orleans and his allies, and all those of their party, rebels, and authorising everyone to oppose them and treat them as enemies of the throne. It was the first time that a public statement to this effect had ever been made, and thus the first time that the country as a whole realised that it was now in fact involved in civil war. To make the situation still plainer, all those with Orleanist sympathies were ordered to leave Paris; and Waleran de Saint-Pol had strict instructions to prevent any Orleanist entering the city and obtaining access to the king.

These proclamations were to have just the effect that Burgundy wanted. But even before they could have been widely known, wherever the Orleanist army passed, the people, armed with whatever weapons or even implements they could find, rose against them, since it naturally seemed to them, ignorant as they were, that the allies were trying to provoke an armed conflict for no sufficient reason. Even the inhabitants of some of Charles' own towns, like Beaumont, fled rather than help him. All the same, on October 4th he and his allies reached the outskirts of Paris where, being refused entry, they encamped at Saint-Ouen. Two or three days later they laid siege to Saint-Denis. The inhabitants defended themselves as best they could but, as they had no troops to help them, they surrendered on the 11th.

The news of this victory filled the Parisians with fear lest Charles meant to seize the sacred symbols of royalty kept in the great abbey there, as a first step towards seizing the throne. Rumours to this effect must have been circulating as soon as the siege began, for to calm them, on October 9th, a long list of lords of the Orleanist party wrote[20] to the heads of the University of Paris, as representatives of the people, protesting against the accusation that Charles wished to supplant the king, and stating that if they had believed such a thing they would never for a moment have served him. They were doing so out of sympathy with his desire to avenge his father's death, and his wish to rescue the king from his state of servitude. To prove this they sent the king a copy of the long letter that Charles had himself sent him in May. Unfortunately some colour was given to the suspicions of the people when Armagnac and the Constable Albret forced the monks of Saint-Denis to hand over to them some of the queen's treasures in the abbey's keeping, to help pay their troops. This so outraged the monks that they at once sought authority to excommunicate the Orleanists.

The day after the taking of Saint-Denis some of Charles' soldiers had scored another victory when about fifteen hundred of them, but not under his leadership, had taken Saint-Cloud, with its bridge. This filled the citizens with panic, since it meant that they were cut off from all the supplies that came up the river; and as they were terrified of the Gascons and Bretons who, as usual, were scouring the countryside, looting everything they could lay hands on and laying the villages waste, the Parisians dared not leave the city to seek the necessities of life that were usually brought in to them. It is difficult to understand why, with time on their side and Paris thus at their mercy, the Orleanists did not attempt to fight their way in and try to obtain access to the king before Burgundy arrived. Still more puzzling is the failure of the Orleanists to intercept the Burgundians and do battle with them before they reached Paris, when they might have won a decisive victory. An opportunity was thus lost that might have saved not only Charles and his allies, but the country as a whole, years of bloodshed, upheaval and misery.

After waiting for him so long and in such trepidation, it was no wonder that, when Burgundy rode into Paris with his army one evening in the last days of October, the people turned out with torches and lanterns to give him a delirious welcome, greeting him with their traditional joyous cry of 'Noël!', which had nothing to do with Christmas. His presence so restored their courage that when, on November 9th, his French and English troops left Paris secretly by night for Saint-Cloud, large numbers of the citizens accompanied them. They reached Saint-Cloud early in the morning, took the garrison by surprise and fell upon them. At the same time ships laden with pitch, which they had sent down the river, set fire to the wooden bridge, so that the Orleanists were trapped between the Seine and the vastly superior forces of the Burgundians. A bloody battle ensued and after three hours' fighting the greater part of the Orleanists were killed, against hardly any losses on the other side, and the victorious Burgundians retired, leaving the field covered with dead.

When Charles, still at Saint-Ouen, heard of this overwhelming disaster, he realised that the only course open to him was to retreat to

Orleans with what remained of his army, as winter was now coming on when in any case fighting would cease. On November 13th, while he and his allies were preparing to march home, sentence of excommunication was being pronounced against them on the *parvis* of Notre-Dame. Because of this, none would bury the dead at Saint-Cloud, whose bodies were left for the birds and wolves* to devour. And so, says Monstrelet, "the Duke of Orleans, seeking to avenge the death of his father, incurred great harm and loss of people."[21]

He had indeed, in spite of his unremitting efforts throughout the year, suffered more reverses than at any time yet, and it needed much firmness of purpose not to lose hope that winter, when his fortunes fell lower yet. One of the most urgent tasks before him, if he were to be able to renew his struggle successfully in the spring, was to try to make good his losses both in men and money. But this was now made much more difficult than in the past because he was gradually being stripped of a large portion of his estates. Already in October royal edicts had taken into the king's domain first his town and castle of Chauny and then Crépy-en-Valois, Pierrefonds, La Ferté Milon and Coucy.[22] An ordinance of the king's in the following January confirmed the seizure from Bourbon of his county of Clermont, and from Charles of his counties of Valois and Beaumont-sur-Oise, with the release of his subjects there from their duty to him. But even before this confirmation Count Waleran de Saint-Pol, one of Burgundy's most fervent allies, was put in charge of the confiscation[23] and he carried it out with a destructive zeal more worthy of a foreign enemy than a fellow noble. Even the dauphin took part in this unchivalrous pursuit of a momentarily powerless foe, bringing Charles' towns of Étampes and Dourdan into submission to himself.

The result of this confining of their quarry within the narrow limits of his lands about the Loire was not only to deprive him of revenues in money and resources in manpower from his other possessions but to bottle up in a restricted area the troops he had to keep in being. Their customary depredations, as they lived off the land, not only terrorised the people, making Charles almost as unpopular with his

---

* Wolves were a frequent menace even in Paris itself at that time. The *Bourgeois de Paris* (p. 286) relates that in the last week of September 1438 wolves 'strangled' and ate fourteen people 'great and small' between Montmartre and the Porte Saint-Antoine, while on December 16th they came again suddenly and 'strangled' four housewives.

3 A bust of Louis of Orleans, from a tomb in the Musée Calvet, Avignon

own subjects as he was with the Parisians, but greatly hindered trade in Blois and Orleans. All these things reduced him to such desperate financial straits that we find his physician Pierre de Vaulx, who had been doctor to his father and mother before him, lending him six silver cups to put to any use he would "in the great need wherein he stands".[24]

But desperate though the need of money was, that of men was even greater; so much so that Charles, supported by his allies, took a step which was to cost him dear, in more ways than one. For though they were all jointly responsible, he alone had to bear nearly all the cruel results of it. In January of that winter of 1412 they sent ambassadors to Henry IV of England, asking him to send troops to help them.[25] This was an act no more reprehensible than that of Burgundy in sending the year before. But whereas no conditions had been imposed in his case, Henry saw in this appeal a splendid chance to win back some of the former English possessions in France. He therefore insisted that, in return for military aid, the allies should promise to support his claim to Aquitaine, with a good many towns and castles in addition, and help him to gain possession of them. In addition he demanded that Charles of Orleans should agree to hold his counties of Angoulême and Périgord as a vassal of Henry's, and that after his death these territories should pass into English hands. These conditions were certainly harsh, but they do not appear to have struck the allies as outrageous or impossible. Aquitaine, with Poitou, had been debateable territory ever since its duchess Eleanor had brought it to the English crown through her marriage with Henry II in 1152. The old Duke of Berry could remember how the English, having subsequently lost it, won it back after Crécy and Poitiers in 1360. If the allies admitted Henry's right to it now, there was no reason why the fortunes of war might not soon enable them to break any promises now made.

All the same they could not give an instant assent and, although the final treaty implied that agreement was reached on January 25th, negotiations did in fact drag on for some months. In the early spring Henry IV sent over to France for discussions his second son Thomas of Lancaster, a young man of twenty-two, of whom Charles was to see only too much in the future. During their meetings Charles had a foretaste of what was to come, for the soldiers Thomas brought with him behaved in their usual lawless manner, seizing the wine and the boats of a man whom Charles had to compensate, and digging themselves in at Meung-sur-Loire and refusing to leave until paid to do so.[26]

D   77

Despite such irritations Charles received Thomas courteously and gave him a grey horse as a present.

But Thomas proved a tough negotiator and Charles and his allies, pressed as they were by their impossible situation, were forced not only to accept the territorial demands of the English but to agree that they should pay the wages of their soldiers for three months after they reached Blois.[27] This was a heavy commitment, because the English promised to bring not only the thousand men-at-arms and the four thousand three hundred archers that the French asked for, but a good many more provided by Clarence and other nobles from their own retinues. It was decided that the English expedition should set sail on June 8th, and, all the details having been settled, the alliance was signed on May 18th by Charles and his allies Berry, Bourbon and Alençon.[28] Full of hope once more at the thought of the coming reinforcements, Charles had a few thousand more escutcheons and banners painted in gold and silver for his army, this time bearing the single word 'Justice'.[29]

But while these negotiations had been going on, the situation among his opponents in France had been changing. That winter the king had recovered his wits again—he was always better in cold weather—and learning for the first time of the Orleanist attack of the previous autumn, he decided that he himself would now take up arms against these enemies of his kingdom, as he was easily persuaded they were. During the preparations for his expedition, copies of the letters from Orleans and Berry to Henry IV fell into the king's hands and filled him with indignation—not so much, it would seem, because of their treasonable aspect as because he had thought the princes were devoted to him.[30] When the letter were read in Council on April 6th, the first Wednesday after Easter, the members of it, which included Burgundy, of course used them to strengthen the king's resolution to take up arms against the Orleanists, a decision that the University and all the Parisians heartily applauded.

A new plan of campaign was formulated: to march south and attack Berry and the two Gascons, Armagnac and Albret, who were all in or near Bourges, together with Bourbon. Accordingly on May 4th the king had the *oriflamme* brought from Saint-Denis and, with the dauphin, led his troops south, accompanied by John the Fearless and his forces, together with some of his own allies. Hearing of this, Henry IV, who had been jubilant at the prospects this treaty opened for him of winning back some former English possessions, and confident of success, on

May 16th sent a letter[31] to the burgomasters and *échevins* of some of Burgundy's chief towns, asking whether they intended to support their lord in his harmful plan to lay waste *his* land of Guienne and those of his dear cousins the allies. To which of course they replied that they did.

They arrived outside Bourges at the end of the first week of June and laid siege to the city. The old Duke of Berry, who was never really a fighting man and wanted nothing better than to enjoy in peace all the treasures that he had gathered in his beautiful city of Bourges, at once loyally offered to yield it to the king or the dauphin but not, he said, to certain persons whom the king would do better without. Rather than that, he would defend it to the uttermost, and he had indeed pledged some of his most precious possessions to enable him to do so. As Burgundy's presence made his offer impossible for the king to accept, an assault was at once launched from both sides and carried on sporadically for some time without either gaining a distinct advantage, although both armies suffered losses, and a certain amount of damage was done to the besieged city. To break this stalemate Burgundy was anxious to use his artillery to launch the great stone cannon-balls that would soon have brought matters to a head by destroying Bourges itself. He was prevented by an order from a most unexpected quarter.

The Duke of Berry, who had no sons of his own left, had recently made his godson the dauphin his heir. This fifteen-year-old boy, who presumably was seeing Bourges for the first time, was suddenly so overwhelmed by the senselessness of destroying this fair and noble city, with its magnificent cathedral, one day to be his, that he found courage to stand up to the all-powerful father-in-law who had so long held him in tutelage. He first forbade the hurling of those great stones by anyone whatever "on pain of losing his head."[32] Then, as if emboldened by his own act, he went on to say that in any case the war had gone on far too long; it was harmful to the king and the kingdom, and it would be better to let his uncles and cousins help and serve him rather than fight them. Apart from Charles' letter of defiance, it was the first time since Burgundy had murdered his cousin that anyone had stood up to him and he was greatly taken aback. However, as the dauphin represented the royal authority, Burgundy could only accept his commands and proclaim his own readiness to make peace.

This was now the general desire in the royal army, which was beginning to run short of supplies, while the Orleanists were apparently well provisioned. Accordingly on July 15th, after the siege had lasted forty days, the opposing sides met outside the city walls to decide what should be done. As the king by this time was once again 'absent', the discussions were between the dauphin and Burgundy on one side and Berry on the other. The seventy-year-old duke, who came fully armed and wearing his Armagnac scarf, wept as he embraced the dauphin and handed the keys of the city to him. To Burgundy he said half-jestingly and half-sadly: "Fair nephew, when my fair brother your father was alive there was no need of a barrier between us, we were of the same mind, he and I."[33] To which Burgundy gave his customary reply that he was not to blame.

A decision that they should all meet later the next month in Auxerre to conclude a peace was quickly reached. The two armies and their leaders then set out on their return journey. On July 21st they halted at a small place called Argenvières on the left bank of the Loire, opposite La Charité, where Berry received a formal document in the king's name declaring the treaty with England null and void and ordering him to denounce it, which he did in a letter next day addressed to what he called "his very dear and beloved nephew" Henry IV of England and his sons.[34] This shabby piece of double-dealing on his part accomplished, the whole cavalcade crossed the Loire to La Charité, where they met representatives of Charles of Orleans and his brothers, who were presumably on their way south to obtain news. These emissaries were told what had taken place; whereupon they were forced to agree to the peace in the name of their masters, and promise that they would bring them Auxerre to swear it themselves.

No effort is needed to imagine the effect on Charles when he heard this news. There appears to have been singularly little liaison between him and his senior allies at that time, but he must have known of the attack on Bourges, and it could hardly have entered his head for a moment that his friends there would abandon the struggle at the very moment when they knew he was assembling English allies to prolong it, in their name as well as his own. To have surrendered Bourges itself out of loyalty to the king was one thing, but to agree to make peace on the abominable lines of the Treaty of Chartres was quite another. The Duke of Berry's compliance over that was perhaps understandable, old as he was, unreliable as he had often proved, seeking chiefly his own ends, and always unhappy at being torn between two loyalties. But that Armagnac and the Constable, not to mention Bourbon, should have given in in this way must have seemed to Charles incomprehensible, as indeed it was. As for Berry's lighthearted renunciation of the treaty with England over the head of Charles, who had been its main negotiator, that was not so much incomprehensible as unpardonable, revealing as it did such a complete disregard of Charles' position in the matter.

For apart from the shock of being let down by his French allies, there was the practical problem of what to do now with his English ones, who at that very moment were preparing to sail for France. They would have as much reason to be angry at having come, at great expense, for nothing, as Charles at being defrauded of the victory he might have won with their help—a victory that would have allowed him to make his own peace terms instead of, as now, being obliged to accept whatever the king, dominated by Burgundy, might impose. His meeting with his English allies would be bound to be both painful and humiliating, and perhaps costly too. Another awkward thing was that he would have to make them wait for it, since he could not disobey the king's command to go to Auxerre on August 20th, for what was likely to prove an even more humiliating ordeal.

It was no wonder then that when Charles rode into Auxerre, accompanied by Philip of Vertus, he wore his customary suit of solemn black. But sombre though the two brothers may have looked, in that brilliant gathering of nobles, ecclesiastics, and citizens of the main towns which had assembled at the royal command, they made as brave an appearance as they could, at the head of some two to three thousand men-at-arms. They arrived two days late, when rumours were already circulating that perhaps they would not come; and the peace meeting was held that same day on a richly adorned stage set up in a field outside the walls of Auxerre.

There, on August 22nd, Charles and his brother Philip had to sign documents renouncing their treaties with the English, and to set their hands, with Burgundy, to another renouncing all alliances against him, including of course that with the English.[35] It is difficult to understand how Charles could once again have brought himself to pronounce that oath as far as Burgundy was concerned, having now no longer the excuse of childish inexperience that could exonerate his similar conduct at the time of Chartres. One can only assume that, abandoned on all sides as he now was, a feeling of the hopelessness of it all made him yield momentarily to a tendency to indifference and resignation—'nonchaloir' as he called it—which was to grow in him with the years, but rarely showed itself in youth. There is no doubt too that, though he could be brave in warfare and had strength to endure adversity, there was also a streak of weakness in him, as other events at Auxerre showed.

He and his brother must have appeared pathetically alone at that crisis. Perhaps that is why the royal letter[36] charging him and Philip to keep these oaths is curiously personal in tone and couched in more affectionate terms than usual, so that one wonders whether the young dauphin, who may even then have been beginning to feel the sympathy for Charles that he showed not long afterwards, had had a hand in it, especially as the document states that it was drawn up at a meeting of the king's Council "held by my lord the Duke of Guienne." It begins by sending the brothers "greetings and love" and reminds them, rather unnecessarily one might think, that their promises to keep the peace bind also the little Count of Angoulême and "our very dear and very beloved niece, your sister"—the six-year-old Margaret, who presumably so far had not shown any warlike intentions.

The only advantages that Charles obtained from the Peace of Auxerre were that the excommunication against his party had been lifted before the meeting took place, though no doubt less as a favour to them than to make it possible to treat with them; and he was promised that the estates that had been seized in the previous winter should be restored to him with—singular generosity!—no demand for reparation for the damage that those which had fallen into the hands of Waleran de Saint-Pol had suffered (among other things he had sold the lead piping at Coucy). It was in fact some time before Charles was able to get these back; but the king did however immediately return Chauny, even though it had been incorporated in the royal domain, with permission to raise 60,000 gold florins in taxes imposed thereon.

When all the business was concluded a solemn *Te Deum* was sung in the cathedral, after which the dauphin gave a great dinner, followed by games and entertainments, in the course of which the wretched Charles was made to mount the same horse as Burgundy, a humiliating spectacle that filled the simpler people among the watching crowds with amazement, as being nothing short of a miracle that perhaps presaged a hope of peace. This treaty does in fact seem to have created a widespread impression that the civil war was now over. On Saturday, August 27th, when Henri de Marle, chief president of the *Parlement*, who had been at Auxerre, read the terms of it to the assembled members of the two chambers, he gave them also a brief outline[37] of the main events of the struggle with what he too always calls "the Orleans children", in the tone of one winding up an account of an unfortunate episode. (It is, incidentally, astonishing to learn from that speech that, in the comparatively few clashes of arms that had occurred, twenty thousand lives had been lost either in fighting or through sickness, including eight thousand of the royal and Burgundian armies during the siege of Bourges.)

A gruesome sign of the better relations that were now thought to exist between the two factions, was that the skeleton of Jean de Montagu, which had been hanging from the gibbet of Montfaucon for the past three years, was taken down, reunited with the head, and given to Montagu's friends to bury in holy ground. This followed upon an announcement by the dauphin at a Council meeting on September 12th, attended by Burgundy, Bourbon, Philip de Vertus and many others, to the effect that Montagu's death had greatly displeased him, as being the result of a hasty judgment dictated by hatred and not by justice—yet another condemnation of his father-in-law by the young dauphin.

Charles was not present at that meeting. He had other things to think about, above all the results of that unfortunate treaty with the English, for which the day of reckoning was yet to come. Henty IV had taken his side of the bargain very seriously. Taxes had been raised to pay for the expedition, and a long list of individuals and cities had offered money to cover its expenses while it was in England. He had appointed his son Thomas of Lancaster as the leader of it and in July had created him Duke of Clarence, and made him his Lieutenant of Aquitaine, which the king now regarded as his. Clarence was to be accompanied by Sir Thomas Beaufort, the third son of John of Gaunt, on whom the king then conferred the title of Earl of Dorset and the office of Admiral of England; by Edward Duke of York and his brother Richard, Earl of Cambridge; and finally by a hardened old campaigner, Sir John Cornwall, who was in fact a brother-in-law of the king, destined to play a harsh part in the life of Charles of Orleans.

The army under their leadership had been mustered at Southampton at the beginning of July, but was delayed by contrary winds and only crossed to France on August 9th and 10th. They landed at Saint-Vaast-la-Hougue, in the Cotentin, whither the Count of Alençon had gone joyfully to meet them. But by the time they arrived he had heard the news of the disastrous peace and, not knowing what else to do, he returned to his own castle at Alençon, leaving Clarence to lead his army slowly to Blois, destroying many of the places they passed through *en route*, no doubt as an expression of their feelings on learning that their services were no longer needed.

It was only when he eventually reached Blois that Clarence received from a herald the letter that Berry had written from Argenvières on July 22nd, and from two other heralds similar letters from Orleans, Bourbon, and Albret—presumably sent later—and also, he surprisingly says, one from Burgundy too, informing him that because their treaty had gravely displeased Charles VI he had ordered them to revoke it. They therefore released Henry from his promises—an unfortunate way of putting it, to say the least. Clarence addressed his reply to Berry,[38] but did not answer until September 6th, explaining the delay by saying that, as the letters were addressed to the king his father, he had at first hesitated whether to open them. Having done so, he could hardly believe that such letters could come from such princes, in view of the pledges that they had signed with their own hands. As for the letter from Burgundy, this filled him with astonishment, since the English had no treaty with him, having refused to make one because they were bound to the princes. If they had not been they would have accepted his offers. Clarence therefore prayed Berry and his allies to remain true to their bond. Having sent off this very reasonable letter, he obviously intended to remain where he was, waiting for the next move.

Charles of Orleans and the Duke of Berry were both at Vincennes with the king and queen when Clarence's letter reached them. It was clear from it that he had no intention of calmly returning to England with his army, and that he still expected them to keep their side of the agreement. The day of reckoning had indeed come, and Charles sent some of his most trusted advisers to negotiate on his behalf. One of these was his chamberlain Raoul, Lord of Gaucourt, an old friend and contemporary of his father's and always a loyal supporter of the house of Orleans, who was to play a considerable part in the later history of this time.

During the six weeks that the talks with Clarence lasted, Gaucourt was constantly on the road between Blois and Vincennes, presumably bringing to Charles and his uncle Berry reports of their progress.[39] These must have been painful hearing, for the English insisted on keeping to the letter of their bond and, where finance was concerned, both Clarence and Cornwall were to show themselves shrewd bargainers on their own account. There is a tendency among French historians to consider that the financial demands of the English on this occasion were excessive, but there are no real grounds for supposing that they exceeded the total cost of engaging such an army for the period agreed upon. It is true that it might have been greatly reduced if that army had returned home without delay, and by the way it had come. But it must be remembered that Henry IV had appointed Clarence Lieutenant of Aquitaine and it was therefore not unnatural that he should wish to visit that territory while he was in France, and to lead his army home that way.

The treaty with the English was finally signed on November 14th,[40] at Buzançais on the Indre, by the four commissioners appointed by Charles to act for him and his allies: Raoul of Gaucourt, Lionel of Braquemont (another of Charles' chamberlains), Jean Chomery, one of his secretaries, and Guillaume de Tignonville who, it may be remembered, had been Provost of Paris at the time of Louis' murder. The total money payment had finally been settled at 210,000 gold *écus*.[41] By far the greater part of this, 176,800, was to go to Clarence for his own household and expenses for the wages of the men-at-arms, and for certain lords and captains under his command. The two Yorks and Dorset were to have comparatively modest shares, amounting to 11,600 between them. There was a very small sum – 225 – for Clarence's chancellor. But Sir John Cornwall exacted for himself and his household 21,375. Over and above all this, Clarence obtained a promise that he should receive an extra 50,000 gold *écus* for himself personally.[42] Whether the total was excessive or not, it was certainly so huge by contemporary standards that it was quite beyond the capacity of the combined princes to pay in ready money, or in the foreseeable future. Clarence therefore, in accordance with the custom of the time, demanded not only jewels but seven hostages as security. And the grasping Sir John Cornwall added an unpleasant little clause to the treaty to the effect that, after all the payments due to Clarence had been made, the hostages should remain in his hands until he had received the whole of his 21,375 gold *écus*.[43]

To provide jewels as pledges never seems to have been any great problem for those treasure-laden princes and on this occasion the Duke of Berry was able to supply the greater part of the demand in the shape of a magnificent cross of gold and precious stones, valued at 40,000 *livres*. But hostages were another matter, and the burden here fell entirely on Charles and was to weigh on him for a large part of his life. It was the custom at that time to send as hostages those who were nearest to one in blood or, if there were not enough of these, the friends or servitors whom one valued most highly. This was a comparatively easy matter in the case of great kings, members of large dynasties. But Charles, as we know, had only two close male relatives, his brothers Philip and John. Philip of Vertus was too essential a helper in his cause for him to dispense with. And so the lot fell on the twelve-year-old John of Angoulême.

The other six Charles chose from among members of his household, many of whom had served his father before him, and whose names occur over and over again in the Orleans records: Archambaud de Villars, Macé le Borgne, Guillaume le Bouteiller, Jean de Saveuses, Jean Davy and Hector de Pontbriant. There is a natural tendency to think of this virtual banishment of John of Angoulême at such an early age as a tragic event even at the time it occurred, partly because of what was to happen to him afterwards. But in fact there was no reason then why it should have seemed so to him. Hostages were released when the debt they guaranteed was paid, so that he might hope his brother would be able to ransom him before long. In the meantime as a prince, and the nephew of a king, there was every likelihood that he would be well treated. His life at Blois since the deaths of his parents could hardly have been a very cheerful one; this development at least brought an element of change and adventure into it. And as he was to be accompanied by six men whom he must have known well, he would not be alone.

Charles made all possible provision for him, and sent him off in as much style as he could. A week before the treaty was signed he had sent an esquire of his stables to buy from a physician in Blois, for the price of seventy gold *écus*, a black hackney, a quiet mare with a long tail, for John to ride when he went to join Clarence.[44] Macé le Borgne, who had accompanied him on other journeys, was to go with him; but Charles also ordered his treasurer to pay out a considerable sum to enable several persons, who were also to accompany his brother, to attire themselves suitably for the journey. And of course John was provided with money for his expenses on the way. By the terms of the treaty, the army was to return to England by January 1st 1413, but Clarence and his fellow nobles lingered in France much longer than that, for he signed a receipt for some of the money which Charles sent him at Bordeaux in the following April. However, when messengers took a much larger sum in gold from Blois to Angoulême in August 1413, they had to ask the Duke of York and the Earl of Dorset what they were to do with it, as Clarence had at last returned to England, taking John of Angoulême with him. Even so, both on the journey south and during that long waiting period, the young Count of Angoulême had an opportunity to see the lands from which he took his title, which he may well never have seen before and was not to see again for many years afterwards.

By the time the events of that sad November were over, Charles' financial position was almost desperate. Innumerable demands had been made on him in recent months. On several occasions he had had to ransom men who had been taken prisoner fighting for him at Saint-Cloud.[45] There was a payment of 3000 *livres* for the wages of the men-at-arms and archers in his army covering several years past. People who had suffered damage at the hands of the English troops had to be compensated. The commissioners who had acted for him in the negotiation and signing of the treaty had to be paid for their services. He even had to reimburse Clarence's chancellor for drawing up the treaty itself. The French clerks whom his secretary Jean Chomery had engaged to make the necessary copies of it had to be paid; and there was the cost of the paper, parchment and wax for that too.

And always in the background was the thought of the huge debt that the treaty had imposed on him and, as a necessary addition to it, the realisation that large sums would be needed for the expenses in England of his brother and the other six hostages until he could redeem them. Yet, in the midst of such a sea of troubles, Charles found time and thought to send a gold ring set with a diamond to his duchess Bonne in Armagnac[46]—not a present up to the old sumptuous Orleans standards, but at least a token and a remembrance.

Even the most indifferent could hardly have failed to realise his need at that crisis in his life, and for once the king and his Council came to his aid, though at no cost to themselves. On November 23rd they issued letters[47] empowering Charles to raise 40,000 *livres* in taxes on his own lands in order to pay his brother's ransom, and assessing the quotas due from the different towns. The Orleans officials obviously lost no time in trying to obtain money by these means, for already by December 15th certain parishes reported that they could not pay, as all their inhabitants had been killed by the English.[48] Clearly it was not going to be easy to obtain this money, and the royal decree cannot therefore have done much to induce a cheerful frame of mind in the young duke, who had just celebrated his eighteenth birthday.

Charles might indeed have been forgiven if he had then abandoned hope, for never had his situation and prospects looked blacker than at the end of that year. His army had been defeated in the field at Saint-Cloud; his allies had let him down at Bourges; he had been humiliated at Auxerre, and again before his English allies. He had impoverished himself for the war and all to no purpose; and now he was burdened by a huge debt to the English that had also robbed him of his youngest brother. Finally, in spite of the royal promise he had still not been able to regain possession of his estates, for Waleran de Saint-Pol had pushed his insolence to such lengths that he refused to hand them over unless Charles reimbursed him for the money he had paid his soldiers to take them! When Charles refused, Waleran burnt Pierrefonds to the ground, an act Charles could not avert. Apart from all these personal adversities, Burgundy was still dominating the king and misgoverning the kingdom.

Yet, although all occasions had so informed against him, Charles' spirit was still not broken nor did his resolution fail. All the same, throughout the dead of that winter of 1413, it was difficult to see what further steps he could possibly take to achieve what still remained his single aim. It was then, when his own situation was at its most desperate, that the march of events began to play into his hands. And though he could not have known it as the winter months dragged by in Blois, some faint gleams of light in the prevailing darkness were soon to show. Burgundy's star had reached its zenith and before long would begin to wane, while that of Charles began a slow climb up the sky.

CHAPTER SIX
Winter 1413–Winter 1415

THERE was by now something so rotten in the state that the festering discontent of the people was before long to erupt like sores on a diseased body. In an attempt to remedy the situation the Estates General met on January 30th and decided that each province should prepare an account of its own grievances. In Paris the University and the chief citizens drew up their report[1] together and in mid-February it was read to the king. It covered every aspect of the existing situation and those responsible for it: the quarrels between the princes, the civil war, the pillaging by the soldiery, the corruption and excessive numbers of those responsible for the national finances, who misappropriated them for their own profit, neglecting all the services for which the royal treasury was responsible; and, almost worst of all, the fact that the *Parlement*, the sovereign court of justice, was in the hands of young and inexperienced people instead of wise men of age and experience, and that it was impossible for the poor to obtain justice. The holders of other high offices were similarly condemned. The report then outlined a sweeping scheme of reform and called on the dauphin, the Duke of Burgundy and his allies to help put it into effect. Such massive public indignation could not be ignored and an official decree, known as the *Ordonnance Cabochienne*, was issued on May 26th promising the desired reforms.

The reason for this name was that, while these deliberations were going on, the most violent section of the Parisians, that corporation of the butchers which had already intervened to some purpose when the Orleanists were marching on Paris eighteen months earlier, now took matters into their own hands once again under a new leader nicknamed Caboche. He was a skinner of beasts and he exercised such an influence over his fellows that they became known as Cabochiens. But many other citizens, among them even certain municipal officials, joined forces with him; and it is symptomatic of the fear that this movement inspired in high places that the promised reforms should thus have recognised it. Once again the rebels adopted a cap, a white one this time, as their symbol, and so powerful did they become that even the dauphin and other princes of the blood thought it more prudent to wear one too, just as later Louis XVI wore the cap of the revolutionaries.

Once again, too, Burgundy supported the butchers, making them believe that all their troubles came from the Orleanists, and hoping by their means to rid himself of all who opposed him. Encouraged and sometimes accompanied by him, they began to break into the houses of those whom they suspected, arresting whom they would, from clerks and minor officials of the court to prominent citizens and noblemen. Rather surprisingly, one of those they turned on was the powerful Pierre des Essarts, Burgundy's nominee as Provost of Paris and, according to Nicholas de Baye, "sovereign governor of the finances" of the realm. Even Burgundy could not save him and he took refuge from the butchers in the Castle of the Bastille. But on April 28th a great concourse of them gathered outside and demanded that he be handed over to them, which he was.

They then went to the dauphin's palace, where they broke into his rooms and arrested the queen's brother Louis of Bavaria, and with him the Duke of Bar. The butchers were accompanied by Burgundy, and once again the young dauphin found courage to stand up to his father-in-law and said: "Know for a certainty that a time will come when you will repent this, for matters will not always go according to your wish."[2] To this, Burgundy insolently replied: "My lord, you will be able to consider these things better when your anger has cooled." And the butchers added their jeers to his. But the dauphin's courage could not save the prisoners, whom Burgundy led away to his own Hôtel d'Artois. Thereafter a veritable reign of terror began. Many of the victims, including Pierre des Essarts, were beheaded. Fortunately for them, Louis of Bavaria and the Duke of Bar were spared. Others, whose actual lives were not in danger, were subjected to exorbitant fines, had their houses ransacked and went in constant fear.

But before long the dauphin's words to Burgundy proved prophetic, and the ordinary people of Paris, finding that the butchers by their brutal methods were creating a situation that was worse than the one they sought to remedy, turned against them. Much more important, they turned at the same time against Burgundy too, recognising at last that the man whom they had so long considered their champion was in fact in large part responsible for the ills they endured. As soon as they realised this, fickle as they were, they turned instead to the old Duke of Berry, whom they had always appeared to dislike and even despise.

He happened at that time to be in Paris, prudently wearing his white cap, and the citizens requested him to take over the government of the city.

This sudden and unexpected swing of popular opinion was one of the most significant events in that long-drawn-out civil war, and certainly one of the most hopeful auguries for the success of the Orleanist cause that had occurred during the four years of their hitherto unavailing struggle. Charles was swift to take advantage of it. He himself had remained in Blois all that winter, but he had not been inactive. In February he had ordered Pierre de Mornay–Gauluet–his governor of Orleans to send from house to house, summoning all his able-bodied and skilled subjects to prepare to go to Paris to join his army and help the king.[3] In March he had published throughout his land, to the sound of trumpets, letters listing all that Burgundy had done against the king and himself. The usual jewels were sold to defray expenses, this time a crown of gold and jewels which fetched 5650 *livres*.

As the year wore on he kept in touch with events in Paris. Although the Cabochiens had the city gates guarded, and attempted to prevent any unauthorised entries and exits, a surgeon in Charles' service, named Gérard Pion, managed to get out of the city several times to bring him news, although on one occasion, in May, he was forced to escape almost naked–a state of things he was no doubt able to remedy with the ten gold *écus* with which Charles rewarded his courage.[4] Another of Charles' informants was his brother Philip of Vertus, who also managed by disguising himself to elude the guards. This, incidentally, was an escape that greatly annoyed the Duke of Burgundy when he heard of it, for he was still hoping to win this young man to his side by marrying him to one of his daughters, a marriage first agreed at the Treaty of Chartres and brought up again during subsequent agreements, but which the obviously reluctant bridegroom had always managed to avoid.

In July, while the terror in Paris was still at its height, Charles and some of his allies, especially the Count of Alençon, held an assembly to discuss how to get the king and the city of Paris out of the clutches of Burgundy. Alençon, who was one of the most generous of Charles' allies, is said to have paid the expenses of it,[5] and Charles sent an embassy from it to the king protesting against the arrests and executions that had taken place, offering his services in the cause of the peace made at Auxerre, and once more claiming the restoration of his lands.[6] Both the king and the dauphin were grateful for these offers and summoned Charles to go to them at Vernon, to discuss plans further.

They were in that region at the time for the marriage of Burgundy's brother, Philip, Count of Nevers, to the sister of Charles d'Artois, Count of Eu; and as Eu was a friend of his, Charles had a twofold reason for going. If Burgundy had hoped by this marriage to win the Count of Eu to his cause he was disappointed, for this young man of twenty-one seized the occasion to sign a pact with Charles of Orleans on July 27th[7] and sent his own armed forces to join those of the allies. As a result of the meeting with the king and the dauphin yet another treaty, the Peace of Pontoise, was drawn up, this time at last with Charles as one of the main negotiators, and on terms that he could accept without shame. One of them was that any prisoners taken by the Cabochiens who were still alive should be liberated. On July 31st Charles and his allies marched to Paris with their troops; and on August 1st the articles of the Peace of Pontoise were read before the king in Council.

The butchers were naturally enraged that their prisoners were to be released, but they were now powerless and had to submit. The rest of the population were overjoyed at this release from their reign of terror, the bells of Paris were rung, masses for peace were said, there were processions and many days of rejoicing. When, at the king's command, the Dukes of Bar and Bavaria and other illustrious prisoners were released, the general rejoicing spread to the court. The most jubilant there was the dauphin himself, who certainly had cause to feel a sense of triumph. Always an extravagant young man, delighting in fine clothes, he celebrated the occasion by having made for himself beautiful robes of violet cloth, adorned with a great white cross and embroidered with gold leaves and the device "Le droit chemin". In the midst of this rejoicing Burgundy judged it prudent to return to Flanders. His departure still further increased the general sense of well-being, among court and people alike, and the Duke of Berry, who was now captain of Paris, rode freely about the city, acclaimed by all. At long last the Orleanists had become the popular party and, as an earnest of their restoration to favour, one of them, Tanguy du Châtel, who had been a trusted officer of Louis of Orleans, was appointed Provost of Paris in succession to the hated Pierre des Essarts, and remained a staunch supporter of the dauphin from thenceforward.

Charles of Orleans seems to have taken no part in this first outburst of relief and joy. It is noticeable that, whether deliberately or not, ever since Auxerre he had never appeared where Burgundy was. But also there is reason to believe that, after the proclamation of the Peace of Pontoise at the beginning of August, his health compelled him to return to Blois, for in his archives there is a document dated August 5th[8] recording a payment for "several items from the apothecary's and pills prescribed" by his physician Pierre de Vaulx – the doctor who had lent him silver cups in his time of need. What this indisposition was is not known; perhaps the sudden change from years of frustration and unavailing effort to royal favour and the hope of justice had brought it on; but whatever it was, it clearly was not serious for on the 29th of that month, that is after Burgundy's departure, we find Charles in Paris, where the king had summoned all the leaders of the Orleanist party to join him. On the way thither, at Orleans, Charles had bought shirts and handkerchiefs for Philip,[9] who accompanied him, but he had apparently not given any particular thought to his own attire, and arrived in the festive capital wearing his customary black, in sign of mourning for the father who was still unavenged.

This sad appearance was so at variance with the general atmosphere of rejoicing that the dauphin begged his cousin, to whom he showed particular affection, to leave it off and adopt the same royal colour that he himself had chosen. What was more, he wanted his cousin's robes to be an exact copy of his own. For Charles, who since his adolescence had never had any occasion, let alone the heart, to indulge in the pleasure of rich raiment, the temptation to let himself go for once must have been strong. He had by no means forgotten the reason why he had always worn black; but now that he had become a welcome and even a cherished member of the royal circle, there was hope that soon he would achieve that justice against Burgundy that was still his one desire. For was not the dauphin's wish, in an age when colours had great significance, a way of associating the Orleanist cause with himself?

So Charles yielded to his cousin's whim and at the end of August bought from a Parisian draper enough violet-coloured Brussels cloth to make four cloaks, three of them being for his chamberlains, of whom Raoul de Gaucourt was one, A jeweller was commissioned to make little gold leaves to adorn them, another craftsman to attach them to the garments and finally they were embroidered with the dauphin's device "Le droit chemin". The chamberlains' cloaks had leaves of silver-gilt. The document[10] recording these transactions gives the names of all the people employed in them and one can imagine the haste with which they worked to get them ready in time for the state entry into Paris (which sounds like another of the dauphin's ideas) that Charles and some of his allies—Anjou, Bourbon, Alençon, Vertus, and possibly also Arthur of Richemont, that younger brother of the Duke of Brittany, —were to make on September 1st.[11]

They entered Paris through the Porte Saint-Jacques to the sound of trumpets and were welcomed by Berry and Bavaria, the Chancellor of France, the Bishop of Paris and many ecclesiastics, and the provost with many citizens. They must have made a splendid sight as they rode through the streets, for the dauphin had now supplied the other allies with violet cloaks too and they wore parti-coloured red and black head-dresses. At the Hôtel Saint-Pol the king received them with every sign of pleasure and gave them a great banquet. A day or so afterwards Charles' remaining allies, the Count of Armagnac and the Count of Albret, arrived too; and on September 5th all the princes, with the exception of course of Burgundy, attended a great meeting of the Council in the great chamber of the royal hôtel. There, all the princes on their knees swore to keep the peace; the allies were reinstated in all their honours; the Cabochiens were imprisoned in the Châtelet or banished from Paris[12] (Caboche himself and many of his followers fled to Burgundy); and once again Coucy and Pierrefonds were restored to Charles.[13]

All that autumn and throughout the winter of 1413-14—indeed until the following April—Charles remained in Paris, living presumably in one or other of the two chief Orleans houses, the Hôtel de Behaigne near the Louvre or the Séjour d'Orleans on the other side of the river. Nothing is known of his movements at this time, but there is evidence of some of his preoccupations. As a young prince of the blood now living at court, he obviously had not only to be richly dressed himself but to keep up a great and splendidly-clad household. The accounts reveal, for the first time since he had succeeded, a lavish expenditure on stuffs and furs. He had for instance a cloak of white satin trimmed with fur.[14] In September no less than forty-one garments embroidered with his device of a nettle, as well as with "Le droit chemin" were made, presumably for members of his staff, and six surcoats. These last were probably for himself, since a few weeks later a jeweller of Paris made jewels in the shape of "small, trembling leaves, to be used for ornamenting six surcoats." This last payment, incidentally, is dated November

23rd, 1413, and suggests that he was approaching his nineteenth birthday, on the following day, in a much more cheerful frame of mind than he had known since the death of his father. He had to play his part on court occasions too. In December there is a record of his having sent in haste from Paris to Melun two of his minstrels because the queen had asked for them.

All this princely life did not make him forget his continuing desire to clear his father's reputation and to obtain justice against his murderer, and one can hardly doubt that it was due to Charles' own efforts that during January the learned doctors of the University of Paris began a prolonged examination of the famous 'defence' of Jean Petit, with a view to denouncing it. As it had been composed by a theologian, university etiquette demanded that theologians should judge it. Petit had supported his monstrous case with copious quotations from Holy Writ, the Fathers and other revered authorities. All these could not simply be brushed aside without disrespect; but it might be found that they had been misinterpreted. As the speech had been a long one, this process took time, and before anything could come of it the restored calm of life in Paris was suddenly shattered. Fortunately this upheaval worked in Charles' favour.

The disturber of the peace was as usual Burgundy. By no means prepared to take his fall from favour lying down, ever since the meeting at the Hôtel Saint-Pol the previous September he had been writing to the king, protesting that as he had not been present at it he did not consider himself bound by the oaths sworn there to keep the peace. But now it was his turn to have his pleas ignored. So on February 8th he appeared with his armed forces marching towards Paris. When the news of this was brought to the dauphin, he at once ordered all the Orleanist princes in Paris to assemble their men and join him before the cathedral, whence they marched to the Hôtel de Ville. There it was decided that each prince should with his forces man a different part of the city and its walls. The dauphin himself commanded the Bastille, Berry the Temple, while Charles was at Saint-Martin-des-Champs close to the Porte Saint-Martin.

The gates of the city were closed and Burgundy's messengers refused entry. He therefore withdrew to the heights of Montmartre, where his army was clearly visible to the watchers on the walls, and occasionally shot in messages on the point of arrows, protesting that he had come with peaceful intentions. His hope was that his old friends the butchers would spread this report and come and join him, perhaps persuading other citizens to do the same. But the allies frustrated this hope by having him proclaimed a murderer and a traitor, and no one stirred. So after waiting a fortnight Burgundy marched his army back to his own territory, humiliated for a second time.

It did now seem as if fortune's wheel had come full circle as far as Charles was concerned. For just as in the past, when Burgundy's star had been in the ascendant, his sudden interventions had always turned the tide of feeling against Charles, as against Valentina before him, so now his latest manoeuvre had the opposite effect, and roused his one-time supporters at court and in the University to act with unwonted speed against him. Even while Burgundy was withdrawing his troops from Montmartre, a great concourse of learned men of the University, together with the Bishop of Paris and many other prelates, were meeting to hear the findings of the theologians who had examined Petit's speech. They ignored the more absurd charges against Louis of Orleans, such as that of sorcery, as having been included chiefly to impress the populace. But they pronounced the charges of tyranny and the various forms of wickedness that hung upon it baseless. It was therefore decided that the defence be condemned and the text of it publicly burnt.

Accordingly on February 23rd 1414 these authorities assembled on a platform specially erected on the *parvis* of Notre-Dame and there, in the presence of the citizens who had flocked to see the spectacle, a professor of theology in a loud voice denounced as erroneous and iniquitous the case that Petit had built up in defence of his master's deed, whereupon the text of it was consigned to the flames. On March 6th this action was approved by a royal letter.[15]

So after his six years' struggle Charles had at last the satisfaction of knowing that, although Burgundy still remained unpunished for his crime, an indefensible crime it was now admitted to have been, committed against a victim whose reputation was now publicly cleared of all the foul charges that had for so long darkened it. It was not the revenge which Valentina, in the wildness of her final grief, had asked for, but it was a first step towards that justice which was probably all she wanted, and all that Charles too, reasonable and civilised by nature, wished and expected to achieve.

When Burgundy heard what had happened, he at once determined to rely on his own armed strength to regain if possible his old authority and dominance. As a gesture of defiance to the king and to Charles, he sent garrisons to occupy Compiègne, which was a royal town, and Soissons, of which Charles was lord. This insolent and rebellious act provoked the Council and even the king to retaliate, as Burgundy had no doubt hoped it would. On March 2nd the Council, in the presence of the queen and the dauphin, declared war on Burgundy, and in the first week of April the king himself took the field, together with the dauphin, to lead the royal troops assembled at Saint-Denis. They were joined by Charles with his men-at-arms and bowmen, among the latter the Scottish archers under John Stewart. His friends and allies went too: his brother Philip, Armagnac, Albret, Alençon, Richemont and Eu. And now, instead of the white cross, which Monstrelet calls "the noble and pleasant ensign that the king and his predecessor kings of France had always worn",[16] Charles VI, the dauphin and all the princes wore the white band or scarf of the Armagnacs. The Orleanist cause had indeed triumphed.

As that short campaign progressed it seemed at first that even greater triumphs lay in store for Charles. The inhabitants of Compiègne and Soissons, Péronne and Bapaume quickly surrendered to the king, especially as Burgundy made no attempt to come to their aid. But although the royal and allied armies had been largely unopposed, the investing of each town, together with the long marches in between, had taken time, so that it was July 28th before they reached Arras, where this time Burgundy was awaiting them. There is no evidence as to whether or not he was dismayed by their successes so far; the presumption is rather that he had been harbouring his strength in the hope of one decisive battle.

He had been in Arras all that summer preparing to defend it not only by fortifying its circumference with walls and ditches, but by a sort of scorched-earth policy in the surrounding country. So when the royalist army arrived they found that the trees which might have masked their movements had all been cut down, while any building—houses, hospitals and even churches—in which they might have billeted themselves had been burnt to the ground. They were thus forced to camp in completely open country, while inside their ramparts of fortification and desolation Burgundy and his fighting men awaited them. From these positions the opposing sides fired lead cannon-balls at each other throughout August without any appreciable gain on either side. For all that, the Orleanists had every reason to hope that, even if they did not manage to take the town by assault, a siege prolonged until the besieged began to run short of supplies and arms, which must inevitably have happened as the year drew on, would force Burgundy to surrender on terms that they could have insisted should include atonement for his crime and which would nullify his power for the future.

This hope was dashed in the first days of September when an offer of an immediate peace came from the Burgundian side. From Charles' point of view it was a fatal offer, as it revealed the fundamental difference between his war aims and those of the king. As the king saw it, the purpose of the campaign had merely been to bring a rebellious subject back into obedience; so if the rebel offered to surrender and make peace, the end had been achieved and he was only too glad to accept. No thought of pursuing his brother's murderer had entered his feeble mind. And when one of the Orleanist lords, outraged by such weakness, went to the king's tent to demand how he could contemplate peace with the "evil, false and disloyal man who killed his brother", the king, whose wits had obviously begun to wander again, answered that his "fair son of Orleans", as he was now wont to call Charles, had forgiven Burgundy everything.[17]

Nor was there any hope of resistance to be found in the dauphin. Ever since Péronne, he had been much in the company of the Countess of Hainault, Burgundy's sister and staunch supporter, who was the mother-in-law of his younger brother John of Touraine. The dauphin had enough courage to defy his father-in-law from time to time, but he could not withstand the constant tears of the countess, who was for ever reminding him of the many ties which bound his family to hers, and begging him on her knees to make peace between them. In any case he much preferred peace to war, as he had already shown at Bourges.

So, to the dismay of the Orleanists, the king and the dauphin agreed to yet another peace, that of Arras. Burgundy himself was not present when it was proclaimed outside the king's tent on September 5th, but was represented by his brother Anthony, Duke of Brabant, and their sister of Hainault. Burgundy's absence on such an occasion may imply that he himself had not really desired to make peace at this juncture, but had been overborne by his forceful sister. But to judge by his subsequent conduct it seems more likely that he was merely using this agreement by proxy as a way of ending the siege of Arras, while at the same time secretly reserving for himself the power to disclaim the peace later on, on the grounds that he had not agreed to it in person.

On his behalf two more or less empty promises were made. The first was that he would surrender to the king Arras and the other towns that he had taken, although these would of course naturally remain part of his dukedom. Secondly, it was agreed that he would make no more alliances with the English, with whom he had signed a secret treaty[18] as recently as the previous May, offering to share with them the spoils of the present campaign if he were victorious. In return he obtained forgiveness for anything that had been done since the Peace of Pontoise; and was further promised that if anything had been done against his honour it would be righted. If the king and the dauphin had not enough perspicacity to see how easily Burgundy might use this last clause to have the recent indirect pronouncement of his guilt cancelled, Charles of Orleans certainly had. This was bad enough, but on top of it he was once again enjoined to repeat the humiliating terms of the Treaties of Chartres and Auxerre, promising to make peace with Burgundy and forgive and forget all the past.

This time it was too much. He was no longer a child to be dominated by his elders, nor a defeated young man to be browbeaten, but a prince of the blood of equal standing with Burgundy and, moreover, an ally of the king. It was insulting, too, that he should be asked to swear, when Burgundy had not even troubled to come and do likewise. So when the dauphin asked him to, Charles found courage to disobey and, bowing low, he replied with his habitual quiet courtesy: "my lord, I am not obliged to swear an oath, for I came only to serve My lord the king and you."[19] But the dauphin replied: "Fair cousin, we beg you to swear to the peace." Charles, desperately seeking some way out, then said: "My lord, I have not broken the peace and ought not to swear. May it please you be content." But the dauphin would not be content and for the third time he pressed Charles to swear, at which, now roused to anger, Charles said: "My lord, I have not broken the peace, nor have those of my council nor my party. Make those who have broken it come here into your presence and swear to you, and afterwards I will do your pleasure." At that the dauphin too grew angry, so much so that the Archbishop of Rheims and some others felt bound to say to Charles: "My lord, do as my Lord of Aquitaine bids you." The deadlock had to be broken and so, having made his true attitude abundantly clear, against his will Charles swore to keep the peace.

Encouraged by his resistance, the Duke of Bourbon also tried to evade the oath by delaying tactics when it came to his turn to swear, but the dauphin cut him short saying: "Fair cousin, we pray you talk no more about it." So he too had to swear, as did after him without further protest the other princes and all the prelates except the Archbishop of Sens, brother of the unfortunate Jean de Montagu, whom Burgundy had caused to suffer such an ignominious death. When his turn came he said to the dauphin: "My lord, remember the oath that you and all of us swore when we left Paris, in the presence of the queen." But the dauphin was by now in no mood to be reminded of any such oath to bring Burgundy low, and he brushed the Archbishop's protest aside also, repeating: "Speak no more of it. We desire that the peace should stand and that you should swear it." Further resistance was impossible, but as he too took the oath the Archbishop made it clear that he did so unwillingly by saying: "My lord, since you wish it, I will do it."

After this painful ending to a campaign so auspiciously begun, the return to Paris from which the royalist and Orleanist forces had set forth with such determination and so brave a flourish, could only be an anti-climax. But, defrauded of a decisive victory over his enemy though Charles had been, his position was not really worse than it had been in the previous winter. John the Fearless had in fact gained nothing by the peace, except a promise of which in the event he did not avail himself. It had not restored him to his previous power and influence at court, or in the Council, and when it was concluded he had no option but to return to his own lands. Charles on the other hand had had a chance to make a courageous stand in the presence of his enemies, as well as of his followers and the dauphin. In spite of his opposition he retained his now favoured place at court and was still, it seems, on friendly terms with the dauphin, who stayed with him on their way home at his castle of Chauny, where Charles engaged a tumbler and his three children to entertain him.[20] They were both after all still young men, the dauphin sixteen and Charles nineteen, so it was natural that they should enjoy such harmless amusements.

But on their return to Paris serious matters were not forgotten and, as though to reassure Charles that the recent peace treaty did not imply a change in the royal attitude to Burgundy, on January 5th, 1415, the eve of Epiphany, the king had the obsequies of his brother Louis solemnly celebrated in Notre-Dame. With him were Charles, his brother Philip and their allies Berry, Anjou, Bourbon, Alençon, Richemont and Eu, all clad in black. A tremendous throng of citizens filled the church. Only the dauphin was absent, having gone to Melun to see his mother and his sister the Duchess of Brittany.

Jean Gerson, Chancellor of the University, and one of the greatest and most influential scholars and divines of his time, preached a vigorous sermon that must have warmed Charles' heart. He praised Louis without reserve, saying that he had governed the realm better than anyone since his death, while as for John of Burgundy, although he did not think he should be put to death, he ought to be humiliated in order to recognise his sin and make due satisfaction for it for the salvation of his soul. And finally, he defended the condemnation and burning of Jean Petit's speech against any who might criticise it. On the following Monday the king held another service in the Chapel of the Celestines, where Louis was buried, and after that another in the College of Navarre. These solemn ceremonies were virtually the last acts in the long drama of Louis' death and all that followed it, and Charles could perhaps feel that he had achieved the aim he had pursued so steadily.

With this debt of honour to both his parents paid, Charles might at last have felt free to cast off care and enjoy his life to the full, if it had not been for the obligation to ransom his brother John and the other hostages, and to do everything in his power for their maintenance and well-being, since to provide for these was no part of Clarence's duties. These obligations had been constantly in his mind during all the events, whether grim or cheerful, of the past two years, and whenever he could he sent such sums as he could manage. He had begun his attempts to pay off the main debt of 210,000 écus in the spring of 1413,[21] while Clarence was still lingering in Bordeaux, and he continued, even during the campaign against Burgundy in the summer of 1414, to send several small sums on account. However, Berry, Alençon and Bourbon were contributing too, so that Charles had not the whole responsibility for it, and might reasonably hope with their help to pay it all off before long. There is in any case no evidence that Clarence had yet begun to press for payment of these sums due to his fellow nobles as well as himself, since after all he had the hostages and jewels as security. It would have been discourteous, too, to insist too quickly, especially as Charles, with his habitual generosity, was sending him presents while he was still in France: a bay courser for himself, and a very special gift to take home to his duchess, a forceful lady much older than himself, (whose first husband had been John Beaufort, Marquess of Somerset), in the shape of a head-dress known as a *floquart*, made of white satin adorned with silver besants, in a linen-covered case.

In spite of that Clarence evidently began, towards the end of 1414, to bring up the question of those 50,000 *écus* he had exacted as a personal gratuity for himself; and in November and December Charles and his uncle Berry sent him small contributions towards that: 1500 *écus* in November and 2140 in December.[22] The grasping Sir John Cornwall also began in 1414 to press for payment of the 21,375 *écus* promised to him; and in view of the stringent conditions with which he had hedged that promise round, Charles and his uncle obviously thought it wise to try and discharge that particular debt as soon as possible; so by October 1414 they together found 11,375 – more than half of it – and Cornwall returned a rich object of gold, garnished with pearls and precious stones, which he had held as security for it.[23]

Charles would no doubt have been able to make larger contributions to the main debt if it had not been for the far more urgent need to send money for the subsistence and expenses of his brother John and his fellow hostages. He had ordered some Florentine merchants in London to send John and Archambaud de Villars 2000 *écus* in December 1413.[24] But in the following March he heard that they were all suffering great want in England in Clarence's keeping, and on getting this distressing news Charles at once instructed his Treasurer-General Pierre Renier to pay John 6000 *écus* for himself with 5000 for his attendants (he presumably was allowed some servants), and another 1000 for the expenses of Macé le Borgne, Guillaume le Bouteiller, Jean Davy and Jean de Saveuses. These sums were to be taken from the revenues for Normandy. In June of the same year Charles sent another 2000 to John and Archambaud, this time through merchants in Lucca and Florence.

Yet in spite of all these drains on his resources Charles was able, during the winter of 1414–15, to indulge in many of the pleasures proper to a young prince of the fleur-de-lis. It was one of the very few occasions in his life when he was able to enjoy socially the company of his younger allies, most of whom were in Paris at that time. One of his closest friends, the Count of Alençon, was on January 1st 1415 raised to the rank of duke, partly as a recompense for his services in the late campaign, but also because, says Le Religieux, "this lord surpassed the other princes of the blood by the charms of his person and manner, and possessed a rich patrimony."[25] To be raised to the highest rank in the land largely for one's looks is a delightful reason and was considered "a mark of particular distinction" even then; clearly Alençon dazzled them all, for Juvenal des Ursins too says he was indeed "a most handsome lord."[26]

As for Charles himself, what his appearance was like, either then or at any other time, remains unknown, for there is no portrait of him, nor any description. It was in fact most unusual at that time for any comment to be made on a man's looks, such as those on Alençon. But if there is no reason to suppose that Charles was handsome, or even good-looking, an exchange of *ballades* which would appear to have taken place then between himself and the Marquis de Garencières, a friend of his father's, gives the impression that he was a gay and light-hearted youth who enjoyed teasing this old friend, and knew how to take it well when Garencières teased him in return. For the subject of Charles' *ballade* was that the God of Love was complaining that Garencières was trying to encroach on his authority, and had called on all the men and women who accepted his rule to come to his aid. In his reply Garencières claimed that it was rather Charles who was usurping the rights of Cupid, whom he asks to punish the young man, saying he is 'un homme de mauvaise vie'. He is, Garencières goes on in the next verse, 'un enfant malicieux', in whom no one should trust, as he has deceived more than two people in France, and is in fact 'le prince de Bien Mentir'. In the envoy he prophesies that with gifts like these

> Vous verrés icellui venir
> A grant honneur, n'en doubtez mie.

Charles' other chief friend and ally, the Duke of Bourbon, was an easy-going, light-hearted character, fond of sport and with a weakness for women. He too came into the limelight on January 1st, which seems to have been a day of general rejoicing and pleasure, by creating a new order of knighthood, composed of personally-selected knights and esquires, each of whom was to wear on his left leg, in honour of his chosen lady, a prisoner's iron hanging from a chain, gold for the knights and silver for the esquires.[27] These were to be worn every Sunday for two years until they found an equal number of knights and esquires willing to fight them "to the death", for Bourbon was also a brave and bold soldier. But he was by no means the devoted servant of only one lady. It was a court, after all, where the pursuit of physical pleasure of all kinds, even to the point of debauch, was general, and

Bourbon himself always remembered in later, sadder years, how much he had enjoyed such pleasures with less reputable ladies.

From a *ballade* which Charles addressed to him many years later, it appears that Bourbon used sometimes to take his young cousin with him on these expeditions.* Although in that *ballade* Charles declares that he no longer has any desire for such things, he admits that in the past he acquitted himself nobly. And in another poem, written when he was older still, he says that in youth

> Amoureus fus, or ne le suy ge mye,
> Et en Paris menoye bonne vie.

For all that, the whole tone of the poem to Bourbon seems to suggest a man for whom, though by no means prudish, that particular pleasure of the flesh never had anything like the attraction it had for Bourbon. He was obviously by nature more tender and devoted than passionate, and more faithful too. And it is perhaps significant that he, almost alone of the great nobles, never had any bastards; even his brother Philip had one.

Certainly his tastes in general ran far more to aesthetic enjoyments and pleasures of the mind. The elaborate details of the splendid garments he ordered for himself at this time indicate an artistic delight in the beauty of such things. But he seems to have taken as much pleasure in the attire of others as in his own, like his father before him, who was always giving rich garments to his fellow nobles and even to the king his brother; for when he and Philip of Vertus went with some friends to visit the queen at Montargis at the end of January, on the occasion of a visit by her daughter Jane, Duchess of Brittany, Charles had nine surcoats of his favourite bronze-green cloth, their sleeves adorned with silver worked to represent scales, made for all of them to wear.[28] For what must clearly have been another very special occasion that winter, Charles had made for himself a garment whose sleeves were embroidered down their whole length with 960 costly pearls, forming what the account for it describes as "the words of the song 'Madame, je suis plus joyeulx'".[29] The most precise instructions for this elaborate fancy were given. Four pearls were to be used to make each of the 142 notes, making 568 altogether, and 392 for the words.

But apart from rich robes and the customary New Year presents,

* See page 190 below.

his favourite gift at this time was that of his own knightly Order of the Camail. This seems to have been an elaboration of an Order of the Porcupine, which his father Louis is said to have instituted in about 1393, or even possibly on the occasion of the birth of Charles, although there is no formal record of it. This is said to have consisted of twenty-five members, including the head of the Order. They wore magnificent robes and the collar was a rope of twisted gold chains, from which hung a porcupine of fine gold.[30] Charles kept the porcupine but seems to have substituted a slightly different collar, which he called a Camail* and renamed the Order after it. Although there is some evidence that at one moment, much later in his life, he too intended to limit membership of the Order to twenty-five,[31] it is clear that he never did so, because he made such constant gifts of it, either in gold or silver, to people of every degree, that he obviously regarded it merely as a personal device which he gave both as a reward to those who had rendered him some special service, and as a mark of favour, no doubt in a richer form, to allies and distinguished foreigners.

Another reason why Charles may not have wholeheartedly followed the Duke of Bourbon in all his amorous escapades was that, if we may judge by what is thought to be the first poem certainly by him that we have, he was in his youth very much imbued with the ideals of courtly love, that demanded of the lover devoted service and unswerving fidelity to one lady only. We have no means of knowing exactly when this poem, called *La Retenue d'Amours*, was written, but there are good grounds for supposing that it was at this time, for the active and anxious life he had had to lead during all the years of his adolescence were hardly conducive to such creation, and the fate that was to overwhelm him at the end of this brief care-free season certainly dried up the fount of his poetic genius for some years to come. It is a poem very much in the style of the time, obviously influenced by the *Roman de la Rose*, an

* It is impossible to determine exactly what this collar, or chain, looked like. The word *camail* generally meant the neck-piece, either of chain-mail or leather, that descended from the back of the helmet and protected the neck, although it was also used for a neck ornament. It seems likely that in the case of Charles' order it was a collar made to look like the links of chain-mail, as one can see it roughly executed on the statue of Dunois at Châteaudun (see illustration). On the other hand a document in the *Chambre des Comptes* (BM., *Add. Ch.* 3150) describes how Charles gave one of his esquires "a silver collar shaped like a *camail* with a golden porcupine".

allegory full of those personifications of abstract ideas so dear to the poets of the Middle Ages.

In it he relates how in his childhood Nature put him first in charge of Dame Infancy, who brought him up tenderly, suffering neither Care nor Melancholy to come near him. When he grew older Nature handed him over to Dame Youth, who says it is quite time he made the acquaintance of the God of Love. This terrifies him, as he has heard of the pangs that love makes his servants suffer, and feels he is too young to bear them. But Youth reassures him, promising that he will not be made to love against his will, and so he goes with her to the manor where Love dwells. The God receives him amiably, repeats Youth's promise, but says that all the same he will have to yield in the end.

He then calls Beauty, telling her that she must tame him. Alone with her, he cannot resist stealing a glance at her, and as soon as she catches his eye, she shoots a dart straight through it into his heart, which begins to laugh for joy at the tickling sensation. But he himself is furious at having been so easily caught, and works himself into such a state that he falls pale and ill at the feet of Love. The God merely laughs and mocks him for his feebleness, so he turns to Beauty, the "jeune, gente, nompareille Princesse", who persuades him to yield and pleads with the God for him. Though clearly rather irritated with him by this time, Love accepts him as a subject. He is made to swear some oaths, one being that he will love in one place only, without desiring or seeking to change; and to promise, without swearing, that he will strive to-wards certain ideals, one of which is that he will study to make songs and *ballades*, as these are things that serve Love. How well he attained this ideal we know. The God then orders his secretary, Good Faith, to give him his letter of appointment (the *Retenue d'Amours*), which Loyalty seals, and in exchange takes his heart, saying that his doctor, Hope, will see that he manages without it until he finds a lady who will give him hers.

Long though this poem is, it is never for a moment tedious as such medieval allegories often are. The narrative flows easily, the versifica-tion is extraordinarily mature for so young a writer and, by some magic of his own, even the personifications of abstract concepts take on a certain liveliness under his pen, as they were notably to do in his later work. But what gives this poem its chief interest is not only the fact that it is the first of his that we have, but the frankly autobiographical aspect of it and its revelation of his personality. He makes no attempt to conceal that he is writing about himself. On the contrary, Youth announces him to the porter at Love's manor as Charles, Duke of Orleans, and presents him to the God himself as a young prince

> sailly de la maison de France,
> Creu ou jardin semé de fleur de lis.

Having made himself known in this way, Charles proceeds to paint his own portrait with the greatest simplicity, showing himself not only as a young man anxious to avoid suffering if at all possible and dreading complications such as those of love, but also extremely shy, like all young people who

> perdent tost contenance
> Quant en lieu sont ou n'ont point d'acointance.

For all that he cannot resist Beauty. He reveals his already urbane and adult attitude to life in the kind of amused detachment with which he views these youthful weaknesses. And even more in the pleasingly dry, even sly, humour that peeps out from time to time, as when he relates how Love, in welcoming him, remarks that in times past he knew his father well, and several other members of his family, who occasionally entered his service. Such things illumine him and bring him closer in many ways than any chronicle of the outward events of his life.

Since this poem was obviously autobiographical the question arises, who then was the unnamed lady and who was Beauty? In view both of Charles' temperament and his public position at court, it seems inconceivable that he can have written it for anyone but his wife, Bonne, or meant it as anything but an allegory of how he came to love her. It was of course true that he had already had a wife before he married her; but on the occasion of that earlier marriage he was only eleven, and so too young to have dreaded the pangs and complications that love might bring, as he may well have done at fifteen, when it was arranged that he should marry the child Bonne, whom he had never seen. It is therefore not unreasonable to conclude that in this poem she is both the unnamed lady who is to give him her heart to replace his which Love had taken, and also Beauty, the "young, gentle, matchless Princess", whose first look sent that dart into his heart, and there kindled the love that, arousing as it did an equal constancy on her part, so far from bringing him pain was later to be one of his few consolations. A final proof that the poem referred to her may be found in the fact that, among the *ballades* which everything indicates were certainly addressed to her when he was far from her, years afterwards, there is one in which he reminds her of that early ceremony when Love bound them together:

> Belle, bien avez souvenance,
> Comme certainement je croy,
> De la tresplaisant aliance
> Qu'Amour fist entre vous et moy;

and he goes on to recall the letter of appointment which Love's secretary, Good Faith, then drew up and Loyalty sealed.*

Although the *Retenue d'Amours* clearly belongs to this first part of Charles' life, to judge from internal evidence it was not the only poem that he wrote then. There are nine other *ballades* that definitely give the impression that they were written in the early days of his love and that it was Bonne who inspired them. Even the use of her name as an adjective seems to suggest this, in such lines as

> Belle, bonne, nompareille, plaisant

the first of a poem in which he says with a simplicity that sounds sincere,

> Car je devins vostre loyal servant,
> Le premier jour que je peux regarder
> La grant beaute que vous avez sans per.

And though we have no portrait of Bonne, she comes very much to life in one of his most beautiful *ballades* in praise of her. She is

> Fresche beauté, tresriche de jeunesse,
> Riant regard, trait amoureusement,
> Plaisant parler, gouverné par sagesse,
> Port femenin en corps bien fait et gent,

Five stanzas describe her many qualities, among others that

> Elle fait tout si gracieusement,
> Que nul n'y scet trouver amendement;

and

> Bonté, Honneur, avecques Gentillesse
> Tiennent son cueur en leur gouvernment.

* See Appendix II

4 John the Fearless, Duke of Burgundy, by an unknown painter of the French School, now in the Musée de Besançon

He thinks God has sent her into the world to show the full range of these high qualities, with all of which he has so liberally endowed her. Her mere aspect would chase away sadness from anyone afflicted, for

> C'est Paradis que de sa compaignie.

And yet he insists that his praise is not partial:

> Je ne dy riens que tous ne vont disant:
> De ces grans biens est ma Dame garnie.

This last line well illustrates Charles' mastery in finding, for repetition at the end of each stanza as the *ballade* form demanded, lines whose direct and simple statement of feeling, expressed in a beautiful rhythm, engrave them in the memory: "Car je vous tiens pour ma seule maistresse", "Ma seule souveraine joye" and so on.

But if these poems do indeed reveal what a place Bonne held in his heart, the mystery of her whereabouts at that time still remains unsolved. It is unlikely that she was at Blois in the winter of 1414–15, for when the King of Sicily (the Duke of Anjou) was about to go there then Charles thoughtfully sent "two antique, pointed diamonds" for his sister Margaret and his little daughter Jane to give to "their dear cousin".[32] If Bonne had been there, he would surely have sent something for her to give too, or at least mentioned her. In any case her place would more properly have been with her husband Charles in Paris in that winter when he was at last tasting some of the pleasures of life; and one would like to suppose that she was indeed there, and that the message of that pearl-embroidered sleeve of his, "Madame je suis plus joyeulx" was addressed to the sixteen-year-old girl who had married him in the days of his despair and who must have rejoiced to know that he was at last "plus joyeulx", and to share with him that happy time which, although they could not guess it, was the last they were ever to know together.

PART TWO

WHILE Charles and his fellow princes were enjoying court life in Paris during the winter of 1414–1415, and taking at last their full part in the king's Council, a threat not only for their own future but for that of the whole kingdom began to raise its head. It had indeed been hanging over them for a long time, but curiously enough none of them, and certainly not the king or the dauphin, realised the danger that now menaced them from England and was in the end to reduce the country to a worse state of defeat and degradation than any it had hitherto known.

As the situation then stood between the two countries, it was not surprising that the French should have been slow to foresee what was coming. It was over half a century since their crushing defeats at Crécy and Poitiers had made the English, by the Treaty of Brétigny, lords not only of Calais but of all the rich provinces of Aquitaine. Of the princes of the blood now living, only the old Duke of Berry, who was twenty at the time, could remember that. Since then the tide had turned against the English and by 1375 the French armies, under their great commander Du Guesclin, had driven them out of all their French possessions except Calais and a mere coastal strip of Gascony. Any retaliation the French might have expected for this was prevented by the death of Edward III and the accession to the English throne of Richard II who, though born and brought up in France, had none of his warlike grandfather's desire to rule it.

Throughout his reign, except for a few sporadic coastal raids, there had been peace between the two countries. Richard's marriage with Charles VI's little daughter Isabelle in 1396, and the long truce which followed it, were enough to lull the French into the belief that this ancient strife was over at last. Richard's tragic end, so soon after that marriage, did not greatly disturb this belief; for his successor, Henry IV, although occasional raids into France still occurred during his reign, had had enough to do at home keeping the throne he had usurped, without thinking seriously of conquests abroad. For this reason both the Orleanists and John of Burgundy had tended to regard him more as a useful ally in their own civil strife than as a possible enemy of their country, and did not scruple to reveal its internal weakness to him.

The young man who succeeded Henry in March 1413 could not have seemed to the French at first potentially any more dangerous than his father had been—indeed less so, because of the indulgences of his youth. They were to learn, as the English did, that once he had the reins of power in his hands Henry became a very different man. Very soon after his accession it was clear to his advisers that the main ambition of his reign was to revive Edward III's claim to the throne of France; and in the pursuit of it he developed that complex character that sometimes made it difficult for his own subjects to understand him and certainly must often have puzzled the French. Though brave and warlike by nature and a brilliant strategist, mere conquest would never have satisfied him. A man of firmly-held religious beliefs, and devout practices, he had a deep need to be convinced that he might "with right and justice make this claim."

To that end he lent a willing ear to any arguments, however specious, in support of it and was able to shut his mind to the two facts that, in French eyes, invalidated any such pretentions on his part: their Salic law, which debarred anyone, French or English, from claiming through a woman, as Henry did through Edward III's French mother, the Princess Isabelle; and the fact that, like his father, he had usurped the English throne, thus weakening any claim to theirs even if the Salic law had not existed. Brushing all that aside, and convinced of the justice of his cause, it was easy enough for Henry to believe in his divine right to the French throne and to see himself as God's chosen instrument to free his subjects, the French, from the sorry state to which their present rulers had reduced them. And so, within a few months, the hot-blooded, impetuous youth had become a grave, determined man, keeping his own counsel, self-assured to the point of arrogance, courteous in his normal bearing but a stern disciplinarian, able to be ruthless and even cruel when justice, as he saw it, seemed to demand it, and, where his ambition was concerned, so self-righteously set upon his goal as to be able to justify to himself any methods whatever that he took to reach it.

To the French, or indeed to anyone else, those methods must have seemed extremely devious, to put it mildly. Henry's first act, in July 1413, was to set on foot negotiations to prolong the existing truce with France. Nothing could have pleased the French better and meetings to discuss the terms of it took place that summer and autumn.[1] No problems arose and, by January 1414, the truce, to last until February 1415, was publicly proclaimed in both England and France.[2] At those meetings the proposal that Henry should strengthen the links of parentage and alliance with France by marrying Charles VI's youngest daughter Catherine, then only thirteen, was also put forward and Henry gave a promise, to hold good until the 18th June, that he would not consider marrying anyone else.[3] But no conditions were then mentioned.

However, before that date expired, Henry had taken two other steps. During the spring, as we know, he had been negotiating privately with John of Burgundy at Arras, a treaty whereby each was to help the other.[4] This was signed on June 4th. Thus assured of Burgundy's co-operation, or at least of his non-interference in the event of an invasion of France, Henry had already come further into the open with his own people, and on May 31st he appointed a Commission to negotiate conditions for his marriage with Catherine.[5] These were to be no less than the restitution of his 'rights' that were being withheld by Charles VI: the crown and what was virtually the then kingdom of France—Aquitaine, Normandy, Maine, Touraine and Anjou. In addition Henry asked for a dowry of 2,000,000 crowns for Catherine. In July he sent an embassy to Paris to put these modest proposals to the French.[6]

But either Henry's eagerness to get on with things had misled him, or his information on movements in France was faulty, for when the embassy arrived in Paris only the Duke of Berry was there to receive it, as the king, the dauphin and the princes were besieging Arras. Berry admitted the ambassadors to the Council where they delivered their message. To the French, who had supposed that the purpose of the embassy was merely to settle the normal conditions for such a marriage, it must have seemed a very odd way of asking for a bride, to demand her father's crown and country at the same time, in addition to vast sums in hard cash, so much so that they found it impossible to take these ridiculous and baseless pretentions at all seriously. But as nothing could be settled in the king's absence the ambassadors were forced to depart, promising to return later.

The non-fulfilment of this mission seems to have incited the impatient Henry to take a further step in revealing his plans at home. Even if he knew of it, he had no reason to fear the Peace of Arras, made by the king and the princes with the Burgundians at the beginning of September, since at the end of the same month Burgundy had already broken one of the conditions of it by renewing his secret treaty with Henry. So the latter now definitely resolved on war and in November summoned Parliament to ask its help in the recovery of his 'inheritance'. Parliament at once voted the necessary sums "for the defence of the kingdom and the safety of the seas", to be provided in the following year. The king's Council went even further, definitely urging him to prepare to invade France, although at the same time they advised the sending of another embassy first.[7]

This second embassy arrived in Paris at the beginning of February 1415. It had already been agreed by both sides that the truce, due to expire that month, should be prolonged until May. The embassy this time was a particularly impressive one, consisting of some six hundred persons. Great ceremonies were held to entertain them, particularly a magnificent tournament which lasted three days and in the course of which Charles VI himself, evidently enjoying one of his lucid intervals, jousted with the handsome, newly-created Duke of Alençon, while Charles of Orleans fought 'very cordially' with Burgundy's brother, Anthony Duke of Brabant.[8] It was perhaps the fantastic luxury, and it may be licence, of the festivities provided by the French at this time that made Henry V, when he heard of it, come to the conclusion that they were a nation wholly sunk in worldly pleasures and even debauchery.

One gets from the chroniclers the impression that the ambassadors became more and more impatient at this continuous revelry and the difficulty of getting the king and his Council to attend to the business on which they had come. The chief reason for this was of course that the French still persisted in considering that business to be the marriage of Henry V with Catherine, an idea that pleased them but did not seem particularly urgent. In reply to the slightly decreased but still preposterous demands of the English for lands and money[9] – the duchies of Aquitaine and Normandy, and 1,000,000 crowns for Catherine – the French, with surprising generosity, and anxious to preserve peace, made quite notable offers both of some provinces and towns and a dowry of 800,000 crowns. When the ambassadors stated that they had no authority to accept less than the full demand, Charles VI proposed that he should send an embassy to London to see if a reasonable agreement satisfactory to both sides could not be reached; and at the end of March the ambassadors returned to report to Henry the failure of their mission.

Another reason why the French failed to perceive the threat that lay behind these approaches from England was that they were at that time far more preoccupied by their own domestic situation. It was necessary that the terms of the peace treaty, hastily agreed at Arras, should be put on a firm basis and properly ratified on both sides. To that end Burgundy's sister, the Countess of Hainault, and his brother Anthony, Duke of Brabant, who had acted for him at Arras, came to Senlis at Christmas and were received by the dauphin at Saint-Denis. Many meetings and discussions with him and the Council (of which Charles of Orleans was now a member) took place during the following weeks and were in fact going on during the visit of the English ambassadors. Burgundy's brother and sister seem to have been so eager for peace—Anthony of Brabant in particular never abetted his brother in his evil schemes and was always trying to improve relations between him and the Orleanists, says Perceval de Cagny[10]—that they recklessly made promises on his behalf that their own revelations about his past perfidy must have made them realise were worthless. They had already assured the king at Arras that he had sworn on the gospel that he had never had any alliances with the English, and they now repeated this assurance, weakening it by saying that, if there had indeed been anything of the sort, thenceforward he would renounce it entirely. They also promised that Burgundy would banish from his lands, and hand over to the king, Caboche and the other traitors.

Finally agreement was reached, the peace was publicly proclaimed in Paris on February 24th, and on March 13th all the members of the Hainault-Brabant mission, together with all the Orleanist princes and many ecclesiastics, swore to it in the presence of the king. But still this was not the end of it, for the king's letters embodying the terms had to receive the oaths and the written agreement of the main officials in all the chief towns of Burgundy's territories, and finally of himself. To obtain these the dauphin sent mission after mission throughout the spring. The task of the emissaries was greatly helped not only by Burgundy's brother and sister but also by his only son, Philip Count of Charolois, then a young man of nineteen, later to play a great rôle in the life of Charles of Orleans. By the end of April all the necessary signatures had been obtained except one: that of Burgundy himself.

The main drive behind all this had been supplied by the dauphin who, during the winter of 1415, had begun to take the government very much into his own hands. Although not only Shakespeare but most serious historians have regarded him as a frivolous, irresponsible youth, he had, from the time of the Bourges campaign of 1412 onwards, consistently shown a desire to end the strife between the princes and pleaded that they should unite for the good of the kingdom. Now he showed himself in yet another light. One night in April, while the court was at Melun, he went with a few followers to the Louvre and there ordered the seizure of large sums of money which he had been informed the queen was hoarding in different private houses—she had long been accused of sending some of the royal funds to her relatives in Germany. He then summoned the chief members of the University, with the Provosts of Paris and the Provost of the Merchants and many prominent citizens, to a meeting at which his Chancellor, the Bishop of Chartres, told them how, since the beginning of the king's reign, the princes had robbed the royal treasury for their own ends. As chief culprits he named the late Dukes of Anjou, Burgundy and Orleans, and the present Dukes of Berry and Burgundy. A notable exception was the present Duke of Orleans, Charles. In future the dauphin was no longer going to tolerate such conduct, he would take the administration of the realm into his own hands and correct these abuses. He then sent orders to the princes to return each to his own lands.

Burgundy of course took this action of his son-in-law's very ill and seized the occasion to send him emissaries to protest against some of his actions. But the main object of their mission was to report an objection which the Duke had brought up as a reason why he had not yet signed the treaty. This was the king's refusal to pardon those Parisian rebels, Caboche among them, who with their families had taken refuge with Burgundy ever since their banishment in 1413. It was no doubt not so much care for them as a desire to convince the Parisians in general that he was still their champion that made him insist on this. When the dauphin angrily refused to listen, the emissaries told him roundly that, if he did not do what their lord asked, he would not sign nor keep the peace and, they went on, "if you are attacked by your enemies the English, neither he nor his vassals and subjects will arm for you or serve and defend you".[11] This reference to a possible English invasion, of which he alone appears to have been aware, and his open admission of what was in any case the attitude he had decided to adopt, signature or no signature, was surprising from the usually secretive duke. But the dauphin seems to have seen in it nothing but a typical threat from his father-in-law, to force him to comply with his demand. This objection to the treaty was to be the first in a series which Burgundy put forward all that summer, while waiting for Henry to move.

Meanwhile Henry had been waiting impatiently for the arrival of the promised embassy from France, which he seems to have imagined would follow hot upon the return of his own. When it did not, on April 7th he sent Charles VI a letter which is a masterpiece either of hypocrisy or self-delusion.[12] Henry began by protesting that ever since he came to the throne he had striven with all his might for peace between their two countries. That is why he had sent ambassadors to transmit his claims, which were only as modest as they were because he was convinced that this was in accordance with God's wish. He could not understand why Charles should take so long to settle this question and that of the marriage. He reminded him that they must both one day answer to God for their conduct and, since he himself had set the public good above any private interest, all the guilt would be that of Charles if he caused his subjects to suffer because he refused to hand them over to their rightful lord.

On the 16th the French king replied mildly that he too wanted peace, sent Henry the names of the ambassadors he proposed to send, and refrained from further comment. Before this reply could arrive, Henry had written again, on April 15th, a letter so revealing that Le Religieux, the most official of the chroniclers, considered it his duty to reproduce it as "a document precious for history".[13] In it, Henry protested once more that he was inspired neither by avarice nor any desire for domination, but solely by his consciousness of his rights. He ended by urging Charles not to suppress his own desire for peace, since their "deplorable divisions" were responsible for the schism in the Church and were fomenting the disorders of the whole world. On April 26th Charles replied, promising to make every effort for peace.

As soon as Henry had despatched these letters, he began his preparations to invade France. Throughout May and June he was busy collecting his forces and transport. He had plenty of time for this for the French, curiously enough, appear to have been completely taken in by what Juvenal des Ursins calls his "gentle manner of writing",[14] and his pious protestations, and still did not suspect him. They therefore saw no reason to hurry and it was only on June 17th that their embassy, led by the tough and eloquent Archbishop of Bourges, left Calais. On reaching England they were conducted to the king, who was at Winchester, already on his way to Southampton.

The negotiations began on the day after their arrival, and lasted for nearly four weeks. The French repeated and increased somewhat their previous extremely generous offers, both as to money and land, and at first it looked as if Henry were inclined to accept. But then his attitude stiffened again, and when his spokesman, the Bishop of Winchester, gave his final answer it was obvious that the king had never had any intention of accepting less than his first outrageous demands. Winchester announced his decision in a most ungracious and even truculent speech, full of accusations against the French. It was clear, he ended, that Charles did not really want peace and so Henry must now have recourse to other methods to secure his rights. This so enraged the Archbishop of Bourges that, having asked permission to speak, he gave as good as he had got, informing Henry that their offers had not been made out of fear, but to avoid the spilling of innocent blood, and pointing out that not only had Henry no right to the throne of France, he was not even the rightful King of England, "nor with you", he ended arrogantly, "can our sovereign lord safely treat".[15]

After this there could obviously be no further discussion and on July 26th the French returned home, while Henry proceeded to Southampton, whence on July 28th he addressed a final letter[16] to Charles VI, lamenting the 'hatred' that had broken out between them and saying that, although now ready to fight, conscience bade him make one more effort. "Friend, give us what is our due, restore our heritage . . . unjustly torn from us, or at least those things that we have asked for out of respect for God and in the interests of peace." And by way of an insulting anti-climax he offered to make a slight reduction in the amount demanded for Catherine's dowry.

On their return the French ambassadors, reporting the failure of their mission, openly declared their opinion that Henry's letters, "although they appeared to be full of moderation, concealed at bottom much malice and perfidy",[17] and that while he was offering peace and union in gentle terms, his one aim was the destruction of their kingdom, for which he was levying troops. They had discovered that already a great army had embarked for a month past at Southampton, though none yet knew its destination. Moreover a few of the French had found out through private enquiries that many secret treaties of alliance existed between Henry and Burgundy. At that the eyes of the king, the dauphin and the whole court were unsealed at last. On August 23rd, Charles VI replied to Henry's letter that all men could witness that he had sought peace by all reasonable means, that he did not fear threats and that, if any came to attack his kingdom, they would find him ready to repel force by force.

In the meantime, without waiting for that reply, Henry had set sail from Southampton on August 11th. On the 15th the English landed at Harfleur and laid siege to it. The governor of the city was Raoul, Lord of Gaucourt, who had been one of the signatories of the Treaty of Buzançais in 1412. Charles of Orleans had subsequently made him captain of his great castle of Coucy. Under his leadership Harfleur held out for three weeks but at last, despairing of receiving any help from the dauphin, who had indeed no forces to send him, the garrison was forced by hunger and loss of life to surrender on September 22nd. It had been a cruel siege on both sides, for the English had suffered much from dysentery because of the heat. The Bishop of Norwich, who had been one of Henry's ambassadors to Paris in the previous February, died of it, as did Michael de la Pole, Earl of Suffolk; while the Duke of Clarence and other noblemen were so ill that they had to be sent home, as had many of the fighting men too.

While Harfleur was being besieged, the king and the dauphin at last began to assemble their forces. Most of the great feudatories were of course summoned, not only to go in person but to bring with them their own military vassals. But when it came to Charles of Orleans and John of Burgundy, the king doubted the wisdom of bringing together the two princes whose dislike of each other he well knew the Peace of Arras had by no means removed, in case discord should again break out between them and disrupt the unity of the royal army. He therefore commanded each of them to send five hundred 'bacinets', as the men-at-arms were called from the name of the steel helmets they wore, but not to go in person. Burgundy, who, even as late as September, was still exchanging letters[18] with the king about his various grievances, forbade his vassals to answer the king's call, but said he would go himself. In the event, however, his subjects, to their credit, flouted their lord's orders; but Burgundy himself broke his own promise and cautiously stayed away from the scene of action, as he so often did.

Charles of Orleans, on the other hand, also disobeyed, but more worthily, for he not only sent the required men-at-arms but went in person. All that summer, ever since the dauphin had dismissed the princes from Paris in April, he had been living quietly in his own duchy, looking after his family responsibilities. These were varied. At one end of the scale we find him authorising the purchase of an A B C in parchment with gilded letters for his four-year-old daughter Jane,[19] and at the other there was the unending business of finding money for the debt to the English and for the maintenance of John and the other hostages. He had in fact been sending considerable sums for their keep all that winter, and in March and May he made payments on account to both the Earl of Dorset and the Duke of Clarence.[20] But economise as he might for these demands—and his personal expenditure that summer was little enough—he still had princely duties to fulfil, costly presents to give and guests to entertain. In September, for instance, the Duke of Anjou stayed at Orleans with his duchess, the remarkable Yolanda of Aragon, and the dauphin's twelve-year-old brother, then known as the Count of Ponthieu but one day to become Charles VII.[21] This was possibly the first time that Charles saw the boy with whom later he was to be so much concerned.

But as soon as the call to arms reached him in that same month Charles acted with the utmost speed. He bought a complete armour of steel and a bay horse for himself, and two more horses for two of his pages.[22] He called up his men-at-arms and archers and made arrangements for the payment of their wages.[23] A desire not to leave any old debts outstanding seems to have possessed him too, for on September 15th he ordered his treasurer, Pierre Renier, to repay his old physician, Pierre de Vaulx, for those six silver cups he had lent the duke nearly four years earlier.[24] When all was in order, Charles set out on the long ride—some 250 miles—to Rouen, whither the king and the dauphin had already gone, and where he found a large part of the army and many of his friends and allies assembled: the Dukes of Berry, Alençon and Bourbon, the Counts of Eu, Vendôme and Richemont, and the Constable Albret. Anjou soon joined them. Another familiar figure was Marshal Boucicaut, one of the great French captains and an old friend of Louis of Orleans; and, closest of all to Charles, his faithful Pierre de Mornay, who had fought beside him in all the campaigns against Burgundy, and whom he now appointed commander of his men-at-arms.

Henry V meanwhile, after spending some time consolidating his position at Harfleur, had decided to march to Calais, against the advice of the majority of his Council, who wanted him to return to England at once, in view of the approach of winter and the sickness of so many of his army, of which only about 6000 remained fit for service (5000 men-at-arms and 1000 archers). The reason he gave was that he wanted to see something of the country that he considered his. He felt confident the French would not disturb him on this journey, but equally sure that if they did attack him his troops would be victorious. He therefore set out at the end of the first week in October, with his uncle the Duke of York and his brother the Duke of Gloucester and the remnant of his army. They took a northerly route near the coast in the hope of being able to cross the Somme at the ford of Blanche-taque near Abbeville, where Edward III had crossed after the battle of Crécy. As soon as the French received news of his march, and its direction, Charles VI despatched an advance-guard of his army, under the leadership of Marshal Boucicaut and the Constable Albret, with orders to prevent Henry's crossing of the Somme. With them went Alençon, Vendôme and Richemont. They took a quicker, more southerly route and reached the river three days before the English. When Henry arrived there, hearing that Blanche-taque was guarded, he turned east up-stream in the hope of finding another crossing-place.

After the departure of their advance-guard, the main French army also set out for the Somme. The command was given jointly to the Dukes of Orleans and Bourbon. They led their troops by a still more southerly route, heading direct for Amiens where there was a chance that they might intercept Henry; but when they arrived on October 17th the English had already passed the town as they marched east along the south bank of the river. The French therefore proceeded to Péronne and installed themselves there. Henry V meanwhile, finding every crossing-place blocked by the French on the other side of the river, ceased to follow the main course of it and headed for a point much further up-stream and south of Péronne. There at last fords were found, and by the evening of the 19th the whole army had crossed safely and were encamped for the night near a small place called Athies. The men by this time were worn out by the length of their march and the dysentery from which many of them were suffering. They were hungry too, as their rations had given out and they had to depend on what the sullen and hostile peasants would give them. But at least they were now across the Somme; and as yet they had no knowledge of the size of the French army round Péronne, only about six miles to the north of them, nor of that army's intentions.

As to these, the French themselves had at first been divided, the older and more cautious, like the Constable, being for defensive and delaying action in the hope that, when the English found the first crossing guarded, hunger would make them surrender. But when they saw the determined way Henry was heading up-stream they sent to ask the king and the dauphin for permission to fight. A Council meeting, attended by Berry and Brittany, agreed that they should, and the king wrote to inform the Constable of the decision. Consequently, as soon as they heard that the English had now crossed the Somme, on the morning of October 20th Charles of Orleans, Bourbon and the Constable sent three heralds to Henry's camp to tell him that they knew he had come into France to conquer their country and depopulate their cities, and that they had consequently assembled to defend them and would fight with him wherever he wished. Although Henry, knowing the state of his army, had hoped to avoid such an encounter, he remained unmoved and replied that he did not intend to seek them out, that he would continue to march straight to Calais at his own pace, and that if they disturbed him on his journey they might find him where they would, but it would be at their utmost peril.

After the heralds had departed, Henry put on his coat-of-arms and ordered all his nobles and knights to do likewise. He also ordered the archers to cut themselves long staves sharpened at both ends, since he had heard a report that the French intended to try to break the lines of his archers by a cavalry charge. By these signs his weary troops knew what now lay before them, possibly that day or the next. But by the next morning there were no signs of an immediate attack, so they took the road again in heavy rain and marched past Péronne where, to their surprise, there were now no signs of the French. But a mile or so out of the town, where a road branched off to Bapaume, they saw from the churned-up state of the muddy ground that huge numbers of marching men and horses had recently passed that way.

It was the first sight, and an awe-inspiring one, that the English had of the size of the army whose determination to fight them they now knew. But when and where the fatal encounter would take place remained terrifyingly unknown. There was nothing for it but to march straight ahead, continually on the alert for an attack that might come at any moment and find them in some disadvantageous position. For the next three days they marched without seeing any sign of the enemy, who were following a parallel route to the east of them but gradually closing in. On the morning of the 24th, when they had already covered half their journey to Calais, Henry and his advance-guard, from a high ridge at Blangy on the little river Ternoise, beheld for the first time the immense French army filing across the valley below and cutting off the route they themselves were following. It was clear that the battle could not now be long delayed; and clear too, seeing that the French were just ahead of them, that it was they who would choose the site of it.

It is difficult to understand why, the choice being theirs, the French threw their advantage away; for that same day they went only a little farther and finally encamped by the woods of Tramécourt, which certainly enabled them to cover the direct route to Calais but left hardly any space for their vast forces between the Tramécourt woods and those surrounding the castle of Agincourt on the other side of the route. Seeing what they had done, Henry billeted his army in and about the village of Maisoncelle about a mile to the south of the French. Night was now falling and as it wore on each side prepared in its own way for the battle that awaited them on the morrow. The hungry, sick and exhausted English, feeling they had little chance against such vast opposing forces and certain of death, after praying and confessing spent the night in fitful sleep and talk, with no heart to disobey the king's command that the whole camp should keep silence. The French, certain of an easy victory, and so in the highest spirits, warmed themselves by camp fires, drank, jested, and threw dice for the prisoners they felt confident they were going to take, while the great numbers of their different servitors, and their horses, continually moving about, churned the ground into a morass in the rain that fell all night but did not dampen their spirits.

By now a force of some fifty or sixty thousand[25] had assembled. In answer to an appeal from the king urging all noblemen accustomed to bear arms to rally to his forces, more and more of Burgundy's subjects from Picardy, Artois, Flanders and Hainault had hastened to join, his brother Philip Count of Nevers and his brother-in-law the Count of Hainault among them. The king had twice sent special messengers to Burgundy's son Philip of Charolois too, begging him to come, as indeed he longed to do. But by his father's orders his governors forcibly restrained him by shutting him up in the Castle of Aire near Saint-Omer. At this the young man wept; and so great was his disappointment that to the end of his life it remained one of his greatest regrets that he had not been at Agincourt "to live or die there".[26]* What made his situation

* Philip's distress at his enforced absence from the battle was so genuine that, when it was over, he gave orders that all the bodies that remained unrecognised and unclaimed on the field (for those of the nobles were taken away by their servants to be buried in their own lands) should be interred in great trenches on the spot, at his expense, with a thorny hedge round the site to prevent wolves from digging them up. Five thousand eight hundred were so buried. Monstrelet III, 122.

even more bitter was that practically the whole of his household slipped secretly away to join the army; for a great wave of patriotism and excitement had now swept the country, and men were hastening to Agincourt from all parts.

It is hardly surprising that Charles of Orleans appears to have been one of the most elated of them all. Still more of his allies were now with him, Edward Duke of Bar and his brother John among them, so that now the only ones missing of all that company that had supported him for so many years were the Dukes of Anjou and Berry, who had remained with the king in Rouen; the Duke of Brittany who, when the decision to fight was taken, had left with some thousands of his followers to join the army but only arrived on the day after the battle; and Charles' father-in-law, the Count of Armagnac, whose absence on such an occasion seems inexplicable, warrior as he was, and his brother Philip of Vertus, whom Charles may well have deliberately kept away.

Thus surrounded by friends all equally confident of victory,* Charles, as though unable to wait for his first sight of the enemy, ordered his friend Arthur of Richemont to assemble some two thousand of his bacinets and archers and to go with him during the night right up to the English camp. At their approach some of the English archers discharged a few arrows at them, to which the French replied, but as they had not intended more than a brief reconnaissance, the French soon withdrew. All the same, Charles had taken a risk and for this exploit on his return he was knighted—an honour customarily conferred even on great nobles when they first distinguished themselves in the field.

The next day, St. Crispin's day, both armies were afoot before dawn. King Henry, outwardly calm as always, after hearing mass three times, rode among his men on a little grey horse, heartening them with his words, his belief in the righteousness and justice of his cause, and his splendid presence in shining armour with a magnificent jewelled crown over his helmet. The English battle order was simple and practi-

* It became a habit, in later English accounts of the battle, to put boasting remarks into the mouths of the French nobles before the fight began. The Metrical History, thought to date about thirty years later, credits the Dukes of Orleans, Bourbon, Bar and Brabant (who was not there that night) with such remarks, and it was this fashion which Shakespeare followed in Henry V, Act III, Sc. 7. But none of the contemporary chroniclers, English or French, mentions them.

cal. Henry himself commanded the main body in the centre, with Lord Camoys on his left and the Duke of York on his right. Bands of archers in compact, wedge-shaped formation, were distributed between the men-at-arms; but the main blocks of archers, in a slightly curved formation, stood on the two flanks. The French battle position, much more elaborate, betrayed their fatal faults of character: none would accept the authority of the others, each wanted to win the utmost glory for himself, with the result that all strove for a place in the front line, putting their archers behind them and so rendering them useless. In the final disposition there fought side by side in that front line the Dukes of Orleans and Bourbon, the Counts of Eu and Richemont, the Constable and Boucicaut. A second line, with the archers in between, was commanded by the Dukes of Alençon and Bar. As the field was so narrow that there would not have been space for them all if they had been mounted, nor could they have manoeuvred on horseback, all the princes, knights and men-at-arms in the first lines were on foot, almost rooted in the mud by the tremendous weight of their armour and equipment. On their two flanks were detachments of mounted men-at-arms, and behind them another line, also mounted.

Thus drawn up the two armies stood facing each other for some three or four hours, motionless. Realising the effect of this on his exhausted men, Henry decided that he must take the initiative. His army therefore moved slowly forward until they were within bowshot of the French, when they halted to give the archers time to drive into the ground, at an angle slanting outwards towards the enemy, those long, sharp-pointed stakes they had dragged over the weary miles, and which now were to prove their worth. Protected behind this fence, as one man they then let fly a hail of arrows that darkened the sky as they whirred with blood-curdling hiss through the air, pierced the visors of the French knights and tore great gashes in the horses of their flanking cavalry.

There could be no more standing still after that, so, lowering their visors to protect their eyes, the French of the first line now in their turn came on, the mounted and those on foot alike. But the horses, thundering at full tilt and arriving first, were riddled with arrows and impaled on those sharp stakes. Tearing themselves free and maddened by their wounds, many threw their riders, whom the English at once slew, and then, charging back, careered into the advancing nobles and men-at-arms, overturning many of them, so that in a few minutes all was in wild confusion. Yet still the nobles and men-at-arms in that first French line kept on until they reached the English lines and the combat was engaged. But the French were now packed so closely together that they could not raise their arms to use their weapons or to defend themselves. Thus many were knocked down by blows from the English lances or swords and once down found it impossible to rise again in their heavy armour, with no pages to help them. Many were hacked or battered to death where they lay and others, not even wounded, were slowly crushed or suffocated under the growing weight of fallen bodies that soon lay in mounds over the field.

When the men-at-arms in the second French line saw what had happened to those in the first, some of them began to leave the field. The Duke of Alençon who, with the Duke of Bar, was in command, followed and strove to rally them but, having failed, mounted his horse and himself rode back into the thick of the *mêlée* where he wounded the Duke of Gloucester.[27] The king came to his brother's rescue and his guard immediately overpowered Alençon who, finding himself on the ground at their mercy, stretched out his hand to the king, giving his name and surrendering to him. But before the king could take the hand, a soldier killed the duke with a great blow of his battle-axe. So perished the splendid young prince who had been made a duke less than a year before because of his great beauty. Late in the day the Duke of Brabant, who had striven so hard to heal the rift between his brother John the Fearless and the princes, galloped up, having ridden so fast to join the army that he had left all his followers behind. When he found that the battle was not only engaged but nearly over, not stopping to put on his armour he seized a weapon and plunged into the turmoil with a rallying cry of 'Brabant!' But he too was immediately overborne and slain.

Although these are the only two recorded instances of outstanding French courage in the battle, many thousands of others lost their lives fighting on that memorable day. In addition, hundreds more were killed in cold blood. When the main strife was over and the English soldiers were busy taking captive those who were wounded or lying helpless on the ground, the mounted men-at-arms in the third French line, who all that time had stood motionless, began to move through the Tramécourt woods, looking as if they intended to attack from the rear. On observing this, Henry, fearing that if the prisoners he had sent to the back saw their countrymen coming to their aid, they might try to escape and join them, gave orders that all prisoners except those of high rank were to be killed. His soldiers, appalled at the idea of giving up their captives, whose ransoms or sale to their lords were the only reward that all their toil would bring them, were reluctant to obey, so the king ordered a band of two hundred archers to do the dreadful deed. And there, as they stood waiting to be led off the field, uncounted numbers of French men-at-arms were quickly cut to pieces, most of them, since they were in armour, by having their helmets removed and their heads hacked off.

By nightfall, when the English soldiers had finished their work of stripping the corpses of their armour and possessions, the flower of the French chivalry and men-at-arms lay, bloody and naked, on the desolate muddy field. Among them were not only Alençon but other friends of Charles – the Duke of Bar and his brother John, and the Constable Charles of Albret; while in addition to Brabant, John of Burgundy had lost his only other brother, Philip of Nevers, and numbers of his nobles. Altogether it is estimated that between seven and ten thousand Frenchmen died at Agincourt that day, seven or eight hundred of them nobles, against a total loss of five hundred on the English side, the most notable of whom were the Duke of York and the young Earl of Suffolk, whose father had been killed at Harfleur.

In addition to the thousands of dead, the list of whose names fills many pages in the French chronicles, the French losses included some fifteen hundred prisoners, all men of rank, most of whom had been taken because, hampered by their armour in the clash, they could not defend themselves. Among these were the Duke of Bourbon, the Counts of Eu, Vendôme and Richemont, Marshal Boucicaut and, most illustrious of all, Charles of Orleans. He and Richemont had been discovered, as had many others, under one of those piles of corpses, Richemont slightly wounded, Charles not at all. With the other prisoners they were led to the king's quarters in Maisoncelle. Those of the highest rank became his property, while the lesser nobles were assigned either to the lords who had captured them or to those who had bought them, often for very small sums, from the ordinary soldiers who had taken them, since only those of knightly rank had a right to ask ransoms.

The next day Henry V took the road to Calais "through those heaps of patriotism and blood",[28] with his prisoners riding between the advance-guard and the main army. The king behaved very courteously to his noble prisoners, and especially to Charles, the most distinguished of them. During a halt for rest he sent him bread and wine, but Charles would neither eat nor drink. When he heard this Henry, thinking he had refused out of displeasure, rode up to him and said "Fair cousin, how is it with you?" "Well, sire," answered Charles.[29] Then Henry asked him why it was that he would neither eat nor drink, to which Charles replied that in truth he was fasting. Such a reply might have made a more sensitive man than Henry suppose that his young captive was feeling too wretched to eat. But Henry, never very quick at perceiving the reactions of others, and perhaps genuinely meaning to be modest, urged his cousin to be of good cheer, saying that he knew God had given him the victory not because he deserved it but to punish the French; and if what he had heard tell was true, this was not astonishing, for it was said that never was a country so full of every kind of sin and vice, so sunk in sensual pleasures of the grossest sort, as France, so that it was no wonder God was angry. No doubt there was truth in this, as far as the nobility and many of the court officials were concerned, but it was hardly a tactful moment to rub it in, especially to a youthful prisoner the difficulties of whose life hitherto had hardly permitted him to indulge in all those vices, even had he wished to. And why Henry should have thought that this view of his victory would help his young captive to be of good cheer is difficult to understand.

Charles had at that moment only too many reasons for sorrow. Death, though it may be that he did not yet know it, had just robbed him of some of his closest friends and supporters. He had been torn brutally away from others whose counsel and affection he had always been able to rely on during the difficult years of his youth: the old Duke of Berry, the faithful Gauluet and, closest of all, his brother Philip, his constant supporter. Moreover, consoling though it may have been to know that he was going into captivity in the company of many others of his allies, this very fact meant that the cause for which they had all striven for so many years was left undefended. His enmity against Burgundy because of his father's murder was now a thing of the past. But, over and above that, Charles and his party had genuinely striven to rescue the king and the dauphin from the clutches of John the Fearless. Of all the princes who had opposed him, only the Count of Armagnac could now be counted on to continue the struggle, as Anjou and Brittany had always been inclined to sit on the fence, and Philip of Vertus was too young to be an effective leader. Burgundy must even then be rejoicing in the knowledge that that terrible battle, from which he had so carefully kept away, had virtually rid him of all his opponents and left him free to pursue his aims, as he was now fearfully to do. The king had further talks with Charles, and the other prisoners too, as they rode along, and one chronicler who was there affords some grounds for hoping that they were not all on the same theme, for he says that the king comforted them kindly "as one who well knew how to do so."[30]

They certainly needed some encouragement, for the journey was a long one. When they reached the Castle of Guines, Henry sent the bulk of the army straight on to Calais, but kept the prisoners with him and spent several days in the castle. By the time they reached Calais the army had already sailed for home, but the king stayed for a while, being joyously received and fêted by the whole population—an odd experience for the prisoners to see their own countrymen welcoming the king who had brought their country so low.

While he waited there for ships to be made ready to carry him and his prisoners to England, their number was increased by the arrival of Raoul of Gaucourt and the other prisoners taken at Harfleur, whom Henry had released before Agincourt on parole to rejoin him later if he won that battle, but who now were to go into captivity with the others. The king, who set great store by chivalrous behaviour, treated them all with great courtesy and consideration, inviting them to a banquet one night, though it must rather have taken the edge off their appetites when in the course of it he repeated his set-piece about his victory being God's punishment for their evil ways.

Those days of waiting provided Charles of Orleans with the opportunity to despatch some business of his own. On November 9th he gave money to his three pages for their journey home.[31] Had they perhaps the sad task of taking back to Blois that new steel armour that Charles had ordered for the battle? For now, like the other prisoners, he had to change it for a damask robe that the king had ordered to be given to each of them. But humiliating though it must have been for any French prince, accustomed to sumptuous clothes, to have to wear such ready-made garments, Charles was not denied his princely standing, and was allowed to send for his secretary Robert de Tuillières[32] to join him at Calais and go with him to London, since it was obvious that he would need clerical assistance immediately for the ordering of his duchy during his absence.

By the 11th of November all was ready and Henry V, with his nobles and the prisoners, embarked for England. A terrible storm arose when they were at sea so that, as if the heaviness of their hearts was not enough, the French prisoners had to endure the agony of sea-sickness, a plight that probably none of them, and certainly not Charles, had ever experienced before. So fierce was the storm that it was four days before they finally landed at Dover on November 16th. After a day's rest there they proceeded to Canterbury where the Archbishop came out to meet the king, who went to pray in the cathedral. Their progress then took them by slow stages through Rochester and Eltham to Blackheath, which they reached on the morning of the 23rd. There the Lord Mayor and twenty-four aldermen in scarlet came from the City of London to meet them, together with a crowd of some twenty thousand lesser citizens, all on horseback, and dressed in red, with parti-coloured hoods of red and white, and devices descriptive of their different crafts.

At the approach to Tower Bridge the figure of an enormous giant had been erected, with the keys of the city in his left hand; and at the entrances to the different streets on the way to St. Paul's great decorations of different kinds had been set up, in the form of castles, towers and columns, the structures covered with cloth painted to look like white marble and green or red jasper. At all these key points there were choirs either of venerable old men, young boys or beautiful young girls, the former clad like Old Testament prophets, apostles, martyrs and kings of England, and the girls and boys all in white with glittering wings and jewelled locks, dancing and singing psalms and hymns of praise to God. In Cornhill the venerable prophets, clad in crimson and gold, as a symbolic sacrifice let loose masses of sparrows many of which alighted on the king's breast and shoulders. But he himself, clad in a purple mantle, never relaxed his grave expression as of one conscious of being not an earthly conqueror but an instrument of divine justice. After he had prayed in what was then called "the church of the apostles Peter and Paul", the citizens led him to the Thames where he embarked, at 3.30 in the afternoon, for the Palace of Westminster, which was richly hung with tapestries and adorned in his honour and that of the illustrious prisoners who accompanied him.

But for the Duke of Orleans and his companions, no matter how courteously the king treated them, the day must have been as painful as for any foreign captive following the chariot of some victorious Caesar acclaimed by the crowd on his return to Rome. Once again it was the month of November, so often ill-fated for Charles in the past. And the day of the procession through London was the eve of his twenty-first birthday.

CHAPTER EIGHT
December 1415–August 1422

THE first seven years of Charles' captivity in England, coinciding as they did with the last seven of the life of Henry V, were to prove some of the most eventful both in the history of his own country and the lives of his family and friends. But he who hitherto had taken a leading part in public affairs in France as head of his own political party, and acted at the same time as a father to his own small family, was now an exile, powerless to influence either his country's destiny or the lives of those nearest to him. Because of this his name almost entirely disappears, for the time being, from the narratives of the contemporary French chroniclers, and figures but rarely in those of English. However, it appears in nearly all of the very large number of Orleans archives of that time which have survived, in many official English documents, and sometimes in the letters of the king himself. And from these dry bones, merely factual and largely concerned with administrative details though they mostly are, springs not only the material story of his life in those dramatic years, but something of the character and preoccupations of the still youthful prince who had to endure them.

At first the king seems to have felt a genuine desire for the well-being of his prisoners and an understanding of their personal needs. Soon after they all reached London he gave a massive and detailed order for furnishings of all kinds:[1] beds, curtains, coverlets, blankets, mattresses and bolsters, carpets and so on, for the rooms that they were to occupy in his palaces in and around London where they were at first kept: Westminster, Windsor and Eltham and, for some of them, the Tower. Safe-conducts were freely granted for their own servitors to bring over personal possessions they needed, and to receive instructions for the administering of their affairs in France. These safe-conducts mostly lasted for one month, and allowed the servitors to bring horses, armour and goods of all kinds for their masters. Every now and again these documents reveal something of the character and pursuits of particular prisoners. Among the first people the Duke of Bourbon sent for were four of his falconers,[2] who presumably came to train others in his methods of hawking, a sport which he was obviously permitted to enjoy even in captivity. Bourbon's need for immediate distraction is not surprising in one who had always enjoyed physical exploits, and whose not very strong character was soon to reveal its lack of fortitude in adversity. He knew, too, that he need not trouble himself about the affairs of his duchy, since his able wife Mary, daughter of the Duke of Berry, was more than competent to conduct them in his absence.

Charles of Orleans, both by temperament and circumstances, was in a different position. As in former years, there is no evidence that his wife Bonne was present in his duchy or took any part in the administering of it. On the other hand Charles fortunately had, as we have seen, many faithful officers, some of whom had served him ever since he suceeded his father, a few of them having belonged to Louis' household also. They now remained at their posts to carry out his instructions or, when he was not able to send them, as members of his Council, to assume responsibility for him. Their names now recur so frequently in the family archives that they begin to seem like familiar friends. Chief of them was Guillaume Cousinot, whom Charles had appointed Chancellor of Orleans and head of his Council; and he stood too *in loco parentis* to his master's brothers and sister and his young daughter. Nor did this kindly man forget the other young brother in England, for in spite of all his duties he found time to write a short chronicle of French history, called the *Geste des Nobles*, especially for John of Angoulême. After Agincourt, when Cousinot probably had less time for writing, this chronicle becomes a series of very short chapters, in which he jotted down particulars of contemporary happenings likely to be of interest to the youthful exile, whose treasured copy of this book still exists.[3] Next after Cousinot the most important was Pierre de Mornay (Gauluet), who had been Governor of Orleans in Louis' day and now held the rank of Marshal, as well as being one of Charles' chief councillors and Chamberlains.[4] Both Cousinot and Gauluet were held in high regard in the king's court and served his cause as zealously as they watched over the interests of their own master.

After them, the names that occur most frequently are those of the officers responsible for the finances of the duchy, and of Charles' secretaries. The Treasurer-General was still Pierre Renier, and it was generally he whom Charles directly, or sometimes one of his senior representatives, ordered to make all the necessary payments. But, important and reliable official though he was, his work was double-checked, and every command, either to Pierre Renier or to any other officer, to make a payment, had to be accompanied by another to the *Chambre des Comptes* to allow for this sum in the accounts of the officer concerned. All these instructions were kept, together with the receipts for the payments in question. The head of the *Chambre des Comptes* and chief auditor was Denis Mariète who, like Pierre Renier, had held his post for many years, and an arduous one it must have been. The majority of these commands begin with the statement that they are the result of letters from Charles, but it seems probable that in many cases this was a mere formula, for it is hardly possible that he could have been consulted on the literally hundreds of items whose details have been preserved.

The secretaries who visited him most frequently were Robert de Tuillières, Hugues Perrier and Jean Chomery, one of the signatories at Buzançais. The first of these, as we saw, had gone to his master even before he left Calais, and he and Hugues Perrier and others were allowed to cross to England with him, since there was urgent business for Charles to attend to even while he was on his way to London. From Rochester, for instance, on November 20th and 21st he sent orders[5] nominating officers for various important posts. Two days after his arrival in London he appointed Jean le Fayel Governor of the Duchy of Valois and the County of Beaumont.[6] Many similar appointments were continually made thereafter and those who had served him faithfully were not forgotten. Such indeed was the burden of this secretarial work that the visits of the secretaries became very frequent in the first years of Charles' captivity. Their journeys must often have been laborious. For instance, early in 1416 one of Charles' chamberlains had been ordered to take a sumpter horse to England, laden with extra clothes and bedclothes both for Charles and his brother John. But in Amiens the horse was taken ill and its rider had to leave it behind. Fortunately by the time he passed through Amiens again on his way home, the horse had recovered and he was able to take it back to Paris with him.[7]

One of the things that understandably troubled Charles, now that he was no longer able to control his own affairs directly, was whether in future he would be able to afford the salaries of the numbers of officials of all ranks on whom he must henceforth rely. Such was his anxiety that, only a month after he reached England, he sent an order that all wages were to be suspended for one year.[8] Six months later he modified this, at least in the case of the newly-appointed Governor of Valois and Beaumont, and also the captain of the castle of Beaumont, by ordering that they should be paid something on account.[9] It says much for the devoted service he was able to command that there is no evidence that any of his staff left their posts because of this drastic order. In any case they would, of course, have continued to live at their lord's expense; and the knowledge of the straits to which he was now reduced, and of the huge sums that he had to find for the English and the hostages, was apparently enough to appeal to the understanding of such loyal and devoted servants.

At the same time Charles was anxious that his young family should not suffer materially because of his absence, and laid it down from the outset of his imprisonment that they should continue to live as before.[10] They were obviously continually in his thoughts. In March 1416 he bought a silver-gilt goblet, with a lid embossed with various animals, in a leather case, as a present for his six-year-old daughter Jane.[11] And in the autumn of that year payment is ordered of a modest sum for hose and "his other small necessities" for his bastard brother John, now about twelve. Later still there are payments for slippers, not only for the two girls and the bastard, but for their fools, both male and female. It is pleasant to think that, amidst so much that was sad there had been no attempt, where the children were concerned, to cut down on these laughter-makers, so indispensible to a medieval household.

But Charles himself had no fools now to take his mind off his troubles. In the first year or two of his imprisonment he seems to have relied for consolation rather on certain priests, for though he was never a deeply pious man, such as his brother John became, he had the normal unquestioning faith of his time, and duly fulfilled the religious observances and works required of him. It was therefore no doubt at his request that in January 1416 the prior of a monastery of Celestines went to England to see him, and later that year a chaplain accompanied Hugues Perrier.[12] Perhaps it was these priests who encouraged in him that reflection which he was later to say chiefly sustained him at that time: that he had been captured while performing his duty loyally, and that God would be pleased with him for this and would help him.*

Certainly he had need of all the spiritual support he could get to help him bear the unrelievedly melancholy news from France. When the king and the dauphin had returned from Rouen to Paris, after hearing of the terrible disaster at Agincourt, the dauphin had sent for Bernard of Armagnac to bring his followers to defend Paris against the troops

* See p. 333 below.

that John the Fearless was already mustering. But the royal party had barely arrived when, on December 18th, the dauphin himself died, from what cause is not known. Unpopular though he was—Cousinot describes him as "pompous, lazy, useless, cowardly, timid"[13]—he had at least stood up to Burgundy, had been kindly disposed to Charles and seemed genuinely to desire peace. His younger brother John of Touraine, who succeeded him, was very much under Burgundy's thumb, married as he was to the duke's niece, Jacqueline of Hainault. So there was now no one but the aged Duke of Berry to try to put an end to civil war, since Armagnac was too much of a fighter to desire it. And none could tell when Henry V might not take it into his head to invade France again, to follow up his success at Agincourt.

For the moment, however, he was intent rather on consolidating his position at home. In spite of the prestige that his victory had brought him, his throne was not altogether secure, since Edmund, Earl of March, had a better claim to it. Moreover, Henry had as yet no son, while the Earl of March had as heir his five-year-old nephew Richard, who had become Duke of York after the death of his childless uncle Edward at Agincourt. Another constant threat to Henry was James I, King of Scotland, who had been a prisoner of the English for some ten years past; and one of Henry's fears was an understanding between the Scots and his French prisoners, whom he could never be sure were not plotting against him. In the circumstances it might be best, he thought, to use his French prisoners as pawns in diplomatic negotiations for a peace with France on the basis of his original claim to her throne, rather than risk another invasion to try and conquer it, especially as a successful campaign would be a very costly venture to prepare.

While the king's mood was thus apparently undecided, the question of a possible peace was brought to a head by a visit from the Emperor Sigismund, always then called King of the Romans. In March 1416 he had gone on a visit to Paris, where he was lavishly entertained by the king and the dauphin, together with Berry, Anjou and Armagnac. During his stay he came to share their distress that so many of their relations and allies were held captive in England, so much so that he conceived the idea of making peace between the two countries. Accordingly at the end of April he sailed from Calais, and arrived in London at the beginning of May. Henry also received him with much magnificence and gave up his own Palace of Westminster to lodge the emperor and his vast retinue. This was increased shortly after his arrival by that of the Count of Hainault, who brought a large following of his own. He in turn was followed soon after by the Archbishop of Rheims, with a suite of thirty.

One of the splendid occasions that Henry arranged to gratify Sigismund's love of costly entertainment was a great banquet in Westminster Hall. No doubt it was partly in order to impress Sigismund with his kingly magnanimity that the other guests of honour at this feast were the French prisoners. Charles of Orleans sat on Sigismund's right, with Bourbon next and the others thereafter in order of rank, while on the emperor's left were the Count of Hainault and the other chief nobles of his own party. Such treatment was enough to make Charles and his fellow prisoners hope that perhaps their release was near. They would have had the more reason for such hopes if they had known that at one point during his talks with the emperor, Henry had suggested taking them all to Calais with him for one of the meetings between himself and Charles VI that Sigismund proposed.

But in spite of the continual discussions that took place during the emperor's stay of nearly four months, agreement was never reached. Henry, in a rather obscure communication addressed to the Viscount of Kent on June 13th, blamed the prisoners for this, implying that they had refused to agree to the conditions proposed, without saying what these were, and were working against him and Sigismund.[14] But it seems equally likely that this time it was the French who were to blame for the breakdown of negotiations; and the Frenchman chiefly responsible for this was Charles' father-in-law Bernard of Armagnac. He had chosen that moment to lay siege to Harfleur by land, while his Genoese allies blockaded it by sea, thus preventing Henry from provisioning his newly-won town and forcing him to send troops and ships to defend it. When the Count of Hainault carried to Paris, at the end of June, proposals for a three-year truce during which peace talks should be held in Calais or Boulogne, Bernard dissuaded Charles VI and his Council from accepting them, saying that he did not trust Henry and felt sure his aim was merely to have the siege of Harfleur raised so that he might be the freer to prepare an invasion.

This lack of co-operation on the part of the French alienated Sigismund's sympathy from them, and on August 15th, in Canterbury, he signed an alliance with Henry in which he recognised him and his dynasty as Kings of France as well as England, and agreed to support him thereafter.[15] On August 24th Sigismund left Canterbury for Calais, whither Henry followed him on September 4th. On October 1st they were joined there by Burgundy, who came with a retinue of no less than eight hundred persons. Their discussions lasted until October 17th, when Henry returned to England.

Ill though all this boded for any further prospects of peace with France, the captives did not relinquish the hope which the preliminary negotiations with Sigismund had bred in them. In those comparatively early days it would appear that they were able to communicate with each other freely, and were thus able to lay plans. On January 18th 1417, therefore, Charles of Orleans and John of Bourbon, together with Marshal Boucicaut, put forward to the king a proposal that if Raoul of Gaucourt were allowed to go to France, with the twofold purpose of arranging peace and securing their speedy liberation, they would stand surety for him in the sum of 40,000 *écus*, if he did not return to England by March 31st. The Bishop of Durham, who was Chancellor of England, and one or two nobles whom Henry informed of this proposal, had some doubts about the wisdom of it and the bishop offered to go and discuss it with the prisoners at Pontefract (from whence the prisoners' document is inexplicably dated, though there is no evidence that any of them were there at that time). These doubts were apparently resolved and on January 27th the king granted a licence for Gaucourt to go.[16]

It was at this point that the Duke of Bourbon's sole concern for himself began to reveal itself. Unbeknown to his fellow prisoners he had a secret interview with the king, at which he begged that he, too, might be allowed to go to France to negotiate. After Bourbon had left him the king wrote in his own hand a long and secret letter[17] to Sir John Tiptoft, whom he had accredited to Sigismund, describing Bourbon's offers as far as he could in the Duke's own words, – "in substance as follows, save that he spake French" – and empowering Tiptoft to tell Sigismund of them. Bourbon, he said, had promised first that he would try and persuade Charles VI to give up a number of French towns to Henry who, he had heard, had offered in that case to renounce his claim to the French crown – "a great and reasonable proffer", Bourbon called it. If Charles VI refused, then Bourbon would hasten to join Henry as soon as he invaded France and do homage to him as the true king of it. Indeed, he stated that he and many of his fellows had been looking into Henry's claims lately and now realised the justice of them in a way they had not before. His only condition for this offer to sell his country was that he himself should be allowed to keep all that was his. So eager was he to get away that he wrote also to the Chancellor, as Henry of course knew, offering to hand over two of his own sons and other lords as hostages, and to pay 240,000 *écus*—a sum larger than the debt which had crippled Charles of Orleans for so many years—if only Henry would let him go.

Reckless though these offers were, Bourbon was thus far only involving his own conscience in making them. But in his anxiety he then forgot his loyalty to his fellows and told the king that he had talked them round, that they all wanted him to go, and even went so far as to say he thought it likely that some of them would act as he intended to. This did not take Henry in for, as he reminded Tiptoft at the beginning of his letter, whenever he had talked of possible peace terms with his prisoners and told them, in reply to their questions as to what his conditions would be, "that they should know me (as of right they ought) for their sovereign lord", it was always said "by the Duke of Orleans in the name of them all, that thereto they neither might nor could answer." It was no doubt this firm stand taken by Charles in the name of all his fellows that Henry was referring to in his letter to Kent of the previous June, when he blamed the prisoners for refusing his peace conditions.

In the event Bourbon's willingness to implicate his fellows availed him nothing for, although Henry told Tiptoft that he had granted him leave to go, in the end Gaucourt went alone. In any case Bourbon's going would probably have been profitless, for Henry assured Sigismund through Tiptoft that nothing would now deflect him from his purpose to renew his invasion of France later in the year.

The different attitudes adopted by Charles and Bourbon at this time sprang not only from their opposed conceptions of honour but from their individual temperaments, which adversity was already developing. Whereas Bourbon, excitable and with few resources in himself, continually chafed against his lot, his cousin Charles, although his junior by fourteen years, seems to have accepted his situation with fortitude, realising no doubt that, as the senior French prince, he was a trump card in Henry's hand that the king would certainly not relinquish without some immense concession in return. It must have been for this reason that, at this stage, no question of a ransom for him had yet arisen: Charles was beyond price and became more so as death continued to decimate the ranks of his faction in France, to whom his presence would have meant so much. In June 1416, the old Duke of Berry died, leaving no male heir, so that a large part of his great estates – Berry and Poitou – reverted to the king, who gave them to the new dauphin, John. Less than a year later, in April 1417, he too died, to be followed to the grave in the same month by the Duke of Anjou, King of Sicily. So now Bernard of Armagnac was the only tried leader left to support the cause of the king and Charles of Orleans against Burgundy, as well as against the English. The new dauphin, Charles, was only fourteen.

Of more immediate concern to Charles was the continuing need to find the remainder of the money due to Clarence and his fellows. As we have seen, ever since the Treaty of Buzançais in 1412 he had at different times paid considerable sums, but the total was so large that to settle it entirely was inevitably a slow business. In those earlier days he had had some help from Alençon and Bourbon, and some from his great-uncle Berry too. But now that Alençon was dead and Bourbon a prisoner, those two sources had dried up. The news of Berry's death too was therefore most alarming, both to Charles and John. It is generally supposed that the brothers never saw each other in England,* but they were certainly in communication with each other, for it seems to have been John who reminded Charles of a sizeable loan that their father Louis had once made to Berry, which had never been repaid. Now that Berry's executors would be winding up his estate, this was obviously the moment to claim this money, and for Charles to try and exact the other sums he had counted on from Berry. Accordingly the brothers sent their claims to France only three months after Berry's death. The old debt to Louis was acknowledged and presumably paid. But the other claims were rejected, or put off for the time being, after which no more was ever heard of them.[18]

This refusal to help was a desperate business for Charles, as there is good reason to suppose that Clarence, who must also have realised that Charles' credit was not now as good as in Berry's time, was beginning to press him for the still unpaid part of the debt. A new agreement between them, drawn up on May 22nd 1417,[19] was obviously the result of much discussion, which could only have taken place at Clarence's instigation. Charles fortunately had in England at that time his faithful secretaries Robert de Tuillières and Jean Chomery to help him, and Raoul de Gaucourt was also present and acted for him with them.

* See Appendix I

Although two of the creditors, Edward Duke of York and his brother Richard Earl of Cambridge, had died in 1415, the sums promised to them still figured on the list, to be paid to their heirs.

This new agreement set forth the manner and dates of future payments, and the forfeits due if these promises were not kept. It was no doubt largely with a view to assessing his financial position because of it that Charles had an inventory, both of his books and of his other goods in Blois, made in May.[20] That same month he borrowed a large sum of money from a merchant in Paris and sold him a quantity of jewels, including a superb gold crown studded with gems.[21] And he sent orders from Westminster to Cousinot and other officers to entrust plate and jewels to the value of 41,000 *livres* to certain other merchants of Paris, who were to send him the cash equivalent to England, against a promise to repay the loan within a year from the following All Saints' Day. If the repayment were not made by that date, the merchants were to be assigned not only certain rents of the duke's estates in a long list of towns—Caen, Bayeux and Provins among them—but also all his revenues from taxes on those estates, beginning on October 1st 1418.[22]

In spite of all these efforts, it proved impossible to find the total sum due within the time-limit set, and the heavy debt continued to burden and harass Charles as before. It is strange that John of Angoulême's main biographer should acuse Charles, once he got to England, of entirely neglecting his brother's needs and thinking only of his own ransom,[23] since not only was there no talk of a ransom for him until many years later, but great numbers of the documents in the Orleans *Chambre des Comptes* concern the attempts he made to raise money for John. Indeed there are so many, covering a period of thirty years from then on, that the mere reading of them is as wearisome as those attempts must have been. Charles racked his brains for sources of revenue and never seems to have omitted a chance to appeal to anyone likely to help, so that one has the impression that messengers were constantly on the road in France carrying appeals from him on behalf of his brother. Yet in spite of all his efforts he was never able, during the whole of his imprisonment, to find the total sum that would have procured John's release.

Very soon after Charles had signed the new agreement with Clarence, an abrupt change in his circumstances took place. Ever since his capture he had been kept in the different royal palaces in or near London. One of his instructions to his staff is dated from Windsor, another from "the palace of London",[24] which presumably meant the White Tower, and he was sometimes at Westminster too. If we compare the riverside White Tower, where the king himself often lived, with the Louvre, the more intimate Palace of Westminster further upstream with the Hôtel de Saint-Pol on the banks of the Seine, up-stream too, and Windsor in its forest with Vincennes in its great woods, there were enough similarities between the lay-outs of the two capitals for Charles not to feel himself in too strange a place. Most of the nobles about him spoke or could understand French. And there were the frequent visits of different members of his household at Blois to keep him in touch with his home affairs and bring him all he needed.

As recently as the previous March, Robert de Tuilières and Jean Chomery had brought him a long list of goods,[25] some of them wearing-apparel (such as six pairs of bronze-green hose and twelve head-dresses of fine linen-cloth from Troyes,) but most of them luxurious objects of his former daily life, nearly all stamped or adorned with his arms, among them what sounds like a fine leather dressing-case containing two big combs, a mirror and two razors with ivory handles decorated with his arms in enamel. The most evocative of all the items are the last on the list: three pounds of a kind of nougat from Lombardy, and seven pounds of quince marmalade, which seems to indicate an unusually sweet tooth. There were also two boxes of Genoese *triacle*, which was an antidote against the venom of animals. Later in life there is evidence that Charles took a particular interest in poisons, but why he felt he needed this safeguard in England we can only guess. His servitors brought all these things freely and easily to their master, who lived by no means as a prisoner but rather according to his rank, at the king's expense. Nor is there any mention at that time of anyone's being appointed to guard him.

But now this London sojourn came to a sudden end. The king was then preparing to leave for his second invasion of France, and before he went something apparently happened to make him feel that it would be unwise to leave Charles in London during his absence. Henry does not say what it was, he merely refers to "certain reasons especially moving us at present",[26] a formula he frequently used. At that time, when Charles had been so deeply preoccupied with financial matters, it is difficult to imagine what actions of his could have caused the king anxiety. Whatever the reason, Henry decided to put him in the custody of one of his most loyal and confidential servants, Robert Waterton.

He had already had experience as guardian of illustrious personages, for the little Richard Duke of York lived under his care, and at different times since March 1416 he had had charge of Arthur of Richemont, the Count of Eu and Marshal Boucicaut.[27] Although he had so far never received a penny of the £100 a year he was promised for the little duke, nor even of the 23s 4d a day for each of the three Frenchmen—and was not indeed paid until after the king's death—he continued to discharge the tasks entrusted to him and now accepted the guardianship of Charles. Waterton was Constable of Pontefract Castle and it was there that on June 1st 1417 the king ordered him to conduct Charles and to keep him there for the time being.[28]

Pontefract was at that time one of the largest castles in Yorkshire, a great fortress surrounded with walls and towers, its huge keep hollowed out of fifty feet of the rock on which it stood. Founded in the eleventh century, much of its structure dated from the twelfth and thirteenth, so that one can imagine it to have been a stern and comfortless dwelling in that bleak northern climate, very different from Charles' own castles in the gentler country of the Loire and the Seine valleys. Grim associations hung about it for him too, for he must from boyhood have heard from his first young wife, Isabelle, how her husband Richard II had been done to death there in some way that had always remained mysterious, and was perhaps the more terrifying for that.

In actual fact Charles' life there may well have had its agreeable side, for Waterton, to judge by the scanty references to him that we have, was a kindly man who, as we learn later from a letter of the king's, used to invite the duke out to his country house—a house of which some small portions still remain—at Methley, about six miles from Pontefract. There Charles met Waterton's family and it may not be too fanciful to suppose that it was his pleasure at finding himself welcomed by a family again that made him, that August, give Waterton's wife, Cicely, a gold goblet, while the two children got a silver necklet each.[29] These things were specially made according to orders taken to London by one of Charles' many servants, who came to London several times that summer in connection with the payments recently agreed with Clarence. Among other things they brought with them those 41,000 *livres'* worth of plate and jewels which it was originally intended should be handed over to merchants in Paris.[30] For Charles had now acquired the services of an Italian merchant in London, who had gallicized his name as Jean Victor, and who from then on undertook financial transactions for his master, keeping an account of the purchases he made for him and submitting it occasionally for the duke's approval and signature. One such, a roll sixty centimetres long, is approved in his own hand: "I, Charles, Duke of Orleans, state that I am very satisfied with the above account."[31]

Now satisfied that Charles was in safe keeping, Henry set sail for France again, and the news soon after he landed there on August 1st must again have been unwelcome hearing for his prisoner. Working in what looked suspiciously like agreement with Henry, John the Fearless marched towards Paris at the same time. So great was the threat that he had always represented for the allied princes that Bernard chose rather to defend the city against him than Normandy against the English. Although no actual fighting broke out between them, Burgundy undermined any hope of French unity by winning Queen Isabeau over to his side and proclaiming her regent. In this capacity she announced that her young son Charles, the dauphin, had no authority, and that her orders alone must be obeyed, the king once again being incapacitated.

With the country thus divided under two rulers, a kind of paralysis seemed to seize even Bernard of Armagnac, who had become Constable after the death of Albret, and thus all that winter and the following spring Henry swept victoriously on, conquering one Norman town after another, unopposed by any save their inhabitants. By the end of May practically the whole province, with the exception of its capital Rouen, was in his hands, and still the Armagnacs remained in Paris, waiting on events there.

Those events, when they came, were terrible. On the night of May 28th, a force of Burgundians was let secretly into the city, where they marched to the Hôtel de Saint-Pol and seized the witless king. Many Parisians rose to join them and then set about massacring all the Armagnacs they could lay hands on. Bernard tried to hide from them, but they ferreted him out and killed him, and over five hundred of his followers, taking prisoner a great number of prominent citizens, including nobles and ecclesiastics, whom they suspected of Armagnac sympathies. When finally the Bastille fell it looked as if Burgundy, who had prudently stayed away while this slaughter was going on, had at last realised his ambition and was not only undisputed master of Paris but virtual ruler of the country.

So indeed it must have appeared to Charles, when the news of the death of his father-in-law, the last of his former allies and his only senior relation, reached him in Pontefract. But very soon afterwards there was to be news of resistance from a quarter unexpected enough to fill Burgundy with dismay and Charles with surprise and pride. Of that massacre in Paris there was one important survivor: Tanguy du Châtel, Provost of Paris, had managed to save the dauphin and take him to Melun, where he was safe. He was a timid, uninspiring figure, haunted by the thought that he might be illegitimate, as his mother always declared he was; but he could at least be made into the head of a party to oppose both Burgundy and the English, if anyone could be found to stand by him and help him to form it. It was at this point that Philip of Vertus, now twenty-one, who had hitherto played the rôle of devoted but dependent young brother to Charles, emerged as a leader to be reckoned with.

During the winter of 1418 Philip took command and, with a pre-science apparently unique among his peers, began to prepare for the English attack that he foresaw must soon spread south from Normandy. The Orleans accounts show him buying armour for himself,[32] and sending to the family lands at Asti for a black courser, while he procured arms and recruited troops locally. He strove, too, to find allies to help in this resistance and at the beginning of May we find him rallying John, Duke of Alençon,* aged fourteen, and Louis, Duke of Anjou,[33] who was fifteen, the youthful heirs of Charles' old supporters. Another youth who joined the dauphin's army at that time was the fifteen-year-old Charles, Count of Clermont, heir to the imprisoned Duke of Bourbon. He had been captured by the Burgundians at the time of the May massacre but had managed to escape. It must have seemed strange to the exiled prisoner to think of this band of young men and boys now leading what without them would have been a lost cause. In later life he was to know some of them well.

When the dauphin fled from Paris, then, to the territories that still remained loyal to him—Anjou, Poitou and Berry—he found Philip and his allies with their troops all ready to help him. He himself had brought what remained of the Gascon soldiers and there were also—a most

* The young Alençon did not need much rallying, for Perceval de Cagny, the family chronicler, says (p. 110) that at the age of eleven, a few months after his father was killed at Agincourt, he led a richly-dressed company of 400 horse to join the forces of the king, who found him "a very beautiful child". So he had evidently inherited his father's looks.

valuable addition to his army—some Scottish archers under the command of John Stewart, Earl of Buchan. They had not long to wait for action for in June, while Henry was beginning his long siege of Rouen, other parts of his army began to push south. That month messengers had to be sent post-haste to warn the inhabitants of the Beauce to take shelter in the fortresses and castles there.[34] In July, copper cannon and crossbows were sent by messengers "hastening night and day" for the defence of Meung-sur-Loire, which the English were attacking in great force. At the end of September, when the fall of Cherbourg freed the army under Clarence, the danger in the Orleans territories became greater still, so much so that an 'esquire carver' of Charles' household was sent from Blois to Amboise to see if Margaret and Jane could be lodged there. But the dauphin's army under Philip stood firm.

It is not improbable that it was the unexpected strength of this resistance that made Henry V, who all this time was besieging Rouen, begin to wonder whether it would not be wise for him to enter into an alliance with the dauphin, by way of keeping the civil strife going in France and thus allowing him a freer hand when at last Rouen should fall. During that autumn he set out his ideas on the subject in a long document for consideration by his Privy Council.[35] One aspect of the matter on which he particularly sought their opinion was the question of the prisoners. If the dauphin should ask that the Duke of Orleans and the rest of the prisoners should be what the king calls 'put to finance' for the strengthening of his party, should this be done? If so, should it be all of them or some? If not all, which should and which should not? Should any be let out before he had paid his full sum? If so, what surety should be taken for those that were allowed to go? "And in especial this is to be advised first and most for the Duke of Orleans, and next for Bourbon and so forth for the remnant". The reply of the Council is not recorded, but on October 26th an embassy was appointed to treat with the dauphin. But there is no evidence that any discussion with him ever took place; and as far as Charles was concerned this possibility of release, and of seeing again the brother whose staunch loyalty to the dauphin's cause was at least in part responsible for it, remained a matter between the king and his Council and never reached the duke's ears. But one significant fact emerges from this abortive consultation: this was obviously the first occasion on which a ransom for Charles had been considered.

Unaware of these thoughts passing through his ally Henry's mind,

John the Fearless continued to triumph in Paris. On November 3rd, thanks to his now powerful position, he was able to have the sentence against Jean Petit, that had never ceased to rankle in his mind, revoked at a mass in Notre-Dame attended by representatives of the Council, the Church and the University. One can only hope that the news of this never reached Charles. The ceremony can hardly have seemed other than a hollow mockery to such of those present as still remembered this old story, but according to Monstrelet,[36] John was pleased by it. It was the last triumph he was to know.

In the following January Rouen was finally forced by hunger to surrender, so that Henry became lord of all Normandy. He then represented such a threat to the kingdom that the dauphin sent ambassadors to Burgundy, suggesting that they should unite against the English. This could at best have been an alliance between sworn enemies, for the dauphin had now taken the title of regent. All the same there was something to be said for it. But Burgundy was so full of suspicion, as it was soon to prove that he had reason to be, that it was September before he agreed to a meeting. It was fixed that this should take place on the 10th, at Montereau on the river Yonne. The dauphin and some of his court went there to await the duke, some of them waiting on the bridge which Burgundy would have to cross. When he and his retinue met them in the middle of it, in the ensuing press John the Fearless was stabbed to death. The whole thing happened so suddenly that none could say who struck the fatal blow, although afterwards there were many accusations. Juvenal des Ursins for one roundly asserts that it was Tanguy du Châtel who, he says, pushed the duke by the shoulders, saying "You go first", and then clove his head with an axe from behind.[37] Although the guilt was never with certainty laid at anyone's door, it seemed more than likely that the attack was premeditated, and the Burgundians naturally accused the dauphin of complicity in it.

Whether they had intended the murder or not, the Armagnac party could not but rejoice that at last their arch enemy had met his end in a way that they felt to be a judgment on him. As for Charles, he had occasion to say publicly many years later that when the news of John's death reached him he was greatly distressed at it, realising that because of the manner of it the kingdom of France was in greater danger than before. One can well believe that, humane and civilised as he was, he would never have approved of such brutal, eye-for-an-eye methods.

Although the new Duke of Burgundy, Philip of Charolois, known as 'the Good' was a very different man from his father and had by no means always approved his actions, he was filled with genuine grief at his death and swore to avenge it on the dauphin. To that end he joined forces so whole-heartedly with Henry that he, on his side, gave up all thoughts of an alliance with the dauphin, and consequently of releasing his prisoners. On the country, he now became more than ever determined to keep them under strict guard in England, fearful lest they should escape or plot against him; so much so that he wrote at this time to the Bishop of Durham:[38]

> I would that ye . . . set a good ordinance for my North Marches, and specially for the Duke of Orleans and for all the remnant of my prisoners of France, and also for the King of Scotland; for as I am secretly informed by a man of right noble estate in this land that there has been a man of the Duke of Orleans in Scotland and accorded with the Duke of Albany . . . that there should be found ways to the having away specially of the Duke of Orleans, and also of the king . . . Wherefore I will that the Duke of Orleans be kept still within the Castle of Pontefract, without going to Robertes place or to any other disport, for it is better he lack his disport than we were deceived.

The Chancellor presumably obeyed the king's command and deprived Charles of what must have been a blessed occasional escape from the grim castle to Waterton's country home at Methley, where there was some kind of sport to be had, the game of tennis perhaps, of which his father had been so fond, or even a chance to ride and hunt. But the seeds of doubt, once sown in the king's mind, were not easily cast out and on October 1st, only three weeks after the murder of John of Burgundy, he wrote again from Gisors to the Chancellor,[39] urging him to keep special watch over the Dukes of Orleans and Bourbon. Every line of this letter with its repetitions breathes anxiety: "For their escaping, and principally the said Duke of Orleans, might never have been so harmful nor prejudical unto us as it might be now, if any of them escaped, and namely the said Duke of Orleans, which God forbid". He therefore bade the Chancellor to see that Robert Waterton "for no trusting, fair speech nor promise that might be made unto him, nor for other kind of cause, be so blinded by the said Duke that he be the more reckless of his keeping." The Chancellor is to enquire "if Robert of Waterton use any reckless governance about the keeping of the said Duke" and if so to write to him about it "that he be amended".

As a result of this correspondence the Council judged it wiser to change the guardianship of Charles and Bourbon, putting the latter in the care of Waterton and giving the custody of Charles to Sir Nicholas Montgomery. In the minutes[40] recording this there is no reference to any change of residence, but it does not seem likely that Charles remained at Pontefract. This arrangement was, however, modified not long afterwards, Bourbon being returned to the care of Montgomery, while Charles was transferred to that of Sir Thomas Burton.[41] He was warden of Fotheringhay Castle in Northamptonshire, so the probability is that Charles was sent there then, as we know he was certainly there a year later.

If so, it must have been a pleasant change from Pontefract to this castle in a gentler countryside, set on its little hill encircled by the river Nene. For all its remote situation Fotheringhay Castle, of which only some foundations now remain, was an important royal stronghold. In the village church of St. Mary lay buried the bones of Edward Duke of York, whose body had been boiled down, according to the custom of the time, after he had been killed at Agincourt. Charles had the company of some of his fellow-prisoners there, for Arthur of Richemont, the Count of Eu and Marshal Boucicaut were all in the custody of Sir Thomas Burton at this time.[42]

One would like to know what had caused these sudden suspicions on the king's part. It seems very unlikely that Charles had been plotting with the Scots or anyone else as, to judge from the absence of safe-conducts in 1419, he received no visits from France in that year. Moreover there is evidence that, just at that time, his thoughts were wholly set upon the everlasting financial problems that harassed him, and that he was feeling particularly solitary and neglected by his own people, so much so that on September 3rd 1419 he wrote a long letter in his own hand to his Chancellor Cousinot, and to his Treasurer-General, reproaching them for not helping him more.[43] It is a most human document, revealing vividly how wearing the cares, the monotony and the constantly deferred hopes of his solitary existence must have been, to force the usually even-tempered and philosophical young duke to adopt for once a tone of querulous complaint and, at moments, sharp reproof.

He has, he says, written to them several times on behalf of his financial agent, Jean Victor, who has paid on his behalf a considerable sum out of his own money towards the debts, and now is in need himself because, he rather bitterly remarks, "one cannot live nor incur expenses with nothing, as you may well suppose." He therefore presses them to send money for Victor as soon as they can "and in addition as much more as you can for the necessities and affairs of my said brother, myself and the said hostages, or otherwise the said Jean [Victor] will be undone and will fail us all when we are in need." That is why he has written to them several times, "but it seems to me that you pay little heed to my letters and neglect them. I am therefore writing to you this time once for all. You must see to it that whatever happens this time there must be no failure and no more delay. And do not think that the said money has been spent in follies nor ill-advisedly, but be sure it has been used with my knowledge and by my order. . . . . I do not intend to write to you again on this; but I am thinking of finding for my needs other servitors more diligent in obeying me and fulfilling my orders than you are."

After this little outburst of ill-humour he softens and says that if they can hasten the deliverance of his brother "he and I will be most grateful to you and very pleased." And he goes on to tell them how grateful he is to the Count of Vendôme, who has offered to let him raise money on his lands; but Charles wants them to ask the dauphin to let his officers see to this for him—a characteristic desire to spare his own people this delicate task.

At the end of this long letter Charles refers to one he had received from Cousinot written on the previous July 16th, saying among other things that he was sending one of Charles' servants to him to discuss the whole business of his master's needs, a statement that made him "very pleased and joyous." He urges them to use all possible means with the King of England (for the safe-conduct) "so that the coming of my said servant may be as soon as possible, and thus by him I can send you my wishes about all my needs". And to end on as cheerful a note as he can he tells them that he is "in good condition and health, by Our Lord's mercy". When one realises that six weeks had passed since Cousinot's letter was written, and that the secretary announced in mid-July had not arrived at the beginning of September, the asperities of Charles' letter are understandable, especially as, from a reference in it to "Robert de Tuillières, whose soul may God keep", it is clear that this faithful secretary had recently died. The knowledge that he would not see again the familiar face of this man who had accompanied him on his first going to England and whose frequent visits since then had done so much to keep him in close touch with his own people, must have deepened his sense of loss and exile.

As for Henry's suspicions of Waterton's reliability as a guardian, there is no doubt that he was on good terms with his charge. Charles' habitual patience, his courtesy, his cultivated mind and the sense of humour and amused irony which he revealed later in his poetry, must have made him a pleasant and attractive prisoner to guard. But there is no evidence that Waterton was thereby induced to fail in his duty. Had he perhaps written too glowingly about his charge to the king? Whatever the reason, Henry obviously thought it wise to remove Waterton from the office of guardian to any of his prisoners at that time. Yet he was by no means in disgrace. He continued in friendly correspondence with his sovereign, to whom, in a letter of the following April,[44] he wishes a happy marriage and a good peace. These hopes were inspired by the news of Henry's successful negotiations with the new Duke of Burgundy, Philip the Good, which on May 20th 1420 resulted in the Treaty of Troyes, whereby Charles VI recognised Henry as his only true heir and disinherited the dauphin, whom he accused of horrible crimes. Less than a fortnight later, on June 2nd, the long-talked-of marriage with the Princess Catherine at last took place; immediately after the wedding Henry returned to his fighting, conquering in swift succession Sens, Montereau, Melun and finally the Bastille and Vincennes.*

Whether or not it was that these triumphs had induced a mellower attitude in Henry towards his prisoners, on June 8th, by his orders, Charles of Orleans and John of Bourbon were brought to London by their respective keepers, Sir Thomas Burton and Sir Nicholas Montgomery, to appear before the king's Council "for certain reasons particularly moving us", wrote Henry in his accustomed phrase, as usual without saying what.[45] What happened there is not recorded in the minutes, but on July 20th Bourbon was allowed to go with a deputation to Dieppe,[46] to try and negotiate financial and other terms for his own liberation. In that same month Henry freed Arthur of Richemont,[47] that he might persuade his brother the Duke of Brittany, who had been changing sides with bewildering rapidity, to remain on Henry's, where he happened to be for the moment—a vain hope as it turned out. The

---

* The fact that Henry had married the youngest of the six daughters of Charles VI did not of course affect his political position in France or mean that he was accepted in Paris as a conqueror.

departure of Arthur, his companion at Fotheringhay, and the knowledge that Bourbon was going to France too, while he remained behind, must have increased Charles' sense of the hoplessness of his position; but he had no possibility of finding money, even if there were any question of a ransom, which there still was not; and he would hardly have betrayed the dauphin's cause while his brother Philip was continuing to fight for it.

Philip was indeed the dauphin's most valued counsellor at that time, so much so that on one occasion the dauphin sent a hundred men to escort him, for greater safety, when he went from Blois to Amboise for consultations. The young count and his messengers were constantly on the road, keeping in touch with his Scottish allies and his loyal towns.[48] So much of the fighting for the past two years had been over the Orleans territories, both in Valois and around the Loire, that the economic situation was becoming more and more serious for Philip to face (and perhaps accounted for the difficulty in sending Charles all the money he needed). The devastation caused by the armies made the peasants so fear the soldiery that they dared not venture on the roads to go and cultivate what bits of land they could. Consequently provisions became more and more difficult to procure and the value of money dropped further and further. Other necessaries for the war were in short supply too, and we find Philip sending an armourer to Orleans to see if there were any steel coats of mail for sale.[49] And when a boatman took Philip and his officers from Blois to Montils he was given a carpet of Philip's with a design of ears of corn as security for payment.[50]

Since so much depended on him the loss to the dauphin's cause must have seemed irreparable when, at the end of July, Philip of Vertus suddenly died. The cause of his death is nowhere stated. He was certainly not killed in battle, though he may have been wounded, for there is a record of fees paid to the doctors who cared for him "from the day that he took to his bed,[51] and the indications are that he died at Beaugency, where he appears to have had a house.[52] If the cause was not a wound but a malady, it must have seized him unexpectedly, for all the actions taken subsequently by the officers of his brother's household show how unprepared for his death they were. On July 26th a sergeant was paid to announce at the cross-roads in Blois, and at the market-place outside the town, that if any to whom Philip owed money presented themselves to his executors they would be paid.[53]

These executors of his will, of whom Cousinot was one, on September 2nd drew up a list of his modest personal possessions and household goods, and sold most of them. But they retained a few things to give as souvenirs, "As much to the ladies Margaret and Jane of Orleans and to the Bastard of Orleans, that they might remember the late Monseigneur and be obliged to pray God for him, as to other people to whom the late Monseigneur was beholden". There is no record of any souvenir being sent to Charles. When all these matters were concluded Philip was buried, with as much pomp as could be afforded, in Blois on November 26th,[54] two days after Charles' twenty-sixth birthday,

Yet even now the House of Orleans was not left unrepresented and leaderless. Just as Philip had so ably taken his brother Charles' place, so now the young bastard John, whose quality Valentina had so early discerned, begins at this time, though still only sixteen, to step into the foreground, where not long afterwards he was to play a glorious rôle, not only as his brother's champion but as one of the greatest captains in French history. Three years before this, Charles had made him a present of a horse[55] and he must early have become used to going about on his own, for he was in Paris at the time of the massacre of the Armagnacs in May 1418. Although he fortunately escaped death on that occasion, he was taken prisoner by the Burgundians, who held him in their territory until August 1420 when, on instructions given by Philip of Vertus before his death, a considerable sum was paid to one of the dauphin's esquires,[56] who delivered him from the Burgundian who held him. He would appear to have been in the thick of the mêlée on the night of the massacre for in the course of it he lost his silver *Camail*, a loss that must have grieved him, so much so that Philip's executors gave him instead the one that had belonged to Philip "with a gold porcupine and a big pearl hanging on the neck of the porcupine".[57] The only other object he inherited suggests how far by now the House of Orleans had declined from the old, sumptuous days: it consisted of a length of fur from one of Philip's robes, which a furrier in Blois had been ordered to scrape and do up "so that it might be more seemly to present to the Bastard of Orleans."[58]

On December 1st, a few days after the burial of Philip, Henry V entered Paris and was royally received by the chief citizens. At the end of that month he returned to England with his wife Catherine, after an absence of three and a half years. He left his uncle the Duke of Exeter as lieutenant in Paris, while Clarence remained to carry on the war against the dauphin. Greatly though the latter's cause had been weakened by the loss of Philip, he was continuing to resist the English, with the help of his invaluable Scottish allies. Although most of their actions hitherto had been defensive, on March 22nd, 1421, at Baugé, they inflicted a massive defeat on the English, killing the Duke of Clarence among others, and taking some notable prisoners, including the eighteen-year-old Earl of Somerset and his brother Edmund (both sons of the Duchess of Clarence by her first marriage to John, Marquess of Somerset, who had died in 1410), and also the Earl of Huntingdon.

The news of this at once bred in Charles' family in Blois, and in himself and John in England, eager hopes for their release through an exchange, and the speed with which Margaret and Jane acted is a measure of their longing for the return of the prisoners. On April 1st, only a week after the battle, they and the Chancellor Cousinot sent letters to the dauphin at Tours, begging him to write to the Scottish lords who had actually taken the prisoners, to put before them the possibility of an exchange, against ransoms, between two of the prisoners and Charles and John.[59] On the 21st Cousinot, on Charles' orders, went himself to see the dauphin and the Scottish lords, with the same proposal. At the same time Cousinot sent letters, through their Scottish captors, direct to the two main English prisoners. A month later, on Charles' instructions, a messenger was sent to the Duchess of Clarence and the Duke of Exeter, who were both in France, to see if they would not agree to exchange a certain Thomas Beaufort* against John of Angoulême, as Charles himself had suggested that John should have priority in this matter. But it was all to no avail.

It was hardly a moment to expect clemency from Henry. Not only was the death of his brother Clarence a great blow to him, but the defeat at once began to alter the balance of power. On May 8th the Duke of Brittany, far from being mollified by the release of his brother Arthur, and impressed by his brother-in-law the dauphin's victory, signed a treaty with him at Sablé, not far from Baugé. The dauphin consolidated this by giving Charles of Orleans' sister Margaret in marriage to Brittany's brother Richard. According to Cousinot's *Geste des Nobles*,[60] Charles was not pleased by this marriage, though Cousinot gives no reasons. If Charles could have foreseen the good results, for his own family and for France, that were later to come of that union, he might

* See pp. 178-9 below.

have approved of it at the time.* Perhaps his displeasure, if indeed he felt it, was due merely to sadness that this important event in his sister's life was settled without reference to him. And whatever his feelings were, he ordered a singularly exquisite Book of Hours as a wedding present for her.[61] Another matter from which he was then excluded was the formal betrothal of his eleven-year-old daughter Jane to the young Duke of Alençon, to whom she had first been promised when she was four months old. This was another forging of a political link, for Alençon was a nephew of Brittany through his mother Mary, Brittany's sister.

Encouraged by his recent victory and these alliances, in June the dauphin began to threaten first Chartres and then Paris, which brought Henry back with all speed to France. The small but fresh army he brought with him was more than a match for the dauphin's troops, and during the ensuing months they were gradually pressed back until they were once more fighting all over Charles of Orleans' territories. By the spring of 1422 these reverses caused the dauphin to lose heart, and he abandoned the struggle and retired to live quietly in his temporary capital, Bourges. The Duke of Brittany, influenced no doubt by the dauphin's defeatism, turned coat once again and recognised the Treaty of Troyes. Nevertheless, all that summer fighting continued, with the French and Scots still defending the Orleans lands against the English. But for Henry the end was now drawing near. He had been so ill with dysentery since the spring that in the end he had to be carried in a litter with the army, not being able to sit his horse. In August he was taken to Vincennes, and in the castle there, on the 31st, he died.

On his death-bed he remained lucid to the last, still protesting that he had only undertaken these wars to gain his rights, and exhorting his brother, the Duke of Bedford, and his uncle the Duke of Exeter, to continue them until peace was won, and never to give up Normandy. Bedford was to have the government of Normandy and, if the Duke of Burgundy did not want it, the regency of France too, while Exeter was to remain Governor of Paris. Moreover, if Monstrelet is to be believed, even in those last moments the king did not forget his French

* Francis, the son of that marriage, eventually succeeded to the dukedom of Brittany and became one of Charles' most loyal supporters. And it was Francis' daughter, Anne of Brittany, who, on marrying Louis XII, the son of Charles of Orleans, finally united the dukedom of Brittany and the Kingdom of France.

prisoners for, he says,[62] he charged the Duke of Bedford: "And take care that you deliver not from prison my fair cousin the Duke of Orleans, the Count of Eu and the lord of Gaucourt. . . . until my fair son Henry reaches years of discretion (*l'âge compétent*), and for the others, do as it seems good to you." If he did give this charge on his death-bed it merely shows how much this matter was on his mind, for he had already included an instruction that Charles should never be released until he himself had completed his conquest of France, in the will that he had drawn up at Dover more than a year before. This ended with the words: "I have made this will be myself and written jit in hast with myn owen hand, thus enterlynet and blotted as hit is, the IXth day of Jun ye yere of oure Lord MCCCCXXI, and of my regne ye IX."[63] His "fair son Henry" at the time of his father's death was a baby of nine months.

IT is unlikely that Charles heard of Henry's depressing last instructions concerning his prisoners, if indeed they were uttered, or learnt that he had also embodied them in his will. Some time after the king died, and certainly by December of that year, 1422,[1] he was transferred to the care of a certain Sir Thomas Comberworth in the castle of Bolingbroke in Lincolnshire, a royal stronghold (now destroyed) that had belonged to John of Gaunt, and where Henry IV had been born. The news of the king's death might rather have seemed a hopeful event to one like Charles who had been his personal prisoner, his fate closely bound up with the progress of the war in France, which had been so much Henry's main preoccupation. With the king dead, there was a chance that the situation there might change.

Any such hopes were quickly doomed to disappointment. It was not long before Charles heard of the latest developments in France, for just before Christmas he received a visit from three of his officials – Jacques Boucher, his Treasurer-General, who seems to have succeeded Pierre Renier, Hugues Perrier and Jean le Mercier – who came with six servants and twelve horses, bringing not only a further contribution of money for John's ransom, but jewels of gold and silver and letters too.[2] Whomever the letters were from, they could not have brought the prisoner news of much comfort. His godfather, Charles VI, had died on October 21st, only two months after Henry V, and when he was lowered into his grave at Saint-Denis on November 11th many French partisans of the English had publicly cried "Vive le roi Henry roi de France et d'Angleterre".[3] The fact that the Duke of Bedford was the chief mourner at the funeral, which was attended by none of the French nobles, no doubt accounted for this. But since on October 20th the partisans of the dauphin had proclaimed him King of France at Mehun-sur-Yèvre, it was obvious that the country was now in some ways more hopelessly divided than ever.

Five months later, in May 1423, Boucher, Perrier and Mercier came again.[4] Pleasant though it must have been for Charles to see these faithful friends, their visit must have indicated that no end was foreseen to his captivity, and the news of the most recent events in France made it only too clear why. On April 17th a treaty had been signed at Amiens between the English and the Burgundians, whereby Henry VI was recognised as King of France and England. To strengthen this alliance two marriages were arranged. The first was that of the Duke of Bedford to Anne, sister of Philip of Burgundy, and the second that of Arthur of Richemont to Margaret, Philip's eldest sister.[5] Rather belatedly, Arthur had accomplished the mission for which Henry V had freed him in 1420, and his brother the Duke of Brittany, forgetting his previous treaty with the dauphin in 1421, had now joined the Burgundian side, for the time being at any rate, as, by his marriage, Arthur did also. With their forces thus consolidated the English and Burgundians resumed their operations against the dauphin's army that summer and were for the most part successful. It was therefore clear that the situation in France offered Charles no hope of help from his own country.

Although the war there was going as Henry V had hoped it would, his death had created a far from satisfactory state of things in England, and this too affected the position of Charles. It was because Henry's desire to retain and increase his territorial possessions in France was of paramount importance to him that he had appointed the elder of his two brothers, the Duke of Bedford, Regent of France; for, although still only thirty-three, he was both a wise and experienced administrator and a fine soldier. This meant that the office of Lord Protector of England fell to the younger brother, Humphrey Duke of Gloucester. Although a lover of learning and the arts, he was also an ambitious, quarrelsome, unscrupulous and headstrong man, whom Henry himself had not trusted, a distrust he revealed by an order that, on occasions when Bedford happened to be in England, he was to replace Gloucester as Protector.

Henry's feelings about this brother were shared by Gloucester's peers and the other members of the Council, of which he was of course the head. He returned their dislike in full, with a particular hatred for his uncle Henry Beaufort, Bishop of Winchester, who was the Chancellor. The constant clashes between Gloucester on the one side, and the Chancellor and the rest of the Council on the other, were to bedevil the whole of Henry VI's minority, creating a situation not unlike that which had prevailed during Charles of Orleans' adolescence in France, with Gloucester continually stirring up trouble as John the Fearless had done, and posing as the friend of the Londoners as Burgundy had posed as the champion of the people of Paris.

With these domestic problems on their hands the Council had little attention to spare for the war in France and were content to leave the prosecution of it in Bedford's able hands. And if he did not share Henry V's anxieties about Charles' possible connection with it, the Council too were obviously prepared merely to leave him where he was. So in May 1423 they reached a new agreement with Sir Thomas Comberworth,[6] promising him a larger payment for his care and expenses in looking after the prisoner. Even so it was less than that previously paid to Robert Waterton at Pontefract or Sir Thomas Burton at Fotheringhay; for it seems that the cost of keeping their illustrious involuntary guests was beginning to be a matter of some concern to the Council. With the exception of Arthur of Richemont, and of Marshal Boucicaut who had died at Pontefract in 1421, they were all still in England.

For Bourbon too had returned. After Henry V had released him temporarily in 1420 he had spent months in France, struggling to find the 100,000 gold crowns that were to be the price of his freedom, and to fulfil his own offers to persuade his eldest son, the Count of Clermont, to serve the English king, and hand over his second son, Louis, with some of his chief subjects as hostages. But all his efforts proved vain, and a few months after the death of Henry V the wretched duke, whose health was gradually being undermined by hope deferred, was sent back to England.

It was presumably because of the cost of maintaining these two royal dukes whose keep, as the king's prisoners, was a charge upon the state, that at a meeting on January 26th, 1424, the Council decided that from the following Easter onwards they should pay for their own expenses.[7] This was a most unusual decision, and it was no doubt in order to inform him of it that Charles was brought to London by Sir Thomas Comberworth on December 26th and kept there (Sir Thomas had a house there) until the following February 2nd.[8] There is no record of what either Charles or Bourbon thought of this change in their circumstances. Morally there were two or three ways of looking at it. Henry V might almost be said to have taken a certain pride in the two princely prisoners his great victory at Agincourt had brought him, and for whose welfare and safety he felt responsible; and they on their side could not fail to have been aware of the importance they had in his time and had now lost, for the present at any rate. Yet although they might be said to have lost status by ceasing to be the king's guests, even though

captive ones, it would also make their position in future less humiliating not to have to live merely on what they were offered.

Whatever importance such moral considerations may have had, the
financial aspect of the change was certainly the more pressing both for
Bourbon, who needed every penny he could get for his ransom, and
for Charles, continually harassed to find the sums needed to set his
brother free. There is nothing to tell us how the new arrangement
worked in either case. Presumably such money as their own people
managed to send them for their keep had to be handed over to their
guardians to spend on their behalf; and in Charles' case, if we are to
believe Monstrelet,[9] those guardians made such a good thing out of it
that this was one of the reasons for the later reluctance to set the prisoner
free. One concession that this new arrangement secured for Charles was
the right to have wine sent from his own lands duty-free, and this he
lost no time in ordering. Even before April 1424 his faithful servitor
and banker, Jean Victor, who during the past year had been more than
usually busy helping Charles and his brother John, and their cousin the
Count of Vendôme too, with loans, brought some over for him and
thereafter there are frequent mentions of considerable consignments.[10]

One can only hope that those pleasant wines of the Loire valley
softened for Charles the misery of having nothing but the trivialities
of daily life with which to concern himself, while in France his brother
the Bastard and his son-in-law Alençon were continuing to fight for
the dauphin. It was particularly cruel to have to endure forced inactivity at that time when the news from the battlefield was bad. Although
the dauphin's forces, recently increased by fresh Scottish contingents
under the newly-arrived Earl of Douglas, greatly outnumbered the
combined English and Burgundian armies, they were heavily defeated
in August 1424 in a battle at Verneuil, in Normandy, where the Duke
of Bedford killed the Earl of Douglas, and that old Scottish campaigner,
the Earl of Buchan, whom the dauphin had made Constable, was also
slain. Of more importance to Charles was the fact that John of Alençon
was taken prisoner. He was to remain a captive for three years, thus
condemning his fifteen-year-old wife, Charles' daughter Jane, whom
he had married only a year before, to that same virtual widowhood that
the duke's own fate had inflicted on Bonne d'Armagnac.

After such dramatic events the ensuing stalemate in the war in France,
that lasted for the next four years, was at least a time of lessened anxiety
for the absent prisoner. A probable reason for this comparatively slow

prosecution of the war was that Humphrey of Gloucester was creating such unrest in England at the end of 1425 that the Council, fearing an outbreak of civil war, sent for the Duke of Bedford, who arrived in January 1426 and had to remain for sixteen months before he could restore the situation to comparative calm. In his absence from France he left his army there in charge of the Earls of Salisbury and Suffolk, and the fighting continued sporadically, with small gains and losses on both sides, but no major victories, although the dauphin's army had been strengthened by the presence of two new leaders.

One of these was Raoul of Gaucourt who, in spite of Henry V's alleged deathbed ban, was allowed to return to France in 1425,[11] although he had not then completed his ransom. He was in any case in a different category from the Agincourt prisoners, having surrendered at the fall of Harfleur. His final liberation was arranged as an exchange with the Earl of Huntingdon, who had been a prisoner in France since the battle of Baugé in 1421.[12] The other new recruit to the dauphin's side was, rather surprisingly in view of his recent Burgundian marriage, Arthur of Richemont, who "surrendered and became French", as Cousinot puts it.[13] In 1425 the dauphin gave him the vacant office of Constable, but he was for some time looked at askance by the dauphin's other loyal leaders, the Bastard, Gaucourt and Bourbon's son the Count of Clermont, who together stoutly defended the lands of the absent duke as the war gradually approached his territories.

During the four years while this state of suspense continued both in France and England, the only practical matters that Charles had with which to fill his thoughts in his virtually solitary confinement in the castle of Bolingbroke were the everlasting financial affairs of his brother, for the money for whose release he was still being pressed. John's circumstances, too, were causing Charles anxiety, for after the death of Clarence at Baugé in 1421, John had been transferred to the keeping of Clarence's duchess, who sent him to their castle of Maxey in Northamptonshire. She seems to have treated him more harshly than her husband did, so that at times he had not enough to eat. To help relieve his needs Charles gave him the proceeds of the salt-tax (*gabelle*) in Orleans and elsewhere. The gift evidently meant a great deal to John, whose autograph letters of August and December 1427, asking for the money to be sent by special messenger, have a touching urgency.[14] At the same time Charles was doing what he could for some of the other hostages.[15]

Because of all these calls upon him at that time, but chiefly for John's sake, in 1427 Charles agreed to a very considerable sale or pledging of many of his possessions at Blois, not only furnishings and jewels, but his precious library. In March of that year, 1427, his constant visitors, Hugues de Saint-Mars and Hugues Perrier, came to England bringing with them a more important official, John of Rochechouart, Lord of Mortemart, who was one of Charles' councillors and chamberlains.[16] On the 17th, at Canterbury, whither Charles must have been allowed to go to transact this important business, he signed an authority for John of Rochechouart to sell all these possessions for him.[17] (Before Rochechouart returned to France, Charles bought a mule from him.[18] It is pleasant to think that, at a time when he had to give up so much, he was at least able to acquire an animal to which he must have taken a fancy, for he always seems to have preferred mules to horses.)

On his return to France Rochechouart signed, on June 1st, a receipt for the goods he had taken.[19] The items, which are described in great detail, give a vivid idea of the furnishing of a princely house of the time. Among them are many tapestries of wool, silk and gold thread, whose subjects are all given: Theseus, Charlemagne, the vices and virtues and so on. Other furnishings include bed-covers of cloth of gold and silk, room-hangings, somthing described as "leathers to spread in summer-time," "three big mattresses covered with vermilion silk and stuffed with cotton" and "half another mattress . . . that the late Monseigneur de Vertus . . . had cut in half and took the other half to Tours." Among the rich and sometimes jewelled objects there is a minutely-described and very elaborate board and set of pieces for the game of tables, once belonging to "the late Madame d'Orleans, the elder" – which might be either Charles' mother or his first wife Isabelle – and something called a *chappel* (probably a short cape) made of white and coloured peacock's feathers, spangled with gold, in a leather case, which took the Bastard's fancy, for he bought it for sixty gold *écus*. The one really splendid object that Charles decided to part with at that time – a great cross of gold, garnished with pearls and precious stones – he entrusted to Hugues de Saint-Mars and Jean le Mercier to take to Avignon, where the Lombard merchants traded, and sell it there.[20]

The thought of selling all these things, which in any case he had not seen for twelve years, could hardly have mattered much to Charles as his circumstances then were; but the decision to part with his library at Blois, including even those precious manuscripts that had been dedicated to Valentina, must have been a terrible wrench for him. And now he had to face the thought of never seeing any of them again. All but four or five of the eighty-five volumes listed for Mortemart to take appear in the 1417 inventory.* An anxious moment arose over the transfer of one of them, the great bible whose translation had begun under Louis of Orleans. In March 1427, when the dauphin was staying in the castle at Blois, he had sent one of his servants to borrow it from Pierre Sauvage "pretending that he wanted to read it."[21] Thereafter, in spite of repeated requests from Mortemart, Pierre Sauvage and others, he refused to give it back until considerably later.

One consolation for Charles in parting with these particular books was that he had with him in England nearly a hundred more volumes which his servitors had brought him from time to time, or which he had received as gifts from friends.[22] The inventory of these, which was drawn up after hisr eturn to France†, reveals that the majority of them were of a much more serious nature than those which were to be sold, and from it one can divine what were his chief preoccupations during his captivity. There are no romances and no classical authors except Seneca. No less than seven of the books are treatises on medicine. This might be thought to indicate either that he had a tendency to be hypochondriacal or that his health caused him anxiety while he was in England; but as some of them are ancient works it is more likely that medicine was a subject in which Charles was so interested for its own sake that he collected books about it, or was given them by his friends. Thus one of these volumes was a gift from one of his officers, Jean le Fuzelier; Pierre Sauvage, one of his secretaries, gave him another, and two more were presents from his lifelong friend and doctor, Jean Caillau. These treatises, written at a time when medicine so often concerned itself with a man's temperament, may very likely have provided, for one who had only too much time to think about himself, wise guidance in general. One of them that begins 'Maladie est une mauvaise disposition' suggests as much. In addition to medical books there were no doubt lessons to be drawn from one whose subject was *L'Information des Princes*, from another on the government of kings and princes, which apparently came from one of his servants, beginning

---

* See page 143 above, and Appendix III.
† See Appendix III.

'a son especial seigneur', and a third whose title speaks for itself–
Consolation a ung grant seigneur estant en tribulacion'.

But for the spiritual sustenance and consolation which he must have
needed in this long trial of his patience and fortitude, Charles relied
chiefly on edifying works, and by far the greater part of his library in
England consisted of such things as the Bible, breviaries, psalters,
missals and books of hours, lives of the saints, the Virgin and Christ,
the works of St. Augustine, St. Gregory and St. Jerome, and collections
of prayers and devout meditations.

Proof of how much his reading in this kind meant to him is to be
found in the fact that he had made for him in England two manuscripts
containing what one may presume were the prayers that had a particular appeal for him and that he read most frequently. The bigger of these
two is an exquisite manuscript written in a beautiful hand in double
columns on very fine vellum and illuminated.[23] It contains a great many
prayers addressed to different saints, several of them English, which
seem to suggest that he had read similar texts in English and had them
translated. Among other prayers are one for those who suffer "a cause
du government des peuples" one for prisoners, and one for a man in
adversity, tribulation and grief, ending 'Misericors'. Another is a prayer
to support misfortunes patiently. The other manuscript is shorter[24] and
consists mainly of a series of extracts from the works of St. Bernard,
St. Augustine, Hugh of St. Victor and John of Hovendene.

In addition to these manuscripts, the perfection of whose writing
proves them to have been the work of professional scribes, presumably
at the duke's orders, the inventory of his books mentions two others
written in his own hand, both of which have until recently been thought
to be lost.[25] One of them has still not been found but the other, described
in the inventory as "a paper booklet written in my said lord's hand,
containing several prayers" has, it is claimed,* recently been identified.
If this claim is justified, as it may well be, this very personal-looking
and rather shabby little notebook, so obviously used for jotting things
down almost anyhow, without regard to the actual writing and with frequent erasures and alterations, is as poignantly evocative of Charles'
sojourn in England and the ways in which he filled the long, lonely
days, as are the boards for his favourite games of chess and tables, which
are also listed in the inventory, and a beautiful manuscript entitled
De Ludis Scachorum, giving the rules for playing all these games, and

* See Appendix I, both for the books of prayers and the little notebook.

with annotations in his own hand, which he may well have made during those monotonous years.

But much more evocative still is the mention of a manuscript described as "The book of my Lord's Ballades, with his arms on the clasp" and which contained all those that he wrote in captivity. This particular manuscript has not yet been identified with certainty, but from several contemporary copies its contents are known.[26] Although, except in one or two instances, the poems were not dated, their subject matter reveals to a great extent the periods of Charles' imprisonment to which they belong. And from what we know of the different circumstances of it, it would appear that he wrote a number during those six years or more that he spent at Bolingbroke, when he had so few outside distractions and had to rely not only on his love of reading and meditating, but on that greatest of all his resources, his gift of poetry, to feed not only his mind and spirit, but his heart too. What it meant for an absent lover to be able to express his feelings in this way he tells us himself:

> Loué soit cellui qui trouva
> Premier la maniere d'escrire;
> En ce, grant confort ordonna
> Pour amans qui sont en martire;
> Car quant ne peuent aler dire
> A leur dames leur grief tourment,
> Ce leur est moult d'alegement
> Quant par escript peuent mander
> Les maulx qu'ilz portent humblement
> Pour bien et loyaument amer.

That Charles was speaking of himself when he wrote those lines is obvious. And so full are the *ballades* that he wrote then of memories, hopes and fears, of longing and of suffering, all expressed with the utmost simplicity, that it would be difficult to doubt their sincerity, or that, although he never names her, they were addressed to his wife, Bonne, from whom he had been so long separated. The terms that he constantly applies to her: 'Jeune, gente Princesse', 'Jeune, gente, nompareille Princesse,' are the same as those that he made use of in the earlier *ballades*, written when he was still in France, to praise her whom he then called 'Ma seule souveraine joye'. And he underlines this when he calls her: 'Belle, nompareille de France' and 'Ma joye, mon seul souvenir'. In these *ballades* that must certainly have been written during those first fourteen years of his captivity, his love for her and the varying emotions it causes him are his sole themes. In the early days in England, when he first finds himself

> Loingtain de vous, ma tresbelle maistresse,
> Fors que de cueur que laissié je vous ay

he intends, until he can see her 'gent corps plaisant et gracieux' to put a brave face on things:

> certes j'endureray,
> Au desplaisir des jalous envieux,
> Et me tendray, par semblance, joyeux.

and he assures her that

> Vostre toujours soye, jennes ou vieulx,
> Priant a Dieu, ma seule desirance,
> Qu'il vous envoit s'avoir ne povez mieulx,
> Autant de bien que j'ay de desplaisance.

That his heart remained faithful to her throughout those years of separation can hardly be doubted, for there is never any wavering in his protestations, nor diminution in their warmth:

> De ma part je vous fais promesse
> Qu'en un propos me tiens tousjours,
> Sans jamais penser le rebours
> C'est que seray toute ma vie
> Vostre du tout entierement.

He will never forget her:

> Belle que je tiens pour amye,
> Pensés, quelque part que je soye,
> Que jamais je ne vous oublie.

He has left her his heart, his most treasured pledge; nothing could take it from her except death:

> C'estoit mon cueur que j'ordonnoye
> Pour avecques vous demourer,
> A qui je suis entierement.
> Nul ne m'en pourroit destourber
> Fors que la mort tant seulement.

But gradually the long pain of separation and loneliness eats into him. Sometimes physical desire for her so overwhelms him that he hugs his pillow and cries aloud:

> Quant en mon lit doy reposer de nuis,
> Penser m'assault et Desir me guerrie:
> Et en pensant maintesfois m'est advis
> Que je vous tiens entre mes bras, m'amye;
> Lors acolle mon oreiller et crie.

and again:

> Ardant desir de veoir ma maistresse
> A assailly de nouvel le logis
> De mon las cueur, qui languist en tristesse,
> Et puis dedens par tout a le feu mis.

He longs to see her again but fears he never may; if that cannot be granted he wants only death:

> Belle, que tant veoir vouldroye,
> Je prie a Dieu que brief vous voye;
> Ou s'il ne le veult accorder,
> Je lui suply treshumblement
> Que riens ne me vueille donner
> Fors que la mors tant seulement.

And again:

> Pour ce que veoir ne vous puis,
> Mon cueur se complaint jours et nuis,
> Belle, nompareille de France.

All this frustration and suffering wrenches from him the marvellous line: 'Je suis cellui au cueur vestu de noir.'

He continually begs her to remain as loyal to him as he is to her:

> Soiés seure, ma doulce amie,
> Que je vous ayme loyaument.
> Or, vous requier et vous supplie
> Acquittiez vous pareillement.

She would appear to have written to him from time to time and these signs of her continuing remembrance of him fill him with joy:

> . . . humblement vous mercie,
> Car par escript vous a pleu me donner
> Ung doulx confort.

Once indeed she was moved to write him a little *chanson* herself, which he put in his manuscript, and quoted in one of his own poems:

> Mon seul amy, mon bien, ma joye,
> Cellui que sur tous amer veulx,
> Je vous pry que soyez joyeux
> En esperant que brief vous voye.
>
> Car je ne fais quequerir voye
> De venir vers vous, se m'aist Dieux,
> Mon seul amy, mon bien, ma joye,
> Cellui que sur tous amer veulx.

It was not a very original lyric and obviously full of echoes, but it touched him to the heart, and the suggestion that she was trying to come to see him filled him with hope:

> Je sens ces motz mon cueur percer
> Si doulcement que ne sauroye
> Le confort, au vray, vous mander
> Que vostre message m'envoye.
> Car vous dictes que querez voye
> De venir vers moy; se m'aid Dieux,
> Demander ne vouldroye mieulx,
> En esperant que brief vous voye.

To keep him in good heart he begs her

> Jeune, gente, nompareille Princesse,
> Puis que ne puis veoir vostre jeunesse,
> De m'escrire ne vous vueilliez lasser;
> Car vous faictes, je le vous certiffie,
> Grant aumosne, dont je vous remercie,
> Quant il vous plaist d'ainsi me conforter!

This message from her raised his spirits to such a pitch that, as though to relieve them, he gives his fancy rein in a poem full of those favourite personifications of his, relating how, at the instance of his lady, Hope has engaged Comfort to bring her over to him by 'la nef de Bonne Nouvelle'. He prays for 'un plaisant vent venant de France' to bring the ship quickly over the sea of Fortune into the port of Desire, and prays Hope to guard it from the sea pirates that are in league with

'Dangier' who, in his language, stands both for danger and, by a sort of verbal association, the 'pays d'Angleterre'. He carried this joyful note on through several other *ballades*, all peopled with the same fancies. And to Bonne herself he developed a charming fantasy of how he keeps the heart she left with him wrapped up in a head-scarf placed, for greater security, in the coffer of his memory. To keep it nice he has often washed it in the tears of Piteous Thought and dried it in the fire of Hope. He therefore trusts that she is keeping the heart he gave her locked up in Good Will. In another *ballade* he relates how he keeps in his thought a mirror he bought from Love, in which he always sees the beauty

> De celle que l'en doit nommer
> Par droit la plus belle de France.

In addition to the *ballades*, two of the four poems that he called *Caroles* seem also to be addressed to Bonne, one of them with the refrain 'M'avez vous point mis en oubly?' and the other which begins and ends with the poignant short line 'Las! Merencolie' which one can almost hear sung to a lute.

But it was not in Charles' nature to grieve only for himself during his captivity. He was not merely a lover separated from his beloved. He was a great prince of the fleur-de-lis, who was paying the price of his country's defeat at Agincourt. That defeat, as Henry V had so bluntly pointed out to him after the battle, was in large part due to the degradation into which France had sunk. Even if Charles himself had not realised this at the time, he obviously brooded over it during the years of captivity, until the pain it caused him became unbearable and broke out in one of his greatest poems, a long *Complainte* that is like a cry addressed to the 'Trescrestian, franc royaume de France!', the line with which each stanza ends.

It is a most noble poem, which opens with his regret that his country, once a pattern to all others for honour, loyalty, courtesy, prowess, has now sunk so low. The reason, he states frankly, is that her great pride, gluttony, laziness, envy, lack of justice and lechery have caused God to punish her. But she need not despair, for God is full of mercy and will heal the country if humbly prayed. To encourage her and summon up her pride in herself again, he reminds her of her ancient greatness, of such symbols of it as her war-cry 'Montjoye', her arms with the three golden fleur-de-lis on the azure ground, the *oriflamme* which once led her to victory over her enemies, the sacred unction with which her kings were crowned, the popes who honoured her and the great champions that Christianity once found in her: Charlemagne, Roland, Oliver, Saint Louis. Therefore she must not depair, but strive to live again as once she did, and God, Our Lady and the saints will forget the past and help her. The poem ends movingly with his simple admission of how he wrote it while he was still young and in prison, but already filled with that ardent desire for peace which later inspired him with a still greater poem:

> Et je, Charles, duc d'Orlians, rimer
> Voulu ces vers ou temps de ma jeunesse,
> Devant chascun les vueil bien advouer,
> Car prisonnier les fis, je le confesse;
> Priant a Dieu, qu'avant qu'aye vieillesse,
> Le temps de paix partout puist avenir,
> Comme de Cueur j'en ay la desirance,
> Et que voye tous tes maulx brief finir,
> Trescrestian, franc royaume de France!

It seems probable that, situated as he then was, Charles wrote this poem more to relieve his own pent-up feelings of regret and sorrow for the past, and to comfort himself with hopes for the future, than with any .dea that it could serve some purpose at the time when he wrote it. But curiously enough, while he was still at Bolingbroke, this unspoken rallying call of his to his own country to find again her ancient virtue was, as it were, echoed in France itself by another voice, a wholly unexpected one, the voice of the young peasant girl, Joan of Arc. Stranger still, it was in large part the thought of him, held captive in England while his enemies were ravaging his lands that he was powerless to defend himself, that impelled her to undertake her hazardous mission. We have her own word for that when she declared at her trial that she knew very well that God loved the Duke of Orleans, and for that reason she had more revelations about him than about any man alive, except him whom she called her king;[27] that God had sent her an angel as a sign of the merits of the king and the good Duke of Orleans; that Saint Margaret and Saint Catherine had told her she would cross the sea within three years to bring the duke back, and that if she had been allowed to continue for three years, she would have had enough English prisoners to achieve this. It was in fact against the chivalric

Photo. Archives Photographiques, Paris

5 The Bastard of Orleans, Count of Dunois, a statue at the castle of Châteaudun

code of the time for an enemy to attack the lands of an absent lord, especially of one whom he held captive, and there was indignation in France that the English should do so. But that a simple shepherdess in far-away Lorraine should have shared this indignation is not the least of the many mysteries about her.

It would be pleasant to think that Charles himself had the consolation of knowing that this strange champion had arisen to defend not only his cause but that of France itself. Although he never made any reference to her, there is no reason why he should not have done, since both his brother the Bastard and his son-in-law Alençon became her daily companions-in-arms, and we know that he was kept in touch with their exploits. It was in gratitude for all the Bastard had already done and was doing that, in March 1427, Charles, writing from the village of Bourne in Lincolnshire,* had made an outright gift to him of his own County of Porcien in Champagne, to be held by him in future in direct homage to the king. Charles gave him also the manor of Champ-le-Roy in Romorantin,[28] south of Blois. Not only Charles but the dauphin had reason to be grateful to the Bastard at that time; and in 1428, after he had driven the English out of Châteaudun in the County of Dunois,[29] the dauphin made him Count of Dunois, although as often as not he continued to be called, and to sign himself, 'the Bastard'.

Soon afterwards Charles was to have even greater reason for gratitude to his brother, for in July 1429 the war, that had continued sporadically for so long, suddenly flared into fierce action. The Earl of Salisbury, who had gone to England to seek reinforcements, returned with a fresh army and marched swiftly towards Orleans, taking many of the duke's strongholds—Meung-sur-Loire, Beaugency, Jargeau and Châteauneuf-sur-Loire—on the way. By October he, and the Earl of Suffolk who had joined him, reached Orleans and there prepared for their six-month-long siege of the city, which the Bastard held on behalf of his brother and as the dauphin's lieutenant-general.

When Joan, full of her belief that she could raise the siege, reached

* Although there is no official record of a move to Bourne, Charles must sometimes have been taken to places in the vicinity of the castles where he was imprisoned. There is, for instance, one document written at Peterborough, where he is not otherwise known to have been. Many structural repairs were carried out at Bolingbroke just before he was sent there, and it was possibly the continuance of these that made it necessary to lodge him elsewhere at times. (See *The History of the King's Works*, II, 572.)

the castle of Chinon and asked to see the dauphin in March 1429, one of the first people she met there was the Duke of Alençon. He accepted and believed in her from the first, and she on her side became devoted to him, partly because he was Charles' son-in-law, always addressing him as 'gentil duc' or 'mon bon duc'.[30] He testified later that he heard her say that her mission had four aims: to beat the English, have the dauphin crowned at Rheims, deliver the Duke of Orleans and raise the siege of his city. At some moment during her long wait for the dauphin's permission to set out for Orleans, Alençon took her to see his young wife, Charles' daughter Jane, who told her how much she feared for her husband, who had only come out of prison two years before, that they had had to spend a great sum for his ransom, and that she would give much if he might remain with her. To this Joan replied: "Madame, do not fear, I will send him back to you safe and sound, and in even better state than he is in now."[31]

Alençon was not able to accompany Joan when at last she set out with a convoy for Orleans, for he was still on parole, not having yet quite finished paying his huge ransom, which had left him "the poorest man in France",[32] and had obliged him, among other things, to sell his great castle of Fougères to his uncle the Duke of Brittany. Raoul de Gaucourt, who had been Governor of Orleans since 1425, accompanied her instead, leading her and her convoy, as the Bastard had instructed, to the south side of the river, which he crossed to meet her. When she rounded on him for not having had her taken to the side where the English were, telling him that God had sent her because He "had taken pity on the town of Orleans and would not allow the enemy to take both the duke and his town", and the wind veered at that moment to make the crossing possible, his belief in her divine mission was confirmed.

After the victory the Council of Charles of Orleans felt it incumbent on them to show their gratitude to the Maid, for her deliverance of their lord's chief town from the hands of the English, by making her a gift. It may be that, being themselves in Blois, none of them had met Joan (although she had passed through there) or knew anything of her other than her great deed in raising the siege. And it does not look as if they had thought of asking advice from her companions-in-arms, all of whom well knew that she cared only for such things as would serve her military purposes—as Alençon had realised the moment they met at Chinon, where he gave her a horse as soon as he saw how well she could ride and manage a lance. Left to their own devices, then, the Council chose the most unsuitable gift that could well be devised for Joan; and the bill still exists[33] for the costly robe of fine vermilion Brussels cloth, lined, with a head-dress of pale green, both trimmed with white silk, all of the very best materials and costing thirteen gold *écus*. The records state that it was given to her by the Council "having regard to the good and agreeable services that the said maid had rendered them at the encounter with the English, ancient enemies of our lord the king and ourselves." What Joan said in acknowledging the gift is not recorded.

She had in any case little time for such matters then, for as soon as Orleans had been relieved, she and the Bastard with the other captains sought out the dauphin, who had now reached the castle of Loches, to obtain permission to pursue the enemy and strive to recapture the Loire towns so recently taken by the English. The dauphin agreed to the proposal and sent Alençon with them. They were victorious everywhere and at one hard-fought battle, at Jargeau a little to the east of Orleans, they took prisoner the Earl of Suffolk who, after the death of Salisbury, had been in command of the English forces at Orleans. It was a grim day for him, for during that same battle two of his remaining brothers (the eldest had died at Agincourt) were killed, while the fourth was taken prisoner with him.[34] This holocaust might well have been the end of the Suffolks, if the Earl had not had the good fortune to be a captive of the Bastard, who not long afterwards granted him his liberty on easy terms, a magnanimity that was to stand his brother of Orleans in very good stead.

Now that Joan had liberated the main towns belonging to Charles round the Loire, she marched to Rheims for the coronation of the dauphin, thus completing the second of her fourfold aims. But thereafter virtue seemed to go out of her and she was unable to galvanise the new king into further action or to win further victories. However, although she had neither wholly conquered the English nor liberated Charles, she had contributed more than she knew to both these aims. Her successes, and the fear of her supposed witch-like powers that she had instilled in the English common soldiers, weakened their morale and made it difficult to recruit new troops. To restore their self-confidence and their sense of national pride, the Duke of Bedford suggested that the young king should come to France. To make such a step effective he must first be crowned in England.

Henry VI, then a child of eight, was crowned in Westminster on November 6th 1429. Even before that, any royal letters concerning his cousin Charles of Orleans had always been couched in terms of affection quite unlike those used by his father; and now that he was king he was to take a much more liberal and generous line concerning his royal prisoner and his ultimate release than either his father or his Council had done. It is indeed not impossible that he had a hand in an alteration in Charles' circumstances that occurred soon after his coronation, although this might also have been a result of the general awareness that resistance in France was still a force to be reckoned with, and that French prisoners therefore still had importance. Whatever the reason for it, at the end of December 1429, Charles' six-and a-half years' sojourn in Lincolnshire was brought to an end. Although the keeper to whose care he was now consigned was not necessarily an improvement on his previous guardian, a change in itself must have been welcome; and it was at least something to feel that he was not quite forgotten by his captors. In the event the change proved a stepping-stone to a happier fate.

Another event that autumn that boded well for him, although he could not then have known it, was the arrival in England in November of Isabella, daughter of King John of Portugal and grand-daughter of old John of Gaunt, on her way to Flanders to marry Philip the Good of Burgundy. A few years later Charles was to have reason to feel the utmost gratitude to this remarkable princess.

CHAPTER TEN
1430–1432

THE man to whose care Charles of Orleans was transferred was that tough old campaigner, Sir John Cornwall, whose debtor he had been ever since the Treaty of Buzançais in 1412. With the money that Cornwall had gained from the wars in which he had spent his life—either in recompense for his services or by way of ransoms for the prisoners he had taken—he had built himself a castle at Ampthill in Bedfordshire, on a splendid site commanding great views of the country round (a castle now demolished). And it was there that Sir Thomas Comberworth brought his prisoner on December 29th, 1429.[1] We are not told why Sir John had become the keeper of Charles, but from what we know of him it seems not unlikely that he had himself asked for the position, the better to keep an eye on the duke's finances, in order to extract the sums that were still owing to him.

Charles had not been a month with Cornwall before the latter brought him to London on January 27th, where he stayed for some two or three weeks. The reason for this visit is unknown, nor do we know where the duke lodged while he was there; he was certainly not with Cornwall then, as the latter received no money for him at that time. This we know from the fact that it was decreed in the following May that, with the exception of those three weeks, Cornwall should be remunerated at the same rate as Comberworth had received for the past two years, for as long as Charles should remain in his custody.[2] These payments to both Comberworth and Cornwall were made by the king "for their great labours and expenses" in looking after their prisoner who, as we know, paid for his keep.[3]

Cornwall endured this great labour of keeping Charles for two and a half years, a period that for his captive must have been a time of considerable suspense, as the tide of war between England and France ebbed and flowed, bringing him increasing financial difficulties. But it brought him, too, fresh evidence of the efforts of his brother the Bastard to help him with these, efforts that before long were to bring an important amelioration of his lot in other ways than the merely financial. Before those things happened, however, the actual events of the war were enough to fill the waiting duke with anxieties for both his country and his kin. The Duke of Bedford's wise counsel had proved right, for when at the end of April 1430 the young Henry VI crossed to Calais with a freshly recruited army, the war flared up anew and the Burgundian troops flocked to help their English allies lay siege to Compiègne.

At the news of this, Joan of Arc managed to escape from the galling inactivity of Charles VII's court at Bourges, and at the end of May she entered the besieged town with her former companions-in-arms Alençon and Gaucourt who, with the Bastard, had won many strongholds from the English earlier in the year in the lands round the Seine north of Paris. But whatever hope Joan's presence may have bred in the defenders of Compiègne, it was to be quickly dashed. For on the evening of her arrival, when she sallied out of the town with Alençon and Gaucourt, she and her soldiers were at once cut off and the Maid was taken prisoner by the Burgundians, who were to keep her in prison for five months before their duke finally sold her to the English. With Joan now out of the war for good, the spirit seemed to go out of the French soldiers, in spite of the courage of the Bastard and his friends. One after the other they lost to the English the places that had been won earlier in the year, and by July 29th the young Henry VI, who all this time had been at Calais, was able to make a state entry into Rouen. Not long afterwards the English resumed once more the government of Paris.

The direct result of these English successes on Charles of Orleans was that, in September, the English in Rouen ordered that in future all the revenues from the Norman possessions of both Charles and Alençon were to be collected in the name of the English king,[4] and presumably kept by him. This reduced Charles to even worse financial straits than before. But in spite of it he had some fresh hope then because, for the previous six months, the Bastard had been working on an ingenious plan to help him to free John. Nothing could better illustrate the Bastard's loyalty and devotion to his brothers than these efforts on their behalf, especially when he was at the same time engaged in defending their lands; nor reveal more clearly his general magnanimity than the method of helping that he now proposed.

There was in the keeping of Tanguy du Châtel, the Provost of Paris, an English prisoner called Sir Thomas Beaufort, who had been captured at the battle of Baugé in March 1421. His identity is obscure, but for some reason the Duchess of Clarence was particularly anxious to secure his release.[5] It was perhaps because of pressure on her part that the Bastard of Orleans now suggested to Tanguy an arrangement whereby his brother Charles should try and find Beaufort's ransom of 28,000 *écus*, in return for which Beaufort promised that, when released, he would see that that amount was deducted from the sum still owed to the Duchess of Clarence for John of Angoulême.[6] The second part of this rather complicated plan concerned the Earl of Suffolk who, it will be remembered, had been taken prisoner by the Bastard at the battle of Jargeau in June 1429. The Bastard, between whom and his prisoner a mutual sympathy seems to have sprung up, offered in February 1430 to release him on parole, provided he paid his agreed ransom of 20,000 *écus* to the Duchess of Clarence as yet another contribution to the freeing of John of Angoulême.

All concerned agreed to this plan and Charles spent much of his time both that year and the next desperately trying to collect the 28,000 *écus* needed to free Beaufort. And he showed his gratitude to the Bastard by creating him Count of Périgord in July 1431, and appointing him Captain of the castle and town of Blois.[7] Since the Bastard freed Suffolk soon after the arrangement had been made, presumably the latter kept his part of the bargain by paying his own ransom to the duchess. But it seems unlikely that Charles managed to collect the total sum demanded for Thomas Beaufort, although it appears that he may have managed to pay a good part of it; for seven years later, in November 1436, Jean le Fuzelier approached Tanguy du Châtel for a loan of 23,000 *écus* "guaranteed by the finance of the late messire Thomas de Beaufort".[8] Whether or not Tanguy had in the meantime allowed Thomas to return and spend his few remaining years in England we do not know.

It is strange, and sad, to reflect that, during twelve months of that period while the Bastard was striving so diligently to help his brothers, from May 1430 to May 1431, Joan of Arc, who had done so much to assist both Charles and the Bastard, was first languishing in prison and then enduring the cruel trial that was to end with her burning by the English at Rouen on May 29th. Naturally enough, her English judges called no French witnesses to speak for her, so that it was only at her rehabilitation twenty years later that Dunois, Alençon and Gaucourt were able to pay their tributes to her.[9] Any attempts to rescue so closely-guarded a prize would no doubt have been out of the question for them, but it is impossible that her old companions-in-arms, and particularly the Bastard and Alençon, should not have chafed at their inability to help her. As they could not, at least in striving to help Charles the Bastard was indirectly helping Joan to achieve one of her four aims. He appears indeed to have been so intent on these efforts of his, and the journeys in which they involved him, that for the time being at any rate he took no part in any French resistance to the English, who continued on their successful way until, by November, Henry VI was able to enter Paris in state, there to be crowned King of France in Notre-Dame on December 16th 1431. Thanks to the Bastard's freeing of him Suffolk was able to be present. Henry only spent ten days in his new capital, leaving on the 27th for Rouen and Calais whence, on February 9th, he returned to England.

For Charles at that time it must have seemed as if the future held no hope at all. With the best will in the world his brother the Bastard had not been able to help him. In 1432 came the sad news that his only child Jane, Alençon's wife, had died aged only twenty-two. It is probable, too, that it was just at that time that a worse sorrow still befell him, cutting the dearest of the links that still bound him to his own country and his past life. His first warning of it came with the news that his wife, Bonne, had fallen ill. For a time she rallied but not for long, and this more cheering news was followed by that of her death.[10] No document survives to tell us what was the disease that killed this young woman, still only in her early thirties, nor where she died. But there can be little doubt that, of the poems that Charles wrote in England, those that express his anxiety at hearing of the illness of his love, and his despair at the news of her death were addressed to Bonne* and were written to ease his pain at his cruel loss, the sharpest personal grief that he had yet had to bear. They are perhaps the most beautiful of all his *ballades*.

Even before this fatal news he had sometimes feared that he might never see her again. After the poem in which he had lamented that he could not see her youth, he seems to have passed through a period of increasing despair and hopelessness that wrung from him the cry 'Hélas! la verray je jamais?'. He girded against Fortune for the length of his exile:

> Les maulx que m'avez fait souffrir,
> Il a ja plusieurs ans passez;
> Doy je tousjours ainsi languir?
> Hélas! et n'est ce pas assés?

* See Appendix II

He could bear everything but his absence from Bonne:

> Tous maulx suy contant de porter,
> Fors un seul, qui trop fort m'ennuye,
> C'est qu'il me fault loing demourer
> De celle que tiens pour amye;

But to chase away his melancholy he comforted himself with the remembrance that she had once written to him:

> C'estes vous de qui suis amye.

He had indeed tried to lessen his longing by taking part in such innocent pleasures as the traditional processions of May Day, but when one of these happened to be wet it suited his mood better:

> Le premier jour du mois de May
> S'acquitte vers moy grandement;
> Car, ainsi qu'a present je n'ay
> En mon cueur que dueil et tourment,
> Il est aussi pareillement
> Troublé, plain de vent et de pluie.

So great is his depression that for the first time doubts of her enter his heart. He reminds her how she had freely promised to love him as long as he lived,

> Non pour tant, me fault vous ouvrir
> La doubte qu'en moy est entree,
> C'est que j'ay paeur, sans vous mentir,
> Que ne m'ayez, tresbelle nee,
> Mis en oubly; car mainte annee
> Suis loingtain de vous longuement,
> Et n'oy de vous aucunement
> Nouvelle pour avoir liesse;
> Pour quoy vis doloreusement,
> Ma Dame, ma seule maistress.

The pains of doubt were soon changed to a real panic of anxiety when the news that she is grievously ill cast his heart into such despair.

> Qu'il souhaide piteusement la mort
> Et dit qu'il est ennuyé de sa vie.

He tries to comfort his heart by telling it that Fortune could not be so cruel as to take her from this world, but he cannot, and he implores God to cure her. In the following *ballade* he celebrates the news he has received of her recovery. But this short-lived relief is quickly followed by the news of her death, that draws from him one of the most beautiful and poignant of all his poems:

> Las! Mort qui t'a fait si hardie,
> De prendre la noble Princesse
> Qui estoit mon confort, ma vie,
> Mon bien, mon plaisir, ma richesse!
> Puis que tu as prins ma maistresse,
> Prens moy aussi son serviteur,
> Car j'ayme mieulx prouchainnement
> Mourir que languir en tourment,
> En paine, soussi et doleur!
>
> Las! de tous biens estoit garnie
> Et en droitte fleur de jeunesse!
> Je pry a Dieu qu'il te maudie,
> Faulse Mort, plaine de rudesse!
> Se prise l'eusses en vieillesse,
> Ce ne fust pas si grant rigueur;
> Mais prise l'as hastivement,
> Et m'as laissié piteusement
> En paine, soussi et doleur.
>
> Las! je suy seul, sans compaignie!
> Adieu ma Dame, ma lyesse!
> Or est nostre amour departie,
> Non pour tant, je vous fais promesse
> Que de prieres, a largesse,
> Morte vous serviray de cueur,
> Sans oublier aucunement;
> Et vous regretteray souvent
> En paine, soussi et doleur.
>
> Dieu, sur tout souverain Seigneur,
> Ordonnez, par grace et doulceur,

De l'ame d'elle, tellement
Qu'elle ne soit pas longuement
En paine, soussy et doleur!

This anguished cry of grief is followed by several more *ballades* recording the pains that his realisation of his loss cause him. One of them, telling of how her death makes him feel the vanity of all earthly things, seems like a forerunner of Villon's 'Ballade des dames du temps jadis':

Quant Souvenir me ramentoit
La grant beauté dont estoit plaine,
Celle que mon cueur appelloit
Sa seule Dame souveraine,
De tous biens la vraye fontaine,
Qui est morte nouvellement,
Je dy, en pleurant tendrement;
Ce monde n'est que chose vaine!

Ou vieil temps grant renom couroit
De Creseide, Yseud, Elaine
Et maintes autres qu'on nommoit
Parfaittes en beauté haultaine.
Mais, au derrain, en son demaine
La Mort les prist piteusement;
Par quoy puis veoir clerement
Ce monde n'est que chose vaine.

On New Year's Day (presumably the one following her death) he remembers how he used to wonder what present to give her; but now that Death has taken her out of this world all he can do is to pray for her soul:

Non pour tant, pour tousjours garder
La coustume que j'ay usee,
Et pour a toutes gens moustrer
Que pas n'ay ma Dame oubliee,
De messes je l'ay estrenée;
Car ce me seroit trop de blasme
De l'oublier ceste journee,
Je pry a Dieu qu'il en ait l'ame.

183

Tellement lui puist prouffiter
Ma priere que confortee
Soit son ame, sans point tarder,
Et de ses bienfais guerdonnee,
En Paradis et couronnee
Comme la plus loyalle Dame
Qu'en son vivant j'aye trouvee:
Je pry a Dieu qu'il en ait l'ame.

Quant je pense a la renommee
Des grans biens dont estoit paree,
Mon povre cueur de dueil se pasme;
De lui souvent est regrettee:
Je pry a Dieu qu'il en ait l'ame.

When May Day came round and, according to a prevailing custom, lovers had to choose between the flower and the leaf, Charles chose the leaf

Car la fleur, que mon cueur amoit
Plus que nulle autre creature,
Est hors de ce monde passee,

and he wanted no other. Without Bonne he feels he has lost his way and become 'l'homme esgaré qui ne scet ou il va'. All the customary feasts have lost their savour for him. On St. Valentine's Day, when he hears the birds 'parlans leur latin' as they choose their mates, it only reminds him that he has lost his.

But after a time a good doctor comes to ease his grief. He is called Nonchaloir (indifference or resignation) and from now on 'Nonchaloir' becomes one of the favourite characters in Charles' gallery of abstract personifications, along with 'Dueil', 'Tristesse', 'Espoir', 'Destresse', 'Douleur', 'Pitié' and of course 'Dangier'. 'Nonchaloir' reconciles him to his fate, and in thought he buries Bonne under a 'stone' of gold with blue sapphires that signify Loyalty.

J'ay fait l'obseque de ma Dame
Dedens le moustier amoureux

and resolves 'N'en parlons plus', for

De riens ne servent plours ne plains:
Tous mourrons, ou tart ou briefment:

CHAPTER TEN

Nul ne peut garder longuement
Le tresor de tous biens mondains.

But however resigned and philosophical he tried to be, he could not escape the sense of loneliness that wrung from him that bitter cry 'Las! je suis seul!'

FORTUNATELY for Charles a change of scene, a change of company and a change of preoccupation were at hand to rescue him from the pit of loneliness and despair into which he may well have fallen. By means of them he was enabled, at this critical period of his life, to break the bonds of frustrating inactivity that had held him captive for seventeen years, and play a part in the politics of the time that was in the end to lead to his own release.

The Earl of Suffolk's readiness to help Charles in the matter of John's ransom will be remembered. Although nothing had come of that, Suffolk did not forget his gratitude to the Bastard, which had moved him to it, and not long after his return to England from Paris, where he had been in charge of the ceremony of Henry VI's coronation, he showed it in a different way. In July of that year, 1432, Sir John Cornwall was created Baron Fanhope.[1] Whether because of this elevation he wished to be released from his custody of Charles, or whether a change of guardianship for the duke was in any case officially decided, is not known. Nor do we know whether Suffolk himself asked for the care of the prisoner or whether he was chosen for the office for some other reason. The relevant Privy Council minute[2] says that the Treasurers were empowered to "treat with the Earl of Suffolk to take Charles, the king's prisoner", but no doubt that merely refers to the practical arrangements they were to make. From all his subsequent relations with the duke it seems safe to infer that it was at Suffolk's own request that in August 1432[3] Charles was transferred to his keeping, and thus entered upon what was without doubt the happiest period so far of his captivity, in the company of a man of like tastes and aims with his own, without whose great power and influence with the king and in the country he might never have seen his own land again.

William de la Pole, the third Earl of Suffolk, was then a man of thirty-five, just two years younger than Charles. His father had died of dysentery at Harfleur, and William had succeeded to the title after the death of his elder brother Michael at Agincourt that same year. He entered the king's service when Henry V invaded France again in 1417, and had spent the next fourteen years fighting in all the campaigns there, in positions of increasing command and authority, until his capture at Jargeau in 1429 and again, after his release, until the coronation of Henry VI. But although he was a brave soldier he was also, like Charles but in a lesser degree, a poet and a lover of letters. During his brief period of imprisonment he had written several poems, chiefly *ballades*, addressed to his absent lady on the usual themes of faithful love and the pains of absence.[4] In addition to this poetic gift he had two other characteristics that distinguished him sharply from the majority of his fellow English nobles: an instinctive liking for the French, even while he was fighting them, so strong that it evoked an answering sympathy in them; and a political sense that enabled him, as time went on, to realise the folly of this war that had robbed him personally of a father and three brothers, and had reduced both kingdoms to a state of impoverishment. It was therefore to the cause of peace that, after his return with the king, he dedicated himself.

But first Suffolk had affairs of his own to attend to. His own chief estate was at Wingfield, on the border between Norfolk and Suffolk, where he possessed a moated, crenellated castle of which the towered entrance gate and part of its flanking walls, with the foundations of the chapel, still remain. But he had for some time been equally at home in the village of Ewelme in Oxfordshire, where his family had close links with that of the Chaucers, who were lords of the manor there. These links Suffolk forged more firmly in 1431 or 1432 by marrying Alice, Thomas Chaucer's only daughter and thus the grand-daughter of the poet, who succeeded to the manor of Ewelme on the death of both her parents within the four succeeding years. Thereafter she and her husband divided their time between Wingfield and Ewelme, endowing both with beautiful buildings. In both places their houses were the resort of civilized company where poets like Lydgate, who had been a great friend of Thomas Chaucer and whose main centre was at Bury St. Edmunds, in the same county as Wingfield, were made welcome.

For Charles to find himself in such company after so many comparatively solitary years must have been like coming into the fresh air from a stuffy room. Although as a royal prisoner he was still always under strict surveillance by special guards (it was no doubt partly for the expense of providing these that Suffolk was paid 14s. 4d. a day),[5] he was also frequently in the earl's company and went with him occasionally from his castle at Wingfield to his father-in-law's manor in Oxfordshire.[6] Charles was thus able to enjoy both the poetic melancholy of the flat pastoral lands of Suffolk and the more intimate charm of the little village of Ewelme, cradled among gentle slopes, with its clear stream running close to the manor. Now again, too, he could sometimes enjoy the pleasure of feminine company, of which he may well not have had much since those far-off days when Robert Waterton used to take him from Pontefract to his own home at Methley, until Henry V put a stop to those occasional diversions. Added to all these things was the agreeable fact that he was with people who loved his country and spoke her tongue.

But Suffolk was too energetic and enterprising a man to allow his prisoner to idle away his days in the tranquil enjoyment of country scenes and civilized company. The presence of this great prince of the royal house of France could but reinforce the earl's growing sense of the folly of war between their two countries, a view that, as we know, Charles had long held, seeing in peace the only hope of restoring his land to her ancient greatness; and it was not long before Suffolk involved the willing duke in his schemes in the cause of peace. Although none of their peers in England seems to have shared their views wholeheartedly, many were beginning to feel that the war had gone on long enough; and at the same time a sense of the futility of continuing hostilities was gradually being born in France.

The coronation of Henry VI in Paris had made no difference to the war, which the dauphin's forces under the Bastard had continued to wage briskly against the combined armies of Bedford and Burgundy. But in August 1432, just before Charles was handed over to Suffolk, the Duke of Bedford was taken ill during a battle fought in sultry heat at Lagny on the Marne, where the English were defeated by the Bastard and his army. A few months later the death of Bedford's young wife Anne of Burgundy loosened the ties between him and her brother Philip, who that autumn signed a temporary truce with the dauphin, as both he and the English still always called him. These events seem to have bred a kind of war-weariness in the English faction in France, which led to a peace-meeting at Auxerre in the last weeks of 1432. Henry VI, and the Dukes both of Burgundy and Brittany sent ambassadors to it, but the dauphin's representatives, who were for the moment in the stronger position, arrived late and imposed conditions which the other side felt unable to accept. The meeting was therefore adjourned until the following March, when it was agreed that they would assemble at Corbeil or Melun.[7]

One of the conditions insisted on by the French side was that the Agincourt prisoners should be conducted to some place in France where they could give their advice and counsel. Suffolk of course immediately saw the valuable rôle that Charles, the most important of the remaining captives, could thenceforth play if Henry VI and his Council would consent to this condition; and Charles himself hardly needed pressing to serve this cause that meant more to him than his own liberation. It is not difficult to imagine what it must have meant for him to be brought thus into the world of action again, after so many years of isolation from it. He entered into it wholeheartedly and from then onwards until his release he appears clad in a new vigour and firmness of purpose, while losing nothing of the patience that had always upheld him.

During that winter of 1432–3 therefore, encouraged of course by Suffolk without whose help he could have done nothing, he lost no chance of urging the young king to accede to that French condition, and of offering to do everything in his power to persuade his countrymen to discuss and accept reasonable terms if he were allowed to sit at the council table with them. He felt sure that the princes and others who had always been of his party would come to a peace conference if he asked them to. It was as if the mantle of his leadership of the Orleanist faction fell on his shoulders once again. Pressed thus by Charles and Suffolk, the king agreed to the proposition in general and informed the dauphin that he would bring the 'captive lords' to Calais, if the French would be willing to come and meet them there. Charles for his part sent messages, through the members of his own household, to his French friends begging them to come. When the time of the conference drew near, Cardinal Beaufort, the Chancellor, and the Dukes of Bedford and Gloucester went to Calais to await the French lords, to whom the king had sent the necessary safe-conducts to admit them to this piece of English soil. Charles was only to be allowed to join them there after his French friends had actually arrived. In the meantime he was sent to Dover to await the summons; and as the French had asked for the Agincourt prisoners in general, the Duke of Bourbon was sent to wait with him.

The meeting between the two cousins must have been a moving one, for as far as we know they had not seen each other for eighteen years, when they went their different ways after Agincourt. They had not lost all contact for at some point, presumably just before Bourbon was allowed by Henry V to go to France in 1420 to try to collect his ransom, Charles sent him a *ballade* beginning with good wishes for the success of his mission:

> Puis qu'ainsi est que vous alez en France
> Duc de Bourbon, mon compaignon treschier,
> Que Dieu vous doint, selon la desirance
> Que tous avons, bien povoir besongnier.

He then went on to give him a message for Bonne, 'Car un amy doir pour l'autre veiller'. All he asks is that he should tell his lady how it grieves him to be separated from her 'doulce compaignie'. If Bourbon pretends that he does not know who she is, Charles tells him he need merely seek the most accomplished lady there is; and he ends by begging his cousin 'Souviengne vous du fait du prisonnier.' It is a charming poem, without a shade of envy for what then seemed Bourbon's better luck than his, and surprisingly light-hearted considering that he himself had then been a prisoner for five years.

The only other interchange that we know of in the following years was when Bourbon sent Charles a present of some 'blans connins', to remind him, by means of a salacious pun ('connin' being both a rabbit and having also an easily-guessed, less innocent meaning), of the gay times with ladies they had enjoyed togethet in the past. In the *ballade* he wrote to thank Bourbon for his gift, Charles tells him he has forgotten all that and put all thoughts of physical love out of his mind.

> Quant aux connins que dittes qu'ay amez,
> Ils sont pour moy, plusieurs ans a passez,
> Mis en oubly; aussi mon instrument
> Qui les servoit a fait son testament
> Il est retrait et devenu hermite;
> Il dort tousjours, a parler vrayement,
> Comme celui qui en riens ne prouffite.

He urges Bourbon to try and do likewise, but the lusty, amorous duke was obviously unable to do so, for in 1423 there is a reference to a bastard he had managed to beget in England.[8]

After Bourbon returned from that long-ago fruitless journey to

France, he had never ceased to bombard the king and his Council with wordy documents begging to be released, on promises to fulfil within specified dates all the original conditions he had proposed but never been able to keep, and even, in his despair, frantically adding others, such as a promise to pay for the release of the two sons of the Earl of Somerset, "John and Thomas, brothers", taken prisoner at Baugé.[9] His insistence grew as his health degenerated and that had begun early. Even in Henry V's time we are told that the king had felt pity and compassion for him on account of it.[10] By 1429 it is recorded that, as a result of the different illnesses he had suffered, his limbs were so weakened and, as it were, broken, that he would no longer be able to bear arms even if he had to. But though they saw these things the English stuck to their demand that only after he had kept all his promises and paid would they let him go. From March 1427 Bourbon had been in the keeping of the Duke of Bedford, it is not said where but presumably at some house of his in England. But in 1428 Bedford had complained that the charge was too burdensome for him; and so in December 1429, when Charles left Bolingbroke for Ampthill, Bourbon was sent to take his place with Sir Thomas Comberworth.

It was there that Charles sent him, before their meeting at Dover, what is one of the most beautiful as well as one of the most self-revelatory of his *ballades*. Every line of it breathes the joy and hope that he was beginning to feel at the thought that the peace he had so long desired was now not far off. But in the midst of his rejoicing at this, he does not forget his dear cousin, for whose sufferings during his long captivity Charles has nothing but compassion. He longs, one can see, to cheer him with the idea that they may soon see each other again, and that peace will bring him release at last. Yet it is obvious that he does not wish to be too explicit as to this, perhaps for fear of raising hopes that might in the end be disappointed once more.

> Mon gracieux cousin, duc de Bourbon,
> Je vous requier, quant vous aurez loisir,
> Que me faittes, par balade ou chançon,
> De vostre estat aucunement sentir;
> Car quant a moy, sachiez que, sans mentir,
> Je sens mon cueur renouveller de joye,
> En esperant le bon temps avenir
> Par bonne paix que brief Dieu nous envoye.

Tout crestian, qui est loyal et bon,
Du bien de paix se doit fort resjoir,
Veu les grans maulx et la destruccion
Que guerre fait par tous pays courir.
Dieu a voulu Crestianté punir
Qui a laissié de bien vivre la voye;
Mais puis apres, il la veult secourir
Par bonne paix que brief Dieu nous envoye.

Et pour cela, mon treschier compaignon,
Vueilliez de vous desplaisance bannir,
En oubliant vostre longue prison
Qui vous a fait mainte doleur souffrir;
Merciez Dieu, pensez de le servir,
Il vous garde de tous biens grant montjoye
Et vous fera avoir vostre desir
Par bonne paix que brief Dieu nous envoye.

Resveilliez vous en joyeux souvenir,
Car j'ay espoir qu'encore je vous voye,
Et moy aussi, en confort et plaisir
Par bonne paix que brief Dieu nous envoye!

Although it is clear from this *ballade* that Charles knew Bourbon had suffered much, it is doubtful whether he realised to what a state of pitiful decrepitude the gay companion of his younger days had now been reduced, although he was still only just over fifty; and one can imagine what a shock the sight of him must have given Charles, and how painful were the six weeks that they spent in each other's company, as the time dragged on at Dover with no signal for them to proceed to Calais. For neither the dauphin nor his representatives, meeting at Corbeil, took any notice of Henry's message or made any attempt to get in touch with their countrymen. Well might, as Henry said, the "captive lords have been much troubled and displeased" at this neglect.[11] For Bourbon this last disappointment was the final blow. He returned to his solitary northern prison with all his hopes now gone, and less than a year later his shattered health gave way completely and he died at Bolingbroke on January 15th, 1434.[12] On February 12th Sir Thomas Comberworth was authorised to distribute his possessions locally, while his servants were given safe-conducts to return to the duchess and his son in France, to try to obtain money to pay his creditors.[13]

As for Charles, nothing could better illustrate his moods during those weeks at Dover than the *ballade* he wrote then, one of the best known of all his poems, as he gazed across the sea towards France:

> En regardant vers le païs de France,
> Un jour m'avint, a Dovre sur la mer,
> Qu'il me souvint de la doulce plaisance
> Que souloye oudit pays trouver;
> Si commençay de cueur a souspirer,
> Combien certés que grant bien me faisoit
> De voir France que mon cueur amer doit.
>
> Je m'avisay que c'estoit non savance
> De telz souspirs dedens mon cueur garder
> Veu que je voy que la voye commence
> De bonne paix, qui tous biens peut donner;
> Pour ce, tournay en confort mon penser.
> Mais non pourtant mon cueur ne se lassoit
> De voir France que mon cueur amer doit.
>
> Alors chargay en la nef d'Esperance
> Tous mes souhaitz, en leur priant d'aler
> Oultre la mer, sans faire demourance,
> Et a France de me recommander.
> Or nous doint Dieu bonne paix sans tarder!
> Adonc auray loisir, mais qu'ainsi soit,
> De voir France que mon cueur amer doit.
>
> Paix est tresor qu'on ne peut trop loer.
> Je hé guerre, point ne la doy prisier;
> Destourbé m'a long temps, soit tort ou droit,
> De voir France que mon cueur amer doit!

It was characteristic of his new attitude that this upsurging of love for his country, and the memories it brought of the 'doulce plaisance' he had once enjoyed there, instead of merely increasing his sadness at his exile now served to confirm his hatred of war and to strengthen his resolution to work harder than ever for peace. It had been cruelly revealed to him that there was little to hope for from the dauphin, and it was perhaps his disappointment over his failure of his natural lord to take advantage of his promised presence that caused Charles to take a very grave step shortly afterwards. But he had not lost faith in the willingness of his French friends to help, and as soon as he returned to Wing-field he began once again to urge the king to make use of him and those of his fellow nobles on whose support he felt sure he could count.[14]

There remained, however, one French prince, the most powerful of all, who could easily ruin Charles' plans if he opposed them, Philip of Burgundy. The long enmity between his house and that of Charles, and his espousal of the English cause, made it seem only too likely that he might. But fortunately he was himself at that time reconsidering his own position and gradually coming to the same conclusion, as to the necessity of peace, as was Charles. He knew that the truce he had signed in the previous autumn with the dauphin had aroused the anger of the English and he was beginning to think that to reach an under-standing with Charles might be the most politic step he could take at that stage. In July, therefore, he sent an embassy to England, charged with a threefold mission: to discover the present attitude of the English to the war, and the possibility of peace; to sound the prevailing opinion concerning himself; and to try to see the Duke of Orleans and discover his views on all these matters. The leader of this embassy was Hue de Lannoy, lord of Santes, and having fulfilled his mission he stopped in Lille on his way home to send his master a very full account of all he had seen and done, in a despatch that reveals him as a born writer.[15]

He had first met the king, whom he calls "a very beautiful child and well-grown", out hunting near Guildford with his uncles Bedford and Gloucester and other nobles; and Henry had at once enquired, in French, after Burgundy's health and whereabouts. On a later occasion the envoy was able to have a long conversation with the young king, who told him of his disappointment that the dauphin had disregarded the peace overtures both at Auxerre and at Corbeil, taking no notice of the fact that Henry had sent the prisoners to Dover to be available for talks. Henry assured de Lannoy that he knew Orleans was ready to work for peace and had made this known to his officers in France. The king was at pains to tell him what the war was costing, giving him statistics; and he informed him that he was going to assemble the Three Estates to decide what should be done. From other sources the embassy heard that this Parliament was to be called on July 8th and was likely to continue all August. The great numbers who were going to attend it would there decide whether to try and make peace or to raise a very large and powerful army. "For from what we can perceive", said de Lannoy, "they very well know that the affairs of France cannot long continue in the state in which they now are."

On their first arriving they found that almost everyone was ill-disposed towards Burgundy, but as time went on this impression was softened. The king, Cardinal Beaufort, the Chancellor, and the Earl of Warwick all expressed confidence in him. Still warmer in his protestations of belief and hope in Burgundy was the Earl of Suffolk, whom de Lannoy saw many times.

It was no doubt only through Suffolk's connivance that the ambassador was able to see Charles since, wrote de Lannoy, "we perceived by many ways and means that the said English do not take it with good will that either we or any of your people have any communication whatever with my said lord of Orleans." The occasion of their first meeting sounds, in fact, as if it had been expressly arranged to seem a chance affair, for de Lannoy says that when he called, he found the earl was rising from dinner and his prisoner with him. His account of "how we have spoken to my lord of Orleans: what he said to us, what we have been able to discover about him and his affairs" is by far the most interesting part of his report. De Lannoy obviously knew how anxiously Burgundy would read all this; and that and his own gift for vivid reporting enabled him to capture not only the very accents of the duke but to divine other things that he would have said if he could; and to sense, too, the tension and expectancy that gripped Charles at that critical point of his career.

Immediately he arrived, de Lannoy said, "my lord of Orleans took us by the hand, and asked us very anxiously how you were, and where you were, and we told him the truth, and how you recommended yourself very earnestly to him, and that you desired to know of his good health. To which he answered us that he was in good bodily health, but that he was distressed because he was spending the best part of his life in prison." Hue de Lannoy encouraged him by saying that good might come of that if, as a result, he became a mediator of peace between the two kingdoms, in which case he would have no need to complain of the pains and dangers he had endured. To this Charles answered, "Here is my good cousin of Suffolk, who knows how I have always offered myself to the King of England and the lords of his Council, to be employed therein, and I still do so; but I am like a sword, shut up in a scabbard, of which a man cannot avail himself unless he draws it; and I have always said, and still do say, that I can be of no real use unless I speak to some of my friends in France, by which means I might help to advance the business; and it appears to me that if I might have a conference with some special friends I have, I might therein be of much service. For I believe that there are, among the greatest lords in the court of my lord the King of France and those of his party, persons who would act and who would be very pleased to act according to my counsel with regard to the general peace. And by the faith of my body, so much do I desire the said peace that I would that I might be the cause and means of having it well accomplished, that it should endure hereafter, and that seven days after this were brought about, that I might suffer death. And I venture to say before you, my fair cousin of Suffolk, that my good cousins of Burgundy and Brittany can do more for this, after the principal parties, than any prince alive."

The envoy replied that he knew for certain that his master also wanted peace as much as anything in the world and would help with all his might.

"And then said the Earl of Suffolk to my lord of Orleans: 'My lord, I have always told you that my lord of Burgundy is well-disposed towards peace.' And Orleans replied: 'Of this I have no doubt; for I well know that neither he nor I are the cause of the evils which have come upon the kingdom of France; and of this I formerly spoke to you, messire Hue, and believe me I am still of the same mind.' And then he pressed my hand and, what is more, squeezed me by the arm very strongly, and this he did twice; and I very well saw that he did not dare say what he would much have wished. And then he began to say again 'I wish that the King of England would employ me on these affairs, making himself sure of my person, for I do not in the least desire so much to treat of my own deliverance as of this said peace. And I dare say aloud that I could therein be of as great an assistance, or greater, than any man alive.' To which my lord of Suffolk said to him, 'Well my lord, it would be a pleasure to the king to hear of this said peace, and employ you in it, for you know that he has now given safe conduct to certain of your people to come to you.' To which my lord of Orleans replied, 'You speak truly, fair cousin, for I shall shortly see Camail, my herald.' Then he began to ask me once more very anxiously about you and your health; and truly he could not refrain from speaking thereof, praising you very much and wishing very earnestly that he might be able to see and speak to you."

So reluctant was Charles to bring the interview to an end that when de Lannoy took leave of him he begged him to come and see him again, which Suffolk promised him he should.

But before that happened de Lannoy received a visit from one of Charles' guards, a barber of the Earl of Suffolk's called Cauvel, who told him that he was a native of Burgundy and a loyal subject of its duke, and was employed to guard Charles because he spoke French. For that reason Charles put more trust in him than in anyone else in the house. Charles had obviously charged him to tell de Lannoy more explicitly some things he had felt but had been unable to say himself. It had been rumoured, said the barber, that Charles hated Burgundy and had threatened if ever he got free to make war on him. This was untrue for "before your arrival" said Cauvel, "as long as I have been near him, I have heard him say marvellous much good of my lord of Burgundy, showing that he loves him with all his heart, and he has spoken to me more of him than of all the rest of the lords of France". Cauvel went on to say that, if Burgundy should wish it, he felt confident of finding some way of carrying a letter to him from the Duke of Orleans, "by which he may know his good will". De Lannoy thanked him and charged him to tell Charles that he might count absolutely on Burgundy's help in securing his deliverance, and on his answering love.

Even the knowledge that Cauvel had taken his message was not enough to satisfy Charles' craving to be able to communicate with Philip of Burgundy himself. When the ambassadors went the next day to take leave of him and Suffolk, Charles asked his keeper, "My fair cousin of Suffolk, might I not write a letter to my good cousin of Burgundy?" To which the Earl, obviously not wishing to humiliate him before the ambassador, replied, "My lord, you shall deliberate upon it before night." But the next morning "my lord of Suffolk sent us by the said Cauvel a letter addressed to you, which we send you, but the said Cauvel told us that my said lord of Orleans could not then have leave to write to you." It was no wonder, when we learn of frustrations such as these, that both Charles' herald Camail, and Jennin Cauvel, "the one in the absence of the other", told the envoy that, "if the dauphin and the lords of his party will not hear of peace, and by this means of the deliverance of my said lord of Orleans, nevertheless my said lord of Orleans has no intention to allow himself to be ruined, nor will he always live in the state in which he now is. But they have heard him say that if he could have spoken to you, my very redoubtable lord, to my lord the Duke of Brittany, or to the bastard of Orleans, his brother, he could easily find means for his deliverance."

After reading this despatch, neither Charles nor Philip could have been in any doubt that they could count on each other's support. But even more than for its political importance, this rare document is precious for its revelation of the human sentiments of these two great princes at this moment of their lives. Although Charles had spent most of his youth in striving to avenge the murder of his father at the hands of Philip's father, he was magnanimous enough not to wish to visit the sin of the father on the son, and of large enough mind to put the good of his country before any personal quarrel. Nor must it be overlooked that Philip too was ready to forget that Charles' brothers had been fighting against him for many years past, in support of the dauphin whom he still considered responsible for the murder of his own father. Charles himself seemed to indicate a desire that both of them should shake off these ancient grudges when he told de Lannoy that neither he nor Philip was the cause of the evils which had come upon the kingdom of France. But over and above these views, which might still be in part due to perspicacity, de Lannoy makes it plain that each felt himself drawn to the other by an instinctive sympathy and trust; and that on Charles' side this sympathy had ripened into a genuine affection strong enough to be remarked by those around him as something pregnant for future good.

With the Burgundian envoy's assurances to encourage him, on August 14th Charles submitted to the Parliament, which had been sitting since the beginning of July, a document embodying the proposals and decisions on which he had been working for many months past.[16] It was a very long and detailed document, in legal and often repetitive Latin. Although the text gives the impression of having been drawn up by someone versed in the drafting of treaties, Charles was at pains to state in the second paragraph that he alone, of his own free will, was the author of the substance of it, uninfluenced in any way either by the king or any of those near him. In that same paragraph, too, he gave an inkling of the gravest decision he had reached, when he referred to the many offers he had already made to "my Lord Henry, King of the French and of England and Lord of Ireland".

The most immediate of his proposals was that a peace conference should be held on the following October 15th, either somewhere in Normandy or at Calais. If this was agreed, he could answer for it that a long list of French nobles would attend it, for they had assured him that they would. His list did not include the Duke of Burgundy, since he had not been allowed to communicate with him, even by messages sent through his herald as he apparently had with the other princes. But it was an important list for all that, headed by the name of the Queen of Sicily, that intrepid Yolanda of Aragon, Duchess of Anjou, who had been virtually a mother to the dauphin since his own mother Isabeau made no secret of her dislike of him, and had brought him up with her own children: Louis, the third duke, René,* Charles, and Mary, who became the dauphin's wife. The fact that this wise and prudent princess, who knew the dauphin as well as anyone, had consented to attend the peace conference herself (although only if it were held in Normandy, not in Calais, a stipulation made also by the Duke of Brittany and the Count of Armagnac), certainly seems to indicate that she also had little faith in him, and realised that a firm hand over him would be necessary if the meeting were to achieve anything. In addition to these three names, Charles' list included Brittany's two brothers, Arthur of Richemont and Richard of Étampes, who was Charles' brother-in-law; the Duke of Alençon, his son-in-law; and the young Count of Clermont, Bourbon's son, among others. Once the date and place were fixed, Charles promised to communicate them to the princes immediately. He was confident that, provided a reasonable share of lands and lordships were made for the dauphin, a general and lasting peace could be concluded. And as a guarantee he offered to remain in England himself for a year after the signing of it, or even longer if the king wished, although he asked that when this time was up he would be set free without ransom.

Charles then came to the other promises which he was prepared to make, if it should happen after all that an immediate peace was not concluded. Although the document does not expressly say so, these promises seem designed to enable the English to take over the lordship and governance of France with the consent, as far as possible, of Charles' countrymen. By far the most important of them was his repeated statement that he would recognise Henry as the true King of both France and England, and was ready not only to pay homage to him and his heirs after him as their liege man, but to serve him against his enemies in France until such time as he had obtained the monarchy

---

* René succeeded to the Dukedom of Anjou on the death of his brother Louis in 1434, but was always known as the King of Sicily.

and brought the whole kingdom into obedience to him and his law. To facilitate this he further offered to hand over to Henry his own main towns, Blois, Orleans and Châteaudun among them, together with all his castles and strongholds, and to send his subjects in them to fight for him, promising to punish as rebels any who would not also swear allegiance to the English king. He went even further and offered to persuade a long list of towns which did not belong to his apanage to swear obedience to Henry too.

In addition to these offers of his own he assured the king that all his friends in France would be as ready as he was to recognise Henry and and his heirs as their rulers, and went so far as to promise that some of his non-French friends, like the Dukes of Milan and Savoy, would join alliances in support of the English king. In return for all this Charles merely asked that his own subjects, once they had become liege men of the English king, should still be allowed to retain the ownership of their former lands and titles, or given others of equivalent value, and that Henry should maintain them in their former liberties. Finally, for himself, Charles asked that, when some part of his promises had been implemented, the king would allow him to leave England; and that when they had all been kept, he should be released entirely from captivity, with no ransom exacted either by the king or his heirs.

Some French historians have roundly condemned Charles for these promises, accusing him of selling both his country and his honour.[17] And certainly on the face of it by modern standards they do appear at first sight startling if not shocking, especially when one remembers his proud refusal in 1417 to recognise Henry V as his king, when Bourbon was ready to do so. But actions can only be fairly judged in the light of circumstances prevailing at the time, and by contemporary codes of accepted behaviour and practice. In 1417 France had in Charles VI a universally recognised king, even though he may have been feeble-witted, and both Charles and Bourbon had long been his loyal subjects. When Bourbon offered to recognise Henry V in his stead, he did so solely to regain his own liberty, without regard to the views of any of his fellow princes and indeed without their knowledge, and at a time when the English invasion had achieved only the victory of Agincourt. Charles' offer, on the other hand, was made first and foremost with the aim of ending a war that, seventeen years later, had brought his country into a state of abject ruin such as she had rarely known, and as the result of his mature belief that her own sovereign prince was powerless to save and govern her.

He was confident, too, that none of his fellow nobles would condemn his action, believing rather that they would support and imitate him. His attitude to the English king and the dauphin was, after all, no different from that of Philip the Good of Burgundy, who had long fought for the one against the other, and whom none appeared to blame for it. As for the offers of territory, not only had the French themselves accepted for many years past that much French land, in Guienne and Gascony, and Normandy too, was an English possession, but very soon after, when peace discussions began, the official French representatives voluntarily offered to cede further great territories to the English. It is true that they stipulated that the English king should hold them as a vassal of the French monarch and not as an autonomous lord; but at a time when powerful French vassals, such as Burgundy and Brittany, were themselves virtually independent princes, such a condition was more theoretical than real. It seems evident, then, that Charles' contemporaries would not have regarded his offers as in any way outrageous or treasonable; and they certainly afford proof of what he had told de Lannoy, that his desire for peace far outstripped his desire for his own freedom.

As things turned out, Charles was not to be called upon to fulfil these promises. A letter from the king, dated the following day, makes no reference to them, being wholly concerned with the proposed conference.[18] It is addressed to all his office-bearers in both England and France, of whatever degree, and to their "friends, allies and well-wishers". After referring briefly to the dauphin's failure to take advantage of his attempts to meet his wishes earlier in the year, the king informs them that his fair cousin the Duke of Orleans has offered to bring his friends and kinsfolk, with other nobles and members of the dauphin's Council, to a meeting to be held at Calais on October 15th. This letter, like that of Charles' in some ways, is obviously a summing up of decisions taken some time previously; for the king then goes on to tell his subjects that he has sent safe-conducts to all those whom Charles names (with the exception, incidentally, of the Duke of Brittany), and also to a good many others, including fourteen of those officers of Charles' household whose names are so familiar because of their frequent journeys to see their master. The king therefore commanded all his subjects to facilitate by every possible means the journey of any delegate who came their way, these orders to remain in force until the first of January following.

After all these careful preparations, Charles had to suffer the disappointment of seeing his bright hopes dashed and his confident beliefs prove unfounded, for the conference never took place. Although the king sent the Cardinal with the Earls of Suffolk and Warwick to Calais at the appointed time, none of the French turned up. The only explanation that can be found for this failure comes from a letter which the Count of Armagnac wrote to Charles' Chancellor Cousinot two years later.[19] From this one gathers that Charles, fully expecting that now that he was a principal in the affair, he would be taken to Calais at the outset, had merely invited his friends to meet him there 'au bien de la paix' and reserving all the details of his plan for when they did. The invitation was obviously too vague to inspire them to accept it, quite apart from their usual reluctance to go to Calais. But no such explanation can account for the case of Burgundy, to whom Henry VI had written personally on August 14th,[20] and who also, in spite of his eagerness for peace as reported by de Lannoy, did not turn up. In the circumstances, and looking at it from his own angle, it was not surprising that Henry VI, in a later letter to the Duke of Brittany,[21] spoke of the "strange manners" of his adversaries, telling him too of the danger, not to mention the expense, that there would have been if he had sent the Duke of Orleans anywhere but Calais.

A more likely reason for the failure of the French to attend was that that summer, at the time when Charles was making his plans, an unexpected change was coming over the scene in France. In June, through the connivance of the Duchess of Anjou and her daughter, Mary (the wife of the dauphin), Arthur of Richemont, the Constable, seized the person of the all-powerful Duke de la Tremoille, who had been the evil genius of the dauphin ever since his coronation at Rheims five years before, keeping him from his capital and from all affairs of state. Yolanda sent her third son Charles to take his place, and under their joint impulsion the dauphin summoned a great assembly to meet in July under his leadership. His captains meanwhile—Richemont, the Bastard, Alençon and Clermont—continued to fight the English troops on their soil, and so successfully that in July of the following year, 1434, the Duke of Bedford, whom the Commons had begged to remain in England as Protector, had to return to France to take up his old position as commander-in-chief and governor of the territories under English rule, where there was much unrest. All this of course meant that Charles' appeals to his friends to attend a peace conference, especially one with the conditions he proposed, could not have arrived at a more inopportune moment.

In these resumed hostilities Burgundy, despite that momentary defection which had so angered the English, returned to his old allegiance and fought on their side. But he no longer had any real stomach for the war and was increasingly convinced of the need for peace. The importance of ending the hundred years' strife between England and France was at that time gradually becoming recognised outside their boundaries. Earlier in the year the Council of Basle had sent embassies to both Henry VI and Charles VII exhorting them to make peace, and Burgundy was astute enough to see that France would gain much by acting as a principal organiser in the matter. As a first step towards this he now turned his mind to ending the civil discord in his own country. Family alliances afforded a good basis for this, for both Arthur of Richemont and the Count of Clermont were married to sisters of his. He therefore invited them to meet him at Nevers at the end of January 1435 (the month when Clermont succeeded to the duchy of Bourbon on the death of his father in England), where they were not long in agreeing on the preliminaries to be followed for the calling of a meeting which it was proposed should be held at Arras in the following August. During their discussions Burgundy for the first time referred to the dauphin as "le roy Charles", a fact significant both of his own changed allegiance and, no doubt, of the greater esteem in which the French king was beginning to be held in general. In mid-February heralds were sent to London, Paris and Basle to report the result of their meeting.[22]

Thereafter Burgundy's influence quickly became paramount. During the meeting at Nevers the Duke of Bedford had left Paris for England. When Philip of Burgundy arrived in Paris in April he was everywhere greeted as the harbinger of that peace the people had longed for for so many years. Some of the citizens, especially the young women, waited on his duchess, that Portuguese princess Isabella who had passed through London on her way to Burgundy in 1429, to implore her good offices for peace, and she told them, "My good friends, it is one of the things of this world that I most desire, and for which I beg my lord both day and night, seeing as I do the great need there is of it."[23] She assured them that she knew for certain that her lord had a great desire for it too. She had good reason to know it, for there is no doubt that his attitude was largely due to her influence, an influence which he had the unusual grace, for a great prince of his time, to recognise and defer to more and more as time went on. Philip informed the English Council in Paris that now the French would never accept Henry VI as their king, but that peace they must have. In May he sent de Lannoy to England again, to urge Henry VI to send envoys to the conference;[24] and heralds were also despatched to Spain, Portugal, Denmark, Poland, Italy and Sicily, urging them too to appoint delegates to attend.

Henry VI rather resented the appeals from the Council of Basle, since he felt that he had been doing his best to call a peace conference already. Nevertheless he answered them in June,[25] offering to send envoys to Basle to treat of it. To find now that Arras and not Basle was to be the seat of the meeting, and that the initiative for calling it was in the hands of their former ally Burgundy, could hardly have been welcome to the English, especially to those among them who, like Humphrey of Gloucester, both hated Burgundy and were all for prolonging the war. This perhaps accounted for the tough attitude that their delegates, the Archbishop of York, Suffolk and Hungerford[26] among others, were instructed to take at the meeting, which they had perforce to attend, since all Europe was to be represented there. There were, in fact, such numbers of delegates, all with their retinues, that it was some time before all were lodged and the negotiations could begin.

When they did,[27] negotiation was hardly the word for the discussions that took place, for the English made not the slightest attempt to meet the French point of view and stuck stubbornly throughout to Henry's claim to the throne of France. It was as if the long shadow of Henry V had fallen over them, taking no account of all that had happened since his day. The French on the other hand showed themselves surprisingly generous, offering, in addition to the traditional English holdings in Gascony, Guienne and Picardy, almost the whole of Normandy and a long list of important towns in the south-west of France, all to be held as vassals of the French crown. Besides all these concessions, amounting to about a third of France proper, they offered the hand of a daughter of France for Henry VI and a liberal payment. In return they demanded that Henry VI should renounce his claim to the crown. They asked too that a reasonable ransom should be fixed for Charles of Orleans and that in the meantime he should be freed from his parole

6 Philip the Good, Duke of Burgundy, portrait by R. Van der Weyden, at Bruges

and imprisonment. This was a very important clause, for it was the first time that a ransom for him had ever been mentioned. But it was all in vain. For the English it was the crown or nothing, since, as they saw it, if they had that, all these other things would be theirs anyway. The conference therefore broke up and on September 6th the English delegates returned home.

Their attitude was not one to persuade Burgundy to resume his alliance with them. A week after they left Arras he therefore obtained a dispensation from his oath of loyalty to them at the Treaty of Troyes in 1420, and instead made his peace with Charles VII by the Treaty of Arras, thus bringing to an end the long feud between the Burgundians and Orleanists that had ravaged the country ever since the murder of Louis of Orleans nearly thirty years before. In the middle of that month the Duke of Bedford died at his house in Normandy. His aim had always been to rule wisely those parts of France which the English had won rather than to conquer more, and he had done this with such consideration and justice that he had found, he said, his king's subjects there as anxious to keep faith "as ever were people, and to me as loving and as kind".[28]

With his moderating influence removed, Gloucester had no difficulty in persuading the Commons to continue the war, extending it now against Burgundy too. But in Bedford the English had lost a commander as well as a statesman; without his help they were no match for the French. In April 1436 the French forces, under the Bastard and Arthur of Richemont, managed to scale the walls of Paris, whose gates were kept locked, and enter bearing the banner of Charles VII. The English, taken by surprise and overcome, were allowed to march out. They continued to fight elsewhere, but the tide had now definitely turned against them. In July, even Calais was so gravely threatened by Burgundy's forces that Humphrey of Gloucester was appointed lieutenant-general of the army to defend it.

In the events of these last three years Charles took no active part. *The Proceedings of the Privy Council* speak of a possible peace conference to be held at Calais in the summer of 1434, to which it was decided to take him. They took the utmost precautions to see that he did not escape on the way, ordering for instance that 'the see be serched'.[29] And they sent a 'remembrance' to Suffolk, to remind Charles of his former offers of help, to find out how he would feel about going to Calais himself if his French friends merely sent ambassadors and did

H 205

not come themselves; and most of all to insist that, if he went, he would do so at his own expense and, what was more, that if the expedition failed of its purpose, he would be expected to pay the king's expenses too. But in spite of all these precise arrangements, no meeting took place at that time, nor is there any other reference to it.

When it came to the Arras conference, however, Philip of Burgundy had expressly charged his envoy, Hue de Lannoy, when he sent him to Henry VI in May 1435, to ask that the Duke of Orleans and the Count of Eu also should be brought to it. He also wrote to Henry to the same effect. Henry could hardly refuse completely so direct a request, but he would only agree that his two prisoners should be brought to some place near Arras, where they could be "easily and comfortably visited", if it looked as if their influence would be useful in persuading his adversaries to make peace. Whether Eu went in the end is not known, but Charles certainly did. But it rather looks as if the arrangements to take him were made without much preparation, for this time there are no Council minutes concerning them, and indeed the only English reference to his going is in one of the London Chronicles, which states that when the Cardinal, with Huntingdon and Suffolk, went to Arras "they brought with hem the Duke of Orlianx oute of England, and whas at Calays ffor to trete as for his party".[30]

It seems likely too that Charles had had no opportunity to warn his allies in France of his coming, for it was to tell Cousinot that he had heard of it from the Bishop of Auch that the Count of Armagnac wrote him that letter already referred to. However, the news of his presence soon became known locally, for a newsletter from Arras, dated August 2nd, remarked upon it and on the fact that he was not to proceed further until agreement was reached at Arras. And the Duke of Bourbon and Arthur of Richemont, who were both at the conference, sent personal envoys to Calais to ask Charles for his views, whereupon he gave them a message stressing the need to make peace without difficulties. But his advice, as we know, was not taken and no official approach seems to have been made. On September 2nd he took the opportunity of being at Calais to write a very short note in his own hand to Duke Amadeus of Savoy, asking for financial help, and on the 8th he returned to England with the rest of the English delegation.[31]

To have been thus excluded from this conference, and to have had no hand in the planning that preceded it, after the central rôle he had played in 1433, was not necessarily upsetting to Charles. Self-importance was never one of his weaknesses. It was peace itself that mattered to him, not who was the peace-maker. If he was now debarred from working actively for it, he could at least use his gift of poetry to persuade all manner of men of the urgent need and lasting benefits of it, and this he did in what is perhaps the noblest of all his poems, illumined with a vision and a social conscience most rare in a prince of his time:

> Priés pour paix, doulce Vierge Marie,
> Royne des cieulx, et du monde maistresse,
> Faictes prier, par vostre courtoisie,
> Saints et saintes, et prenés vostre adresse
> Ver vostre filz, requerant sa haultesse
> Qu'il lui plaise son peuple regarder,
> Que de son sang a voulu racheter,
> En deboutant guerre qui tout desvoye;
> De prieres ne vous vueilliez lasser:
> Priez pour paix, le vray tresor de joye!
>
> Priez, prelas et gens de sainte vie,
> Religieux ne dormez en peresse,
> Priez, maistres et tous suivans clergie,
> Car par guerre fault que l'estude cesse;
> Moustiers destruits sont sans qu'on les redresse,
> Le service de Dieu vous fault laissier.
> Quant ne povez en repos demourer,
> Priez si fort que briefment Dieu vous oye;
> L'Eglise voult a ce vous ordonner:
> Priez pour paix, le vray tresor de joye!
>
> Priez, princes qui avez seigneurie,
> Roys, ducs, contes, barons plains de noblesse.
> Gentilz hommes avec chevalerie,
> Car meschans gens surmontent gentillesse;
> En leurs mains ont toute vostre richese,
> Debatz les font en hault estat monter,
> Vous le povez chascun jour veoir au cler,
> Et sont riches de voz biens et monnoye
> Dont vous deussiez le peuple suporter:
> Priez pour paix, le vray tresor de joye!

Priez, peuple qui souffrez tirannie,
Car voz seigneurs sont en telle foiblesse
Qu'ilz ne peuent vous garder, par maistrie,
Ne vous aidier en vostre grant distresse;
Loyaulx marchans, la selle si vous blesse
Fort sur le dox; chascun vous vient presser
Et ne povez marchandise mener,
Car vous n'avez seur passage ne voye,
Et maint peril vous couvient il passer:
Priez pour paix, le vray tresor de joye!

Priez, galans joyeux en compaignie,
Qui despendre desirez a largesse,
Guerre vous tient la bourse desgarnie;
Priez, amans, qui voulez en liesse
Servir amours, car guerre, par rudesse,
Vous destourbe de vos dames hanter,
Qui maintesfoiz fait leurs vouloirs tourner;
Et quant tenez le bout de la couroye,
Un estrangier si le vous vient oster:
Priez pour paix, le vray tresor de joye!

Dieu tout puissant nous vueille conforter
Toutes choses en terre, ciel et mer;
Priez vers lui que brief en tout pourvoye,
En lui seul est de tous maulx amender:
Priez pour paix, le vray tresor de joye!

That light-hearted, teasing fifth stanza, addressed to the gallants whom war impoverishes and prevents from keeping an eye on their mistresses, whose fancy is apt to stray in their absence, was very typical of Charles, whose later poems show him to have been always ready to see the humorous and human side of things in love and even in still more serious matters. It may be, too, that it was because of an amorous adventure of his own at that time that he had a special thought for lovers then. We have no detailed information about this. The main evidence comes from some of his poems, which definitely suggest that a young English woman had fallen in love with him and that he had responded, in so far as his condition as a captive allowed. Dangerous though it is to assume that sentiments expressed in a poem are necessarily based on actual events, in this case there is at least one piece of supporting evidence. René of Anjou, 'le bon roi René', the second son of Yolanda and himself a poet, later became a great friend of Charles of Orleans and in 1457 spent some time with him at Blois. René was at that time engaged on a long allegorical poem of his own, *Le livre du cuer d'amours espris*, describing famous lovers of his time, and Charles obligingly supplied him with a few details of an episode of his own life when a prisoner in England twenty years earlier, to include in it, which René then summed up in the lines:[32]

> Et tant y demouray qu'en aprins le langaige
> Par lequel fus acoint de dame belle et saige,
> Et d'elle si espris qu'a Amours fus hommaige
> Dont mainte beaux ditz dictié bien prisez davantaige.

We do not know when this episode took place, but there are considerable grounds for supposing it was during those last three years at Wingfield. That undying faithfulness to Bonne, which all his earlier *ballades* protest, make it unlikely that this new love occupied his thoughts until after her death; and the political agitation of his first year at Wingfield would not have given much opportunity for it then. But when, after that, he was forced back again into idle bondage, in a household where he was in close contact with civilized company, such a mutual attraction may easily have occurred, and one can understand what an appeal it would have for a man of forty, as he then was, whose physical nature had been starved for so long and whose affections, too, no longer had any outlet.

Searching the poems as the most likely source from which we may learn this story, there is perhaps some hint of its beginnings in a *ballade* that, from internal evidence, follows the one in which he wrote that, on a May Day after the death of Bonne, he had chosen the leaf as his symbol rather than the flower. In it he describes how, on the morning after that May Day, he awoke from a dream in which he saw a flower who accused him of having, in choosing the leaf, forgotten her, although he had always showed his inclination for her and she had trusted him. Charles is surprised at this, for 'Riens n'ay meffait, se pense je, vers toy'. He tells this 'tresbelle fleur' that he had had no thought of displeasing her, and that in choosing the leaf rather than the flower in that particular year he had but acted as he was bound to. Must he be banished from her because of that? He is ready to honour her, wherever he may be, for the sake of his love for a flower he had loved in times past, and whom he prays God that he may see one day in Paradise. And so he does not ask the forgiveness of this English 'tresdoulce' flower, for he has done her no wrong—'Riens n'ay meffait, se pense je, vers toy!' If this poem is really autobiographical, it seems to imply that the young Englishwoman had supposed his inclination for her to be more serious than it was, not realising perhaps, as well she might not, the depth of the love he had felt for his wife, and his grief at her loss. Charles then, with characteristic gentleness, reveals to her the true state of his heart, showing her frankly the place she holds in it and that he has in no way deceived her.

With the situation thus clear between them, they appear to have embarked on an amorous flirtation together, spiced with a little danger because of the disapproval of her friends and the surveillance under which his English guardians—symbolised as 'Dangier'—keep him. The fact that he expressed his moods and feelings in this affair in the gayer verse form of *chansons* rather than *ballades* indicates their comparative lightness; although as time goes on it is clear that her beauty and her charming ways more and more ensnared him, and gave him the gratifying knowledge that his starved and frustrated senses were not dead and could still respond to provocation, a sensation not easy to distinguish from being in love. Once or twice he frankly admits that he is, rather implying that he had striven not to be:

> Tiengne soy d'amer qui pourra,
> Plus ne m'en pourroye tenir.

He follows this with the definite statement 'J'ay une Dame choisie' whom he describes as being most accomplished whether she dances, sings or laughs. Her charming aspect obviously dazzled him: 'Regardez moy sa contenance' one *chanson* rapturously begins, and goes on to ask if there is one to compare with her 'Entre les parfaictes de France'. The mere sight of her causes him deep pleasure:

> Dieu, qu'il la fait bon regarder
> La gracieuse, bonne et belle

and makes him forget all unhappiness:

> De vostre beauté regarder,
> Ma tresbelle, gente maistresse,
> Ce m'est certes tant de lyesse
> Que ne le sauriés penser.

> Je ne m'en pourroye lasser,
> Car j'oublie toute tristesse
> De vostre beauté regarder,
> Ma tresbelle gente maistresse,

especially when she returns his glance:

> Pour le regard de vos beaux yeaux
> Qui me met tout hors de tristesse.

He blames the head-dresses of the time that conceal lovely faces:

> Levez ces cuevrechiefs plus hault
> Qui trop cuevrent ces beaulx visages,

but at the same time warns about the dangers of gazing too ardently at the beauty who has ensnared him:

> De la regarder vous gardez
> La belle que sers ligement;
> Car vous perdrez soudainement
> Vostre cueur, se la regardez

It was not only her beauty but the charm of her youth that attracted him:

> Quant je voy la doulce jeunesse
> De vostre gent corps gracieux!

It was perhaps because of it that what he calls 'envious persons' made attempts to remove her from him:

> Ou regard de vos beaulx doulx yeulx,
> Dont loing suis par les envieux,
> Me souhaide si tressouvent
> Que mon penser est seulement
> En vostre gent corps gracieux.

They were, he says, always talking to him about it, so that he had to pretend indifference, although he could not keep his eyes from her:

> Mais, pour mesdisans destourber
> De parler sus vostre jeunesse,
> Il fault que souvent m'en delaisse,
> Combien que ne m'en puis garder
> De vostre beauté regarder.

But in case this pretended indifference distressed the young woman, Charles reassured her in two of his most charming poems, both rather alike, which illustrate so well his gift of exquisite simplicity that one of them at least must be quoted:

> En faictes vous doubte?
> Point ne le devez,
> Veu que vous savez
> Ma pensee toute.
>
> Quant mon cueur s'i boute
> Et vostre l'avez,
> En faictes vous doubte?
> Point ne le devez.
>
> Dangier nous escoute,
> Sus, tost achevez,
> Ma foy recevez,
> Je ne sera route
> En faictes vous doubte?

'Dangier' (meaning presumably his keepers rather than her friends) is constantly keeping a watchful eye upon them but would need a hundred eyes, both before and behind, to prevent lovers from getting the better of him. For in spite of all the watchfulness he managed to ask her, in a tiny poem that most vividly conveys the ardour and urgency of the whispered request:

> Le voulez vous
> Que vostre soye?
> Rendu m'octroye
> Pris ou recours.
>
> Ung mot pour tous,
> Bas qu'on ne l'oye:
> Le voulez vous
> Que vostre soye?
>
> Maugré jalous,
> Foy vous tendroye;
> Or sa, ma joye,
> Accordons nous:
> Le voulez vous?

He could see from her expression that she was not reluctant, if only she could get free of 'Dangier':

> Vostre bouche dit: Baisiez moy,
> Se m'est avis quant la regarde:
> Mais Dangier de trop prés la garde
> Dont mainte doleur je reçoy.

However, they must have managed to evade him for there are many *chansons* that speak of kisses:

> Dedens mon sein, pres de mon cueur
> J'ay mussié un privé baisier
> Que j'ay emblé maugré Dangier,
> Dont il meurt en peine et langeur

and

> Dangier, toute nuit, en labeur,
> A fait guet; or gist en sa tente.
> Accomplissez brief vostre entente,
> Tantdis qu'il dort: c'est le meillieur.
> Prenez tost ce baisier, mon cueur,

and one that goes so far as to say:

> Tantdis que Dangier est las
> Et le voyez sommeillier,
> Logiés moy entre vos bras
> Et m'envoiez doulx baisier.

The identity of this young woman who had fallen in love with the romantic prisoner, who was both a great prince and a gifted poet, has long remained a mystery and is still not definitely known.* But it has recently been discovered that the first letters of one of a series of English poems in Charles' own manuscript of his poetry, and which there is therefore some reason to suppose he himself wrote, spells the name Anne Molins.[33] It so happened that there were at least three women of that name in England at that time; but the most likely of the three to have met Charles was the young widow of Sir William, also called Lord Moleyns, who was killed in the French wars in 1428 or '29. She was a first cousin of Alice Chaucer, the wife of the Earl of Suffolk, and a ward of Alice's father Thomas Chaucer. It is therefore not straining possibilities unduly to suppose that, after her husband's death, she

* See Appendix II.

would often have stayed with her cousins at Wingfield and perhaps
Ewelme too, and thus have been there during the years when Charles
was in the keeping of Suffolk.

We do not know how old Anne was at the time, but if she was the
very young woman that Charles depicts, it would be understandable
that any suspicion of a love-affair between their young relative, of good
but not high birth, and this prince of the royal blood of France would
have caused her cousins some apprehension, both for her sake and his,
so that they thought it wise to keep them apart if possible. This may
indeed have had something to do with the fact that, early in 1436,
Charles was moved from Wingfield; but whether it had or not, this
move must have put an end to his chances of seeing Anne any more,
even if he continued to love her. That he did so may seem to be proved
by a few *chansons*, in two of which he laments that he now has to write
to her instead of speaking:

> Ma seule amour que tant desire,
> Mon reconfort, mon doulx penser,
> Belle, nompareille, sans per
> Il me desplaist de vous escrire.
>
> Car j'aymasse mieulx a le dire
> De bouche . . .

and

> Pour vous moustrer que point ne vous oublie,
> Comme vostre que suis ou que je soye,
> Presentement ma chançon vous envoye,
> Or la prenés en gré, je vous en prie,

and another in which he says:

> Car pour un jour qui m'a esté joyeux,
> J'ay eu trois moys la fievre de destresse.

But the most moving poem that seems to speak of this separation is a
long *Complainte*, too long to quote in its entirety. In it he tells how
when he had to take leave of her

> mes yeulx estoient
> En un tel vouloir de pleurer
> Qu'a peine tenir s'en povoient
> N'ilz n'osoient riens regarder,

yet he had to try and hide his tears for fear of causing talk. He would rather not have been born than let his grief be seen. As he had thus to leave her without telling her all he was suffering and

> Maintenant que, contre mon vueil,
> Me fault estre de vous loingtains,

and so can no longer see her beauty, he begs her not to forget him, who will serve her faithfully until he dies:

> Si vous suppli, tresbonne et belle,
> Qu'ayez souvenance de moy;
> Car, a tousjours, vous serez celle
> Que serviray comme je doy.

The fact that René of Anjou says that it was through his knowledge of English that Charles made the acquaintance of his English love implies that the lady had no great knowledge of French. If that were so, and if indeed his own English was adequate for the purpose, there is a possibility that he was the author of seven English poems (six *rondeaux* and a *ballade*) which occur in his personal manuscript of his poems,[34] four of which do very much suggest that they were written for Anne Molins. One of these four is the one that gives her name as an acrostic:

> Alas mercy, wher shal myn hert yow fynd?
> Never had he wyth yow ful aqwaintans;
> Now com to hym and put of hys grevans.
> Ellys ye be unto yowr frend unkynd!
>
> Mercy, he hath ever yow in hys mynd:
> Ons let hym have sum conforth of plesans!
> > Alas mercy etc.
>
> Let hym not dey, but mak at ons amende;
> In al hys woo an right hevy penans,
> Noght is the help that whyl not hym avans
> Slauth hys to me and ever com behynde
> > Alas mercy etc.

There are lines in all four that give the impression that they were written after he had been separated from her. In the second of them for instance he says:

> I most as a hertles body
> Abyde alone in hevynes

and in the sixth he tells her:

> That to my hert it is a grete plesans
> Of your godenes when y remembre me.

But he remained faithful even in absence:

> For in my thought, ther is nomo but ye
> Whom y have servid wythout repentance.

And the one that appears to be the last, written perhaps on the verge of his release from imprisonment, suggests most definitely that he had wanted to marry her, but that she, rather shabbily as it seemed to him, had then failed him.

> Ye shal be payd after your whylfulnes
> And blame nothyng but your mysgovernans,
> For when good love wold fayn had yow avans,
> Then went ye bak wyth wyly frauhyednes.

> I knew anon your sotyl wylenes
> And your danger, that was mad for ascans
> Ye schal be etc.

> Ye might have been my lady and maistres
> For ever mor withouthyn varians;
> But now my hert yn Yngland or in France
> Ys go to seke other nyw besynes.
> Ye schal be etc.

And so this English love-story ended in disappointment for him, but a disappointment not so bitter that he could not contemplate 'new business' in the future, either in England or in France. Indeed, even while he was writing to his English love in 1436, it seems possible that he had been contemplating a possible marriage with Margaret, daughter of the Duke of Savoy, whose husband Louis, Duke of Anjou, the elder brother of René, had died in 1434. It appears that there was then some idea that those responsible for the plan might be able to buy Charles' freedom, if we can judge from the *ballade* that is thought to refer to this matter, and in which he says to his heart:

> Mon cueur dormant en Nonchaloir,
> Reveilliez vous joyeusement,

Je vous fais nouvelles savoir,
Qui vous doit plaire grandement;
Il est vray que presentement
Une Dame treshonnoree
En toute bonne renommee
Desire de vous acheter,
Dont je suy joyeux et d'accort;
Pour vous, son cueur me veult donner
Sans departir, jusqu'a la mort.

It is obvious from the cheerful and even excited tone of this that the prospect of all this filled him with elation and hope, indeed he goes on to say so:

Ce change doy je recevoir
En grant gré tresjoyeusement;

charging his heart to go at once and lodge with her 'Et l'onnourer entierement'. The marriage did not in the end come off; but the story of this little episode certainly seems to indicate that Charles' amorous adventure in England did not after all go very deep.

CHAPTER TWELVE
1436–1440

DURING the two and a half years when Charles had been dropped from the peace-making activities, he appears to have had a very solitary time, for there is no record of any visits to him at that period. But not only did he bear this state of apparent abandonment with his usual patience and fortitude, he managed also to retain that humour that so often flickers in and out of his verses. It was a gay, mocking humour, that enabled him to take a detached and clear-sighted view of himself and his circumstances, without a trace of self-pity. Nothing better expresses it than a *ballade* that he wrote to assure his friends in France that, contrary to recent rumours, he was not dead; some may be sorry to hear it, he says, but his true friends, who love him loyally, will rejoice 'Qu'encore est vive la souris!' He goes on to tell them that he is in good health, and that he spends his time in hoping that peace, 'qui trop longuement dort', will awake one day. Although old age is trying to get a grip on him, youth is still potent in him, and he thanks God for having given him such energy and strength that 'the mouse is still alive'. He ends by recommending that no one should wear black for him, grey cloth is cheaper. It would be difficult to find a less pompous peer of France in that or any other epoch than the author of that poem.

Well though he had endured it, this trying period of suspended animation mercifully came to an end in May 1436, when Charles was transferred from Wingfield to the care of Sir Reynold Cobham, of Sterborough Castle in Surrey. No explanation is given for this change, though the fact that Suffolk, after the failure of the Arras conference, had to return to France in the following October to take part in the continuing war, is perhaps reason enough for his having to give up the guardianship of Charles. For Charles himself, apart from the loss of the company of Suffolk and his family, the change meant a transfer to a curiously similar situation; for Sterborough, like Wingfield, was also a small, square, moated castle, set in the middle of flat land, two or three miles from the nearest village, that of Lingfield. But the now-vanished castle, whose shape is still clearly discernible in the shape of the island in the moat, was much smaller than that of Wingfield, and life there was doubtless on a simpler scale. Sir Reynold was given the same payment for keeping Charles as Suffolk had received.

Remote though Sterborough was, almost immediately after his transfer Charles entered on a period of activity that did not cease until his release, and moved about more freely than he ever had before. It looks very much as though this was due to the king himself. Henry VI was now a youth of fifteen, and was beginning to play an increasingly important part in the deliberations of the Council, thus lessening the influence of Gloucester. Although he may have been weak, he was kindly and humane too, and his attitude towards the Agincourt prisoners, especially Charles, had always been understanding and even affectionate. So now, although it is nowhere expressly stated, it seems likely that it was the king who laid down that, if Charles could find the sum of 20,000 crowns to cover the estimated expenses, he should then be allowed to travel to France, and not merely to Calais, on a mission designed to promote peace.[1] Henry was in close communication at this time with the Duke of Brittany, who seems to have become less fickle with the passage of time; and the king's letters to him show that he was greatly counting on the duke's help and influence in the making of peace. Brittany certainly at this point was to prove himself a useful friend to Charles too.

On hearing of this new possibility, Charles set to work without delay to obtain the necessary money. Even while on his way from Wingfield to Sterborough he wrote from London to Cousinot, asking him to send letters-patent for the officers of his household, letters that would be necessary for the instructions he was to send them.[2] He signed this letter with his own hand, and indeed the hand in which the actual text of it is written also strongly resembles his own. If in fact it was, nothing could better convey his eagerness in the matter. This sense of urgency plainly communicated itself to all concerned in Blois, making them feel that now at last there was a chance that their lord might soon be returning to them. And for the next eighteen months both the Bastard and Charles' chief officials were constantly on the road about his affairs, keeping in touch with the English commanders in Normandy[3] who of course were closely concerned in any plans for peace, and striving to collect those 20,000 crowns.

The prince who showed himself by far the most generous at that time was the Duke of Brittany, who, with help from the Bastard himself, promised half the sum demanded.[4] The only means that could be found of raising the bulk of the remainder was by the sale of lands and titles. Except in the very last resort Charles could not dispose of those territories, especially the royal apanages, from which he took his own titles. The Bastard therefore, with his customary generosity and devotion to his brother, began to sell those counties with which Charles had rewarded his loyal service from time to time: Périgord and Porcien[5]—a sale that proved by no means easy. The need to try every possible means to raise money is well illustrated by the fact that in April 1437 a herald was sent to Bruges to sell a balay ruby to a merchant there;[6] while that summer the relations of Jean de Rochechouart, now dead, were asked to give an account of the still unsold tapestry and jewels deposited at La Rochelle ten years before, and again to sell them.[7] (See page 280 below.)

What added to the difficulty in collecting the 20,000 crowns was that the ordinary expenses of life still continued; and that Charles showed himself as generous as ever, especially where his family were concerned. That family in fact increased at that time, for in January 1437 a bastard of Philip of Vertus turned up from Lombardy, apparently to the surprise of all concerned. Charles, hearing of it, ordered his treasurer to pay the debts of his "fair nephew Philip Anthony of Vertus" and to give him money for his personal expenses.[8] That same year Charles gave handsome pensions to his sister Margaret, Countess of Étampes and to the Bastard, who was also given the captaincy of Pierrefonds, perhaps to compensate for the lands and titles he was surrendering. Nor was John of Angoulême forgotten, for in May Jean Le Fuzelier, who was now general counsellor for the duke's finances, was ordered to pay him 600 gold *écus* annually, as he was finding the salt-tax insufficient for his needs.

Meanwhile the English, or rather it seems the young king himself, was so anxious for Charles to begin his mission that he was prepared for him to go to France as soon as he had received the half of the stipulated sum that Brittany and the Bastard had contributed. The reason is perhaps apparent from the formal permission to go to Normandy which he gave Charles, in a letter dated April 29th, 1437,[9] in which he said that Pope Eugenius IV, the Council of Basle and the Duke of Brittany had all been writing to him exhorting him to make peace. In the same letter he stated that the money he had demanded was for the cost of the duke's journey and those of the people needed for his custody; but he laid it down that, if it were not so used, Charles would

be allowed to take it back to France with him (after his liberation presumably), provided he did not use it against Henry or his heirs. The
next day letters-patent which Jean de Saveuses was to take to France for
the use of the duke were read to the Council and assented to by them.[10]
A hitch in the proceedings then occurred because the 10,000 crowns
had not arrived. But early in July it looked as if they were going to
materialise, and the king instructed his Chancellor in France, the Archbishop of Rouen, to give safe-conducts to the persons bringing the
money.[11] At the same time Sir Reynold Cobham was authorised to let
the herald who came with it speak with Charles.[12]

It now looked as though no obstacle remained to his peace mission
and Charles' excitement at the thought of it shines through everything
he then wrote and did. At the end of August he sent, by a herald, messages to the Bastard, apprising him of his speedy return to France.[13]
He paid a goldsmith in England to make new patent seals for his use.
He sent one of his officers, Benoît de Vaulx, to take letters about his
affairs to the Queen of France, Yolanda's daughter Mary, in Tours. In
September Jean le Fuzelier and Jean de Saveuses were sent to Rouen
to see the Archbishop and the English Council there about the date for
his visit. But it was not yet possible to fix a date because the money had
still not arrived, and was not now expected before January 15th.[14] In
great distress and anxiety about this, Henry VI called a Great Council
to meet at Sheen to tell them of his plan to send Charles to Normandy
and to ask their advice about the finance of it. They suggested that Sir
Reynold Cobham should bring Charles before the Council and he
was accordingly brought to London and taken down to Sheen on the
October 28th.[15] No decisions were taken there, but since there seemed
no reason to doubt that Brittany's money would in the end be forthcoming, it was clear to all, including Charles, that this time the intention
to send him to France was definite.

His conviction that his circumstances were now very soon going to
change and that he was at an important cross-roads in his career, made
Charles, as his way was, take stock of his inner life; and as was natural
to him, he embodied the thoughts that this bred in him in a long poem
called the *Songe en Complainte*, which he wrote a day or two after
returning from Sheen. It is a pendant to the *Retenue d'Amours*, that he
wrote when he was on the verge of manhood before Agincourt, and he
uses in it the same allegorical framework. But the verse in this second
poem is not only, as one would expect, much more mature technically

in its suppleness and richness. It has now become a vehicle in which Charles uses those abstractions, to which even in his earlier work he had always contrived to give a certain personality, to a most moving effect, so that through them we enter into his heart and soul, and share the emotions that filled them at this crucial stage of his life.

He begins with the usual convention of a dream in which he sees before him an old man, whom he thinks he has seen before but whose name he cannot remember. Seeing this, the old man tells him he is Age, and reminds him how he once took him from Infancy and handed him over to Youth; but now he has come to warn him that he has lingered over long with her and that Old Age will soon claim him. It were therefore better, while he still has youth, to give up thoughts of love 'Puisque la Mort a prins vostre maistresse'. If he gives up love voluntarily no one will be able to say 'Que l'ayez fait par faulte de puissance'; they will think it is for sorrow, because he does not wish to love elsewhere

> Puisqu'est morte vostre Dame sans per,
> Dont loyaument gardez le souvenance.

He should therefore ask the God of Love to give him back his heart, that he may leave his service honourably. After all this he wakes up trembling like a leaf, so grim is the thought of Old Age. Yet although he still feels young and is not tired, he admits it is better to be prepared, for then Old Age will treat him more gently. He therefore decides to renounce all amorous exploits and to write to Love begging him publicly to release him from his vow and to give him his heart again.

This narrative prologue fills twenty-two stanzas that carry the reader smoothly along. Then comes The Request, addressed to God Cupid and the Goddess Venus, and this is couched in eight short stanzas of a complicated but elegant metre, of which the first is:

> Supplie presentement,
>   Humblement,
> Charles, le duc d'Orlians,
> Qui a esté longuement,
>   Ligement,
> L'un de voz obeissans,

> Et entre les vrais amans,
> Voz servans,
> A despendu largement
> Le temps de ses jeunes ans
> Tresplaisans,
> A vous servir loyaument.

It goes on to remind the two gods how Death has taken 'sa seule Dame' from him. As he will never fall in love again he begs them to give him his heart back, with a formal letter, drawn up by Good Faith, to say this has been done with their agreement. He will be lastingly grateful to them if they will do this.

After this follows a series of four *ballades*, headed *La Departie d'Amours*, describing how Love first encouraged him to think he might find another lady ready to love him, but then, seeing he is not to be persuaded, promises, as a reward for his faithful service, to give him his acquittance. Having received this, Charles then asks for his heart back. He kneels before Love, who takes his heart, wrapped in a black silk covering, from a case and

> En mon sain le mist doulcement,
> Pour en faire ce que vouldroye.

Then follows a copy of the acquittance that Love has freely given after hearing the plaint

> De Charles, le duc d'Orlian,
> Qui a esté par plusieurs ans
> Nostre vray loyal serviteur.

The acquittance states clearly, to prevent malicious gossip, that he is not leaving Love's service for any fault, but simply because Death has taken his lady and he wishes to be like the loyal turtle-dove who, having lost her companion, only wants to remain alone. Love then sets his seal on the document

> Le Jour de la Feste des Mors,
> L'an mil quatre cent trente et sept.

After this there follow three *ballades* which are the most moving part of the whole poem. In them Charles relates how he is so overcome with grief on leaving the court of Love that the God sends Comfort to help him. Comfort leads him to the manor of 'Nonchaloir' (indifference) where he dwelt in childhood. There he is welcomed and decides to stay until Old Age comes to take him away. The thought of that weighs on his heart when he remembers it; but he thanks God he is still far from it. Feeling now happy and well, he writes to thank Love for all he has done for him, and hopes the God will always be able to prevail over

> faulx Dangier,
> Qui en tous temps vous a esté contraire.

The poem ends:

> Escript ce jour troisieme, vers le soir,
> En novembre, ou lieu de Nonchaloir.
> Le bien vostre, Charles, duc d'Orlians,
> Qui jadis fut l'un de voz vrais servans.

It was rare for Charles to date any of his poems in this way; that he did so now shows what importance for him this crucial time had assumed. The air was thick with the sense of impending events. Later that November the king's Council selected the names of those who were to accompany him to France,[16] and Jean de Saveuses came over to visit him before his journey as did also his herald Porcépic.[17] In December another of Charles' heralds, Montaguillon, went from Blois to Rouen to see Suffolk about it; and just before Christmas still another of them, Camail, came to England to visit Charles, together with the herald of the Duke of Brittany. Another thing that seemed to presage his early departure was that in November his brother John of Angoulême, accompanied by his keeper, Waller, was given permission to "go to the Duc of Orleans, to speke with him in both their keepers sight and hearing, an it seem good to my Lord Cardinal".[18] As far as is known, this was the only occasion on which they met during the years of their imprisonment,* and must have been a special privilege because of Charles' forthcoming mission. When one thinks of all they had both endured, because of each other, since the then youthful Charles had been obliged, twenty-five years earlier, to send his twelve-year-old brother to England as a hostage, the meeting between them must have been more painful than pleasurable on both sides.

The Council now seemed so keen to press on with the sending of

* See Appendix I.

Charles that on January 16th 1438 they decided, as the money had still not yet arrived, to advance the necessary funds to take him to Cherbourg to make peace, "rather than that it should break".[19] But first, with the habitual English caution, in order that all the arrangements should be laid down and accepted on both sides, Sir John Popham, the Treasurer of the king's household, and other envoys were sent to France to discuss them with the Duke of Brittany, who had offered himself as a mediator.[20] They did not leave until mid-March and then first visited the Earl of Warwick, in command of the English forces,[21] so that it was not until May 30th that they reached agreement, in Vannes, with the Duke of Brittany and the Bastard, as to the best way to send Charles over.[22]

And then, after all that preparation, for some reason that remains mysterious, Charles did not go. Stranger still, it appears that he was himself responsible for this, although we do not know why. Had he perhaps received some secret news from France, and did his French friends there, and perhaps Suffolk too, consider that it was undesirable to let the Duke of Brittany be the mediator in this great matter? In May, Jean de Saveuses came to England again, bringing four letters from French knights to Suffolk, who happened to be in England at that time. Saveuses was sent to speak with his master, who was summoned to appear before the Council again.[23] But there is no record of the contents of the four letters, nor of what passed at the Council meeting on July 8th. Charles was at that time again transferred, for unexplained reasons, from Sterborough to the care of Sir John Stourton,[24] a member of the Council and one of the king's faithful supporters, who lived at Stourton in Wiltshire, in a splendid castle, part of which he had built out of his profits from the wars in France. When passing through London on his way there Charles went to see the king.

This we learn from a document,[25] in French, dated July 17th and issued over the signature of Henry VI. It reads like a minute written to record something recently heard and decided. It first states that as the "appointment" made by the king's ambassadors with the Duke of Brittany and the Bastard had not been kept, it was cancelled. The king then goes on to say that the Duke of Orleans had come to see him in person, and clearly admitted that it was "through him or his people. . . and not through us" that he could not go to Normandy within the time set. He had therefore asked that the appointment should be prorogued. He had also asked that in the meantime, while peace plans were being worked on, a truce should be proclaimed "for the relief and consolation of the subjects on both sides." The king had agreed to the duke's request on condition that a considerable sum should be paid, a part of it in gold and silver money, plate and jewels, to be handed over to his representatives in Rouen by the following October 1st; and he promised that if he could be sufficiently satisfied that "his adversary of France" would send ambassadors to Cherbourg he would send Charles about the fifteenth of February 1439 across the sea to Normandy. The document ended with a proviso which almost seems to forsee another breakdown, to the effect that if, through the fault of the king or his people, Charles did not go, the king would refund in the May following such part of the sum of gold money as had been paid.

One is almost tempted to think that Charles' readiness to accept such a distant date for the prorogued appointment with the Duke of Brittany indicates that he did not expect to keep that one either, and must have had good reason for it—perhaps a hope of a better plan. At any rate he does not appear to have been cast down at that time. It may be that his interview with the king had fortified his hope of being set free before long, for from then onwards there is increasing evidence that this kindly young sovereign was totally opposed to the harsh views of his father and his uncle Gloucester where prisoners were concerned. In the preceding May Charles' friend and contemporary, the Count of Eu, had at last returned to France, having been exchanged for the Earl of Somerset, who had been a prisoner there since he was taken at the Battle of Baugé seventeen years before. Charles was thus the last of the Agincourt captives still awaiting freedom. It could surely not be long now.

Pending any further immediate arrangements for him, the English did make an attempt to institute the truce that Charles had advised, and in August the English Chancellor in Rouen sent a letter to the dauphin to suggest it. But the Bastard, who appears to have been the official spokesman and was very much in control of the situation, obviously auspected that this was a scheme to by-pass Charles. He therefore answered that the dauphin would act only as his Council advised, and on that he promised to send them a plain answer shortly. In this plain answer,[26] which he wrote from Blois on September 20th, he stated that the dauphin "the wheche that he called his king", would not treat of a peace or truce until "he hadde sende hys ymbassators into Engelonde to the duke of Orlyaunce, and that he hadde answered again from hym."

An entirely different approach to the peace problem was then made, obviously at the instance of the Duke of Burgundy, for in January 1439 Cardinal Beaufort went to Calais to discuss with the Duchess Isabella the possibility of a conference.[27] It must have been because peace between France and England was, as she had said before the Arras meeting, one of the things that she most desired, that her husband Philip was content to leave the pursuit of it in her hands, a most unusual proceeding at the epoch. It was agreed that a conference should be held during the course of the year, and it was settled that Charles of Orleans should attend it, since the duchess set great store by his presence.

The place finally chosen for the conference was the Château d'Oye, about seven miles from Calais and four from Gravelines. The date selected for its opening was July 6th. As it would be necessary for the French delegates sometimes to visit Calais, in May Henry sent the duchess safe-conducts for a large number of princes.[28] In the event the only delegates who came were the Archbishop of Rheims, the Count of Vendôme and the Bastard, who were chosen to be the French ambassadors. In May also the English ambassadors were chosen: The Archbishop of York led them, with Cardinal Beaufort as mediator. On May 26th they were given very detailed instructions as to exactly how they were to proceed.[29]

No effort is needed to imagine the state of mind of Charles of Orleans at this juncture. In order that he might appear at the conference as befitted his rank, certain articles of dress had been bought for him at Saint-Omer as early as March 1st.[30] He and Sir John left Stourton on May 8th for their journey to Dover. They joined the archbishop and the other ambassadors there and on Friday, June 26th, crossed to Calais. They lost no time in welcoming the French ambassadors to the town, and the next morning the latter called on the Duke of Orleans in the great hall of the staple* and spent the whole day in conference with him there, breaking their talks only when they all went to dine with the cardinal and the archbishop at ten in the morning and to sup with the Earl of Stafford at five in the evening.[31] In addition to the satisfaction of being at last consulted on the questions he had so much at heart, that

---

* A staple was an officially-appointed place where merchants had the exclusive right of purchase of goods destined for export. There were many such in important towns in England, Wales and Scotland, but in the fifteenth century the chief was at Calais and was therefore called simply "The Staple". O.E.D.

day brought Charles one of the greatest joys he had tasted for a long time: his meeting with his brother the Bastard, whom he had not seen since the Bastard was a boy of eleven, and whom he was at last able to thank in person for the devoted care he had taken of his duchy for so many years. The French ambassadors left Calais for Gravelines next morning, but on July 2nd some members of Charles' Council in Blois arrived to see him, and some of his friends who had accompanied the ambassadors remained with him in Calais until July 5th, when they left after vespers.

After these auspicious beginnings it was a great disappointment to Charles to learn next day, when the English ambassadors left Calais for the opening of the conference in the great pavilion that Isabella had had erected near the Château d'Oye, that he was to remain behind in Calais, guarded by his keeper Sir John Stourton, and one or two others charged with the same duty and with the defence of the town. The chief reason for this was that the English had heard from their scouts, who had, with the agreement of the French, been scouring the country-side in the vicinity of Calais, that many Flemings and Picards had been asking whether Charles was to attend the meetings, and rumours had consequently arisen of an intention to try to rescue him. Indeed, throughout the whole of the proceedings the English were obviously haunted by the fear of such an event, so that they never permitted Charles to go to the place where the official deliberations were being held. When he learnt that he was to be excluded in this way, Charles remarked that if he were not there the others would merely beat the air. His prophecy proved only too true.

Discord broke out at the first meeting, when each side objected to the other's terms of reference. The French considered it insulting that the English called their sovereign merely 'Charles of Valois', curiously enough preferring their usual appellation 'Our Adversary of France' as more respectful. The English found the French terms, mentioning as their two main aims the conclusion of a final peace and the release of the Duke of Orleans, obscure and contradictory, although they seem plain enough. It was agreed to redraft both but to begin talks mean-while, whereupon a deadlock was almost immediately reached. The English, true to their instructions, in which the hand of Gloucester is plain to see, once again bluntly and inflexibly claimed the crown of France for Henry VI. They refused to pay homage for the French lands they held; and although at one point they offered to cede the lands

228

south of the Loire, they did this only on condition that they should be held in homage to Henry and in return for an annual rent of £20,000. The French of course utterly rejected these demands.

In the hope that the influence of Charles of Orleans might prevail, it was agreed on July 12th that the duchess and the French ambassadors should confer with him. Accordingly next day all concerned (with the exception of the Archbishop of Rheims ("who had hurt his foot in playing at the ball on the preceding day") met in tents erected about two bowshots from Calais. This was the first occasion on which Charles and Isabella had met, and as each shared so passionately the convictions of the other it must have been a meeting fraught with emotion on both sides. Cardinal Beaufort, who himself genuinely desired peace, was generous enough occasionally to leave them during their talks, which lasted all day, broken only when they repaired to his tent for wine and sweetmeats. Although she well knew his mind, the duchess at one point asked Charles the strange question: "My lord, wilt thou never have peace?" Had he perhaps raised some small objection, or did she want merely to reassure the French ambassadors who were present throughout? If so, his answer must have done so, for he replied: "Yea, though I die for it." What other means of achieving it they discussed is not stated. A pause in the proceedings then ensued, for the next day Isabella sent a message asking that the meetings should be postponed for two or three days, as she had had to go to Saint-Omer to see her husband, who was not well.

When she returned two days later Isabella put to the cardinal a plan from which she hoped much. This was that, as it seemed impossible to reach a final peace, a temporary one to last for 30, 20 or at worst 15 years should be instituted, during which time Henry VI would refrain from using the title of King of France. If, after the treaty lapsed, he wanted to resume it and start the war again, he could do so provided he gave one year's notice of his intention. This rather feminine proposal was obviously based on the commonsense conviction that surely no one would be so foolish as deliberately to restart all this troublesome business after a long interval, quite apart from the changes of circumstances and personalities that time would bring. The plan commended itself to the cardinal, especially as he had been instructed, at the king's particular desire, if all else failed to try and get Isabella or Charles to propose a modified version of it.[32] But when the cardinal told the other ambassadors of it they demanded to see it in writing. The written version was found to include a clause to the effect that Henry VI should surrender his French possessions for the duration of this truce, with the exception of a list of these to be agreed, but these were not specified. Even Charles of Orleans expressed surprise at the difference between the two versions.

In the course of the subsequent meetings, deadlock was again soon reached. The English ambassadors told the duchess they could not accept her formula in itself, without seeing the list of places; that even if the list were inserted they could not conclude a peace of that kind without referring back to their king, and this would take three weeks; and finally they gave her to understand that the list would have to include all the lands they had ever claimed in France—a good two-thirds of the country. Faced with what threatened to be the failure of her plan the duchess, worn out by her efforts, was momentarily reduced to tears, but "whether of rage or grief. . . I know not", says the king's secretary, Beckington. Another long day of conversations outside Calais between herself and her ambassadors on the one hand, and with Charles and the cardinal on the other, failed to advance matters, and on July 29th it was agreed to adjourn the whole conference until September 11th and try to start afresh then.

On August 5th the English ambassadors chosen for the mission embarked for England to lay Isabella's proposal before the king. Charles remained in Calais with the cardinal who, hearing that many people in the town were asking if the duke were still there, posted extra sentinels to keep strict watch. While they waited, nothing happened in Calais itself; but Charles VII, whom Isabella had informed of her temporary peace-proposal, wrote to both her and Charles to say that he on his side could not accept it without the consent of the lords of the blood and his Council, and that they would not be able to meet until September 25th. The French ambassadors had in any case left Gravelines on July 30th, so when the English, having returned from England on September 9th, went to the conference pavilion on the 11th, they found no-one there. When they heard of the letters from Charles VII they decided that there was no point in continuing to confer, especially as the message they had brought back was that the peace proposal was utterly unacceptable—a decision which Gloucester admitted later that he had imposed.[33] But when Isabella heard of this decision she asked for safe-conducts to come to Calais once more to confer with Charles. Her request was granted and on September 15th she came, and spent the whole day with him and the English. But their talk only underlined the general disagreement. Isabella was given in writing the reasons why the English rejected her plan, but all the same she continued to plead for it. When she suggested that the conference should continue after they heard from Charles VII the opinion of his Council, the cardinal refused, accusing the French of delaying deliberately, and remarking that at Arras they had made better offers. This Isabella countered by pointing out that the French were now in a much stronger position than they had been then, and gave him a list of the towns they had taken in the interval. The only decision reached was that a new meeting should be held on April 15th or May 1st 1440. And on October 2nd, after being held up a long time by the weather, the ambassadors returned to England.

Although Charles had been disappointed of his hope that he would be able to make peace, his stay in Calais had brought him many consolations. He may not have been allowed on French soil but he had breathed again the air of France. Apart from his staff he had been surrounded by well-wishers, all eager for his final return, the Bastard chief among them. But perhaps the greatest consolation of all, where his hopes for the future were concerned, was that he had made the acquaintance of Isabella of Burgundy, who seemed to desire his freedom as much as he did himself.

It was obviously thanks to her, too, that he was at last able to communicate with her husband, as he had so longed to do six years earlier when he met the duke's envoy, Hue de Lannoy, and permission had been refused. Even now a regular exchange of letters would perhaps have been frowned upon; but poems were a different matter, hardly to be reckoned dangerous. So although, some years previously, after his *Songe en Complainte*, he had renounced his poetic gift in a melancholy *ballade* beginning

> Balades, chançons et complaintes
> Sont pour moy mises en oubly,
> Car ennuy et pensees maintes
> M'ont tenu long temps endormy,

and going on to complain that his language has become rusty, so that those who knew it when he was 'Jeune, nouvel et plain de joye' must now excuse him, he now had recourse to it again to convey to Philip of Burgundy, in some of the freshest and most spontaneous poems he ever wrote, all his deepest feelings at that critical and exciting moment of his life.

There are altogether five *ballades* addressed to Burgundy, only the first two of which appear to have been written from Calais. The first conveys vividly his delight at being in France not far from his cousin, his desire to learn more about him, his longing for peace and his loyal affection:

> Puisque, je suis vostre voisin
> En ce païs presentement,
> Mon compaignon, frere et cousin,
> Je vous requier treschierement
> Que de vostre gouvernement
> Et estat me faictes savoir;
> Car j'en orroye bien souvent,
> S'il en estoit a mon vouloir.

One of his reasons for wanting peace is

> Que je puisse joyeusement,
> A mon desir, prouchainement
> Parler a vous et vous veoir.

Once again he says how much he hates war, and would banish it entirely if he had his way. In the envoy he sends his *ballade* quickly to Saint-Omer to tell the duke that he is his

> loyaument
> Et tout a son commandement
> S'il en estoit a mon vouloir.

This *ballade* had such an effect on Burgundy that it moved him to try his hand at a *ballade* in reply. It is a poor, halting thing and presumably it was his awareness of his inadequacy as a poet that made him address Charles as 'Mon maistre et amy sans changier'; but it did express his agreement with all Charles' sentiments on war and peace, and his own desire to get him out of prison if it were in his power. Charles' reply is an extraordinary proof that poetry was so much his natural mode of expression that he could dash off something that combines all the urgency of a letter written in a hurry with the calm perfection of a beautifully composed *ballade*. It was written on the eve of his sailing back to England:

> Pour le haste de mon passage
> Quil me couvient faire oultre mer,
> Tout ce que j'ay en mon courage
> A present ne vous puis mander.
> Mais non pourtant, a brief parler,
> De la balade que m'avés
> Envoyee, comme savés,
> Touchant paix et ma delivrance,
> Je vous mercie chierement,
> Comme tout vostre entierement
> De cueur, de corps et de puissance.

He goes on to say he will without delay send Burgundy a message 'loyal, secret et assez sage', telling him all he can find out about the things Burgundy wants to know, and charging him to busy to himself about matters in France. In the next stanza his deep feelings, so long denied outlet, well out. He tells Philip that he is leaving him his heart as security, and will never fail; he asks him to recommend him to his cousin Isabella, and to believe

> Que en vous deux, tant que vivrés,
> J'ay mise toute ma fiance;
> Et vostre party loyaument
> Tendray, sans faire changement,
> De cueur, de corps et de puissance!

The *ballade* ends with his protestation that

> Tout Bourgongnon sui vrayement
> De cueur, de corps et de puissance!

The beautiful rhythm of this last line of each stanza not surprisingly so sang in Burgundy's head that he made it the first of his answering *ballade*, of which the burden is that only Charles can bring peace, and they must pray God for it "Car trop avez souffert douleur". He urges him too not to forget

> L'estat et le gouvernement
> De la noble maison de France,
> Qui se maintient piteusement.

Charles and his keeper arrived back at Stourton on October 14th.[34] Either on his way there or soon after, thanks to the cardinal, he had an audience with the king, from whom he learnt some news that filled him with the deepest pleasure. Although he may not have been aware of it, even before the beginning of the conference the idea of his final liberation had been accepted in principle and the ambassadors had been empowered to discuss the ransom that should be exacted;[35] but in the event they omitted to do this. By the time Charles saw the king, Henry had learnt from his ambassadors of their failure to make peace, and had also heard from Isabella of the proposed dates for the renewal of the conference in the following year. So ardently did the king now desire peace that he quickly wrote to her,[36] agreeing to the proposal. But it was now quite clear to him that peace would never be achieved unless Charles were released, if only temporarily, to help prepare the conference and take part in it as a free agent. The good news that he therefore gave him at his audience was that he was to be temporarily freed to that end, as soon as he could obtain financial guarantees from his compatriots to cover his ransom.

The elation that filled Charles on hearing this news rings out in the *ballade* that he at once wrote to Burgundy to tell him of it and of the king's kindly reception of him, beginning:

> Des nouvelles d'Albion,
> S'il vous en plaist escouter,
> Mon frere et mon compaignon,
> Sachez qu'a mon retourner
> J'ay esté deça la mer
> Reçue a joyeuse chiere,
> Et a fait le roy passer
> En bons termes ma matiere.
>
> Je doy estre une saison
> Eslargi pour pourchasser
> La paix aussi ma raençon;
> Se je puis seurté trouver
> Pour aler et retourner
> Il fault qu'en haste la quiere
> Se je vueil brief achever
> En bons termes ma matiere.

He therefore begs Burgundy to promise to help him financially, for

> Mes amis fault esprouver
> S'ilz vouldront, a ma priere,
> Me secourir pour mener
> En bons termes ma matiere.

Burgundy seems to have responded at once to this appeal, for Charles' next *ballade* to him begins:

> Beau frere, je vous remercie,
> Car aidié m'avez grandement.

As for the other friends whose willingness to help him Charles decided to prove, there exists what would appear to be the prototype of a letter[37] designed to be sent to all his close relatives; a letter that is both dignified and touching in its confidence that the help asked will be forthcoming:

Very dear and very beloved cousin, I commend myself to you. And may it please you to know that after I left Calais, I reached an agreement with the King of England and his Council concerning my deliverance. For which deliverance I need your help. I therefore pray and require you, as affectionately as I can, very dear and very beloved cousin, that you will succour and help me in the way that my brother the Bastard will beg of you in my behalf, as I have and must have trust in you that you will not fail me in this. May it please God, very dear and very beloved cousin, to have you in his holy keeping and to grant you a good life, and long. Written at
in England on the   day of
    Your cousin the Duke of Orleans and Valois, Count of Blois and Beaumont and Lord of Coucy
                                                            Charles.

Charles despatched letters on these lines from Stourton to his friends and relatives on October 26th.[38] At the same time he wrote to the Bastard to ask him to intercede for him, and also to obtain the king's guarantee for the sums that he hoped the queen and the dauphin too would contribute towards his ransom. He informed the authorities of his town of Orleans of his forthcoming return.[39] And finally, in giving the same good news to his own officers, he asked them to send him the ready cash he needed. Having thus done everything he could, Charles had to wait with what patience he might for the outcome of all his requests.

It was a solemn moment in his life, for that November he was forty-five. He marked his anniversary with a ballade in which he mentions it, saying:

> J'ay tant joué avecques Aage
> A la paulme que maintenant
> J'ay quarante cinq;

Age is furious that this game of tennis should have lasted so long, but Charles says he still feels himself strong and powerful enough to keep it up. It is not a very inspired poem. In a much better one, which may also have been written at this time, and which begins with the lovely line 'je fu en fleur ou temps passé d'enfance', he looks back over his life, and with his characteristic philosophy comes to the conclusion that it was not unwise of Reason to cast him into prison, where the fire-brand of foolish desire was quenched in him, and he was able to grow mature as he lay on his prison straw. Now all he prays for is peace, when he will be:

> Tost refreschi, et au souleil de France
> Bien nettié du moisy de Tristesse;
> J'attens Bon Temps, endurant en humblesse.
> Car j'ay espoir que Dieu ma guerison
> Ordonnera; pour ce, m'a sa haultesse
> Mis pour meurir ou feurre de prison.

He had not long to wait, for in December no fewer than eleven of those to whom he had appealed for financial help replied,[40] all guaranteeing large sums for his ransom, so that it looked as though his deliverance was at last in sight. But before it could be planned, another obstacle arose.

There still remained in England one man violently opposed to the freeing of Charles: Humphrey of Gloucester. Of the varied passions that swayed this strange and complex character—his genuine devotion to learning, his recklessly changeable relations with women, his political hatreds, and his obstinate clinging to the aims and ambitions in France of his dead brother Henry V— none were stronger than the last two. High on the list of those he loathed was his uncle Cardinal Beaufort, of whose influence in the realm he had always been jealous. This hatred was so exacerbated by the cardinal's efforts at Calais to work for that peace to which he himself was totally opposed, and to use Charles to that end, that soon after the turn of the year he attempted to pour all the poison of it into the ears of the young king, who wisely suggested that he should put his case in writing.

The resulting document[41] is an extraordinary diatribe, the main aim of which is to accuse the cardinal of every possible malpractice in the way of corruption and graft since the days of the king's earliest childhood. When he comes to the recent peace conference one of his charges is that, although there was a natural enmity between Burgundy and Orleans "for the murder of their fathers like to have endured for ever", the cardinal, by allowing Charles to talk with Isabella, made peace between them "to the hurt of both Henry's kingdoms." He has heard that it is due to the influence of the cardinal that Charles is to be freed, for which purpose he has brought him to London; and he reminds the king that Henry V had said in his last will that Charles should never be freed until he himself had completed his conquest of France and then only with every possible guarantee. What should therefore be done with him now that the enemies in France have so increased in power?

There is no record of any discussion of this document in the minutes of the Council meetings, but there must have been, for sometime during the spring Gloucester followed it with another,[42] in the preface to which he stated that the king had asked certain lords of his Council to debate the good and ill effects that might follow the liberation of the Duke of Orleans, and to bring their reports to him. This they did, but Humphrey, having presumably waited to hear theirs first, found that they had omitted much that should be said against this liberation, which he now set down.

It was well known, he said, that neither Charles VII nor his son the dauphin was able to govern and had to be led, and moreover there was dissension between them. Was it not then likely that the French lords and the Three Estates might ask Charles, whose "grete Subtilitie and Cauteleux Disposition" the English Council well knew, to be their Regent, "he being so nigh of the blood and of such discretion as he is named"; and that he might then heal the dissension and unite the princes, to England's hurt? It was known that the duke considered Charles VII his sovereign, to whom his oaths of homage for his lands were more binding than his promises to Henry VI; the oath of a prisoner is not to be trusted. Then there was the danger to the English possessions of Guienne and Normandy, if Charles were free. His alliances with the

Counts of Armagnac and Foix, and the Lord of Albret, would endanger the former. As for Normandy, now that Charles and Burgundy had made peace, they could easily unite to drive the English out. It might be that in the ensuing struggle many brave English lords would be taken prisoner, for four or five of whom Charles might have been held equal. "He is a great Treasure if such thing fall", said Gloucester, forgetting that never once had there been any suggestion of exchanging Charles against English prisoners in France. Again, if Normandy were lost, what would the realm of England say, remembering the deaths of Clarence and Bedford and so many more, and the great labour and cost expended to keep it? Gloucester then once again reminded the king of what Henry V had said in his last will[43] on the freeing of Charles. In conclusion, as he was sure a large part of the kingdom would not agree that Charles should be freed without his consent, and would blame him if it turned out badly, he protested that he never had and never would agree to it, and in case anything different should be said after his death he had put this in writing and now asked the king to acknowledge this under the great seal.

One can only suppose that it was because Gloucester had stirred up so much discussion on the subject of Charles' liberation that Henry VI failed to send ambassadors to the resumed conference at Gravelines, which he had agreed should be held on April 15th or May 1st 1440. This was odd because in April, May, and even up to June 20th, he was still authorising his envoys to attend, and giving power to the Bishop of Rochester and others to conclude either a truce for two years or a final peace with France;[44] and at the same time sending safe-conducts to more French ambassadors.[45] Charles VII would hardly have been to blame if he too had failed to send emissaries, for he was involved just then in an even more disturbing situation.

He had at last taken his royal responsibilities seriously and was beginning to institute a series of reforms which strengthened the central power. These roused the opposition of the feudal princes, so much so that the young Duke of Bourbon, hitherto a staunch supporter of his king, led a revolt against him known as the Praguerie*, in which he was joined by Brittany, Alençon and Vendôme, who together persuaded the sixteen-year-old dauphin Louis, who hated his father, to join them against him. Fortunately, that able soldier Arthur of Richemont remained loyal to his sovereign, the rising was soon crushed, and

* So named because a similar revolt had recently taken place in Prague.

peace was made between the king and his son. In spite of all this Charles VII sent his chancellor to Saint-Omer at the beginning of May,[46] where he was joined by the Bastard and others. The safe-conducts which Henry had sent them in the previous January were to last until July 31st, and the French did in fact remain in Saint-Omer all that summer. Philip and Isabella of Burgundy had in any case taken up residence in their castle of Hesdin, not far away, for the summer too. Curiously enough, there is no record of any protests or queries sent to England about the absence of their English counterparts.

Charles of Orleans, who seems at that time to have been allowed much more liberty of movement than before[47] was well aware of Gloucester's opposition to his liberation and his enmity with Burgundy. He therefore prudently concealed his own friendship with the latter and revealed the subtle disposition and wary nature Gloucester described him as having by speaking ill of Burgundy in public. This we learn from the long *ballade* that he managed to send him, he says, by a porter in whom he trusted, and that openly begins:

> Pour ce que je suis a present
> Avec la gent vostre ennemie,
> Il fault que je face semblant,
> Faignant que je ne vous ayme mie:
> Non pour tant, je vous certiſſie
> Et vous pri que vueillez penser
> Que je seray, toute ma vie,
> Vostre loyaument, sans faulser.
>
> Tous maulx de vous je voiz disant,
> Pour aveugler leur faulse envye;
> Non pour tant, je vous ayme tant,
> Ainsi m'aid la Vierge Marie,
> Que je pry Dieu qu'il me maudye,
> Se ne trouvez, au par aler,
> Que vueil estre, quoy que nul dye,
> Vostre loyaument, sans faulser.

He goes on to urge Philip to act in the same way towards him. Few must know of their secret dealings until the time comes when he can be publicly known as the duke's friend.

For Charles was still sure that that time was coming and was by no means discouraged by Gloucester's efforts to prevent his liberation.

Throughout the spring and summer he went steadily on with his efforts to obtain money from all sources. Fortunately his king seemed well disposed to him now, and even when he was away from Paris, in the midst of his campaign against his rebellious nobles, he wrote to Charles[48] on April 15th to tell him he was going to send his ambassadors to the marches of Calais. In that same month there is talk of taxes[49] being raised to pay for the ransom, and in May Charles of Orleans authorised the Bastard and others to alienate some of his estates for the same purpose. Fortunately members of his staff were still coming to England to help him with all this business, and fortunately too he was being allowed to import an extra supply of wine,—thirty-five very large jars of it duty free—which must have helped to keep him going during this trying time.

Charles had good reason not to lose hope, for Henry VI had not flinched before the force of his uncle Gloucester's protests and kept firmly to his determination to set his prisoner free. The reasons which led him to this decision were summed up in a long document,[50] said to have been issued by the Council after Charles had left, in answer to certain complaints—prompted by whom, one wonders—that the king had acted too personally in the matter. This document often gives the impression that it embodies the king's own words. It does nothing to excuse his action but is, as it states, "a plain declaration... of the causes that the king was moved by", and those causes reveal his strong sense of justice, generous nature and compassionate heart, not to mention much sound common-sense.

The chief cause was the desire he had always had "above all other earthly things", for a good peace to put an end to the war between England and France. He wanted it, first, because only this would heal the schism in the church. Secondly, because the huge waste of money and senseless loss of life, in the attempt to conquer and keep lands in France, had never, from the time of Edward I down to himself, really achieved anything lasting. Thirdly, in Normandy, the one territory they had clung to, his French subjects, unable to endure "the unbearable sorrow and misery of this war" had gradually fled into the neighbouring lands, leaving Normandy unpeopled. He had heard that his 'adversary' was also inclined to peace, but would never consent unless the Duke of Orleans were freed.

Then, on humane grounds, the king felt that it was contrary to custom and the law of arms to keep a man, honestly taken in war, in a perpetual prison, when he was ready to ransom himself. He had never seen such a case before, even with a prisoner much more likely to do harm if freed. Moreover if he still kept the duke, this would merely benefit those in France who did not want peace, prevent the king from achieving it by the duke's means, and waste all the money that had already been spent on him and that which would come from his ransom, all of which things would be more harmful than if, being freed, Charles were to break his word "as it is not presumed that he would."

As for the supposition that the duke, who is considered a "great and fell-witted man", would be able to give information to the enemy because of his knowledge of English policy and government, that he could not since he had never been privy to the Council, and could not even know anything by report, "from hearing of the which he hath been restrained by his keepers, the which have not been accustomed to suffer men to speak with him, but in their presence and hearing." There are many in France with more experience of political rule and the conduct of the war than Charles, "and no marvel, seeing how the said duke has been kept from the experience of both." As for the suggestion that Charles, by uniting the French princes, might endanger the king's lands in France, if the king could not keep them in spite of this, he should no longer do so. The document ends by remarking that any fears that the adversary might put forward obstructions would be safeguarded by their letters-patent containing bonds and promises, to be delivered to the king "before the said duke be enlarged"—a statement suggesting that it was in fact drawn up before the liberation of the duke but only published after.

Whatever the date of it the king had certainly made up his mind to free Charles by June at the latest, and communicated this decision to him; for on July 2nd there was an exchange of letters between them,[51] ratifying the arrangements for the liberation. That of Charles was couched as a formal request for freedom and began with a moving preface reminding the king how, during the bitter years of his imprisonment, endured with tears and groans, he had never, in speech, writing or deed, with either intrigues or plots, evaded his duty as a prisoner. And so he had spent the greater part of his life, exiled from his native land, his friends and family, useless to himself and others, and, being unable to help himself with his money or his lands, gradually becoming so impoverished that he could now hardly get sums to redeem himself or pay for little expenses, as he had been able to do at the beginning.

But his friends, whose promised sums he listed, were going to help him with his ransom whose total, and the conditions of his freeing, he then stated.

The king in his reply[52] acknowledged the truth of that first paragraph and then himself set out in full the terms and conditions agreed. These were that the duke:

1. would pay 80,000 *écus* immediately;
2. a further 120,000 *écus* within six months, counting from the day he left England;
3. in addition to these sums, a further 40,000 *écus* within the same six months.
4. For maximum security, he would procure from "our uncle and adversary, Charles, King of France" letters approving these terms. If he did not keep his promise, says Henry VI significantly, Charles VII and his son were to refuse to help him and make him return to England as soon as possible.
5. On these conditions he would be freed at once in order to let him procure, with the help of his friends, the sums mentioned. In case of non-payment of these forty days after the expiry of the six months, he would make himself a prisoner again.
6. Concerning the will of Henry V, the king declared that its aim in recommending that the duke be kept prisoner, was to secure final peace between the two countries. Charles had promised to obtain this. If at the end of a year he had failed, he must return to his imprisonment.

On August 16th Charles VII ratified the treaty of liberation, as he had been requested,[53] and the only thing that remained for Charles to do before he could leave England was to find the actual money for that down payment of 80,000 *écus*. This proved far from easy and as late as October Charles was still writing to the Bastard empowering him to sell or pledge some of his lands for that purpose.[54] Meanwhile Henry VI was obviously doing his best to help his prisoner in every way he could; for example when the duke told him of the difficulties he was likely to have in the future to obtain all the money he would need, Henry gave him permission[55] to man a ship of two hundred tons with twenty sailors in which to trade in wine, iron, salt and cloth freely between France and England, with safe-conducts for some two dozen of his people so engaged. At the same time he gave Charles himself a safe-conduct to go where he would "en notre Royaume de France", and to take over two hundred of his officers with him.[56] At the end of October Burgundy came to the aid of Charles once again, by buying Coucy, Soissons and other properties, with the proviso that Charles, if he wished, might redeem them in ten years' time; and ordering the Lombard merchants in London to give Charles the money in his name.[57] So that by the end of that month Charles was able to make that first payment to the king.

On October 28th, the feast of St. Simon and St. Jude,[58] Charles was brought to Westminster Abbey, where, in the presence of Henry VI and all the princes except Gloucester, who left the church in a rage before the Mass began,[59] he swore:

Moi, Charles, duc d'Orleans, je jure sur les saints evangiles de Dieu, par moi corporellement touchés, que toutes choses contenues dans les lettres d'appointement faites entre serenissime prince Henry, par la grace de Dieu roi d'Angleterre, et moi, Charles d'Orleans, ainsi que dans les lettres d'obligation faites ou a faire par moi envers le dit roi, signées ou a signer, en tant qu'elles me concernent, moi, ma partie, ou autrement, par convention, pacte ou promesse, suivant tout leur pouvoir, forme et effet, sans ruse, fraude, cavillation ou mal engin, je les accomplirai et ferai accomplir et observer.

Je jure en outre de ne pas faire usage au prejudice du dit seigneur roi, de ses heritiers ou successeurs, des privileges de droit ou autre, ou des lettres de graces que je pourrai obtenir . . . Sic me Deus adjuvet et haec sancta. Autrement je prie le Tres Haut que l'infraction ou la violation de ce serment (outre la perte de l'honneur sur la terre et une marque indelebile d'infamie) me merite la damnation eternelle, m'associe perpetuellement au diable et a ses anges. Et en signe de fidelement observer et accomplir ce serment, et tout ce qui en depend, j'ecris mon nom de ma propre main.[60]

On November 2nd Charles once again declared that he would pay the promised sums "not by force or in any unlawful way obliged, but of his own will".[61] On the 3rd, the king acknowledged the receipt of the 80,000 *écus* and declared his prisoner officially free.* On the 3rd too a certain Charles Waterby with four servants was chosen to take the

* That same day the king, declaring that Sir John Cornwall, Lord Fanhope, (who apparently had always had some kind of overall responsibility for the keeping of Charles), had "hitherto faithfully observed his charge", now discharged "him and his heirs from any further such keeping". See *Patent Rolls*, Henry VI, 1436–41, p. 430.

duke, with one hundred persons in his company, to France. The Bishop of Rochester, who was to be of the party, as was Lord Fanhope too, was instructed to hear Charles repeat his oath as soon as he landed in France, and to treat at the same time for a new peace-conference. On the 5th the king, who seemed more and more anxious to do all he could for Charles, paid twenty pounds from his own treasure to Garter King-of-Arms and sent him to accompany the prisoner "for his honour" to his own lands. On that same day Charles of Orleans set sail for home. Robert Reff, the writer of one of the Paston Letters, recording that "this same weke shall he towards France", prayed "God give grace the said Lord of Orleans be true".[62] The prayer was granted for, in spite of Humphrey of Gloucester's doubts and fears, so far as the matter lay with him, Charles kept his bond.

PART THREE

PART THREE

CHAPTER THIRTEEN
1440–1444

ON November 11th, six days after leaving Dover, Charles of Orleans entered Gravelines.¹ Now at last he stood once more on French soil. There to meet him were the Archbishop of Rheims, Chancellor of France, with other dignitaries sent by Charles VII to welcome home his cousin. Charles, restored again to his rightful place as the third person in the kingdom, received each of them joyfully, says Monstrelet, who reports all the events of Charles' stay with the Burgundians in the greatest detail.² More heartwarming still was the welcome of Isabella of Burgundy, who had done so much to help him, and of his brother the Bastard. But the moment of greatest emotion for Charles came at his meeting with Philip of Burgundy, whom he had not seen since the winter of 1414–15 when Philip, then Count of Charolois, and a young man of his own age, had come to Paris to strive to heal the breach between his father John the Fearless and the princes of Charles' faction.

As the two cousins gazed at each other, the thought of the murders of their fathers, that had so long estranged them, and the cruel civil war that sprang from those atrocious deeds, so overwhelmed them that at first neither was able to speak. Then Charles, overcome with gratitude at the sight of the man to whom he chiefly owed his freedom, said: "By my faith, fair brother and cousin, I ought to love you above all other princes of this realm, and my fair cousin your wife, for if you and she had not existed I should have remained for ever in danger from my enemies, and I have found no better friend than you." To this Philip replied that it weighed upon him that he had not been able to free his cousin sooner, as he had longed to do. The gates of speech thus unlocked, the two cousins could not stop talking of all the things that each had upon his heart, repeating themselves over and over again as people in the grip of strong emotion will.

Relief and joy at finding himself free at last did not tempt Charles to forget his promises to repeat the oath that he had pronounced in Westminster Abbey before he left London; and on the morning of the following day the Bishop of Rochester, Lord Fanhope and Sir Robert Roos, who had been charged to see that this was done, had the satisfaction of hearing Charles pronounce it at the altar of Saint Nicholas, in the parish church of Saint-Willibrod in Gravelines,[3] a church now destroyed. Charles went further than was demanded of him and on the same day he wrote a letter to Henry VI, recognizing the fact that the king had set him at liberty and promising to keep his oath.[4] Having discharged this sacred duty with, as he was to prove, the full intention of keeping his promises, he left Gravelines with Philip and Isabella and the English representatives and went by water to Saint-Omer, where they all lodged in the abbey of Saint-Bertin, one of the great monastic houses of northern France. There for the next few days Charles held a kind of court, receiving not only kinsfolk, friends and servitors from his own lands, but many people from other parts of France who came to welcome him back.

Although there is no need to doubt the sincerity of his friendly feelings for Charles* and the genuineness of his desire to free him, Philip of Burgundy was not moved solely by such altruistic motives. He was a subtle and complex character, well able to make his kindly as well as his ruthless actions serve his own ends and ambitions. By the Treaty of Arras, concluded after the failure of the conference with the English, Philip had made peace with Charles VII. But the terms of it[5] made it abundantly plain that it was to be not so much a peace between monarch and subject as one between equals; and that of those equals Philip intended to be far and away the more powerful. This was made plain by some general clauses binding the king to make no future alliances without Philip's consent and to promise him assistance in any quarrel of the duke's as though it were his own. But by far the greater number of the clauses concerned the murder of John the Fearless, for which the duke obliged his sovereign, whose responsibility in the matter had never been proved, to sign a humiliating request for pardon and, among other reparations, to transfer to him many lands for which neither homage nor services were to be exacted. And the Burgundians were to continue to wear the cross of Saint Andrew even in the king's presence.

It was clear from all this that Philip intended to retain his position as the greatest of the great feudatories, in the face of the increasing strength of the king's central government. But to that end he must see

---

* Several of the chroniclers lay particular stress on this. Olivier de la Marche (II, 102) says, "There could be no greater love than there was between these two dukes all their lives", and Chastellain (III, 439) says that Charles would not go against Burgundy "even if it were to gain a kingdom".

to it that all the princes of the blood were bound to him by ties of marriage and friendship. Of those princes, Charles of Orleans was the nearest in kin to the king. Even in exile and prison, with such powerful supporters at home as the Bastard and his other allies, he had remained a potential threat to Philip's domination, if ever he should be released and join them. Better then for Philip to secure the gratitude of Charles by being himself the agent of that release, and thereafter to bind the grateful duke to him by every possible tie.

As soon therefore as Charles had enjoyed a few carefree days in the company of his old friends, this binding process began. Monstrelet implies that the various means to that end had at some time previously been put to Charles (presumably by Isabella at Calais), who had agreed to them all, and the chronicler says that now that Charles was again his own master, he repeated that all those promises he had made, being a prisoner, he would now keep. The first of these was that he would swear to the Treaty of Arras, made in 1435, and would command his brother the Bastard to do likewise. The text of it was therefore solemnly read out in the abbey church in both Latin and French, and if Charles had not already realised the extent of Burgundy's power he learnt it then. It must have been an exhausting business to follow the document, for it was very lengthy. But Charles obviously listened both carefully and critically, for when the moment came for him to swear to it on the Gospels he did so with a reservation that must at once have revealed to his audience, both French and English, his noble and magnanimous nature.

For he refused to subscribe to the clause implying responsibility and contrition for the murder of John the Fearless, saying that he had no need to excuse himself for this. He swore by his soul that he had never consented to it, nor known anything of it in advance, and that when later he learnt of it, so far from rejoicing he had been distressed, realising that because of it the realm of France was in greater danger than before. Having thus made his attitude clear, he swore on the Gospels and upon an image of Christ therein, that he would keep the treaty loyally. The Bastard, when his turn came, showed some reluctance to swear, but at Charles' command he did so too.

Burgundy's next step was to make Charles a member of his own family by marriage. During their talks at Calais in the summer of 1439, Isabella had told the still imprisoned duke of her own and Philip's desire that he should, when released, marry their fourteen-year-old niece Mary, daughter of Duke Adolf of Cleves, who had been brought up in their household ever since the death of her mother Mary, a sister of Philip's. Charles may even have had a glimpse of this young girl at that time, since she had attended some of the Gravelines peace discussions with her aunt, although there is no mention of her having accompanied her on her visits to Charles at Calais. Whether or not he had seen her then, he readily agreed to the marriage, and no doubt found the prospect pleasing after all those years when he had been deprived of the daily companionship of a wife, especially as, according to one chronicler,[6] Mary was very beautiful. In July 1440 a papal dispensation permitting the marriage had been obtained.[7] So now Philip lost no time in drawing up a marriage contract,[8] providing a dowry of 100,000 gold *saluts*, 80,000 of them guaranteed to Mary and her possible children by some of the lands, including the barony of Coucy and the county of Soissons, which Charles had ceded to him, and the remaining 20,000 to be at the disposal of Charles himself. On November 16th this contract was ratified and the betrothal solemnised in the abbey church of Saint-Bertin, immediately after Charles had sworn to the Treaty of Arras.

The marriage itself was fixed for the 26th and in the intervening ten days Charles' servants sent to many places in his territories for provisions to furnish the accompanying feasts. But Philip in his lordly way undertook to pay all the expenses, not only of the ceremony itself but of Charles and all his people, and saw to it that it was celebrated with full Burgundian pomp. He himself led his niece into the great abbey church. Charles of Orleans came next, leading the Duchess of Burgundy, accompanied by the Counts of Eu, Nevers and Dunois, and followed by hosts of other nobles, knights and ladies. Many kings-of-arms, pursuivants and heralds added a blaze of colour to the throng, among them Garter, whom Henry VI had specially sent with Charles, and of course the English lords were present too. Minstrels and trumpeters filled the church with music. The marriage sacrament was performed by the Archbishop of Narbonne. At the great feast that followed, the bride and bridegroom sat at different tables in the medieval manner, each in the company of members of their own sex, with the exception of the Archbishop of Narbonne, who sat on Mary's right. Since she, as Duchess of Orleans, was now the senior lady present, she sat in the middle of the main table, with her aunt Isabella on her left. Charles, with Philip, the English lords and many counts and knights, dined together "comme en brigade", says Monstrelet. After the feast the company went to the market place to watch jousts, the ladies looking on from the windows; and after supper small jousts "on little horses", with only six a side, took place, actually in the great hall of Saint-Bertin.

But on November 30th, the day of Saint Andrew, patron saint of the Dukes of Burgundy, these wedding festivities gave place to the solemn ceremonies, held every five years, of the Chapter of the great Burgundian Order of the Golden Fleece, which Philip had created at the time of his marriage to Isabella of Portugal in 1430. They began with a mass in Saint-Bertin attended by all the brethren of the Order, in their rich furred robes and cloaks of scarlet with head-dresses of the same colour. Charles of course was not present at this; but when the members met in Chapter the next day, Philip's first act was to send two of them to ask Charles, presumably waiting in an ante-chamber, if he would agree to be elected one of their number. Having signified his assent he was brought into the great hall, where the chronicler Le Fèvre de Saint-Remy, who was king-of-arms of the Order and invariably known therefore simply as Toison d'or, was waiting with the collar, the mantle and the hood on his arm. Hue de Lannoy, who had done so much to give Charles hope when he came as Burgundy's ambassador to England in 1433, pronounced the speech of welcome to Charles, telling him that the duke and the other members had decided to make him a member "because of the very high renown, valiance and wisdom of your most illustrious person", after which Philip put the collar round his neck and kissed him. He was then clad in the mantle and hood and made to swear the usual oaths.

In return for this great honour Charles then drew out of his sleeve the collar of his own Order of the Camail with its dependent porcupine and put it round Philip's neck. The casualness of this gesture may well have taken Philip aback if he were not prepared for it. And it is tempting to think that the simplicity and lack of preparation with which Charles made the presentation indicate that he regarded with rather an ironical eye the pomp and formality with which Philip conducted the ceremonies of the Golden Fleece. Certainly, even though he was now restored to his rightful position in the realm, Charles never made any attempt to emulate Philip with his own order. But if indeed his action on that occasion did signify that he regarded all this elaborate ritual as merely outward show, it is also possible that his inexperience of the prevailing political situation in the country prevented him from realising that, by creating him a member of his Order, Philip was in fact making still more sure that his potentially powerful cousin should owe allegiance to him above all others. At a later session of that Chapter, the brotherhood also decided to send collars of the Order to the Dukes of Brittany and Alençon, an act that made Philip's motives abundantly clear to Charles VII, when he heard of it, whether or not they were to Charles of Orleans.

When the Golden Fleece ceremonies were over, the English delegation returned to England. There had been no attempt while they were in France to consider the question of peace in a regular assembly. But Philip had paid all of them, and particularly Fanhope, marked attention; and no doubt the possibility of future meetings, for which the duke was known to be anxious, was mentioned in talk between them. At least they had been able to see for themselves the close ties that now bound Orleans to Burgundy, who would no doubt help him to keep his promise to make peace with England. The only matter connected with the past which seems to have been mentioned during those days was when Fanhope, or Sir John Cornwall as both the French and the English still called him, with his usual long memory for any money that was owing to him, obtained from Charles on November 28th, two days after his wedding, a sum of 8,700 gold *écus* described as being a part payment of a larger sum owing to him.[9]

The next few days seem to have been a kind of lull in all the official business, when Charles was able to attend to his own concerns. On one of them, December 4th, he went on a pilgrimage to Notre-Dame-de-Boulogne and had lunch there, returning in the evening to dine and sleep at Saint-Omer;[10] and one can imagine the pleasure it must have been for him to be at last the master of his movements and go where he would—" Aler sans avoir sauf conduis" as he says in one of his poems. He had time to look into his financial affairs too, and as a result he decided that his order of the previous June, whereby no pensions were to be paid for a year, should not apply to his brothers the Counts of Angoulême and Dunois, his sister Margaret, whose husband Richard, Count of Étampes, had died in 1438, nor his nephew the Bastard of Vertus.[11] He was able, too, to have an inventory made of all the books and papers and small objects that he had brought back from England.*

Meanwhile his public obligations quickly claimed him again, and the first of them revealed how quickly the people of France, even those who

* See Appendix III.

were subjects of Philip, accepted the authority of the returned captive. Only a few days after his first arrival at Gravelines a deputation of the citizens of Bruges had determined to ask him to intercede for them with their lord of Burgundy, against whom they had once rebelled and who had sworn, even after peace was established, that he would never visit their city again unless a greater prince than he took him there. Charles persuaded Philip to go there with him and accordingly, on December 11th, both dukes with their wives and retinues set out for Bruges. They were met outside the city by the most important citizens, barefoot, hatless and beltless, who knelt down before them. Mary of Orleans and Isabella of Burgundy begged Philip to forgive them and he, after what sounds a rather artificial show of hesitation, at the prayer of Charles finally did so. The whole episode reads as though Philip had deliberately staged it to honour Charles and make him feel how important he was in Burgundy's eyes. During the following days the citizens showed their gratitude by the usual lavish entertainments: feasts, jousts, dances "as much for their love of their said lord and prince" says Monstrelet, "as to please the Duke of Orleans and those who were with him". In addition they gave Charles many presents.

At the end of that week of festivities, on Sunday December 18th, Philip forged the last link in the chain that was to bind Charles to him, and produced a treaty of alliance[12] for him to sign. By the terms of this each swore to forget past discords and to help each other, in case of need, against any enemy whatever, as though they were brothers. Both agreed to work for peace and to make no alliance with anyone else in the kingdom without the consent of the other. The wily Philip, even if he had no warlike intentions against his sovereign, was of course aware how much it strengthened his own powerful position to have the sworn allegiance of the great prince his cousin. But it is doubtful whether Charles, being himself free from any ambitious intrigues, saw that in it. The part of the document most likely to have appealed to him was that in which the cousins swore to do all in their power to restore peace to the kingdom of France, putting an end to the wars and pillagings that had so long ravaged it, so that justice might reign there as in the past, and thus that "God might be served and honoured there, and the princes, prelates, churchmen, nobles, bourgeois, merchants, labourers and people of all estates be maintained and kept safe, each in his own degree and right, and live in peace and tranquillity, all this for the good of the king our said lord and of his kingdom and subjects." These last words were so much in accord with the hopes and wishes Charles had expressed in his great poem "Priés pour paix" that he might almost have written this part of the treaty himself. Certainly to nothing could he more willingly have put his signature.

Ten days later Charles and his young wife left Bruges on the first stage of their journey home. The ladies of Burgundy's household wept at the departure of the young duchess, who had been brought up among them and had obviously endeared herself to them. At Quesnoy-le-Comte Charles was received by the Dowager Countess of Hainault, sister of John the Fearless, whom he had first seen at Compiègne thirty-four years before when, as a child of ten, he was married to Isabelle of France, while at the same ceremony her daughter Jacqueline was married to John of Touraine; and then again at Arras and in Paris, in 1414 and 1415, when she had striven so eloquently to make peace between her brother and Charles and his king. Now she lavished gifts on Charles, as did most of the towns he passed through, where he was received with as much honour as if he had been the king himself.

His reputation as a peace-loving prince had preceded him and it was hoped that because of his nearness in blood to the king he would be given a great share in the government and so help to restore peace and prosperity in the realm. Not only those in authority felt thus, but everywhere he went, says Monstrelet, "the people had great confidence and hope that through his return and release from prison great consolation would come to the kingdom of France." For that reason they had long desired to see him freed; and now, moved by their hope in him, men and women of every degree flocked to offer him their services. Knights, esquires and ladies desired to become members of his household, noble families begged him to take their sons as pages, and ordinary folk offered to serve him in any way that he would. Even while he was still in Burgundy's territories many of the duke's own subjects had offered to follow Charles and he had delightedly accepted them, so that before he reached Paris he was travelling with a retinue of several hundred followers, including a bodyguard of twenty-four, and apparently finding this quite normal.

Charles VII, however, saw the matter very differently. He had, after all, sent his Chancellor and other ambassadors to welcome Charles at Gravelines and had assumed that his cousin would at once proceed to Paris to see him. Instead of that he had had to wait two months, during which time he received news of the increasing closeness of the links between Charles and Philip, and now latterly of the growing popularity and consequent power of his cousin of Orleans, of whose intentions and personality he was still ignorant. It was therefore natural enough that he should see in him a possible addition to those rebel powers who, under the Duke of Bourbon and his own son the dauphin, had already risen against him during the Praguerie in the previous summer. The news that Burgundy had also made the Dukes of Brittany and Alençon members of his Order of the Golden Fleece, thus binding all the great feudatories in alliance with himself, further confirmed these suspicions which his closest advisers, to whom he had always been prone to listen, did nothing to lessen.

When therefore Charles of Orleans entered Paris with his train at 5 o'clock on Saturday January 14th, he received a message from the king that, although he much wished to see him, he desired him to come privately, bringing none of his retinue, especially none of those from Burgundy, some of whom had probably fought against him. Such a reception, or lack of it, can only have been a shock and a disappointment to the duke, who now found himself in a difficult position vis-à-vis his cousin and sovereign. It was now clear to him, as no doubt it should have been sooner, that it was impolitic to have delayed so long before going to court. At the same time, he could hardly have refused to take part in all the honours and festivities with which Burgundy had greeted him, especially as Philip was the chief architect of his deliverance, whereas Charles VII had done nothing to mitigate his lot during the years of his imprisonment, and only promised to help with the ransom at the end of it. Perhaps when all the ceremonies of his wedding and enrolment as a member of the Order of the Golden Fleece were over he should have made more haste on his journey to Paris. But he could hardly have refused the request to make peace between the citizens of Bruges and their overlord, nor the receptions prepared in his honour all along his route. In any case, whatever reflections the king's message caused him, the implication that he, the third person in the kingdom, had no right to wait upon his sovereign with a retinue was little short of an insult, which even so naturally modest and unworldly a man as Charles of Orleans must resent. He therefore made no attempt to seek the audience that had been denied him.

The absence of a royal welcome was made all the more chilling by the fact that at first only the Constable of the city and a few lords and burgesses came to meet him; and when he went to Notre-Dame, although the choir had been adorned for him, no one was there to greet him. He therefore went to take up residence in the Hôtel des Tournelles. Three days later, on Tuesday January 17th, he went again to Notre-Dame where this time he was fittingly greeted by the Bishop of Paris surrounded by many ecclesiastics, while the great bells were rung and the organ played. When he came out after hearing Mass he was hailed by the people with the customary shouts of 'Noël'! During his stay in Paris the citizens gave him rich gifts and a tax of 3,000 gold *écus* was levied for him,[13] to be paid by the municipality and the clergy, out of gratitude for his declaration that he was going to do his utmost to restore peace.

Although these things may have compensated to some extent for the king's attitude, there was no denying that his reception in Paris was less welcoming than any he had received; so after a week there, he and his duchess left the city in which, even during his youth, he had only for short periods had any reason to feel at home, and went on their way to their own duchy.

Their welcome in its chief town, Orleans,[14] was warm and enthusiastic enough to blot out the memory of their lukewarm reception in Paris. The municipality had been busy with their preparations ever since they heard of his landing at Saint-Omer. They put up scaffoldings in different parts of the town for various mysteries which were to be enacted to entertain him; and a certain pastrycook was paid to nourish two persons who were to take the parts of David and Goliath. Minstrels were sent for from the surrounding towns, partly to keep the people in good heart as they waited for the duke's coming. No doubt a fountain which ran wine helped to this end too. It was perhaps the excitement of all this that caused the mother of Jean of Arc, who had lived in Orleans ever since the martyrdom of her daughter, on a pension paid her by the town, to fall ill at this time, so that an apothecary had to be called for her. When all was ready it is obvious that the civic dignitaries could hardly wait for the duke's arrival. When they heard that he had got as far as Paris they sent off a mounted messenger to find out when he was coming, and another messenger, on foot, set off by a different route on the same errand.

At last, on January 24th, the duke and the duchess arrived. Four hundred children carrying little escutcheons went out to greet them, and it was presumably on the specially-built dais with its ceiling of blue silk that they listened to the address of welcome pronounced by Philippe

Paris. Although the citizens had already been heavily taxed for the duke's ransom, they generously presented him with a bowl containing 4000 gold *écus*. For a fitting gift for Mary they had gone to the trouble of obtaining from Charles' treasurer, Jacques Bouchier, the design of the arms of Cleves, which they had had engraved on a set of plate they had made for her—a delicate way of greeting her as a person in her own right as well as their new duchess. After they had given thanks in the cathedral church of Sainte-Croix they were conducted to the Châtelet, where they were to lodge, together with the members of their court, who were so numerous that the governors of the city, who normally lived there, had to go elsewhere.

For the next twelve days they were royally entertained, not only by the authorities but by those mysteries and minstrels. There were fireworks too, and the people were able to join in the general feasting at tables set up at crossroads in the town. Among other presents which Charles received, one indicated much imagination in the givers. It was a painting on cloth, over four yards wide and long enough to go all round the cloister of the church of Saint-Aignan where it was on display. This masterpiece, which had been made by a citizen of Orleans, showed the whole course of the Loire from Roanne to Le Croisic, with the towns and villages, the hamlets and castles on its banks, as well as its ports and bridges. When it was taken down to be sent to Blois on the duke's departure it was rolled up in thirty separate pieces.[15]

At last the festivities were over and in the first week of February 1441 the duke and duchess reached their journey's end at Blois. There at last Charles saw once again the familiar castle that in his youth, ever since the death of his mother, had been his preferred dwelling-place, and was now to be so again for the rest of his life. The temptation to settle down quietly at once and enjoy life there with his new companion must have been great. But Charles was mindful of the oath he had sworn to Henry VI, and so he had hardly arrived at Blois before he left again on visits to the Dukes of Brittany and Alençon, partly to remind them of their promises to help with his ransom and partly to secure their support when he should be able to arrange a peace conference between France and England.

These visits were in the nature of a family reunion too, for John of Brittany was Charles' brother-in-law, through the marriage of Charles' sister Margaret to Brittany's brother Richard of Étampes. And although John of Alençon had married again after the death of his wife Jane, Charles' daughter, Charles had never ceased to think of him as his own son-in-law; and when they met in 1441 the liking that he had presumably first felt for him as a child was strengthened and became one of the deepest affections of his life, as he was later to show.

These visits resulted in the forming of alliances promising reciprocal support between the three dukes,[16] alliances in which the Duke of Bourbon also joined in April. In securing their goodwill for his peace-making and other aims, Charles was not acting independently of Burgundy, who kept in touch with him through letters and messengers.[17] Strong in these agreements, therefore, by the beginning of April Charles and his fellow princes were able to suggest to Henry VI that another peace conference should be held in the marches of Calais at the beginning of May of that year 1441. Henry agreed and on April 10th[18] chose his ambassadors and empowered them to conclude a truce with France and, if necessary, to prorogue the date of the meeting. Isabella of Burgundy, in the meantime, had gone to Laon to see Charles VII, not only to tell him of the conference that had been arranged but to talk of other matters as well. One that she chose to bring up was the king's refusal to see his cousin of Orleans in Paris in the previous January. And whether it was that she did not handle this subject tactfully, or that the king's conscience was already pricking him about it, he refused to grant any of her requests. What is more, as soon as she left, the king, obviously resenting the way in which Burgundy continued to treat him as someone of secondary importance, revoked his previous authority to him and his fellow princes to arrange peace talks, intending in future to take this initiative himself.

What happened next remains something of a mystery. According to Monstrelet,[19] Charles VII later complained that, although he resented the choice of Calais, he did despatch ambassadors to the conference there; but that the English sent only a simple clerk not of sufficient authority to treat of such high matters, and so no conference took place. If this was so the most likely explanation is that Isabella of Burgundy, having learnt of Charles VII's attitude, presumed that he did not wish the princes to represent him even on this occasion, and so informed them, so that they therefore judged it politic to stay away. As it was by then late in the day, they had no time to inform Henry VI officially of their decision; but news of it reached his officers in Calais, who at once passed it on to London. This supposition is supported by Henry VI's reference to "certain communications received in Calais from both English nobles and French ambassadors", in a letter[20] which he wrote on May 14th. It would seem, then, that on hearing the princes were not going to attend, the king and his Council doubted whether the conference was going to take place and judged it prudent, before despatching their ambassadors, to send merely a clerk to report. Charles VII in the meantime, assuming from what Isabella had told him that the conference had been definitely arranged, sent his own ambassadors in order to show that he had meant what he said. This way of arranging something so important as a peace conference between two great countries may now seem curiously casual, but the diplomatic history of subsequent meetings fully bears out that such things were often in fact conducted in this manner.

The failure to hold this meeting was obviously a disappointment to Charles of Orleans after all his efforts, and it may be that he managed to convey this to the English king. For in that long letter of May 14th, written in French and addressed to his officers throughout the kingdom, Henry VI almost seems to have gone out of his way to stress that it was at "la tresinstant Priere et Requeste de nostre Cousin le Duc d'Orleans", as well as that of his well-beloved cousin the Duchess of Burgundy, that he had agreed that another assembly should be held as soon as possible. To that end, in a document dated nine days later,[21] he granted safe-conducts to last till August 16th to no fewer than twenty-four French noblemen and officials to attend it. The list included many familiar names: in addition to Bourbon, Vendôme and Alençon there were Anthony the Bastard of Vertus, Guy de Rochechouart, Bishop of Saintes (brother of John, who had died) and some of Charles' own servitors, more especially Jean de Saveuses. Yet in spite of all these preparations, no further conference was held that year, for no reason that history records. On the contrary, even while they were making them the English were actively pursuing the war. Although the national coffers were now so empty that in February the king had had to authorise the Treasurer of the Exchequer to sell or pledge the royal jewels for the defence of France and Normandy,[22] by May, within a day of the granting of those safe-conducts, orders were being sent to the Duke of York, urging his speedy departure as lieutenant-general of the forces in Normandy, since sufficient ships were now ready to take the whole army overseas at one time, and the French were reported to be making great progress.[23]

These warlike preparations did not deter Charles and the other princes from continuing their efforts for peace. They now pinned their hopes on coming to terms with the Duke of York. He was well known to the Duke of Brittany, and so in the last week of July, Charles, with the Bastard, Vendôme and Alençon, all joined Brittany to wait for a message which Garter was to bring from the Duke of York.[24] Brittany was not the only one in close touch with York at that time, for Alençon also had been taking a hand in the negotiations, whether with or without the knowledge of his allies is uncertain. He had, by what seem devious means, sent a message to Garter through his Pursuivant earlier in July.[25] And it is possible that his intent was treasonable, for the message informed him of a plot to deliver to the French certain Norman places, held by the English. But whatever his reasons for this action were, he at least served the purpose of Charles and the other princes by stressing their pacific intentions. This we know from the report[26] of the matter which Garter sent from Caen to the Chancellor of England, and in which he wrote:

> Moreover, my lord, I questioned him [the pursuivant of Alençon] respecting monseigneur Dorleans. He told me that the said monseigneur Dorleans, and all the other lords, are waiting only for my arrival; wherefore, if God please, I will be there very speedily. And when I am come thither, what I shall understand and perceive I will write to your lordship in all haste by the said pursuivant Purchase, if the matter requires haste. And it appears moreover that these lords, who have no wish whatever for war, in consequence of their promises, hold themselves together.

The text of the message which Garter brought to the princes is not extant but the gist of it can be deduced from later communications. For after they had considered it they dispersed. Charles returned to Blois, and Brittany wrote to the Duke of York to assure him that "his whole desire was for the boon of peace, for the honour of the king [of England] and for the good of the kingdoms of France and England".[27] On September 5th York replied, sending safe-conducts for Brittany and Alençon to go through Normandy and "le Calaisis" for a peace assembly on November 1st. But once again this plan was destined to come to nothing and indeed, far from promoting peace, it gave fresh impetus to the war.

Charles VII's intelligence service was obviously well organised, for the text of Garter's letter to the English Chancellor was intercepted and translated for him by the captain of his Scottish guard. This evidence that the princes were still conducting negotiations with England independently of him understandably angered their sovereign and made him anxious rather to pursue the war in Normandy than to support them. He had indeed good reason for doing so, for the sins and injustices committed by the English in Normandy at that time were so rife that even Garter commented on them in his report. It must therefore for both these reasons have been a great satisfaction to Charles VII when, in September, his troops re-took Pontoise from the English. As a consequence the English in that same month, so far from arranging an assembly at Calais, had to order more military stores for the defence of it;[28] and in the following month they heard of a French threat to seize Harfleur.[29]

Any hope that Charles of Orleans would be able to fulfil that part of his oath by which he had promised to make peace between England and France within a year of his deliverance was now defeated. But as the English were well aware that he had striven his utmost to that end, they refrained from any reference to the condition binding him to return to captivity in the event of failure, even when, on November 28th, the text of his oath, on parchment "in the which the said Duc with his owne hand hath written his name" was delivered to the Keeper of the Privy Seal in London by Adam Moleyns, Bishop of Chichester.[30] Although Charles had reason therefore to feel released from that clause in his oath, he nevertheless had the cause of peace too much at heart not to continue when opportunity arose to work for it, as he was before long to show. But in the meantime he was free to think of other matters. One of these was certainly the fact that he had not yet been received by the king and so had had no chance to let him know his attitude on many subjects on which there was reason to suppose that Charles VII misjudged him. An opportunity for getting into touch with his sovereign was soon to present itself.

The Duke of Burgundy was at that time planning to hold an important conference with his fellow princes and his first step was to invite Charles to discuss the matter with him. At the end of October, therefore, Charles spent nearly a fortnight in talks with Philip, first in his castle of Hesdin and then at Rethel, where they were joined by Dunois. The plan that Philip unfolded to them was that at this conference, to be held at Nevers as early as possible in the new year, all outstanding matters should be discussed, not only the everlasting question of peace with England, but any individual problems or grievances of the princes attending.

There was to be an important new element however. Philip realised that the time had now come when he could no longer ignore Charles VII, whose growing power was making itself more and more felt. He therefore proposed that the king should be consulted from the outset and his approval obtained not only for the actual holding of the meeting but of the dates suggested. This gave Charles of Orleans the opportunity he had been seeking, and Philip helped him to seize it, for it was agreed between them that it should be Charles who would send the king the details of their proposals drawn up by Burgundy, thus making himself the chief intermediary. It was further agreed that Dunois should be the bearer of Charles' letter to the king, who was then at Saumur. But Burgundy kept control of the situation by sending ambassadors to take his own instructions first to Charles of Orleans, before the latter wrote to the king to tell him what was happening.

Charles lost no time in grasping this chance and as soon as he got back to Blois he wrote the king a letter,[31] every word of which reveals his desire to impress his sovereign with his loyalty and sincerity and his anxiety to do nothing contrary to his wishes. So great was this anxiety that it made him repeat himself overmuch, just as he had in the letter he wrote to Charles VI thirty years before, which the present missive in some ways recalls.

> My very redoubted and sovereign lord [he wrote], I commend myself as much as always and as humbly as I may to your good grace. And may it please you to know, my very redoubted lord, that Jean d'Amancier has sent me the letters that my fair brother of Burgundy and his chancellor have written to me, the which I now send to you, that you may see their contents; begging you that it would please you to let me know fully what it will be your good pleasure that I should do, and if I should go directly to La Charité, or if you desire that I should pass by you; and if it is that I should pass by you, to let me know at about what time I should be there; and if it should happen that you would wish me to take the other road, may it please you to let me know your good pleasure and how, in following it, I should act.

As soon as he knows the king's good pleasure and commands, he repeats, he will accomplish them, as it is right and he is in duty bound. He subscribed the letter: "Written in our Castle of Blois, the 14th day of December. Your very humble and very obedient kinsman, subject and servitor, the Duke of Orleans etc."

This letter seems to have opened the way to the king's good graces for he replied at once, not only sending Charles a verbal answer by Dunois but despatching his Chancellor and another ambassador to say that he had no objection to the proposed conference, that he would be glad to receive the princes at Bourges in the course of it, but that he could only do so if the meeting took place as soon as possible, since he had promised the Count of Albret to take an army to the south-west in March, for an encounter with the English in the lands which they held in Guienne. Charles of Orleans therefore took it on himself to nominate January 28th as the opening date for the meeting. He at once informed Burgundy of this and wrote again to tell the king, begging him at the same time to write and urge that independent and powerful character the Duke of Brittany to attend. The king obligingly did so, although he had written to Brittany only a few days previously. His second letter seems to have confused the duke, for in the end he never turned up at Nevers, perhaps because of his health, as in August of that year he died. His was the only absence, however, and by the end of the month all the princes had assembled. The Dukes of Orleans and Bourbon both brought their wives with them, and it was on this occasion that the chronicler Olivier de la Marche remarked that Mary of Orleans was "a very beautiful lady".*

There was a very full agenda to discuss and the meetings lasted for many weeks, with a month's break for the customary Easter feasting. In the event the princes did not see the king before he left Bourges, but from time to time they sent emissaries to lay their problems and proposals before him and to ask for his views. The question of another peace conference with the English was one of the first matters that preoccupied them and the king's answer to their suggestion that one should be held on May 1st, 1442 alarmed them by revealing his increasing intention to have his own way. He stated firmly that he had had enough of those meetings in the marches of Calais, where sometimes the English had not even turned up. He had only agreed to their being held there while the freeing of his cousin Charles was also under discussion; now the time had come for the French to choose a meeting-place that suited themselves. In any case he pointed out that it would be quite impossible for him to have such a meeting in the following

* See page 250 above.

May, as he would then be with his army in the south-west. He would however consent to one on October 25th and, if that date were acceptable, would even agree that once again it should be held near Calais. This time, however, he wished it to be an important meeting which some of his own faithful allies—the Kings of Scotland and Spain for example—might also attend. To that end he suggested that the princes should send emissaries to England to persuade the English to send ambassadors with adequate powers to treat. And finally he seized this occasion to remind the princes of the former English insistence on holding their French possessions without paying homage to him for them, a thing to which he would never consent, as he was sure they would not either.

Of closer personal interest to Charles was the king's reply to the complaints that the assembled princes had sent him on the duke's behalf, at the same time pointing out his merits to the king. During his imprisonment and since his return, they said, the king had sent him "no substance or provision", although while he was away the king had taken all the taxes and subventions from his lands. They therefore asked the king to restore the places and lordships belonging to Orleans that he had seized, and also to make suitable financial provision to enable him both to sustain his rank and pay his ransom. In his reply the king denied that he had taken any lands from Charles or indeed done anything against him. What was complained of was done in the time of the king his father and the great lords of his blood then living, when Charles was still in France—a reference presumably to John the Fearless. He promised that his cousin should have no reason to feel discontented with the king's help towards his finances. The king well knew that he had long been a prisoner and had suffered much, and was grieved at this. He therefore intended not only to help him himself but to see that his subjects did likewise; and he scored a last point by requiring the princes to play their part in this, in proportion to the lands and lordships they held.

These were no empty promises on the part of the king. When the Nevers conference was over, Charles and Mary travelled south-west with some of the members of their own Council, and on May 18th, 1442[32] joined the king at Limoges, where he had been since the first of the month, the encounter with the English having been put off until June 24th. On the 20th the king gave a great feast for Pentecost at which Charles and Mary, now at last on good terms with their sovereign, were among the guests, together with Richemont, Charles of Anjou and other nobles. The dauphin was there too, and this was probably the first occasion upon which Charles had seen that unpleasant character. Even before Charles had met the king, on May 8th Charles VII had authorised the duke to receive all the taxes levied on his own lands since his return, a sum that amounted to 14,500 gold *écus*.[33] Four days after the feast the king received him in solemn audience and granted him an 'aide'* of no less than 168,000 gold *écus*[34] to help with his ransom, to be raised forthwith, and authorised him also to take for himself the proceeds of the salt-tax on his own lands,[35] normally the prerogative of the sovereign everywhere. Finally he repeated his promise to inform his subjects throughout the country that they must help the duke too. This was to be done by letter, and one gets a vivid sense of Charles' eagerness to profit without delay from this generous offer from the fact that, the day after it was made, he paid the king's secretaries sixty gold *écus* for preparing the necessary documents and 'closed letters' to the king's 'good towns', whose contributions were all fixed.[36] The king had already left Limoges before these letters, of which there were some three hundred, were ready, and so Étienne le Fuzelier and Jean Chardon took them to him at Toulouse to be signed and sealed.

As the king was so easily able to impose on his towns a tax of this kind that would produce so large a sum as 168,000 gold *écus*, one cannot help wondering why this had not been done long ago, to enable Charles to release his brother and the other hostages in England. It may be that the payment of that indemnity, incurred at Buzançais, was considered a purely personal matter for Charles to settle, especially in view of the circumstances of which it was the result. When it came to Charles' own ransom, it was most certainly a duty for the king, the nobles and the whole country to find the necessary sums, as with their combined efforts they were clearly going to do on this occasion. Whether, when he had received the promised 'aide', which no doubt took some time to collect, Charles immediately sent the money to England to pay off the remainder of his ransom that he had promised to settle six months after his return (and which was by then long overdue), is nowhere related; but as equally there is no record of reminders being sent him from England, one must assume that he did. But this sudden wealth

* An 'aide' was a direct tax imposed on all the people, as opposed to taxes on goods.

also enabled him to go to the help of some of his own subjects too, as when he gave part of it to his vassals "considering the poverty to which the war had reduced them".[37] For there were within his own dukedom calls of every kind upon him, for example the annual payment which he, as well as the town of Orleans, made to the mother of Joan of Arc.[38]

After this satisfactory visit to Limoges Charles and Mary returned to Blois, where they spent the rest of the summer of 1442. But Charles' chief preoccupation remained his desire to make peace with England. In spite of the king's prohibition, ever since Nevers he and Burgundy had kept in touch with the English. As a result of these contacts, at the beginning of September Henry VI appointed his ambassadors for the forthcoming conference, which he was at pains to state, perhaps for the benefit of such men as the suspicious Humphrey of Gloucester, had been arranged through the efforts of the "illustrious prince, our cousin Charles Duke of Orleans".[39] But Henry had had enough experience by then to mention in the same document that, if the date should lapse, another should be chosen. By October 7th he was ordering that, if peace could not be concluded, a truce should be entered into; he was further advised, he said, that the truce should be a long one.[40]

Some prophetic instinct seems to have guided the English here, for once again no conference took place. The reason this time was that Charles VII, whose wishes the princes were no longer able to flout, was still campaigning in the south-west on October 25th. The encounter with the English in that region had turned into a regular campaign which lasted until the end of the year and greatly weakened the English domination in Aquitaine. Even when that particular campaign was over, the king remained in the south-west and it was not until the spring of 1443 that he journeyed north again, reaching Poitiers on May 25th.

During that time he had relied on Charles to carry out certain missions for him, clearly realising now that his cousin was a man without personal ambitions, who could be trusted. He showed too an increasing awareness of the duke's general financial situation, imposing a special tax to provide him with the means to carry out these missions.[41] The duke's growing nearness to the king might well have made Burgundy uneasy, if Charles had not shown him, by keeping him in touch with his movements, that it indicated no lessening of his loyalty to his main benefactor and liberator. Thus when the king returned north, Charles wrote to tell Burgundy that he intended to go and see him in order to bring up the Anglo-French peace question again. Burgundy sent an ambassador of his own to go with Charles, and the papal nuncio joined them.

Their meeting with Charles VII took place at Poitiers on June 9th, when the king invited them to dinner. Two of their fellow-guests were the king's brothers-in-law, Charles of Anjou Count of Maine and his elder brother René, Duke of Anjou, 'le bon roi René' (of Sicily). This was probably the first meeting between Charles and René, whose common love of poetry created a bond and obviously attracted them to each other at once. René was younger than Charles, being only thirty-five at the time of this meeting. Charles VII seized this occasion to continue his liberality to Charles, giving him not only a horse but a pension of 18,000 *livres* to help him keep up his state in the king's service.[42] This pension, later increased, was to become his main steady annual income for the rest of his life. The king showed himself favourable to the peace projects, too, and suggested that Charles should ask the Duke of Brittany to approach the English on the matter. Brittany died two months later, before he had been able to accomplish this mission. But his son and heir Francis accepted it instead.

Whether or not it was a result of his intercession, negotiations were set on foot again at the beginning of 1444. But in a document of January 22nd,[43] listing the safe-conducts granted for the next of such assemblies, it is still to his cousin of Orleans that Henry VI gives the credit for proposing them. No doubt therefore it was Charles also who persuaded Henry to accept this time the idea of a meeting elsewhere than near Calais. Another matter that boded well for the next conference was that his old friend Suffolk, now a duke, was chosen to lead the English delegation. He, as we know, had always wanted peace with France, but even so he hesitated to accept the appointment, well knowing that not only some members of the Council, notably of course the Duke of Gloucester, but many members of Parliament and of the public at large were in favour of continuing the war. He therefore foresaw that if he undertook this task, he would run the risk of being subsequently criticised whether he succeeded or failed in it, the more so as there is some reason to believe that the Council also wanted him to prospect the possibilities of a French marriage for the king.

In these circumstances he showed his considerable statesmanship by giving the Council his reasons for asking to be excused, in a speech[44] which he addressed to the king, who was present with the Duke of Gloucester. In this he said:

> I suppose that ye have in good remembraunce how that I have hadde grete knowleche amonges the parties of your adversarie in France as in being in prison amonges them and have hadde long conversacion with the Duc of Orleaunce at all times as that I was his keeper, for the which causes saving thoffence of your highness, me semeth it not according that I be send now in thambassade that is spoken of to goo into Fraunce, and specially for the nomination that your adversairs amonges others made of me for to be sent and come in the said ambassade and that it like your said highness to hold me excused thereof.

This subtle speech had just the effect that he no doubt desired, for the Chancellor at the king's command willed him[45] to go on the embassy, whereupon Suffolk, as a further safeguard, besought the king that he might be accompanied with "sad and circumspect men" so that any opponents might see that the king had confidence in them and, if the embassy should fail, that he, Suffolk, should not be blamed by the king. The king promised that it should be so. And on February 20th a document was published[46] setting forth Suffolk's scruples and stating that the king would hold him exonerated for anything that went wrong.

Thus given full powers, Suffolk from then on conducted his expedition direct with Charles of Orleans and acted with such unusual rapidity that Charles VII was quite bewildered and perhaps even a little irritated by the speed of his progress. This one can gather from the instructions which he issued on March 30th[47] to his own ambassadors, headed by Raoul de Gaucourt, and to Hugues de Saint-Mars, the Governor of Blois, on behalf of the duke, as to what they should say to Suffolk. About three weeks earlier, he stated, the Duke of Orleans had heard that Suffolk and his embassy would shortly land in Calais. The king had therefore appointed officials to meet them and conduct them to Compiègne, where he had arranged that the Duke of Orleans should be waiting for them. He had intended to send his Chancellor and other members of his Council and the *Parlement* there also, and had told Burgundy that he would provide people who would guide the embassy through his territories. However, a week later he learnt, from letters that Suffolk had written to Orleans, that Suffolk was now going to land at Harfleur and travel through Rouen to Le Mans. He had thereupon sent for René and Charles of Anjou, Orleans, Vendôme, and Eu, to ask their advice as to whether there was now any need to accompany the embassy (since Normandy was of course English ground). He had informed Burgundy and some others too of this change of plan and urged them to join him at once. And now he had heard that Suffolk had in fact reached Le Mans and was asking what the king would like him to do.

The message that the king then gave to his ambassadors was simply that he was pleased to hear of their mission. But he charged the Governor of Blois, as spokesman for Charles of Orleans, to tell Suffolk that, as the king was in weak health at that moment, owing to a recent malady, and as neither Burgundy nor the Chancellor had arrived because the king had been expecting Suffolk to land in Calais, it would be better to put off the meeting until after Easter, and that then it should take place in some town loyal to the king, such as Vendôme. It was further suggested that all fighting should cease in the neighbouring territories as long as the conference lasted. Suffolk at once agreed to the stopping of the fighting. But so eager does he appear to have been to see Charles again, and to begin the conference as soon as possible, that he spent hardly any time in Vendôme and pressed on to Blois.

Charles had passed this time of waiting agreeably enough, making the better acquaintance of René of Anjou. He and René exchanged some of those customary Saint Valentine's Day poems, when lovers chose a lady to be their Valentine for the forthcoming year. Charles pretended in his poems that he was now too old for this custom and would rather go on sleeping a little longer. René rallied him, saying 'Il n'est pas temps de vous retraire', but in vain. All the same it was clear that Charles had much enjoyed what he calls this 'beau débat' of 'deux bons'. And the mere fact that he had begun to write poetry again is enough to prove that he was now in a much more relaxed and hopeful mood.

Very soon after Suffolk's arrival at Blois, he and Charles embarked on the Loire to go down to Tours, where the royal family were staying at the nearby castle of Montils-les-tours. They reached Tours itself on April 16th and were greeted at the gates by King René of Sicily, with John of Alençon and Francis of Brittany, the latter gorgeously dressed and with a great cortège, which accompanied them all to Montils. There the king and queen received them most graciously, as did the other assembled princes. The only person who resented their coming was the cross-grained dauphin who, to judge from a letter[48] to some of his own councillors a few years later, took the line that it was not for Suffolk, as an Englishman and therefore an enemy, to treat directly with the king himself. However his ill temper did not spoil the general atmosphere of good-will and friendliness that seems to have prevailed at once and expressed itself in joyful celebrations, such as the traditional May Day procession, when the queen led three hundred gallants out to bring in the May. This was probably due to the fact that, before the two sides began their deliberations, Suffolk brought up the second part of his mission: the marriage between Henry VI and a French princess. The English choice had fallen on Margaret, the fifteen-year-old daughter of René of Anjou. This proposal was accepted both by Charles VII and Margaret's parents, and on May 4th her mother, the Queen of Sicily, left Tours for Angers with her daughter to prepare her for the celebration of her betrothal.

By that time the Duke of Burgundy had arrived and the peace talks began. The usual deadlock at once took place. The French offered to cede to England Guienne, Quercy, Périgord and Calais, but insisted that they should be held in homage to the French crown. The English said they would be contented with Guienne and Normandy, but must hold them in full sovereignty. The realistic Suffolk seems to have anticipated this and so, instead of continuing the usual wrangle, and aiming at a permanent peace, he suggested that they should content themselves with a long truce. It may be that both sides hoped that the Anglo-French marriage would in time resolve their differences, as it was clearly influencing their attitude to each other at that time. The betrothal was celebrated in the church of Saint-Martin at Tours on May 24th, the Duke of Suffolk standing proxy for Henry VI.

On May 28th the truce, known as the Treaty of Tours, was signed at Montils.[49] It was to begin at sunrise on June 15th, to cover all France, England, Ireland and Wales, and at sunrise on July 1st to cover the sea! It was to last until April 1st, 1445. But in the event it lasted for five years, and while it remained in force the people of France enjoyed such peace and prosperity as they had not known for over thirty years. The first person to sign the truce was Charles, Duke of Orleans. It was an honour he had well deserved, and the people of France had reason to be grateful to him.

CHAPTER FOURTEEN
1444-1449

THE Treaty of Tours was not the only event in 1444 of importance to Charles of Orleans. While he was in Blois that April awaiting the arrival of his old friend the Earl of Suffolk, one who was much closer to him was landing at Cherbourg: his brother John of Angoulême. But he did not come there as a free man, and another year was to pass before the brothers met.

It was now thirty-one years since John had been sent to England as a child of thirteen, and the conditions of his imprisonment had been much harsher than those of Charles. During the lifetime of the Duke of Clarence he had been kept in London, but after the duke's death at Baugé in 1421 he had passed into the hands of his widowed duchess. She kept him chiefly at Maxey, a seat of the Beauforts in Northamptonshire, which belonged to her as the widow of the Marquess of Somerset before her marriage to Clarence; but also for some periods at Groombridge in Kent, where she put him in the charge of Richard Waller, a dependant of the Beauforts, who was sheriff first of Surrey and then of Kent.

Although in France John was the fourth person in the kingdom, in England no particular deference seems ever to have been paid to his rank, as it was to that of Charles, whose political importance was always recognised. The Duchess of Clarence was not one to show any kindness to her involuntary guest. And although Charles, as we have seen, was continually sending his brother money for his subsistence, as well as trying to pay off the indemnity that would free him, the calls on his limited funds were so great that John was sometimes reduced to actual want, and was forced to borrow from his servants and keepers.[1] He bore the hardships and monotony of this dreary life with exemplary patience, being both studious and pious by nature. He knew that he could hardly hope for his own release while his elder brother remained a prisoner, even though at least two of his fellow-hostages, Jean de Saveuses and Guillaume Bouteiller, had been set free many years earlier.[2] And he knew, too, that when Charles was at last about to be liberated, the cost of his ransom was going to make him temporarily less able than ever to help his brother. For in October 1440 John had

had to ratify the sales of territory which Charles had to order to find that cost.[3]

But when his brother had at last returned to France, John had every reason to hope that he would now take steps to free him. It is indeed hard to understand why Charles, especially after his own ransom had been paid and he had received so much generosity from the king and his fellow princes, did not consider it his first duty to pay off the remainder of that old indemnity promised at Buzançais—still apparently a considerable sum—and so not only settle accounts with the English but, much more important, bring back to France the brother who had suffered more than thirty years of exile for his sake. Whatever the reason for his failure to do so, it is difficult not to blame him for the apparent thoughtlessness and heartlessness of this neglect. As for John, when year after year passed and he saw his exile apparently being taken for granted, bitterness against his brother began to creep into his mind, and a desperate anxiety lest he should never get away. Fortunately for him, a change in his circumstances, which had taken place before Charles left England, five years later put him in a position where he was able to bring his plight urgently to the attention of those who could help him.

In 1438, as the result of an exchange with the Count of Eu, there had returned to England from his seventeen years of captivity in France John Earl of Somerset,[4] the eldest son of the Duchess of Clarence by her first marriage. Not long after his return his mother handed over the Count of Angoulême to his keeping, a transfer which of course meant that he would be the recipient of any sums paid for John's liberation. It was no doubt his own long experience of the rigours and miseries of exile and captivity that made Somerset a more sympathetic keeper than his mother had been. What was more, Somerset was on very good terms with Suffolk, in whom he had great confidence, and so he would be naturally influenced by the latter's well-known friendship for the Orleans family and his desire to help them. In June 1443 Henry VI appointed Somerset his lieutenant-general for France, and this afforded him the opportunity that was to mean so much to John, for the Earl authorised John's keeper Thomas Gower, to take the prisoner to Cherbourg, where he was able to communicate with his brothers much more freely than from England.

John seized this chance and the letters he wrote, both to Charles and the Bastard, over the next three months, bring this otherwise little-known man very much to life. His first, written on April 9th,[5] was to

Charles, whom he addressed as "My very honoured lord and brother". He began by thanking him for the twenty pipes of wine, for which John had apparently asked him, and said he was going to send them, as promised, to his "honoured cousin and master the Duke of Somerset" who was, he said, "very well-disposed towards my deliverance". He therefore besought Charles to help him "this time"; he had perfect confidence that he would, for if "this time" he failed to get free, "I may well consider myself lost for ever". He asked Charles two things. The first was that he would put his case to Suffolk when he arrived, as he could greatly influence Somerset. The second was that he would put the money he had received from Burgundy entirely at John's disposal, for he had great need of it. It was a friendly enough letter, but there is the first hint of bitterness in those repetitions of "this time", as though he felt that not enough had been done for him in the past. He obviously knew too of Burgundy's generosity to Charles and was resentful at having had no share in it.

Although Charles was at that moment so preoccupied with the truce, he responded at once to this appeal, and by May 12th he and the Bastard had made an agreement with Suffolk whereby, in return for an immediate payment of 12,000 gold *saluts* and a promise of 60,000 more, John should be set free to go in person to collect "certain great sums for which he was a hostage".[6] When one remembers the endless payments made by Charles over the past thirty-two years, it comes as a shock to learn that "great sums" were still outstanding; but in the absence of any statement of the whole account, the matter cannot be clarified. It is also difficult to see what possible justification there could be for this demand for 72,000 *saluts*, which clearly were additional to the "great sums" that John was to try to collect.[7] It would seem unlike Suffolk, as we know him, to be so rapacious, and unlike Somerset too, for he was then a sick man and died five days later. But there is a strong possibility that his wife Margaret had a hand in this, for after her husband's death she was to show herself a very keen creditor, as indeed she needed to be. Whatever the truth of this matter, both Charles and the Bastard seem to have accepted the demand without question, and immediately set about collecting the money in the usual way, by asking their friends to contribute what they could not find themselves.

The news of this agreement was taken to John by his secretary Pierre des Caves and his herald Cognac, who were able to reassure him that Somerset's death would not affect it, since Suffolk had arranged with

John's guardian, Thomas Gower, that it should still stand, and that it would only be broken if the fault came from the French side. Cognac, who was continually in close contact with Suffolk, also told John that the man who was chiefly responsible for the attempts to free him was the Bastard. On learning this, and "many other things" says John, on June 11th he wrote a very warm and grateful missive to the Bastard in which he said that, if he was freed this time, he knew that it was because of him and he therefore prayed him "as affectionately as I possibly can" to take on himself the whole conduct of the affair. He entrusted it to him "as to him in whom I have and ought to have the most perfect confidence".

On the same date John also wrote to Charles, a letter in such marked contrast to this and also to his previous one of April 9th, that one reads it with something of the shock it may well have caused its recipient. It gives the impression that among the "many other things" that Cognac had reported to him was a great deal of gossip adverse to Charles, which John had believed. He therefore felt impelled to send Charles a letter of advice written in such a superior, sneering vein that it is difficult to recognise in it the patient, devoted, younger brother he had always been. Even the opening salutation: "My lord my brother, as one who most should love your good and your honour" is equivocal; after which John at once began to hand out advice. "It is necessary for the good of the peace which you have begun and of which you have the honour, that you should remain close to the king, not absenting yourself for any occupation, for that way lies the advancement of the peace, your honour and profit, and my deliverance. To gain the love of the realm, and to get the king out of those hands that hold him, see to it that by your means he go to Paris. See to it that the marriage with England be speedily consummated, for good reason." After further gratuitous advice on general matters he turned to his own affairs and again begged Charles to help him 'this time'—as though he never had previously—for if his friends fail him "this time for so little, I shall think myself abandoned". He asked Charles to see to the payment of the pension due to him for that year and part of the last, saying rather bitterly that Charles may guess how much need he had of it, "if you have not forgotten what it was to be in danger". He begged Charles to get the king to give him some money to help him meanwhile, for he knows well that when he sees him he will. As a parting shot he warned Charles against Jean le Fuzelier, the trusted governor of his finances, for

John had heard that he was planning some dishonest practice. If Charles lets him get away with this "everyone will laugh at you and not without cause" he tauntingly added. He ended the letter abruptly with no expressions of affection nor even any of the usual courtly formulae.

The only justification for the tone of this letter is that John, believing all he had heard, was desperate with anxiety lest Charles' handling of the peace talks should prevent his own deliverance. It is in fact possible that some of the French king's advisers were not in favour of them and opposed to Charles. Even so, nothing can excuse the near-insolence of such a letter, addressed to the head of his house, nor the priggish tone of one who had no first-hand knowledge of the matters he was writing about. In addition to its other shortcomings it was out-of-date, for it arrived when the truce for which Charles had been so largely responsible had already been proclaimed.

On June 28th John wrote again to the Bastard to say he had heard from Cognac that the Bastard had made himself responsible not only for the 12,000 *saluts* demanded but for the "*scellées*" (sealed promises) signed by the different princes for the remainder, and promising to recompense him for all this. Once again, too, he urged him to spare no efforts to ensure that his deliverance "which you set on foot" should this time be successfully concluded "as in you I have perfect confidence". But in spite of John's perfect confidence in him, even the Bastard was not able to secure his immediate release. He was taken back to England by Thomas Gower, and Charles meanwhile continued to approach his fellow princes—René of Anjou for one—to solicit their help for his brother.[8]

Nine months then passed before John was brought back again, in March 1445, to Rouen this time, and finally freed by Suffolk, who had arrived there in order to marry Margaret of Anjou as proxy for Henry VI. Before he bade Suffolk farewell they had a conversation which John recorded in a document dated April 1st, in which he certified that he had been liberated by the "great pain and diligence" of the Earl of Suffolk, to whom he would always be beholden. But Suffolk, he said, had told him that everything he had done both for the deliverance of "our very dear lord and brother the Duke of Orleans" and his own, he had done not only out of love for them but especially and principally for love of "our very dear and beloved brother the Bastard of Orleans" whose prisoner he had been, and because of the pleasure he had enjoyed when he was in the Bastard's hands. He begged John to let the

Bastard know this when he had an opportunity to do so. So that all might know the truth of these things, John attached his sign manual to this document and his secretary Pierre des Caves added a note certifying that he had been present at the above conversation.

So eager was John to tell the Bastard all these things that already on March 31st, no doubt immediately after that conversation, he had written to him to tell him that he had that day been freed and hoped soon to see him and thank him as the principal cause of his deliverance. There is no doubt that John had every reason to be grateful to the Bastard, for over the years he had tried one method after another of freeing him. We have seen how he strove to arrange that the ransoms of Suffolk and of Thomas Beaufort should be used to help pay off the indemnity for which John was a hostage. Two years later, in 1432, he had spent much time over an attempt to negotiate a marriage for John with Jane, the eldest daughter of the Vicomte de Rohan, drawing up a contract whereby her father should give her a handsome dowry, by far the greater part of which should be used to pay for John's liberty. This plan had obviously filled John with hope, for he sent an almost excited letter to Jane's father, telling him that he and Charles had full confidence in the "sense, loyalty, wisdom and good diligence of their brother the Bastard as their *procureur général* in the matter. But alas for John's hopes, in the following July Jane herself withdrew her consent, feeling no doubt that she would prefer a bridegroom already in France. Even so, messages continued to be sent to Rohan about it in 1434, but in vain.[9] Undaunted by this failure, in 1435 or 1436 the Bastard tried to make another match for his brother John, this time with Margaret, daughter of Duke Amadeus of Savoy[10] and widow of the young Louis Duke of Anjou, brother of René ,who had succeeded him. But this time the plan was foiled by Charles of Orleans, who thought that Margaret would make a suitable wife for himself.* There is even some indication that, when that plan came to nothing in 1437, the Bastard tried to revive the negotiations with the Rohan family.[11] In spite of all the Bastard had done for John, it seems strange that there should be no expression of gratitude to Charles in those letters, nor any apparently addressed directly to him, for throughout the winter of 1444-5 he made continual efforts to raise the promised money, even selling one of his estates, Château Regnault,[12] for the purpose. As a result, when John arrived in Rouen in March 1445 he was able to send

---

* See page 216 above.

him more than 10,000 *écus* "of good weight", and larger sums still in April and August by the time John had reached Blois. Charles had also sent money to his brother's English guardians.

When and where Charles and John first met after John's release is not recorded, but it was probably at Nancy that April. Ever since the proclamation of the truce with England in the previous May the people of France, both rich and poor, had been revelling almost for the first time that century in all the freedoms that the temporary cessation of the war had brought them. When the news of it first reached Paris there was an almost hysterical explosion of joy, expressing itself both in religious processions and in public merrymaking. In July the Porte Saint-Martin, that had remained closed since Joan of Arc had approached the walls of the city in 1430, was opened again; and not only in Paris but in many other walled towns there were people who, for the first time in their lives, left the safety of their enclosures. They were free at last to go out into the country to till their fields and pasture their beasts, no longer fearing the passing bands of soldiers whom they had been forced to feed and house, often being plundered for their pains. As a result they could live on a less miserable diet than that they had endured for so long, for in addition to their own efforts, supplies could now at last come safely into the towns, both by road and water.

Nor was it only the *bourgeoisie* and the peasantry whose spirits rose at this time. The princes and the nobility in general, released for the time being from the strains and stresses of the unending conflict, moved freely about the country and were able to enjoy their own estates in peace. In the autumn of 1444 Charles of Orleans visited some of his– Crépy-en-Valois, Coucy, Pierrefonds and Brie-Conte-Robert–for[13] the first time since his release. He and his duchess spent Christmas at La Ferté-Milon and in March, after further visits, they were in Paris, staying at the Hôtel des Tournelles. They were there on March 15th when the young Margaret of Anjou, still only sixteen, passed through on her way to Rouen for her marriage to Henry VI, for whom Suffolk was to stand proxy. She had said farewell to her parents at Bar-le-Duc and, young as she was, it must have been comforting for her to be welcomed by the kindly duke and his young wife.[14] They accompanied her as far as Poissy, where she was handed over to the Duke of York. From then on she seems to have been almost entirely in the company of her future countrymen, for although the English embassy under the Earl of Suffolk (recently created a Marquess) that had been sent to attend the wedding was both numerous and splendid, hardly any of the French princes and nobility were there to represent France. This seems a strange omission when one considers how important a step in the making of peace between the two countries it was hoped that this marriage would prove to be.

On leaving Paris that April, Charles and Mary went to join Charles VII and his court at Nancy,[15] where they had been since the previous September. Nancy was in the territory of René of Anjou, who was also Duke of Bar and of Lorraine, and he provided the court with a constant flow of entertainments, from elaborate jousts to balls and feasts. Chief among those who excelled in the jousts was a certain young esquire called Jacques Lalain, a type of *preux chevalier* whose sole aim in life was to win glory in such combats. He had been brought in his first youth to the Court of Burgundy by the young Duke Adolf of Cleves, the brother of Mary of Orleans, who had once seen him there before her marriage to Charles. From the account of Lalain's life and adventures written by the Burgundian chronicler Chastellain, it appears that Mary, while at Nancy, was seriously attracted to this young man. Still only nineteen as she then was, it was natural enough that she should have felt drawn to the dazzling young champion, only a few years older than herself, whom the whole court delighted to honour. But though he wore her favours at the jousts, he also wore those of the young Duchess of Calabria, René's daughter-in-law; and wholly imbued as he was with the ideals of courtly love, there is no evidence that Mary's fifty-year-old husband had any cause for anxiety.[16]

While they were at Nancy, John of Angoulême joined them there. After briefly visiting Blois he had at once proceeded to the court, being anxious before everything else to greet his sovereign. Charles VII received him warmly, as did his brother Charles too. John was able to see some of the jousts during his visit, and one day he also watched an elaborate ballet in which many of the nobles took part. This ballet seems to have impressed him greatly, for he noted down the elaborate steps of it in his own hand, together with the programme of the whole entertainment, in a kind of shorthand, on the first of the blank pages of that little chronicle the *Geste des Nobles*,[17] which Charles' faithful Chancellor, Guillaume Cousinot, had written for him while he was a prisoner, and which he must have brought with him to Nancy. The sight of those scribbles in that little manuscript conjures up vividly the sharp change in the circumstances of John's life; the long solitary years during which that chronicle had been one of his few links with events in his own country, and now his sudden transition to the life of a brilliant court at a time when it was enjoying entertainments such as he could never have seen.

Even now he did not enjoy them for long, for at the end of April the court moved to Châlons-sur-Marne, where the revelry ended, for the king had serious matters to deal with. Charles of Orleans did not wait for these, for he had affairs of his own to attend to. So he left the court before it moved to Châlons taking Mary and John of Angoulême with him. They went to Paris, where Charles at any rate remained all May and June. On June 25th his sister the Countess of Étampes joined him there, and together they settled, in the presence of the two notaries, matters arising from their inheritances both from their father Louis and their brother Philip of Vertus.[18] Four days later Charles had a similar meeting with John of Angoulême.

Now at last, with peace reigning in the country for the time being, largely thanks to his efforts, his hostage-brother home again and provision made for all the members of his family, Charles was free to enjoy for a stretch of nearly two years his favourite castle of Blois. An Italian friend of Charles, Antonio Astesan, who saw it first in 1450, said it was so vast that it could lodge several thousand men and horses.[19] But it was not its size and splendours so much as its situation that made it attractive. Set on rising ground it looked down over the sloping roofs of the little walled town to the broad stream of the Loire, spanned by a bridge that even then was three hundred years old. The vast abbey of Saint-Laumer, whose church still stands, known now as Saint-Nicholas, lay on the bank of the river at the foot of the castle hill. Another church, that of Saint-Sauveur, which Charles himself had founded, stood within the castle walls in what is now the Place du Château, but has since disappeared. This church, says the Italian, was as large as that in any castle in France, and chiefly remarkable for its huge organ, which he said had 1400 pipes, some of them large enough for a man to slide through, and whose sound was very sweet. The great forest of Blois lay to the west of the town, while two other forests, those of Russy and Boulogne, stretched away to the south, beyond the suburb of Vienne on the opposite bank of the river, all three of them full of deer and game of all kinds, including wild boar.

One of the first things that Charles did, now that it looked as though he might be able to enjoy a quiet life at Blois, was to put in hand some new building in the castle. He was not one of those princes who built for the love of it, or for personal aggrandisement, as did many of his successors. His main work lay in reconstructing, in stone and brick, the south-western side of the hollow square of the ancient fortress, built a hundred years earlier, to make of it a more cheerful and comfortable dwelling-place. One innovation to this end was that the rooms, instead of opening into each other as was usual, were connected by an outer gallery. Although this considerable construction was later replaced (by the present 17th-century wing of Gaston d'Orléans), one can get an idea of the style of it from a small building of Charles' time in the courtyard on the left of the present entrance. Apart from this, nothing that he built now remains, although of the earlier castle that he knew there still exists the great Salle des États and the Tour du Foix.

Although we know nothing of the arrangement of the rooms in this new wing, it is probable that one of the most important of them was the library; for this now had to house not only the considerable collection that Charles brought back from England, but those that he had left in Blois when he went into captivity, and whose sale he had subsequently authorised. For on his return from England, Charles had experienced what for him must have been one of the greatest pleasures that his release had brought him: of seeing most of the precious books that thirteen years earlier he had had to face the thought of giving up, back in their old places. Jean de Rochechouart, who must have realised what their loss would mean to his master the duke, after selling a mere five, had kept the rest in his own house at La Rochelle, safer there than they would have been at Blois when the war was raging all round it. Rochechouart died in 1435 and on January 25th 1436 his brother Guy, the Bishop of Saintes, returned them all. We do not know whether Charles in England was told of this; if not, the surprise of finding them at Blois on his return must have made the pleasure keener still.*

Apart from the re-installation of the library, there was much work to be done at that time in furnishing and adorning the other rooms in the new wing, to make of them a suitable dwelling-place for Charles and Mary and their court in future years. Fortunately a large part of the wherewithal for this was at hand, for the Bishop of Saintes had sent back not only the books but the other rich possessions that had also been removed to La Rochelle, and had never been sold, in spite of later orders to do so. So there once again were all the splendid tapestries that

* See Appendix III.

Charles had known since childhood, representing such themes as Theseus, and Charlemagne, and allegories like the virtues and vices, and the bed-covers of cloth of gold and silk. Some of these were perhaps rather the worse for storage, for a little later a man had to be employed for several days in cleaning and then rehanging them.[20]

With all these things to supervise, the only absence from his own lands for which Charles found time in those two years from September 1445 to September 1447 was for a short visit at the end of 1445 when he went to attend the quinquennial meeting of the members of the Order of the Golden Fleece. It was held that year in the ancient Château des Comtes in Ghent, and was planned for its usual date of November 30th, the feast of Saint Andrew. But as Burgundy's own arrival was delayed, Charles got there first and had to wait until the ceremonies began on December 11th. They were celebrated with their accustomed solemnity and splendour and Philip went out of his way to pay honour to Charles who, as the third person in the kingdom, was the most noble member of the Order. But Charles for his part, never interested in worldly glory, returned this homage by bearing himself merely as a brother and a knight of the Order. The person who seems to have been chiefly honoured, after Charles, was Hue de Lannoy, who had first met the duke with Suffolk on his embassy to London in 1433, and was now a very old man. There were present also on that occasion Philip's young son Charles the Count of Charolois who, as Charles the Rash, was later to bring the Burgundian dynasty to an end; and on a much humbler level the chronicler Olivier de la Marche, then only a page, who, when he came to write his chronicle later, related in all their details the banquets, masses and jousts that filled the week, and clearly conceived a great admiration for Charles of Orleans at this, his first sight of him.[21] At one of the jousts when Jacques de Lalain, once again a protagonist, was on the point of harassing his opponent more forcibly than the custom of such combats allowed, the humane Duke of Orleans intervened to suggest that Philip should stop the fight by throwing down his baton, which he immediately did.

As soon as these ceremonies were over, Charles returned to his preoccupation with his castle of Blois. But there was one difficult matter to be settled before he could feel free to devote himself to the quiet life there that he loved. It will be remembered that, as part of her dowry, Valentina of Milan had received from her father, Duke Gian

Galeazzo of Milan, the County of Asti. Although this of course meant that the Astesans became the subjects of the Dukes of Orleans, they seem to have been delighted with the transfer and to have developed a loyal and almost emotional attachment to their French overlords. Thus, after Charles was taken prisoner at Agincourt, they were clearly worried as to what would happen to them and sent letters to Philip of Vertus and his Council. The content of these letters, now lost, can be guessed from the reply that Guillaume Cousinot sent them, in which he assured them that:[22]

> You can be certain that my said lord the duke and my said lords his brothers love as dearly and cordially the city and lordship of Asti and their subjects as they do the duchies of Orleans and Valois and the county of Blois or such other lordships as they possess in the world, and have no more desire to relinquish the city and lordship of Asti than they have those of the duchy of Orleans and the county of Blois for several reasons, among which the two principal are, the one for the memory and love of the very wise and valiant lady their mother . . . the other for the very singular love that my said lord of Orleans and his brothers know that the subjects of this lordship have and always have had for the lords of Orleans and the late lords their father and mother.

This warm and sincere letter, through which shines so clearly Cousinot's undying admiration for the duchess he had so faithfully served, as well as the strong feelings of her sons on which he was sure the Astesans could rely, must have done much to reassure them. All the same as time went by, and Charles and John were still prisoners and Philip of Vertus was now dead, in the summer of 1422 they began to think that, in the continual strife between warring dukedoms then prevailing in northern Italy, they would be wise to put themselves temporarily under the protection of Filippo Maria Visconti, Duke of Milan, who was Valentina's brother, and therefore an uncle of Charles. After a show of reluctance he accepted this proposal, and promised to give the county back to Charles when he was freed. He therefore asked Henry V to grant safe-conducts to two officials from Asti to go to England and obtain the agreement of both Charles and his brother John to this transfer.

Henry V duly granted the safe-conducts but before the delegates arrived he wrote to Charles, charging him to do nothing without his own knowledge and consent. Charles at once suspected that the king's intention of keeping control of this matter was to turn it to his own advantage rather than that of his prisoners, and perhaps himself to make an alliance with the Duke of Milan, with possibly disastrous results for him and his brother. He realised therefore that it was essential for them to give their consent to the plan proposed by the Astesans, and in order to do so he thought out a plan which shows what a subtle diplomat he had it in him to be. Although powerless to act himself, he seems to have managed to get from the delegates a copy of the articles to be agreed with Milan. He then sent them away, suggesting to them that on their return journey they should go and see his Chancellor in Blois; and to him he contrived to send by a safe hand the articles, which he had signed, together with a secret letter, informing him of the situation. This letter, written on a single sheet of dark-coloured vellum, still exists, and it is from it that we learn the story.[23] In it Charles empowered the Chancellor to send the articles to Milan, under his own great seal; but instructed him also to persuade the dauphin to let the agreement with the Duke of Milan be concluded in his name, to give the impression that he had forced the hands of Charles' officials. The Chancellor should then write Charles a letter, explaining what he had been obliged to do, but couching it in such a way that he could show it to Henry V without incurring his suspicions that the duke had deceived him. He warned Cousinot to keep all this absolutely secret, otherwise he and his brother would be in peril of their lives. The Duke of Milan must be sworn to secrecy also; and since Charles clearly did not entirely trust him either, he ordered that some of his officials should be sent to Asti as councillors. Whether it was because their movements were being watched, or because they judged it more prudent to do so, these particular ambassadors did not go to Orleans but returned to Asti, whence two others were sent to France, where Charles' plan was duly carried out.

The arrangement with Filippo Maria seems to have worked peaceably enough in the main, but in 1438 he took a step which was eventually to make things difficult for Charles. He appointed Francesco Sforza, a formidable condottiere, as governor of the town and county of Asti. The Astesans were sufficiently alarmed by his appointment to take legal steps to obtain Sforza's consent that he would hand the town back to Charles when released. When in 1440 Charles was freed, he reminded Filippo Maria of his promise to restore his possession to him, but Filippo, though still promising, took no steps to that end. It was presumably to report this unsatisfactory situation to Charles that two knights from Asti came to Orleans in May 1441.[24] They had increasing reason to feel doubtful of Filippo Maria's intentions when, in October of that year, Francesco Sforza married Filippo's only child, an illegitimate daughter called Bianca, whereupon her father gave him still more lands. However, any immediate fears proved unjustified. In 1443 Sforza gave up his office and Dunois was appointed governor in his stead. He paid a visit to Asti in January 1444[25] but he was back on February 22nd and seems to have been an absentee governor for the most part. And in the following July Charles, in his capacity as Count of Asti, sent Raoul de Gaucourt to pay homage to the emperor for his Italian fief.

But after that he again let matters drift on, and curiously enough it was John of Angoulême who tried to spur him into action; for one of the gratuitous pieces of advice which he gave his brother in that disagreeable letter he wrote him from Cherbourg in 1444 was that he should obtain assistance "to obtain your heritage of Lombardy." Yet beyond appealing to Charles VII to support his claim Charles still took no action, and the truth seems to be that, caring so little for power and possessions as he did, he was not anxious to plunge into the negotiations and possibly actual strife that he could see would be necessary if he were to bring matters to a head. Moreover it was certain to be a costly operation. It was all very well for John to give his brother orders in that way, but it was no doubt partly because, even as late as 1447, Charles was still struggling to pay for John's release[26] that he could not embark on the Italian expedition.

Then an event occurred which forced him into action in spite of himself. In August 1447 Filippo Maria died, having taken no notice of an ambassador, Regnault de Dresnay, whom Charles VII had sent him in May to order him to restore Asti to Charles. But more significant than that, having no son of his own he had appointed the King of Aragon as his successor. Faced with this situation, Charles had no choice but to intervene at once and in person since, quite apart from Asti, he had a better legal claim to his uncle's dukedom of Milan itself than Aragon, who had none at all, and a more legitimate one than Francesco Sforza. But to be effective he would need funds and armed forces, and since he had neither he determined to travel to Asti by way of Burgundy, in the hope that Philip, with whom after all he had signed a treaty of mutual assistance in 1440, would come to his aid. In mid-September 1448 therefore, he left for Lyon, where Mary joined him shortly afterwards. Although they were received with great honour there is no evidence that they succeeded in obtaining any funds at that time. Philip did however agree to allow a certain Guillaume de Châlons, Lord of Argueil, who had married Charles' niece Catherine, daughter of the Countess of Étampes, to raise troops for Charles from among his Burgundian subjects. This was not easy, for Philip had had so many little military expeditions of his own on his hands recently that his vassals were not well provided with arms and horses.

While these forces were being recruited, Charles and Mary remained in Burgundy, where Charles met once again the young Olivier de la Marche, whom he had seen at Ghent. When later Olivier came to write his chronicle, he related how Charles took much notice of him because he had always used all his spare time since childhood in trying to write, and the duke, who he says was "a very good rhetorician",[27] took as much pleasure in the works of others as his own. He even implies that the duke helped him to make a little tour of Burgundy. It is pleasant to think of Charles, in the midst of all his practical concerns at that time, having a moment for those things that meant most to him, and enjoying this chance to show kindness to a young beginner. For although he had never had a son of his own, he had a great liking for youth, a liking which he had hitherto had little opportunity to indulge, but which was to find its fulfilment later.

But this little interlude was brief, for at the end of September he left Lyon for Avignon and Tarascon, where he stayed with his friend René of Anjou, King of Sicily, at the beginning of October. Although Charles' army was not impressive, he was gradually getting some financial support, for in October 1447 Charles VII authorised the citizens of Orleans to raise 1500 *livres* "to put him in a position to recover the succession of the Duke of Milan, whose sole heir he is".[28] With his small following he crossed the Alps and entered Asti on October 16th. He received a friendly and honourable welcome from the citizens, who wanted nothing better than to be under the protection of their French overlord again. But the decision did not rest with them alone, for while Charles was on his way, Francesco Sforza, their former procurator, had himself laid claim to the city again, fought a battle with Regnault de Dresnay, the ambassador whom Charles VII had sent them the previous May, conquered his little army and taken Regnault himself prisoner. Charles realised that with his poor following he could

not hope to overcome Sforza in the field. He contented himself, there-
fore, with much more characteristic actions, first sending orators to
Milan to prove his claim to Asti and then laying a formal claim to the
Duchy of Milan itself.

For this latter purpose he made use of two gifted brothers, Nicolo
and Antonio Astesan, as they are always called.[29] Antonio had in fact
brought himself to Charles' notice as long before as 1430, when he sent
him a long letter in verse on the subject of an episode in Joan of Arc's
campaign. On making the duke's acquaintance in person he became
one of his fervent admirers; and he and his brother, at the command of
Charles, set out his claim to the dukedom in a book of which Charles
sent copies not only to Milan but to Philip of Burgundy and Charles
VII. He then settled down and remained in Asti until the following
August (1448), a stay of over ten months. When he left, by now calling
himself Duke of Milan, he took the two brothers with him.

Charles spent a few days in Orleans on his way home, but he must
have been glad to get back to Blois, for he was not in the best of
health at this time. His old friend the doctor Jean Caillau had been
with him throughout his stay in Asti and returned with him, but in Blois
the queen's doctor, Robert Poitevin, was sent for and spent five days
attending on him,[30] for what illness is not known. It was a long time,
too, since Charles had seen his wife, for Mary had remained in Blois
during his absence in Asti, with John of Angoulême for company.
She had had other visitors too, among them René of Anjou's son John
of Lorraine and Raoul de Gaucourt.[31] Charles had been too long away,
also, from events of national importance, the chief of which during his
absence was that in March Dunois, now the captain of the king's army,
had at last forced the English to surrender the important key-town of
Le Mans. They had promised to do this on the marriage of Henry VI,
but had continually put it off. It was perhaps as a result of this that at
the beginning of October Charles VII paid a state visit to Orleans
where he was royally received,[32] and where Charles may have had an
opportunity to talk with him about the matter that now seemed to
preoccupy him far more than any of these Anglo-French affairs: the
need to help his Astesan subjects.

Although he had been able to do nothing for them during his long
stay among them, this had obviously given him a great sense of responsibility towards them, a sense that the daily company of Antonio
and Nicolo, and their devotion to him, kept very much alive, so much so

that he spent the greater part of the next two years in constant visits
to any who might give him either money or men to help the Astesan
cause, beginning with one to the king that November. On all these
journeys Antonio Astesan accompanied him, his task being to turn into
elegant Latin the letters that his master dictated to him from wherever
he happened to be, addressed to his "well-beloved, and faithful, the
commune, the council and the bourgeois of our town of Asti." These
letters[33] are extraordinarily vivid documents, giving such a day-to-day
and optimistic account of the progress of his negotiations that the
Astesans must have lived in the constant expectation of seeing the
arrival of the promised troops, or even of the duke himself, which he
at one time led them to expect, when he wrote from Chauny to say
he had hoped to return to Lombardy sooner, but "one cannot be
everywhere at once."

Whether the main purpose of these letters was to keep the Astesans
in good heart, whether he himself really believed the promises of help
that he told them he was getting, how much he really wanted to retain
the lordship of Asti and, more than that, was anxious for the dukedom
of Milan itself, it is impossible to know. So little had he ever sought
power and territorial aggrandisement that it is difficult to believe he
really desired them now, so late in his life. Yet he may well have felt
that he could hardly let his inheritance go by default without some sort
of effort to keep it, especially as not only the Astesan brothers but a few
more of his Italian subjects had followed him to France, obviously
relying on him to help their countrymen. What is most probable is that
he was influenced by a mixture of feelings, which would explain the
curious discrepancy between the sense of urgency that breathes un-
remittingly in the letters, and the intervals of leisurely existence that
occur from time to time between his visits in pursuit of his Italian
objective.

Thus in the autumn of 1448, after writing from Paris at the beginning
of November that he had good hopes of help from the king and was
going straight on to Burgundy to urge Philip to send troops quickly
"so that you will soon see the results of a gratitude always renewed for
you", he proceeded to spend six weeks with Mary visiting his Valois
estates: Senlis, Verberie, Coucy and Chauny, where her favourite
brother, Adolf of Cleves, joined them.[34] So it was only in the last week
of that year that he reached Amiens, where he saw Philip. Although
Charles and Mary were lavishly entertained there, Charles got only

vague promises of future help from Philip and left after a mere week to return to Paris. The Astesans had sent a messenger with a letter to him at Amiens—an expensive business for Charles had to pay the messenger seven *livres* for his double journey.[35] In spite of Philip's lack of immediate response, Charles still managed to write another letter from Paris, full of confidence in the good will of both Burgundy and the king, before returning, after these first efforts, to spend a peaceful February at Blois. The temptation must have been great to remain there and enjoy life in his castle. It was a time, too, when his presence there might seem to have been the first call upon him, for that spring there were disquieting movements of English troops in the neighbourhood of his Loire estates[36]—movements that in March led to the breaking of the truce that had been renewed from year to year, when the English attacked Fougères, in spite of the fact that they had just granted safe-conducts to Dunois, Cousinot and others to go to England for yet more peace talks.[37]

Even so, Charles felt impelled that spring to set off yet again on his fund-raising mission. He left Blois on March 1st and went first to Romorantin. It may be that his visit was connected with John's marriage; for at some time during 1449 he married Margaret of Rohan, the younger sister of Jane, whom the Bastard had so often tried to obtain as a bride for him. Charles then proceeded to Bourges where he was able to see the beautiful house, still standing today, that Jacques Cœur, the king's financier, was building for himself, and was shown by the clerks of the Sainte-Chapelle the ornaments of the cathedral there.[38] After visiting Moulins, the main town of his friend Charles of Bourbon, he finally arrived in mid March at Chalon-sur-Saône, where he stayed for three weeks.

This visit to Philip of Burgundy was more fruitful than the last had been, for Philip had summoned the representatives of the different states of his duchy to assemble in Chalon and there ordered them to raise funds for Charles of Orleans. They seem to have done this with some reluctance, for although they voted him altogether 10,000 *francs*, they safeguarded themselves against any future demands.[39] It was not a princely sum and probably not nearly as much as Charles needed or had expected; and so he and Mary remained in the duke's territories for nearly another five months, staying in either Tournus, Mâcon or Lyon. But little financial help came of it. The truth probably is that Burgundy, genuinely devoted to Charles though he seems to have been, had no

more wish than had Charles VII to see him add a rich Italian dukedom to his territories. And so at the beginning of September Charles
and Mary returned home, little richer and in many ways poorer, for
wherever they stayed Charles had to dispense constant largesse.

It must have been a refreshing change from the obsessive and
rather humiliating pursuit of his Italian objective to hear, on his return
to Blois, the heartening news that Dunois had won a great victory over
the English and driven them out of Rouen, which they had held since
1419 and whence they had administered their Norman possessions.
This exciting news was brought to Blois by special messenger on
October 28th, and an echo of how welcome it was seems to linger in an
entry in the ducal accounts stating that the duchess gave the messenger
eight *livres* for coming to tell them.[40] This victory was of tremendous
significance since it marked a turning-point in the long-drawn-out
struggle between England and France and may be said to have heralded
the beginning of the end of the Hundred Years War. Apart from its
national importance it was important for Charles, since it meant that
some of his Norman towns and villages were now free again and repairs could be begun in those that had suffered damage in the fighting.[41]
He himself went to Rouen in December and again in the following
January.

Yet in spite of these inducements to remain in his own dukedom,
when summer came Charles felt impelled to return to Burgundy's territories once more to try to inspire him and his rich towns with enthusi-
asm for his Astesan cause. But again he was doomed to disappointment
and, after spending three months in the neighbourhood, he abandoned
for good this personal quest for financial help and set out for home. It
is doubtful too whether he and Mary were now always Philip's guests
on these visits[42], for in the following year Charles sent a costly jewel—a
gold ring set with a diamond flower—to "la dame de Conches" in
Burgundy, who had helped him and his people by putting them up,
and in other ways. The frustration and humiliation of it all had now
obviously become too much to be borne, and thereafter Charles had to
put any active struggle to gain the dukedom of Milan virtually out of
his mind. He continued to use the title, since it was indisputable that he
had the best claim to it; but when in 1450 Sforza had himself proclaimed
duke, Charles made no attempt to combat his claim. Asti was another
matter. He sent Gaucourt there in June 1450 and he continued for a
year or two to try and induce the emperor and even the Pope to invest

him formally with his title to it. There is no evidence that they ever did but this seems to have mattered little to the Astesans, who remained so loyal to him that they continued to send him revenues from his rents.[43]

One reason why it was necessary to get back to Blois as soon as possible was that Mary was in ill health at that time. As usual, no specific trouble is mentioned, and no doubt the fatigue of those everlasting journeys may have had something to do with it; but it was serious enough to need the attendance of doctors both on the way home and when she reached Blois.[44] As for Charles himself, he was now nearly fifty-six and it was clear that he realised the time had come for him at last to settle down and enjoy a peaceful life, full of the pursuits that were truly to his taste. It was almost as though he could hardly wait to do so for, after a short stop in Orleans, where he gave some money to Joan of Arc's brother, Pierre du Lys, "to help him to live",[45] he proceeded down-stream as far as Beaugency by boat. And to add to the pleasure of that delectable mode of travel he indulged on board in two of his favourite games: chess and merels. Like his father before him, Charles played these games for stakes. But unlike the reckless and spendthrift Louis, his son, no doubt by temperament as well as force of circumstances, was but a modest gambler; for the household accounts show that, for chess on July 29th, he took from his treasurer only 25/- and for merels the next day a mere 10/-.[46]*

* The fact that *s* and *d* were used to denote *sols* and *deniers*, and that the sign /- was also current, tends to give records of payments a confusingly familiar look for English readers. See Note on Coinage.

CHAPTER FIFTEEN
1450–1460

THOSE modest games were typical of the kind of pastimes with which Charles filled some of his leisure hours during the years of country life that he was now at last to enjoy. Several long parchment rolls, which have fortunately survived, recording many of the personal expenses of himself and Mary, give a vivid picture of life at Blois and the pleasures they both enjoyed there. This expenditure was far from excessive, especially if compared with that of, for instance, the Dukes of Burgundy; for neither by upbringing nor personal inclination had either Charles or Mary acquired the habit of luxury, even if they had had the means to do so. Mary's father was relatively poor and her child-hood in her uncle's court is not likely to have encouraged spendthrift ways. As for Charles, his tastes had always been much more those of a cultivated country gentleman of a later age than of a great prince of the Middle Ages. Now therefore that he was no longer so harassed by his debts to the English, or at least did not appear to be worrying about them overmuch, his revenues must certainly have been ample both for himself and Mary and the cost of their large but unostentatious house-hold and court; for in addition to the income from his territories, which comprised eight or nine hundred towns, he had the pension of 18,000 *livres* which the king had granted him in 1443, when he also author-ised him to keep for himself the salt-tax in all his lands.

Of the two, Mary's tastes were perhaps the more extravagant, though by no means unduly so for the great lady that she was. On marrying Charles she had adopted for her own that emblem of the *chantepleure* with its falling tears, and the device of "Rien ne m'est plus, plus ne m'est rien" in which Valentina had symbolised her grief at the loss of her husband nearly half a century earlier. The fact that these things had made such a deep impression on her suggests that they were still to be seen on the walls of Valentina's rooms in the castle, or in the chapel of the Cordeliers where she was buried. Or it may be that Charles had told her of them when he first took her there. However she came to know of them, this devotion to the memory of his mother that her cult of them reveals could not but have touched him and been a bond be-tween him and his youthful wife.

Nor was her love of them merely the romantic whim of a young girl, for they are reproduced again and again in her jewels as the years go by, together with her favourite symbols, such as pansies and columbines and clouds. Thus there is a record of a gold ring, enamelled with tears,[1] a little gold necklace with pansies and pendant tears, enamelled white and blue, and another, also of gold with clouds and her device, this time with pendant pansies of white and violet. There was a chain of twisted gold, too, ornamented with three *chantepleures* and with three letters from her device, which was later to be used as a souvenir of a great event; and a large gold *ferrure*, a sort of corset worn to compress the waist and make the stomach protrude in the fashion of the day, which again had on it her device "Rien ne m'est plus", with *chantepleures*. She even had her gold garters enamelled with pansies and tears! The clasp or brooch which held her robe bunched up in front, as they were then worn, was also in the form of a *chantepleure* with tears of white enamel, and she had another of gold as a present for her favourite brother 'Dolf', to fasten a feather on his head-dress.

Mary had other luxurious objects besides her jewels, such as silver *chaufferetes*, which must have been hand- or foot-warmers, and silver cages for birds.[2] She shared in some small measure, too, her husband's love of beautiful books, among which she had her favourites. She had her own copy of her husband's poems, which still exists.[3] A copy of the story of Troilus and Cressida was specially made for her too. On some of the manuscripts which belonged to her, her emblems and her device again appear. And in a particular favourite, the poems of Alain Chartier, she persuaded all her friends to write their names and their devices on the opening leaves, heading the list with her own, "Rien ne m'est plus, plus ne m'est rien", followed by *Cleves*, all written in her own hand.[4]

But Mary was not the kind of young woman to spend her days either in personal adornment or in the care and ordering of her great castle. She was essentially a lover of outdoor pursuits, especially riding, hunting and falconry, and her passion for these things was so well known that anyone who wished to give her a present inevitably chose something that would gratify it. Charles himself bought her a fine saddle trimmed with black velvet and copper-gilt studs, as well as saddles for her ladies, in the summer of 1445,[5] so that she could go riding with them while he was attending to the improvements in the castle. He gave her a beautiful white palfrey too, and also a grey, and she had other horses from other friends, so that during those years at Blois there were about a dozen in the stables, including those used to draw her two four-wheeled coaches painted with her arms, which, like that of Valentina before her, were suspended on springs of some kind, and which she used for journeys and visits. Other gifts were of hounds from, for instance, John of Angoulême, Arthur of Richemont and the Count of Armagnac. Another lord lent her his own hounds, sent by one of his huntsmen, so that she could hunt with them. She was given presents of falcons too, and even Charles VII gave her two quivers full of arrows. Nor was it only animals for the chase that she loved. She had a weakness for all creatures. Two of her pets were small monkeys, one of them a gift from Dunois' wife. This passion of hers must have been known, for soon after her first arrival at Blois a countrywoman presented her with a sheep!

In comparison with all these things Charles seems to have been contented with very little. He enjoyed making small purchases from pedlars who called at the castle on their journeys through the country-side, and sometimes set up their stalls there for a while. From these he bought such things as ivory combs, scissors, writing tablets and a horn ink-holder.[6] Even Mary sometimes patronised these travelling merchants for small things like iron hooks for working her silk embroidery, and lengths of black cloth. Some purchases reveal the more intimate and sometimes astonishingly modern details of their daily lives, such as that of the iron tags for the ends of the fine silk cords which they used to clean their teeth, and a case in which to keep forks. Other things could not be bought locally and Charles had to send to Paris for the twelve glasses (lenses) that his weakening eyesight made necessary for his spectacles, and two cases to keep them in. The same messenger bought no less than 6000 pins for Mary! As well as such trifles, Charles bought a few precious things too, such as a gold signet ring with an agate and his device "Ma voulenté" written round it. He had a gold porcupine made too, but whether for himself or a present is not stated. On the other hand the gold candlestick for reading at night was certainly for himself, as were the rosaries which he almost seems to have collected, as he bought many in England too. As he does not seem to have been exaggeratedly pious, one cannot help feeling that he liked them chiefly as pleasant objects.

Far and away the main treasures on which Charles spent money, however, were books. He had his own scribes and illuminators.[7]

Finely-wrought clasps of precious metals were needed too and often the leather bindings were adorned with metal studs.[8] But in general his books did not rival in sumptuosity those that his father Louis had had made for his library. He acquired them to study them, and not merely for their beauty. His curiosity and range of interests covered astronomy, science, with a particular stress on medicine, philosophy and theology, especially the works of the Fathers of the church, the classics, satirical and moral books, and of course those works of piety—prayers and sermons and meditations—that were to be found in all medieval libraries. Apart from Petrarch there was little poetry, a perhaps understandable omission on the part of one who was himself a spontaneous poet rather than a student of the art.

One of the chief treasures of the library was his personal manuscript of his own poems, which he is thought to have had made at the beginning of this peaceful time in Blois, presumably as a copy of the one he brought back from England.* In 1455 or 56 fourteen skins of vellum were brought "to shape and add to the book of the *Ballades* of Monseigneur"[9]—an enlargement that the rich flowering of his poetic gift at that time made necessary. For what with his own new poems, and the poems by his friends and the officers of his household that he copied into his book, he had had to use up the empty spaces in the top half of the pages, that were originally intended for the musical setting of some of the *rondeaux* and *chansons*. Charles understandably cherished this manuscript to the end of his days. Because he did, and because many of the poems and corrections are in his own hand, this little volume, which fortunately has been preserved, is one of the most moving evocations we have of the princely poet, whose hands so often held it.[10]

It is not difficult to imagine the happy hours that Charles, surrounded by all these treasures, spent in his library while Mary was out hunting, or reading there at night by the light of his candle in its golden stick. Quite apart from his enjoyment of their contents, something of the active physical pleasure that he took in the possession of his books is enshrined in the exquisite calligraphy of the ex-libris, followed by his signature, which he wrote in a great number of them, sometimes adding a few words of explanation as to how he got the book, if it was not one that he had himself had made. Thus we see that some of them were gifts from friends, whom he named, some he obtained through an ex-

* See pages 167 above and 298 below.

change, and occasionally he won one from friends with whom he played at his favourite game of chess. It was his habit to write the ex-libris and his name in French if the book was in French, and in Latin if it was in Latin, e.g. "Ce livre est à Charles duc d'Orlians," or "Iste liber est michi duci Aurelianensi etc., Karolus"; and the explanatory notes would be in the same tongue.

In some of the books is added to the name Charles or Karolus the number forty, in both roman and arabic numerals, XL and 40, with in addition the letter C repeated back to back, thus ƆC, so that it reads for instance XL Charles 40, or XL C 40 Karolus, though the order of the numbers, the symbol and the name varies. There is no explanation in any document of the significance of this formula. The most reason-able explanation that has been given[11] is that 40 stands for the year 1440, which was of such significance in Charles' life as the year in which he was released from prison. If that is so then the reversed C perhaps stands for that first half of his life which was now behind him, while the normal one signified the happy existence he was then enjoying. The number XL also formed part of his device 'Ma voulenté', which he had had inscribed in that gold and agate ring that was made for him; and this device too supports the idea of the year, from which date he who had for so long been subject to the will of others was at last en-abled to exercise his own.

Much though the hours spent alone in his library meant to him, Charles was neither a bookworm nor a recluse. He was not only soci-able by nature but also a deeply affectionate and generous man who loved to be surrounded by his family and friends. This affection rings out in the formula which records a gift of money which he made in October 1450 to his "very dear sister" the Countess of Angoulême, on the occasion of her "joyous and recent coming to the town of Orleans",[12] a visit which may have been his first meeting with Margaret of Rohan, who had married his brother John the year before, and was to prove a devoted wife to him. Whether her husband accompanied her on that visit, and whether he ever did spend much time at Blois is not recorded, for the place he now preferred to live in was his castle at Cognac, where he had established his library, which meant as much to him as that of Charles did to him. But the brothers were now obvi-ously on good terms, drawn together by their common love of books, which they frequently lent each other. And Charles took an interest in the new castle which John had started to build at Romorantin as soon as Charles gave him this castellany in 1448; for in 1454 he went himself to see the work being done both in the castle and its chapel.[13]

He was also always in close touch with his sister the Countess of Étampes and showed her much generosity. And he was good to her son Francis, too, giving him a pension of 1000 *livres* a year as well as his clothes,[14] gifts which must have meant much to this handsome young man, who was comparatively poor, and as a result rather bashful in his youth, since his mother was not able to do much for him. But in 1458 he emerged from his obscure position and succeeded to the dukedom of Brittany. Charles was fond also of Francis' beautiful sister, Catharine of Argueil, who must have admired her uncle's poetry since he took the trouble to have a copy of his poems made specially for her.[15]

Whether or not they also visited the castle at Blois we do not know, but there was one regular member of the household there who was as dear to Charles as though he were of his own flesh and blood. This was Pierre de Beaujeu, grandson of Charles' friend and fellow-prisoner John, Duke of Bourbon. After John's death in captivity in 1434 he had been succeeded by his thirty-one-year-old son Charles who had, as we know, stoutly resisted his father's attempts to procure his own release by persuading his son to obey the English king. Instead, he had from his boyhood fought with Dunois and Alençon against the combined English and Burgundian forces in support of the cause of Charles VII. Being, like all his family, an ardent supporter of the house of Orleans, it was not until the meeting at Nevers in 1442 that he could bring himself to meet Philip of Burgundy on friendly terms, even though his own wife Agnes was a sister of Philip's. But not long after that he retired from public life, a victim of the family complaint of gout, which reduced to immobility, in his early thirties, this warrior who had been "one of the finest bodies, whether on foot or horseback, and one of the most pleasant and worthy not only of the princes but of the knights of France".[16] He died in 1456, and was succeeded by his eldest son John.

Pierre, who was given the apanage of Beaujeu, was one of his three younger sons. As he was born in 1438 he was a child of twelve when Charles and Mary took him to live with them at Blois in 1450 and virtually adopted him. He was thereafter treated in every way as a son of the house. When there were orders for any kind of sporting equipment, they always included some for "Monseigneur de Beaujeu", sometimes referred to also as Pierre de Bourbon.[17] His arms were engraved, together with those of Charles and Mary, on the name-plates of the grey-hounds, and various articles of saddlery and harness were bought for him and his two pages, so he obviously liked to go riding and hunting with Mary. As he grew older he enjoyed other social pleasures, and a gay jacket was bought for him to go dancing at Shrovetide.[18] Perhaps it was dancing that caused him to wear out his slippers very quickly, for on one occasion no less than nine pairs were ordered for him and his servant Jehan de Mas, who presumably accompanied his young master on these occasions. By the time he was sixteen he had a household of eight persons attached to him.[19] The presence of this gay young man was not only a great joy to Charles and Mary, but must have been an added attraction to the many visitors who came from time to time to the court at Blois, especially to the younger of them.

But it was after all chiefly to see Charles the poet that these visitors came. For although, as a great prince, he would naturally have taken no steps himself to make his poetry widely known, those who like René of Anjou or Philip of Burgundy had had a chance to judge its quality had certainly noised his reputation abroad. There is proof of that in a poem by a contemporary poet called Martin le Franc who, writing not long after Charles had returned to France, quotes him as an example of those whom love had made strong and wise:

> Charles, le bon duc d'Orliens
> Nous en peut donner tesmongnage,

he says, and tells those who do not believe him

> Si tu ne me crois si enquier
> Le livre qu'il fit en Inglant.

And to make sure that everyone knows who he is talking about he says:

> De cestui Duc, de cestui prince
> Je parle singulierement:
> Car, en prison, il aprint ce
> Dont nous parlons presentement
> C'est cellui qui nouvellement
> Sailli de l'Angloise prison
> Par le notable appointement
> Du duc qui porte la toison.

From the last four lines here it would appear that Martin le Franc had been at the court of Philip of Burgundy–"the duke who wears the fleece"–when Charles arrived there, and that he had with him there the book of his *ballades* that "he had made in England".[20]

Another who helped to spread a knowledge of the duke's poetry was his Italian admirer and secretary, Antonio Astesan, who had followed him from Asti in 1448. He remained in Blois until 1453 and while he was there he made a copy of Charles' personal manuscript of the poems he had written up to that date. Antonio took this with him when he returned home and during the following years made a Latin translation of the poems, which his brother Nicolo transcribed in a manuscript now in Grenoble, which bears the arms of the duke.[21]

Among the visitors who flocked to the humane and liberal court of Blois were numerous young descendants and connections of Charles' old friends and allies. Although many of them were men actively engaged in the still-continuing war with England, they were lovers of poetry too, a few of them with a real gift for it; and it was certainly in large part this that drew them to that fountain-head of it, the kindly and gifted duke. There were, for instance, John, the son and heir of Charles' close friend René of Anjou, a young man who in 1458 succeeded to his mother's dukedom of Lorraine; James, or Jacques, "Monseigneur de Savoie" as he is always called, the grandson of Duke Amadeus VIII of Savoy, whose daughter Margaret, widow of René's elder brother Louis of Anjou, Charles had once fleetingly thought of marrying; and one always called the Cadet d'Albret, grandson of Charles' old ally the Constable, Charles of Albret, killed at Agincourt, and through his mother Anne of Armagnac, sister of Bonne, a nephew of Charles. His other nephew, the shy young Francis of Étampes, visited Blois too, as did also Charles Count of Nevers, a cousin of Philip of Burgundy, being the son of that Philip Count of Nevers, brother of John the Fearless, who had lost his life at Agincourt; and young Boucicaut, probably a grandson of the Marshal who was taken prisoner with Charles but died in England. Another very lively guest was Jacques, bastard of the Duke de la Tremoille who had had such a sinister influence on Charles VII at the beginning of his reign.

But their visits were only occasional and the hard core, as one might call it, of the poetic court of Blois was made up of the young esquires who formed a considerable proportion of Charles' household which, at one time, numbered eighty-seven people (not including Mary's household of thirty-four).[22] These young men held intermediate positions between the chamberlains, counsellors, senior secretaries and officials of the *Chambre des Comptes* on the one hand, and the throng of lesser functionaries: the valets, huntsmen, barbers, minstrels and of course the more menial servants on the other. Each of them was attached to one or the other of the different departments of the household that looked after the provisioning of it in bread, wine, meat and so on, and their duties were the serving of the ducal family and their guests at meals, in the role of carver, cup-bearer and so on. Humble though these tasks sound, the young esquires who performed them were nearly always sons of good and sometimes noble families, who started as pages and occasionally rose in later life to the holding of high offices, not only under their original master but in the State. They were very privileged young men, for in return for their extremely light duties they not only lived entirely at their lord's expense, but were given wages and their wardrobes as well as the regular and often handsome New Year gifts. And when they had the good fortune to serve someone as generous and kindly as the Duke of Orleans, they often received other presents as well and were treated as young courtiers with whom he enjoyed playing his favourite pastimes of tables, merels and, above all, chess.

But what Charles enjoyed more than anything was the organising of what have sometimes been called poetic jousts or tourneys, but seem rather to have been purely games or perhaps debates, for there is no evidence that there was any element of competition in them. Generally the duke himself would start the ball rolling by writing a *rondeau*, or occasionally a *ballade*, on a given theme; he would then encourage not only the esquires to try and compose a poem of their own on the same theme, but urge his visitors young and old to do likewise. For those who had no native skill there existed at that time books of instructions on such things as how to find rhymes; but Charles himself was always ready to give advice. The most precious of his precepts to them was that which he himself had always followed: to write simply of what came into their heads, without trying to be clever, as one can almost hear him telling them when he wrote:

> Chantez ce que vous pensés,
> Moustrant joyeuse manière . . .
> . . . .
> Laissez coustume estrangiere,
> Chantez ce que vous pensés . . .

Tous noz menus pourpensés
Descouvrons, a lye chiere,
L'un à l'autre, sans priere.
J'acheveray: commencés.
Chantez ce que vous pensés.

From this it would appear that he sometimes reserved for himself the writing of the final poem in the series – a wise precaution since the temptation for the less inspired simply to imitate the master must have been great. But gifted or not, none had reason to fear that the master would despise their efforts. On the contrary he greatly encouraged them by having at least a good number of their poems copied into his own personal manuscript of his own poems, from which manuscript it is that we learn their names.[23] Many of them too were given the further honour of writing their names, with their devices when they had one, in Mary's copy of the poems of Alain Chartier which served her as a kind of album of friends: a further proof of the prevailing atmosphere of easy and lively friendliness that made the court at Blois such an attractive place.

The titles of the themes set were such as to afford scope for any lively mind to embroider richly on them according to fancy and experience. Some were more or less proverbial: 'Chose qui plaist est a demi vendue', 'L'abit le moine ne fait pas', a subject at which even Mary tried her hand. Others were typically medieval and allegorical, affording just the kind of opportunity for those brought up in the tradition of the courts of love to refine upon their emotions, true or feigned: 'Dedans l'abisme de Douleur', or 'Jaulier des prisons de Pensée'. The most topical of these was 'Les Amoureux de l'Observance', in which the concept of the severe Franciscan reform movement known as the *Observance* was applied to lovers, who were to abstain from any kind of licence for the honour of their chosen ladies. Occasionally the themes themselves were expressed in a line of such poetic beauty as must have incited the would-be poets to try and continue in the same vein. One such was 'En la forest de Longue Actente', where Charles, in his contribution in the form of a *ballade*, paints a scene like a primitive picture, describing how he had set forth on horseback to ride along the tracks through this forest, accompanied by more than sixty horses for himself and his officers, having sent his harbingers on in advance to prepare for his heart and himself the 'ostellerie de Pensée' in the city of Destiny. None of the others, Mary again among them, rivalled this.

Photo. Bulloz, Paris

7 Isabella Duchess of Burgundy, a portrait of the Flemish School, in the Louvre

The most famous of all was on a subject set in a line that is again a poem in itself: 'Je meurs de soif aupres de la fontaine'. This series was initiated by Charles with two *ballades* in which he paints a character who only occasionally appears to be himself, compact of contradictory feelings and attitudes, for instance, 'Suffisance ay, et si suis convoiteux', 'A moy cruel, aux aultres piteux', 'En doubte suis de chouse trescertaine'. This kind of psychological exploration, whether personal or general, with its search for evenly opposed qualities and characteristics, was a kind of game which appealed at once to the members of the poetic court, so much so that no fewer than eight of them entered the lists on this occasion, one of them being no less a poet than Villon himself, who there is some reason to suppose may even have been a pensioner of the duke's at Blois for a short time.[24] But it must be said that not even Villon's entry is in a way out of the ordinary. He, with others, has a tendency to repeat some of Charles' lines, and in the end one feels that what attracted the young poets in the theme was the very thing that killed their inspiration, so that it is tempting to think that it was because he had had enough of them that Charles wrote another *ballade*, beginning 'Je n'ay plus soif, tairie est la fontaine', a theme on which Villon also wrote. But once again his *ballade* is by no means one of his best, any more than is that of Charles.

It was not only the young esquires and visitors who took part in the poetic games. Charles' old friend, the companionable doctor Jean Caillau, tried his hand at the fountain-poems too, as a diversion perhaps, since he wrote in his contribution 'Je hay travail, et le repos m'ennuye'. Charles had by then pensioned him off but he continued to attend him and his duchess too when they were ill. He and Charles exchanged poems from time to time too, to tell each other how they were putting up with old age. For apart from the games, Charles liked to keep in touch with his friends in verse. He himself wrote as naturally as he breathed, so much so that his correspondents or interlocutors could hardly help but reply in kind. There was Charles of Nevers, for instance, to whom Charles had addressed a delightful *rondeau* on his leaving Blois, where he had been a guest, urging him

> Pour paier vostre belle chiere,
> Laissez en gaige vostre cueur,
> Nous le garderons en doulceur
> Tant que vous retournez arriere etc.

This moved the count to reply in kind:

> Mon tresbon hoste et ma tresdoulce hostesse,
> Treshumblement et plus vous remercie
> Des biens, honneurs, bonté et courtoisie,
> Que m'avez fais tous deux, par vostre humblesse.

Not very inspired, perhaps, but obviously sincere, as was his statement 'Mon povre cuer pour paiement vous lesse . . .'

This is all we hear of Nevers, but a friend called Fredet, whom Charles had met at Tours in 1447, was a more frequent visitor until, apparently after some hesitation, he decided to get married. Charles, who took a keen interest in the affairs of his friends, had urged him to strike while the iron was hot in this love-affair ('Le fer est chault, il le fault batre') at the same time teasingly counselling him in a half-French, half-Latin *ballade*, not to overdo intercourse, once married:

> Premierement, caveatis,
> De coitu trop a oultrage,

this being a

> Bon regime sanitatis
> Pro vobis, neuf en mariage,

—one of the rare occasions where we see Charles in a ribald mood. Whether for this or another cause the marriage seems not to have turned out well, and Fredet ceased to visit Blois, whereupon Charles sent him a typically gay little enquiry to find out what had become of him, beginning:

> Crié soit a la clochete,
> Par les rues, sus et jus,
> Fredet! On ne le voit plus;
> Est il mis en oubliete?
>
> Jadis il tenoit bien conte
> De visiter ses amis,
> Est il roy, ou duc, ou conte
> Quant en oubly les a mis?

This called forth a reply to the effect that it was because of his marriage that he had become a recluse, and he appeals to Charles for help in his 'grant doleur', an appeal to which Charles, no longer mocking, answered at once that, as soon as he knows the whole story 'Je vous secourray de bon cueur'.

There were a few poetic exchanges with the esquires too, particularly with those who had a genuine talent of their own. Simonnet Caillau (no relation of the doctor's) was one of these, as were Étienne Le Gout, one of the secretaries, Fraigne, whose charming poem 'Et ou vas tu, petit soupir?' called forth as charming a reply from Charles; Benoist Damien and above all Gilles des Ormes, or Ourmes, an esquire-man-carver and a true poet, very dear to Charles, who made him captain of Chambord in 1457, when he was only nineteen. Simonnet, Benoist and Gilles all took part in the poetic games but wrote other *rondeaux* spontaneously. One poem by Damien, 'Pour parvenir a vostre grace', may indeed be addressed to Mary, as another beginning with the same line, by her cup-bearer Thignonville, certainly was.

Gilles des Ormes produced a delightful piece of witty cynicism, which must have amused Charles a good deal:

> Pour bien mentir souvent et plaisamment,
> Mais qu'il ne tourne a aucun prejudice,
> Il m'est advis que ce n'est point de vice
> Mais est vertu et bon entendement.

Those who act thus, he observes in the next verse, are well esteemed and earn high promotion. Those who lie falsely (a pleasant distinction) to harm others maliciously should be punished. Therefore one must take care to 'bien mentir souvent et plaisamment'. Worldly advice like this is a rare theme, however. Most of the young men sang of the pangs of love, which they liked to pretend they were enduring even when they were not; and Charles, who with increasing age considered, or pretended to consider, love as a folly, enjoyed in his answering poems twitting them on their sufferings. In the case of his handsome but shy nephew Francis of Étampes, who obviously found it beyond him to write his own love plaint, Charles did it for him, making him say he has collected a great burden of love-affairs and beg his uncle 'Pour Dieu! ne vous mocqués de moy'.

Of all his young admirers, whether courtiers or visitors, the one whom Charles perhaps loved best was Pierre de Beaujeu's eldest brother John, Count of Clermont, heir of Duke Charles of Bourbon who had retired into private life in 1442. Although John was then only fifteen, his father's retirement brought him into a prominence unusual for his age. Charles VII both liked and esteemed him, so much so that he made him a member of his Council when he was seventeen, and later gave him his daughter Jane, then a girl of only eleven, as a bride. But John was not only a courtier. He was a gallant soldier too, and fought with Dunois throughout 1450 when he was driving the English out of Normandy. In 1454 the king made him his lieutenant-governor in the Gironde and he spent much time in that region.

It was therefore only at rare intervals that he was able to frequent the court at Blois. But the life there was so much to his taste that he continued to return even after he had succeeded to his dukedom in 1456. And if he enjoyed being there, Charles makes it plain how much he delighted in the company of this young man for whom he had a pet name, Clermondois, and whom he used to tease about his family tendency to gout and his apparently weak digestion. He must indeed have been a lovable character to draw from Charles that unusually affectionate outburst:

> Helas! et qui ne l'aymeroit
> De Bourbon le droit heritier,
> Qui a l'estomac de papier
> Et aura la goute de droit!

John, like all the others, had his love-affairs, and indeed appears to have had an illegitimate daughter when he was a mere boy in 1448. He kept Charles in touch with the progress of his affairs of the heart and seems not to have been altogether pleased with the prospect of marrying the eleven-year-old princess—making 'aliance a la riche', as Charles called it in a *rondeau* praying:

> Dieu vous envoye pascience,
> Gentil conte Clermondois.

Perhaps this patience brought its own reward and John found in his young wife the steadfast love he had been looking for, if indeed she is the subject of a poem that sounds more sincere because more simple than some he wrote:

> Duc d'Orleans, je l'ay trouvée,
> Celle qui ayme loyauté.

Charles found in John , as he did also in Gilles des Ormes, an excellent chess partner too, so much so that he gave him one of his most superb books, the *De ludis scachorum Alearum et Mirellorum*.[25]* Written

* See page 160 above.

in a bold, black hand on thick vellum leaves, it consists of three parts: a treatise on the game of chess by the Lombard Nicolas de Nicolai, a famous chess player of the thirteenth century, an explanation of the different games of tables, and a treatise on the game of merels. The chess section contains a whole series of exquisitely drawn illustrations of the last moves necessary to achieve check-mate, a page to each. This splendid manuscript, which had been a constant companion of Charles' throughout his imprisonment, is inscribed in his own hand "Iste liber constat Karolo duci Aurelianensi etc. KAROLUS". It must have been after 1456, when Clermont came into his dukedom, that Charles gave him the book, for as its new owner he wrote on fol. 264^v "Ce livre est au duc de Bourbon Jehan".

In the course of the poetic games, and of his interchanges with his friends, Charles wrote some fifty poems. But in addition to these, so compulsive and prolific was his gift, there are over three hundred others, nearly all *rondeaux* but a few *ballades*, that he composed in his solitary hours during the years at Blois. A number of these he transcribed himself in his personal manuscript, his *Livre de Pensée* as he called it, using 'pensée' as a wide term to express the whole world of his mind and spirit. It was a world that sometimes seemed to him like a blessed refuge, a world in which he tasted the exhilaration of escaping from contentious matters, letting his mind play with thoughts in solitude where, as he wrote

> Il n'est nul si beau passe temps
> Que se jouer a sa Pensee.

It was a world from which, now that he was back in his own country and at peace, he could look back at his difficult youth:

> En mes païs quant me treuve a repos,
> Je m'esbaïs, et n'y sçay contenance.
> Car j'ay apris traveil dez mon enfance,
> Dont Fortune m'a bien chargié le dos.

By contrast with that he could now shut himself up alone and daydream at leisure:

> Tout a part moy, en mon penser m'enclos,
> Et fais chasteaulz en Espaigne et en France;

opening his mind to the ideas that came crowding in: 'Chascun jour j'ay plus de mille propos.' When he retired into his own mind he was surrounded by many of the things he loved best:

> En la chambre de ma pensee,
> Quant j'ay visité mes tresors,
> Maintesfoiz la treuve estoffee
> Richement de plaisans confors.
> A mon cueur je conseille lors
> Qu'i prenons nostre demouree,
> Et que par nous soit bien gardee
> Contre tous ennuyeux rappors.

He makes an inventory of these treasures that he is going to guard against these 'ennuyeux rappors', and one of them is 'Paix, la bien amee'. For he had not forgotten that passionate devotion to peace which he had proclaimed so eloquently while he was in England; and in another *ballade* on much the same theme as the one just quoted, and beginning

> L'autre jour tenoit son conseil,
> En la chambre de ma pensee,

he begins the second verse with

> Il n'est chose soubz le souleil
> Qui tant doit estre desiree
> Que Paix; c'est le don non pareil.

But 'l'ostellerie de Pensée' seems to him a less cheerful place than the 'logeis de Joye', and more like those 'prisons de Pensée' which he made one of the subjects of the poetic competitions, prisons whose gaoler, Care, reminded him painfully of his years in captivity. And indeed there are times when, alone with himself, he knows moods of deep depression:

> Dedens mon Livre de Pensée,
> J'ay trouvé escripvant mon cueur
> La vray histoire de douleur,
> De larmes toutes enluminee.

Although one can never be absolutely sure whether Charles is merely embroidering on some more or less fashionable fancy or accepted poetical theme, or truly expressing his own feelings, there does seem to exist a kind of touchstone in the marked directness and simplicity of those poems that appear to be autobiographical, so that it is difficult not to feel that they come from the heart as well as the mind of the poet himself, both when he is in a light-heatred mood or in one of sadness. And as certain thoughts and moods tend to recur again and again in this considerable body of verse, their perusal gradually paints a picture of the man himself in at least some of his aspects. In the poems that he wrote for and with his servants and his friends, we saw him as the kindly master and companion, indulgent to young men and ready to encourage them, amused by their youthful emotions and given to affectionate mockery and teasing, but not such as to make them feel ashamed or uneasy. In the poems written for himself he is still the same man, but with other moods and feelings as well, seeing himself as clearly as he sees his friends, mocking at himself too, revealing at times a sad awareness that his life has brought him more sorrow than happiness, girding against the onslaught of old age with its loss of power, but in the end facing it with that philosophy that had enabled him to endure captivity.

In a few of these poems he helps us to know him by a direct description of one of his own characteristics:

> J'ayme qui m'ayme, autrement non;
> Et non pourtant, je ne hay rien,

he says, and one recognises the man who, starved of friendship during the years of captivity, responded so eagerly to the friendly offers of Philip and Isabella of Burgundy and became thereafter their warm and faithful supporter for life. In that same poem he laments 'Je parle trop, las!' insisting that this is true. But though perhaps he was given to talkativeness in his merrier moods, in more sombre moments he kept his thoughts to himself, going so far as to turn into a cough the sighs that some inner sadness was causing him, moods that he described in a delightfully simple and sincere-sounding lyric:

> Plus penser que dire
> Me couvient souvent,
> Sans moustrer comment
> N'a quoy mon cueur tire.
>
> Faignant de sousrire
> Quant suis tresdolent,
> Plus penser que dire
> Me couvient souvent

> En toussant, souspire
> Pour secrettement
> Musser mon tourment.
> C'est privé martire
> Plus penser que dire!

That this was a principle which did in general guide him seems likely, for he returned to the subject in another *rondeau*:

> Quelque chose derriere
> Couvient tousjours garder,
> On ne peut pas monstrer
> Sa voulenté entiere.

He was particularly of this opinion

> Quant on est en frontiere
> De Dangereux Parler,
> Quelque chose derriere
> Couvient tousjours garder.

What of the deeper emotions that may still have stirred in him during those years at Blois, at the beginning of which he was still, after all, only fifty-six? Though there is no reason to suppose that his marriage was other than happy, and though friendship rather than love seems, on the surface at any rate, to have been the dominant tendency of his heart at that time, there are certainly indications in the poetry that he was still susceptible to the power of beauty and may even have felt a definite attraction to one lady who appeared to reciprocate his feeling. Quite a few of the poems, both *ballades* and *rondeaux*, are devoted to dialogues and discussions between the eyes and the heart, and though this kind of theme was rather a commonplace of the poetry of the time, that is no reason why it should not have been used to express genuine sentiments. He counsels his heart to close its doors against the temptations of his eyes:

> Mon cueur, pour vous en garder,
> De mes yeulx qui tant vous temptent
> Afin que devers vous n'entrent,
> Faitz lez portes fermer.

It is treacherous of his eyes, in whom he trusts, to try and lead him into folly:

> N'est ce pas grant trahison
> De mes yeulx en qui me fye,
> Qui me conseillent folye
> Maintes foys, contre raison?

It is no good their constantly telling him of Beauty, it no longer pleases him:

> Ne m'en racontez plus, mes yeulx,
> De Beaulté que vous prisez tant,
> Car plus voys ou monde vivant,
> Et mains me plaist, ainsi m'aist Dieu.

For all that, Beauty obviously does still tempt and trouble him:

> Ostez-vous de devant moy,
> Beaulté, par vostre serment,
> Car trop me temptez souvent;
> Tort avez, tenez vous quoy.

> Toutes les fois que vous voy,
> Je suis je ne sçay comment;
> Ostez vous de devant moy
> Beaulté, par vostre serment.

> Tant de plaisirs j'apparçoy
> En vous, a mon jugement,
> Qu'ils troublent mon pensement;
> Vous me grevez, sur ma foy;
> Ostez vous de devant moy.

He begs her to conceal her charming glance, for

> Vostre attrait, soubtil et douls,
> Blesse sans qu'on lui mefface.
> Plaisant Regard, mussez vous,
> Ne vous moustrez plus en place.

In spite of these attempts to resist Beauty there are two charming and very sincere-sounding poems which suggest that Charles did form a real attachment for one lady, who had perhaps made the first move, impelled no doubt by her own feeling for him. In the first of these two there is a line missing from the first verse, which rather gives the impression that it conveyed a genuine feeling:

> Mais que vostre cuer soit mien
> Ne doit le mien estre vostre?
> ....
> Ouil, certes, plus que sien.

He is content merely to know of her love:

> Je ne desire outre rien,
> Mais que vostre cuer soit mien.

But it rather seems as if the lady herself would have liked things to go further. Her feelings were obviously the deeper of the two, and she feared his affection for her might not last. It needs little perception to read this into the guarded sentiments Charles expressed in the second *rondeau*, beautiful enough to be quoted in full:

> Quant je congnois que vous estes tant mien,
> Et que m'aymez de cueur, si loyaument,
> Je feroye vers vous trop faulcement
> Se, sans fraindre, ne vous aymoie bien.
>
> Essaiez moy se vous fauldray en rien,
> Gardant tousjours mon honneur seulement,
> Quant je congnois que vous estes tant mien,
> Et que m'aymez de cueur, si loyaument.
>
> Se me dictes: 'Las! je ne sçay combien
> Vostre vouloir durera longuement';
> Je vous respons, sans aucun changement,
> Qu'en ce propos me tendray et me tien,
> Quant je congnois que vous estes tant mien.

But although Charles was still susceptible to beauty, and capable of tender feelings, he could now look at women dispassionately and mock at them for their follies. The bygone days when he had taken part in the annual celebrations of courtly love were over, too, although he continued to write poems on that day of lovers, St. Valentine's Day, (there are altogether nine of these during those years). But except for one occasion when he rather half-heartedly took his sister-in-law, Margaret of Angoulême, for his 'per', his lady, on that day, his reaction

is always the same as it was when he exchanged such poems with René
of Anjou in 1444. He wakes or is woken up early to go out and celebrate, as the custom was, but after a moment's hesitation as to whether
he shall rise and participate in the ritual functions, he decides to turn
over and go to sleep again. The chief pleasure the day gave him was to
indulge his fancy and his skill in writing Valentine's Day poems, some
of which are charming, especially one which is a dialogue between him
and St. Valentine himself.

He celebrated the first of May in much the same fashion but not so
often—there are only five May Day poems—saying when he heard the
bell ring for it

> il est trop matin,
> Ung peu je me rendormiray.

It is plain that as time passed he was becoming thoroughly lazy. Yet in
the last of this series, he rather pathetically decides to take part:

> Pour moustrer que j'en ay esté
> Des amoureux aucunesfoix,
> Ce May, le plus plaisant des moys,
> Vueil servir, ce present Esté.

But apart from this one flicker, all he wants now is to leave these things
to the young and be at peace himself:

> Voisent faire geunes gens leurs essaiz;
> Plus cure n'ay de pensée soigneuse
> Comme lasse de la guerre amoureuse.

The things he enjoyed most in those days were all the pleasures of
country life, especially the beauty of nature and the seasons, and these
he praised in some of the most charming of his poems, poems so simple
and so true that by their very sincerity they evoke a picture, more
lively than any painted portrait, of the man who wrote them. The best
known of all his poems (which is in fact often the only one that seems
to be known) contains all the sparkle and freshness of the world in
spring that it celebrates:

> Le temps a laissié son manteau
> De vent, de froidure et de pluye,
> Et s'est vestu de brouderie,
> De soleil luyant, cler et beau.

> Il n'y a beste, ne oyseau,
> Qu'en son jargon ne chante ou crie:
> Le temps a laissié son manteau!
>
> Riviere, fontaine et ruisseau
> Portent, en livree jolie,
> Gouttes d'argent d'orfaverie,
> Chascun s'abille de nouveau:
> Le temps a laissié son manteau.

But its deserved fame has robbed some of the others of their due meed of praise. For example one that describes summer's harbingers decorating his lodging:

> Les fourriers d'Esté sont venus
> Pour appareillier son logis,
> Et ont fait tendre ses tappis,
> De fleurs et verdure tissus.
>
> En estandant tappis velus,
> De vert herbe par le païs,
> Le fourriers d'Esté sont venus. . . .

as a result of which sad hearts become 'sains et jolis'. The sight of beautiful flowers, painting their faces in pleasant colours and bathed in sweet scents, rejoices all hearts, and not only human hearts, for

> Les oyseaus deviennent danseurs
> Dessuz mainte branche flourie,
> Et font joyeuse chanterie,
> De contres, deschans et teneurs,
> En regardant ces belles fleurs.

It is only in summer that he can enjoy the pleasures of the country round Blois, which he always longs for when he is away from it.

> Trouvé me suis, pour une fois,
> Assez longuement en Touraine,

and all he wants is

> Que de m'en retourner à Blois.

On one occasion when he is at Orleans, he seizes the excuse that they are going to play there at the *quintaine*, a game he once enjoyed:

> Raisonnable cause m'y maine,
> Excusé soye ceste fois,
> Pour ce qu'on joute a la quintaine,
> A Orleans, je tire a Blois.

He made this journey usually by river, and such voyages afford him occasion for reflection, as when he tells how

> En tirant d'Orleans a Blois,
> L'autre jour par eaue venoye
> Si rencontré, par plusieurs foiz,
> Vaisseaux, ainsi que je passoye;

and at the sight

> Mon cueur, Penser et moy, nous troys,
> Les regardasmes a grant joye

whereupon he launched into allegorical thoughts on the theme of the waters of Fortune, the ship of the world, the oars of Hope and such.

At Blois itself even the little things of daily life inspire his Muse, such as the visit of one of those travelling pedlars, like the one from whom he bought ivory combs, scissors and an ink-holder. Both this pedlar and the duke spring to vivid life in the two poems which Charles wrote after this visit, the first describing how he began by telling the 'petit mercier' that the trifling objects he was selling were worth nothing:

> Riens ne valent ses mirlifiques
> Et ses menues oberliques;
> D'ou venez vous, petit mercier?

But after telling him he will never make a living by selling such baubles, the duke obviously yielded to the normal temptation to turn over the contents of the basket on the off-chance of discovering some treasure among the wares that he continued to decry, so he ordered the pedlar:

> Desploiez tout vostre pannier,
> Affin qu'on y puisse serchier
> Quelques bagues plus autentiques:
> Rien ne valent ses mirlifiques.

But the little pedlar stood up for himself, giving as good as he got, and one assumes that his spirited defence of his trade and the contents of his basket pleased the duke, since he versified it:

> Petit mercier, petit pannier!
> Pour tant se je n'ay marchandise
> Qui soit du tout a vostre guise,
> Ne blasmer, pour ce, mon mestier.
>
> Je gangne denier a denier,
> C'est loings du tresor de Venise,
> Petit mercier, petit pannier!

In fact the pedlar had the last word, saying he could not waste time in staying to talk to the duke while the day lasted:

> Et tandiz qu'il est jour ouvrier,
> Le temps pers quant a vous devise;

so he will leave him and go off

> Et par my les rues crier:
> Petit mercier, petit pannier!

Happy though Charles always was at Blois, there was another place not far away down-stream which he delighted in visiting, and that was Savonnières,* the country-house of Jean de Saveuses, who had been brought up with him as a child and had served him faithfully all his life. It may be remembered that Charles had sent him to England with John of Angoulême as one of the hostages in 1412, but by some means not recorded his release was procured before 1433, and thereafter Saveuses was constantly on the road on the duke's affairs, visiting him in England. Charles rewarded these services with many high offices in his household. He showered gifts on him too, wood for building and warming Savonnières being some of them. Saveuses was unmarried but he had made Savonnières such a pleasant place to stay in that Charles, on a visit when he was apparently a member of a house-party of friends from Sologne and the Beauce, wrote an unusually enthusiastic description of its pleasures; hunting, fishing, games of tables and cards and

---

* This house, now spelt without the final 's', is still there, though much restored.

good food and drink, a varied menu which they needed no pressing to enjoy, after which sleep came easily.

> Aux champs, par hayes et buissons,
> Perdrix et lyevres nous prendrons,
> Et yrons pescher sur rivieres,
> Puis par deça demourons,
> Nous, Saulongnois et Beausserons,
> En la maison de Savonnieres.

> Vivres, tabliers, cartes aurons
> Ou souvent estudierons
> Vins, mangers de plusieurs manieres;
> Galerons, sans faire prieres,
> Et de dormir ne nous faindrons,
> Puis que par deça demourons.

Another *rondeau* singing the praises of this kind of country-life sounds as if it too refers to Savonnières, where Charles enjoyed finding himself one of a company all occupied as their own fancy took them. It begins with a rather curious line stating that one of their pleasures was not only to dine on their boat, but to have supper while bathing:

> Souper ou baing et disner ou bateau
> En ce monde n'a telle compaignie,
> L'un parle ou dort, et l'autre chante ou crie,
> Les autres font balades ou rondeau.

And the next verse speaks of the pleasure of drinking both old and new wines, all of which makes Charles feel that this is the right way to live:

> Quant tout est fait, il fault passer sa vie
> Le plus aise qu'on peut, en chiere lie.

It is rather surprising to find the normally sedentary duke praising, in the first of those two poems, the hunting of partridges and hares as one of the pleasures of life at Savonnières; but though not a passionate hunter like Mary he obviously did take part in such sports from time to time and was very fond of his three hunting dogs Briquet, Baude and Dyamant.[26] Briquet, 'aux pendantes oreilles', was obviously a spaniel of some kind and a wonderful hunting dog, as good as a blood-hound—'Tu ne fais pas miracles mais merveilles'. But he was getting

old, and had earned his rest, so now the dog with the curious name of
Baude, must take his place:

> Laissez baude buissonner,
> Le vieil briquet se repose,
> Desormais travailler n'ose,
> Abayer, ne mot sonner.
> On luy doit bien pardonner:
> Ung vieillart peult peu de chose!

Most of these were, of course, summer pleasures, for Charles took
no pleasure in the world out of doors in winter, and could not understand those who enjoyed it.

> M'apelez vous cela jeu;
> En froit d'aler par pays?
> Or pleust a Dieu qu'a Paris,
> Nous feussions enprés le feu!

he cries, in a phrase with a very modern ring to it.

> Yver fait champs et arbres vieulx,
> Leurs barbes de neige blanchir,
> Et est si froit, ort et pluieux
> Qu'emprès le feu couvient croupir,
> On ne peut hors des huis yssir,
> Comme un oisel qui est en mue.

This is from a *ballade* that may have been written in England where
one can understand that, shivering in the cold, grim castles that were
his prisons, he learnt to hate the winter when the only joy was a good
fire. This was certainly one that Charles revelled in: 'En yver, du feu,
du feu!' he cries.

Charles' variations of mood arising from his susceptibility to changes
in the weather were not, after all, very serious, except as affording him
a constant theme for his poetic fancy to play upon. Much more profound was his sadness at the old age that was gradually establishing its
empire over him. His dread of this seems to have nothing to do with
any fear of death. His own death is in fact something which he never
mentions. No, it is rather that he feels that the years are gradually rob-
bing him of his powers of enjoyment, and removing him once for all
from the ranks of those younger people whose company he so much

enjoyed. In times past when he looked out of the windows of his eyes he could see more beauties than he can at present:

> Or, maintenant que je deviens vieulx,
> Quant je lys ou livre de Joie,
> Les lunectes prens pour le mieulx,
> Par quoy la lettre me grossoye,
> Et n'y voy ce que je souloie:
> Pas n'avoye ceste foiblesse,
> En mains de ma Dame Jeunesse.

He could learn so much more quickly in youth:

> Pieça, en jeunesse fleurie
> Quant de vif entendement fu
> J'eusse apris en heure et demye
> Plus qu'a present; tant ay vesqu . . .

He accuses Youth for having sold him cheaply to Old Age:

> Pourquoy m'as tu vendu, Jennesse,
> A grant marchié, comme pour rien
> Es mains de ma Dame Viellesse
> Qui ne me fait gueres de bien?

The hostel of Old Age is hung with the black of Sadness.

> Mais il convient que je l'endure,
> Puis que c'est le cours de nature.

He tries to resign himself to his age:

> Passer fault nostre temps en paix;
> Veu que sommes du renc des vieulx:
> Devenons saiges, desormais,
> Mon cueur, vous et moy, pour le mieulx.

But making resolutions is one thing and keeping them another, and occasionally he revolts and bursts out:

> Ah! que vous m'anuyés, Viellesse,
> Que me grevez plus que oncques mes!

He will never be able to get used to it:

> Je vous faiz loyalle promesse
> Que ne vous aimeray jamés.

In one or two of the latest poems he speaks as if Old Age had made him almost desperate, but his philosophical nature comes to his aid. He accepts that he must

> De Vieillesse porte livrée
> Qu'elle m'a, puis ung temps, donnee,
> Quoy que soit contre mon desir,
> Mais maulgré myen le fault souffrir,
> Quant par Nature est ordonnee,

and characteristically resolves to make the best use of it that he can, as long as he can remain true to his own ideas:

> Tant que vivre puisse et mourir
> Selong l'escript de ma pensee.

With increasing age Charles became more and more a prey to a temper of mind that was by no means only an effect of it, since it was something with which he would appear to have been born: a tendency to melancholy, or 'merencolie' as he calls it. Of the four temperaments or bodily humours under which the Middle Ages classified all men, he certainly cannot be considered as entirely a melancholic since there was much of the sanguine and something of the phlegmatic in him too. But the vein of melancholy ran deep in him and his allegorical personification of it, 'Merencolie', stalks like a female figure of Fate through all his poetry from youth to age, lying in wait for him at every turn in different disguises and trapping him beyond the possibility of escape. He was aware of the existence of melancholy even in that first poem, the *Retenue d'Amours*, when he remarked that Dame Jeunesse had saved his tender youth from experiencing 'Soing on Merencolie'. In his moments of hopelessness during his captivity, she was naturally there, along with 'Douleur', 'Desplaisir', 'Tristesse' and other unhappy figures. Together with 'Soing' and 'Ennuy' she mocks at his heart for its folly in thinking that it will escape them while in captivity.

> Au lever et au couschier,
> Trouveras Merencolie
> ....
> Par nous n'auras autrement
> Ou royaume d'Angleterre.

In one extraordinary 'medical' ballade he describes all the complaints—
migraines, fevers, cold sweats, gout, colic etc.—that are brought upon
suffering hearts 'Par le vent de Merencolie'—the line which ends each
stanza. And one recalls that desperate cry, 'Las! Merencolie' which
seems to hold all his grief at the death of Bonne.

Once he was back in France again he might have expected that this
sad figure would haunt him no more, but there she still was. However
he was then in good enough heart to attempt to chase her and her
gloomy companions briskly away:

> Alez vous ant, allez, alés,
> Soussy, Soing et Merencolie,
> Me cuidez vous, toute ma vie,
> Gouverner, comme fait avés?

But she is not to be got rid of:

> Ci pris, ci mis,
> Trop fort me lie,
> Merencolie,
> De pis en pis.

And she makes a sudden sinister appearance when he is least thinking
of her:

> Vous ne tenez compte de moy,
> Beaussire, mais qui estes vous?

He cannot escape, she tells him she will always hold "one end of everything". Again he tries to push her out:

> Pour Dieu! boutons la hors
> Ceste Merencolie

In springtime, when she is especially unwelcome, he urges her to hide
herself:

> Allez vous mussez maintenant,
> Ennuyeuse Merencolie.
> Regardez la saison jolye
> Qui par tout vous va rebutant.

He determines to serve her no longer; instead he will stay with 'Nonchaloir' (indifference) who long ago, when the God of Love had released him after the death of Bonne, had promised to look after him:

> Serviteur plus de vous, Merancolie,
> Je ne seray, car trop fort y traveille;
> ....
> A Non Chaloir vueil tenir compaignie,
> Par qui j'auray repos sans que m'esveille.

But she is not so easily shaken off. If he manages to get out of her toils in the evening, she grips him again in the morning:

> En verrai ge jamais la fin
> De voz euvres, Merancolie?
> Quant au soir de vous me deslie,
> Vous me ratachez au matin.

She knocks at his door: 'Qu'est cela?–C'est Merencolye.' He tells his heart to shut it in her face:

> Fermez luy l'uis au visage,
> Mon cueur, a Merancolye,
> Gardez qu'elle n'entre mye,
> Pour gaster nostre mesnaige.

His heart must stop up its ears too, against 'le vent de Merencolie'. It is all to no purpose. He continues trying to get rid of her:

> Allez vous en dont vous venez,
> Annuyeuse Merencolie,

but he remains an

> Escollier de Merencolye
> ....
> Es derreniers jours de ma vye.

He is trapped in her labyrinth and the more frantically he tries to get out, the deeper he penetrates into his windings:

> C'est la prison Dedalus
> Que de ma merencolie.

No wonder that he sometimes felt:

> Le monde est ennuye de moi
> Et moy pareillement de lui.

All the same there were times of respite. She had warned him that if he tried to chase her away by leading a merry life she would come swiftly back – 'Brief revendray de plaine cource' – but for all that he had found that if he surrounded himself with people

> Et qu'on rit, parle, chante ou crye,
> Je chasse hors Merencolye.

And fortunately, during 1457, there were even more than the usual occasions for joyful gatherings at Blois. In March, René of Anjou came with his suite to stay with Charles and Mary there. He had always kept in touch with Charles ever since that pleasant encounter at Tours in 1444, when they engaged in a poetic duel, but only now did he return the visit that Charles had paid him at Tarascon, when he was on his way to Asti. In the meantime he had often sent Charles presents – gilded javelins, silver goblets, etc. – and in return for one of these, received at Blois, Charles had sent him a charming *rondeau* of thanks:

> Vostre esclave et serf, ou que soye,
> Qui trop ne vous puis mercier,
> Quant vous a pleu de m'envoyer
> Le don qu'ay receu a grant joye!

In the same poem Charles expressed the hope that he would see him soon, as he had something to show him 'sus le mestier' – some work on hand, that he thought would please him. To see the poetry that Charles had been writing since last they met would certainly have interested René, who himself was at that time engaged on his own great work *Le Cuer d'Amours Espris*. And it must have been during this visit that Charles told him something of his life in England, and especially of that brief love-affair that he had known there, which René then recounted in that part of his poem which he devoted to Charles, as one of his chosen heroes of love.* The length of René's visit is not recorded, but as that summer, from May to July, was a particularly gay one – the court was entertained by musicians and dancers, there were constant games of tables and chess, and Jouvenal le Nègre, a famous chess-player from Lombardy, who wandered around Europe, playing with anyone who wished to, came and stayed a long time[27] – it may be that René stayed to share in all these, and that it was by way of thanks for his visit that, in August, he sent Charles the gift of a Turkish knife.[28]

Mary also must have enjoyed the presence of René, for she asked

* See page 209 above.

him to write his name and his device in that *liber amicorum* of hers, her copy of Alain Chartier's poems. She too had taken some part in the pleasurable pursuits of that summer, for in July she went hunting, a rather rash pleasure it might seem, if indeed she rode to it, for 1457 was to be a year of great significance for her, and for Charles also. At the end of it, on December 19th, she gave birth to their first child, a daughter, who was called Mary. The long interval that had elapsed without children had perhaps been due to Mary's health for, as we have seen, on several occasions during those restless years of journeys to Burgundy she had been in the hands of the doctors, and as late as 1451 the Duke of Burgundy's personal physician had come to visit her.[29]

But no doubt the peaceful life at Blois suited her better, and there is an indication that, for some time past, she had been hoping that she might conceive; for in an inventory of her jewels, drawn up in February 1456, there is mention of a golden chain[30] with a strange stone in the form of a black unicorn hanging from it, a stone that the superstition of the day credited with the magic property of helping women in childbirth. Another chain, of twisted gold in several rows, with three *chantepleures* on it and three letters from her device, was mentioned in that same inventory. It seems that Mary may have thought it had similar powers for she had it broken up to form a single chain, which she wore round her waist all the time that she was with child. And some time after she was safely delivered, on the occasion of a royal visit she had it broken into three pieces, by someone called the Bastard of Burgundy, of whom we otherwise hear nothing, to whom she gave one of them, while of the other two one went to a certain Monsieur de la Gentuse, of whom again nothing is known, and the third to that favourite brother of hers, Adolf of Cleves.[31]

Charles' feelings at finding himself the father of another daughter nearly fifty years after the birth of the first one, Jane, can only be guessed. But it was perhaps the sight of the infant Mary's puffy face, after a night when she had not slept properly—a sight so unaccustomed for him—that inspired him to write a lyric full of baby language and his habitual humour:

> Quant n'ont assez fait dodo,
> Cez petitz enfanchonnés
> Il portent soubz leurs bonnés
> Visages plain de bobo.

C'est pitié s'il font jojo
Trop matin, lez doulcinés,
Quant n'ont assez fait dodo,
Cez petitz enfanchonnés.

Mieulx amassent a gogo
Gesir sur molz coissinés,
Car il sont tant poupinés!
Helas! che gnogno, gnogno,
Quant n'ont assez fait dodo.

It would be difficult to invent a better word than 'gnogno' to express the mumbling grumble of a toothless child.

CHAPTER SIXTEEN
1453–1465

O F the several hundred poems that Charles wrote during those peaceful years spent mainly at Blois, only one is concerned with a public event. For him poetry remained a very private thing, a vehicle for expressing the moods and emotions provoked by the daily events of his personal life and those of the friends who shared it. It had indeed always been so. Of the *ballades* that he wrote in England, only two had been inspired by the miseries of the unending wars that had brought his country into such a state of moral degradation. Apart from that, even matters that touched him nearly, although at one remove, like the relief of his own town of Orleans by Joan of Arc, called forth no hymn of praise or gratitude from him. That silence was understandable in a prisoner whose watchful guardians might have taken any such poem as evidence of political activity. But one cannot help but feel it strange that he should never have made the slightest reference to the Maid during those years at Blois, when the memory of her was so much in the public mind.

For it was in 1450, the year after the freeing of Rouen, that enquiries into her death, with a view to her rehabilitation, were begun. In 1455, full-scale proceedings were launched and continued for over a year, based on a thorough search for all the evidence and a questioning of all the witnesses who remained alive. Two of the chief of these were, as we know, the Maid's old friends and supporters, Dunois and Alençon, so if Charles had never realised it before, he might then have heard, at least by report, from their own accounts the moving story of how those two young men, both so near and dear to him, had immediately perceived the quality of this inspired peasant girl, unhesitatingly believed in her mission and helped her to fulfil it. Alençon's story in particular of how his young wife, the duke's daughter Jane, had pleaded with Joan to keep her young husband safe for her, must surely have touched Charles nearly. Yet he made no reference in his poetry to any of these things.

Another event closely bound up with his own past that took place at this time was the impeachment and death of his old friend and guardian, Suffolk. His pro-French policy had never been popular, and as the tide of war turned more and more against the English, so violently anti-French did the mood of the country become that, in January 1450, the Commons brought a charge of high treason against the duke (as he had now become) and he was committed to the Tower. One of the chief accusations against him was that he had persuaded the king to release the Duke of Orleans, with whom it was alleged that Suffolk had plotted that Charles would thereafter "by subtill counsell, might and ayde", assist Charles VII to seize Henry's realm of France and his dukedoms of Guienne and Normandy.[1] The manifest absurdity of this charge, belied by the subsequent conduct of both Charles and Suffolk, did not deter the Lords in March from adding their own quota of accusations, most of which were to the effect that Suffolk had used his influence over the king to subvert to his own use and purposes moneys that properly belonged to the Treasury, Charles' ransom among them.

When Suffolk was brought from the Tower and allowed to speak in his own defence, in the presence of the king, the Lords and the Commons, he easily demolished the case for the prosecution, and protested his loyalty to the king. The saintly Henry was not a man to turn against one he had always trusted and it may well have been his influence which saved Suffolk from being condemned to death. But so exacerbated had the hatred of his enemies now become that, cheated of his blood, only his removal from the scene would pacify them. A sentence of banishment from England was therefore pronounced, with the further proviso that for the next five years he must not live in France either. It was a harsh sentence, but it was less cruel than the fate that awaited him as soon as the vessel he had boarded at Ipswich reached the English Channel near Dover. For there some assassins hired by his enemies stopped it, dragged the duke from it into a small boat and with six strokes of a rusty sword hacked off his head and threw his body into the sea.

No one with the affectionate nature of Charles could have heard without grief and horror of the terrible end of this man who had so befriended him, and without whose help he would never have returned to his native land. None could have imagined more vividly than he Suffolk's leave-taking from his wife and son in that castle of Wingfield that had sheltered him during the happiest years of his captivity. But once again there is no echo in his poetry of his thoughts and emotions then. Hear of it he certainly must have done, for that one 'public' poem of his shows how well-informed he was not only about the progress of the war in France, but the effect of it on England. He wrote it in 1453, that dramatic year that saw not only the fall of Constantinople but, in July, the French victory at Castillon in the Dordogne, which virtually put an end to the domination of the English in Aquitaine, which they had held for three centuries. Three years earlier, in 1450, as a result of their defeat at the battle of Formigny, the English had ceased to be rulers of Normandy. So now, with both their dukedoms lost and only Calais and Guines remaining in their hands, the Hundred Years' War was at an end, except for a little sporadic fighting that continued here and there for a few more years.

Charles had every reason to know of all this, for not only was his brother Dunois the victor at Formigny, in which battle his young friend the Count of Clermont also fought, but, rather surprisingly, John of Angoulême also took part in the fighting in Guienne, where Clermont again, as the king's lieutenant for that region, distinguished himself. No wonder then that Charles who, after Agincourt, had felt so wretched at having to agree with Henry V that God was obviously on the side of the English, because of the sinfulness of the French, should now have felt inspired to proclaim with a great cry of joy that God had now changed sides and was punishing the English for their overbearing pride:

Comment voy je ses Anglois esbays!
Resjoys toy, franc royaume de France.
On apparçoit que de Dieu sont hays,
Puis qu'ils n'ont plus couraige ne puissance.
Bien pensoient, par leur oultrecuidance,
Toy surmonter et tenir en servaige,
Et ont tenu a tort ton heritaige.
Mais a present Dieu pour toy se combat
Et se monstre du tout de ta partie;
Leur grant orgueil entierement abat,
Et t'a rendu Guyenne et Normandie.

In the second verse he recalls the old miserable days of France's abasement, when the English tyrannised haughtily over her. And in the third he reveals that he is well aware of the civil strife beginning in England:

N'ont pas Anglois souvent leurs rois trays?
Certes ouyl, tous en ont congnoissance.

Et encore le roy de leur pays
Est maintenant en doubteuse balance;
D'en parler mal chascun Anglois s'avance;
Assez monstrent, par leur mauvais langaige,
Que voulentiers lui feroient oultraige.
Qui sera Roy entr'eux est grant desbat;
Pour ce, France, que veulx tu que te dye?
De sa verge Dieu les pugnist et bat
Et t'a rendu Guyenne et Normandie.

In his concluding stanza he urges his king 'Parfaiz ton jeu, comme vaillant et saige', and his country 'De ton bon eur, France, Dieu remercie.'

This *ballade* is enough to prove that Charles was by no means so sunk in the peaceful enjoyments of his quiet life at Blois as to have lost interest in the events of the wider world. Nor had he become less close to his friend the Duke of Burgundy, even though Philip never appears to have visited him at Blois; and there is in fact no evidence that they saw each other at all for some years after those fund-raising visits of Charles to Burgundy. But Philip knew he could always count on Charles when he needed him and in September 1454 he turned to him for help in a matter on which he had set his heart. His son Charles, Count of Charolois, then a young man of twenty-one, had lost his first wife, the Princess Catherine, eight years previously. His mother, the Duchess Isabella, who never forgot that she was a grand-daughter of John of Gaunt and therefore had "le cueur comme par nature"[2] in England, wanted an English bride for him. But his father, always scheming to strengthen his links with his fellow feudatories, had conceived the idea of marrying his heir to Isabella, the daughter of his sister Agnes, Duchess of Bourbon, and her husband the gouty duke, who had always been slightly hostile to him. Isabella had in fact been brought up in the Burgundian court and both her parents had favoured the idea of the union until Philip informed her father that, in addition to the usual financial dowry he expected with her, he wanted the lordship of Château-Chinon, a Bourbon enclave in his territory. This Bourbon refused to give, and so the matter had stood for several months while Burgundy was away seeing the emperor in Germany about another project that was on his mind.

On his return, in order to resume the negotiations, he invited the

Duke and Duchess of Bourbon, together with their son the Count of Clermont and his wife the Princess Jane, to meet him at Nevers; and knowing Charles of Orleans' gifts as a mediator, and his fondness for the Bourbons, he asked him and Mary to join them there. The meeting was, as usual on such occasions, enlivened by some entertainments; and no doubt because of the presence of Charles, poetic contests formed part of these, to judge by the fact that the two chroniclers, Olivier de la Marche and Georges Chastellain, who were both present, each wrote on that occasion a *ballade* on one of the themes then in vogue at Blois, 'Les Amoureux de l'Observance'. But though it may have been a pleasant social occasion, no way out of the deadlock was found, for the Duke of Bourbon had not been well enough to attend himself and merely sent ambassadors, who maintained his refusal to hand over Château-Chinon.

It was therefore finally decided that the advice of Charles VII should be sought and that the young Countess of Clermont, whom Philip had met for the first time and made much of, should go to intercede with her father. The king approved of the project and sent messengers both to Bourbon, advising him to agree to transfer the lordship requested, and to Burgundy, telling him not to insist too much on this transfer since he had "God's gifts in great measure, and plenty of them."[3] So eager was Burgundy for the marriage that as soon as he got wind of the king's approval, without waiting for his messenger he instructed his duchess, who was in Lille with her son and Isabella, to see that the marriage was not only celebrated but consummated forthwith, before anything should prevent it. His commands were obeyed and Charles and Isabella were privately married at the end of October. Philip, as usual, had got his own way, for Bourbon, bowing to the king's advice, ceded Château-Chinon to him.

Although Jane's intercession with her father had no doubt played a part in securing his approval, Charles of Orleans had also done much to influence the king in the matter. This we learn from a letter which Burgundy sent to Charles from Dijon on November 28th,[4] thanking him for a long one that Charles had sent him on October 18th "making mention at great length of how, after your leaving Nevers, you had been to see my lord the king at the said place of Romorantin, and also that my fair niece of Orleans, your companion, had been there; and how in that place my said king had received you with great good cheer." That letter from Charles is unfortunately no longer extant, but it is obvious from the affectionate and grateful tone of Philip's reply that he not only had good reason to thank Charles for what he had done on this occasion, but had every confidence that his influence with the king would be most beneficial over the next matter on which he wanted his help. For he went on to tell him that he was sending his Chancellor to La Charité, whither he understood that Charles was then going, and where he would learn from the Chancellor the reason for his visit. He was so clearly now counting on Charles' help that he begged him to let him know if any change in his plans should prevent him from going to La Charité.

Charles probably had more than an inkling of what it was the Chancellor would tell him, for ever since the previous February, during a meeting of the princes at Lille, Burgundy had been talking of his intention of going on a crusade. Like the majority of people in Western Europe he had been shocked by the fall of Constantinople the year before, and the idea of avenging and perhaps recovering it appealed to his always restless and adventurous spirit. It was to sound the emperor about it that he had then gone to Germany, and he had promised to sponsor the campaign. Philip had informed Charles VII of his intention, asking, among other things, that he might not only be allowed to levy an *aide* to finance the expedition and recruit troops (two measures that the king's institution of a centralised financial and military system now made necessary), but that he might also take the banner of France with him. Charles VII saw no particular necessity for this crusade, and the idea that one of the most powerful subjects should join it under the emperor did not appeal to him. So he refused.

Having heard all these details from Burgundy's Chancellor in February 1455, Charles went to see the king at Mehun-sur-Yèvre to beg him to reconsider his refusal, and at first received a favourable reply. Encouraged by the news of this, in the following July Burgundy sent a large embassy to his sovereign to obtain his formal agreement. The king was then at Bois-Sire-Aimé in Berry, and thither Charles of Orleans went too, to support the embassy, taking with him his duchess and also John of Angoulême and his countess. But this time Charles' advocacy proved in vain, for the king in the meantime had decided that his kingdom was still not sufficiently safe from threats of invasion by the English for him to equip and finance expeditions such as that desired by Philip. Charles reasoned with him and his Council as best he could, but could not move him. All he could do therefore was to honour the crestfallen ambassadors by accompanying them on part of their return journey, where they were feasted wherever they stopped. Mary and the Angoulêmes accompanied them.

Although Charles of Orleans had not succeeded in changing the king's mind on this occasion, his reputation as a peace-maker must have grown recently, for on May 18th of that year, 1456, even the dauphin wrote to beg him to try and patch up the bitter dissension between his father and himself.[5] The dauphin seems always to have had a certain affection for Charles, in so far as he could feel such emotion for anyone, for when he was a young man, after Charles' return from England, he wrote him a charming letter to say he had heard the duke was looking for a nice, amenable mule and so he would like to give him his; but he would be grateful if Charles could send him a good greyhound in exchange, as they were difficult to procure where he was. He had also contributed to Charles' ransom. But Charles was able to do nothing in reply to his last request, the rift between the king and his son was too deep, and soon afterwards the dauphin took himself to the court of Philip of Burgundy where he remained to the end of his father's reign.

After his performance of all these duties in the service of friendship and peace, Charles was able to resume his quiet life at Blois for two uninterrupted years. But it was not the same carefree existence as at first, for now he could not have been other than deeply troubled by what was happening to his beloved 'son-in-law' the Duke of Alençon. It will be remembered that this originally gay, handsome and brave man had come under suspicion of treachery with the English when he was with Charles and the Duke of Brittany trying to arrange a peace-conference in July 1441. Although knowledge of this came to the king, the matter seems to have been passed over at the time with no particular enquiry into it.

Before long, however, Alençon's behaviour began to reveal what was the probable cause of it. He had never got over the fact that, in order to pay his heavy ransom on his release from captivity in 1427, after the battle of Verneuil, he had had to sell his town and castle of Fougères to his uncle John, Duke of Brittany, who had paid him only half its value and thereafter always refused to return it at any price. John's successors had maintained the same attitude, always protesting that it was theirs by inheritance. This had roused an understandable sense of grievance in Alençon, who had continually begged the king

to intercede for him with the different Dukes of Brittany who succeeded each other very quickly. But this the king could not do, for the
good reason that he really had no authority over the Breton dukes, who
were still more independent than those of Burgundy, not even considering themselves his subjects. Refusing to understand this, Alençon
chose to consider that the king was against him. He began to feel too
that at court he was not received with sufficient deference—a poor
return, he felt, for his services to the king in the field when he was only
the dauphin. He took to complaining about this treatment on all occasions; and his character obviously began to go to pieces in other ways
too, for an exchange of poems with Charles of Orleans implies that the
younger man had taken to excessive drinking.

Finally, in his bitterness, Alençon began to think that the only way
of recovering his lost territory would be to encourage the English to
invade and take it for him; and he started to correspond with them to
that end. He then left his own lands and wandered about, so that if an
invasion should take place he might pretend surprise at it. But unfortunately for him, either because he had enemies or because the royal
intelligence service was so good, in the spring of 1456 some of this
correspondence came into the king's hands. Charles VII was greatly
grieved at finding that one of his own blood was betraying him, and
ordered his immediate arrest. He charged Dunois with the sad task of
arresting his old companion-in-arms, and the Bastard performed it with
his accustomed gentleness and tact.

He went at once to Paris, where Alençon was known to be staying.
It is a poignant thought that the reason for his presence there was that
on May 3rd he had been giving his testimony at the rehabilitation enquiry into Joan of Arc's death. Finding him in his lodging, Dunois
laid a hand on his shoulder, quietly told him why he had come and
suggested that he should at once mount his horse and ride out of the
city with him, so that any citizens watching would suspect nothing.
Taken wholly by surprise, Alençon obeyed at once and without protest.[6] Outside the city they found the other officials whom Dunois had
instructed to wait for him, and together they took Alençon to the king.
On being questioned by the king himself, Alençon insisted that he had
not been a traitor but had merely made alliances with 'certain lords'
who had promised to help him regain his lands. But his guilt was clear
and he was sent to prison where for the next two years he awaited trial.

His case finally came up on September 15th 1458. An impressive *Lit de Justice* had been organised at Vendôme, and was attended by the king himself with all the peers of the realm and many other great lords of the blood and otherwise, together with so many members of the Council, the court, the *Parlement* and other high officers, not to mention churchmen of all ranks, that one has the impression that the whole administration of the country must have stopped while the session lasted. There were three notable absentees. One was Arthur of Richemont, who had succeeded to the dukedom of Brittany only the previous December and who naturally, as the present owner of Fougères, could have felt none too comfortable about the whole thing. He did in fact come to Vendôme but took no part in the proceedings. The second was Philip of Burgundy, who had taken exception to the fact that the king had actually summoned him to come, had said he would only do so if he could bring several hundred followers, and who finally merely sent ambassadors, whom the king reluctantly accepted, but thereafter virtually ignored. The third absentee was the dauphin, who had as we know fled from the court to Burgundy, and whose place was taken by his younger brother. One of the chief persons was Dunois, both in his own right and as representing Richemont in his capacity as Constable. The Duke of Bourbon was there too and, of course, Charles of Orleans.

There is no complete account of the trial, but the texts of a few of the speeches have been preserved. These are all pleas for mercy on one ground or another, for Alençon's guilt seems to have been taken for granted. No speech was more moving than that of Charles,[7] who seems to have spoken last, both for the references it contained to his own past sufferings and experiences, and for the wisdom and generosity of his counsel as to what the sentence should be. It was a subtle speech too, for before he gave that counsel, after first professing his loyalty and obedience to the king, he tried to influence him by reminding him that he was but a man of flesh and blood, and that it was only the mercy of God which had raised him to a position where, as Charles truly said, "none of your predecessors have had the kingdom so wholly in their hands as you have". The king must therefore remember that he is God's lieutenant. Charles excused himself for this plain speaking on the ground of his own nearness in blood to the king, which made it a duty for him to speak his mind.

Turning then to the case to be judged, Charles said he realised that it was one that touched the king and all his kin, himself among them for, said he,

Photo. Bulloz, Paris

8 The *Lit de Justice* trying the Duke of Alençon at Vendôme, in 1458. (Dunois stands below the King, on his right hand. Charles of Orleans is in the back row, next but one to Dunois' right.) From an illustration by Jean Fouquet

It is the most grievous thing that I ever had in my heart; as for the death of the late lord my father (whom God pardon) I was then a young child and did not know how to suffer grief as [I did] when I was held in prison. But at that time I recognised that I had been taken in doing my duty loyally. I therefore comforted myself that God would be pleased with me and would help me, and also that all those of the kingdom of France were for that reason bound not to fail me, when the need should arise, and after my life to recommend me in their prayers.

As for the present matter, he went on, he had found it impossible to believe

until I had it from the mouth of him to whom I was naturally bound by lineage, and bound too to his late father, who had been brought up by my late father and whom I had found so perfect a kinsman and friend; for in the quarrel of my said lord my father he put all his own affairs aside and served me . . . for which reason, and for the love I had for him, I gave my only daughter in marriage to his said son, who is now in question.

But after these personal reminiscences, as though anxious to show he was not trying to sway the court on sentimental grounds and could judge Alençon's actions objectively he continued:

And although he has said in the presence of all those who are here that he had more trust in me and love for me than any other person, he showed it badly to me when he wanted to lose Normandy. By so doing he would have made me lose some of my land, valued at ten thousand pounds of rent, and through that might have come the destruction of the kingdom and of all us French, if we had fallen into the hands of the English, ancient enemies of France.

Charles then gave his view of what the judgment should be. He pleaded against the death-sentence, partly because it would deprive the prisoner of any chance of improving his soul and partly because, since it had been said that his crime deserved the greatest possible punishment, in his view to suffer grief and pain for a long time in prison would be harder than to be delivered by death. "For I have learnt through myself" he said, "that in my prison in England, because of the cares, suffering and dangers in which I found myself, I many times wished that I had died in the battle where I was taken, so as to be rid of the pains I endured. That is why I give this advice, and would not for anything that his life should not be saved." He then agreed that for the safety of the realm Alençon should be held in some safe place, and that all his lands and possessions should be confiscated. But he felt strongly that, contrary to other suggestions that had been made, honourable provision should be made for his wife and children that they might live according to their rank. Finally, and characteristically, he put in also a plea that something should be done for Alençon's servants.

On October 10th, in the hall to which the ordinary people were now admitted, the Chancellor pronounced the sentence of death against Alençon, with the confiscation of all his goods. But he declared that the king in his good pleasure had deferred the execution of the judgment; and as for his possessions, because of the services he had formerly rendered, and at the request of the Count of Richemont, they would be left to Alençon's wife and children, with the exception of his artillery and his fortified places. Of his territories the king confiscated only the duchy of Alençon. The sentence for which Charles had pleaded was therefore in effect granted, although for some reason not stated the credit for it was given to Richemont, who had made no public speech, not being present at the trial. Perhaps his conscience had moved him to plead with the king in private.

It was clear from Charles' speech that Alençon had been present and allowed to speak for himself during the earlier part of the proceedings. But there is no evidence that he was allowed to hear the various pleadings on his behalf, and he certainly was not there to hear his sentence, for this was conveyed to him in his lodging afterwards. There was public indignation at the sentence, which was considered too harsh, for Alençon was obviously generally liked and considered to be weak and misguided rather than criminal. He was taken at once to the castle of Loches, with only his barber to look after him, and confined in those grim underground dungeons that never see the light of day, and on whose walls despairing scrawls of the prisoners can still be seen. There is no mention of the length of time decided upon for his imprisonment, but judging from later appearances of his, it would appear to have been some five years—long enough in such a place.

When all was over, Charles of Orleans must have left Vendôme with as heavy a heart as he had ever known. He did not leave it alone, for with him went Arthur of Richemont, and together they travelled to Fontevrault where they both wanted to see the abbess, Mary, who was niece to them both, being the daughter of Charles' sister Margaret and her late husband Richard of Étampes, who was Arthur's brother. Charles and Richard, who were of the same age, must have had plenty of subjects to talk over together, beginning with their memories of those far-off days, over forty years ago now, when they had both been captured at Agincourt. And now they were closely bound by those family ties too, for three years previously Charles' young nephew Francis, Margaret's son, had married another of Arthur's nieces, and through that marriage had become next in succession to the dukedom of Brittany. He had in fact not long to wait for that inheritance, for Arthur, who had himself only held the title for a year, died only a few months after that journey to Fontevrault. The succession of his nephew Francis to the dukedom of Brittany could only have given Charles pleasure, both because it rescued the young man from his rather restricted and obscure life, and because in him he gained a staunch supporter, as Francis was later to prove.

On returning from Fontevrault, Charles might once again have hoped to be able to enjoy a quiet life at Blois; and certainly there were a few domestic events in store for him, in the bosom of his family, that were to bring great joy to his declining years. But there was now too much unrest in the kingdom, for a variety of reasons, for so great a prince to be able to turn his back on it; and both because of his friendship for Philip of Burgundy, and by virtue of his position so close to the throne, Charles was constantly called on during these last years of his life to play an official part in one way and another.

It was the everlasting tension between Burgundy and the king that first called him from home, in March 1459, to attend meetings of the king and Council at Montbazon. These were held to consider a long list of complaints from Philip. The lack of any particular deference shown to his representatives at Alençon's trial appears to have roused Philip's wrath and induced in him such a vengeful mood that he thought up every possible grievance that he fancied he had suffered since the Treaty of Arras in 1435, as well as a long list of the services which he considered he had rendered the king. These he charged his ambassadors to lay before his sovereign. The king made a masterly and subtle reply, stressing for example that in the campaign to recover Normandy he could not remember that Burgundy had sent him any men-at-arms, though certainly some knights and esquires from the Burgundian lands, who were, he remarked, his own relations and subjects, had joined his army and been paid by him. The ambassadors protested that all this did not really answer Burgundy's two main points, which were to make clear to the king "who my lord of Burgundy had been . . . who he was, and who he wished to remain towards the king";[8] and secondly to enquire if the king was dissatisfied with him, and if so why. They said they were afraid to take back the replies they had been given. The king answered that in his view those replies were a "good and sufficient answer"; but he would send some of his counsellors back to Burgundy with them to make his will and intentions plain.

It could not have been easy for Charles of Orleans, who was there with the Duke of Brittany and other princes of the blood, to listen to all this, torn as he must have been between his loyalty and duty to the king and his personal devotion to Burgundy, whose protestations were so patently unconvincing; especially when it was common knowledge that Burgundy was doing all in his power to support the dauphin against his father. It was clear to all that the king who, ever since he had overcome the rebellious princes in 1439, had been growing in statesmanship, stature and power, was at last able to outface the most powerful of his great dukes, and had reached a point of wisdom where, says Mathieu d'Escouchy, who reports this whole matter in great detail, "by the great sense and good discretion that was in his person" he could resist those of his councillors who wanted him to act against the duke, and instead excused and supported him. All that Charles could do in that situation was to feel grateful for the king's policy and firmly to ally himself with it, for nothing would ever have persuaded him to turn against the friend who had helped him.

As a pleasant change from these affairs of state, there was a happy domestic event in July 1460, when Charles' little daughter Mary, now two-and-a-half years old, made her first state entry into Orleans with her mother and father, and was officially received and fêted by the town, which gave her a thousand *livres*, adding another ten *écus* for her governess.[9] The schoolchildren who had cried "Noël" on her entry were given pears, a great torchlight ball was held in her honour in the courtyard of the Châtelet, which was the ducal residence, at which the ladies of Orleans danced with "Mademoiselle", as she was always called; and most remarkable of all, the poet Villon, who happened to be in prison there at the time, was let out and celebrated the occasion with a poem in which he praised the infant for her "confident bearing" and compared her to the wise Cassandra, the beautiful Echo, the worthy Judith, the chaste Lucretia and the noble Dido.

The reason for these celebrations, which would normally have been unusual for a little princess, was certainly because Charles, thinking himself unlikely to have more children, now considered her as his heir. It was perhaps at that time, and for the same reason, that he began to dream of an alliance between her and his young favourite Pierre de Beaujeu, who had for ten years now been as a son to him. And since he would not be able to leave her his actual Duchy of Orleans, which as a royal apanage would have to return to the king's domain, it seems not unlikely that it was with a view to increasing the possessions that were his to leave that, in that same month of July, Charles, with the support of his brother of Angoulême and his nephew of Brittany, decided to try to drive the usurping Sforza out of the Duchy of Milan, and wrote to the Duke of Modena and the governors of Venice to ask for their help in this enterprise.[10] Charles had obviously discussed this matter with the king, for he and the other two were able to state in their letter that they were writing with his approval and that he was helping them. They promised to send seven or eight thousand horsemen and four to five thousand archers, and this they certainly could not have done without royal assistance. There is no evidence that this approach bore any fruit.

The king's support of Charles in this matter seems a further proof of the benevolent attitude that he had shown his cousin ever since their first meeting at Limoges in 1442. But it is doubtful whether the king now either knew or cared what he was authorising, for he was by then a very sick man. The persistent hatred and malevolence towards him of his son the dauphin, whom he had not seen for years, and the fact that Burgundy was harbouring him and thus threatening one day to resume that power over the throne that his father John the Fearless had exercised over the king's own feeble-witted father, seemed finally to take the heart out of Charles VII, who gradually sank into a state of apathy and fear which made him refuse more than the bare minimum of food and dread that even that might contain poison. It was therefore virtually of starvation that he finally died at Mehun-sur-Yèvre on July 12th 1461.

Since the dauphin, on hearing of his father's death, did not trouble to return to court or to take part in the funeral, it fell to Charles, as now the second person in the kingdom, to bear the brunt of the exhausting ceremonies that this entailed. The town of Orleans voted him a sum of 4000 *livres* to cover the heavy expense of his attendance both at the obsequies and the subsequent coronation and he left at once for Mehun-sur-Yèvre with his brother John of Angoulême. The first of the ceremonies sounds distinctly macabre, for what is described as an image of the king, so lifelike that the people who saw it took it for the man himself, was dressed in the royal robes and placed in a sitting position in a chariot which then, accompanied by Charles and his brother, made the slow journey to Paris, followed by another chariot bearing the embalmed body of the king. The preparations for this, and the journey itself, took a long time, for they did not reach the capital until August 5th. Mary of Orleans and Dunois were waiting for them there, so that Charles had their support during the many masses, vigils and other services which then succeeded one another at all hours, chiefly at the church of Notre-Dame-des-Champs, and at which he, as chief mourner, had many rites to perform, entailing endless bowings to the body as though it were alive. Finally came the slow journey to Saint-Denis, led by Charles in his great black cloak and head-dress, riding on his mule, with more exhausting services until the body was lowered into the ground.

There was of course hardly any interval between these ceremonies and those of Louis XI's coronation in Paris, which took place on August 31st. But this time the leading figure was Philip of Burgundy, and Charles, thankfully one would suppose, was able to watch the coronation procession from a window. But he attended the various banquets and other entertainments arranged by Philip, who was responsible for the arrangement and cost of everything, and who was in his element, outdoing everyone in the glittering splendour of his attire. The people were quick to notice the contrast between him and the shabby king, in his mean grey robes, who did not hide his ill-humour nor even bother to attend some of the festivities. Philip would not have been human if he had not enjoyed the obvious admiration he evoked by his magnificence and his easy manner, as when for instance he rode through the streets mounted behind his niece Mary of Orleans on her horse, as his own had not been ready when she called for him one morning to go to a joust. In all this he never failed to treat his dear cousin Charles with the same solicitousness he had always showed him; but in Louis he obviously felt he had a willing pupil who was now in a position to show his gratefulness for all the kindness and support he had received. Philip was quickly to learn that for Louis gratitude was an emotion that did not exist, and that for him his uncle Burgundy was merely one of the great princes whom he distrusted and disliked equally and against whom he was to spend his reign in bitter strife.

Although Louis, when dauphin, had appeared to be fond of his uncle of Orleans, now that he was king he obviously began to dislike him as much as he disliked the other princes, but in a different way. It was plain to him that he had nothing to fear from Charles, who had never been ambitious and was now old. And it almost seems that it was because he knew this that his twisted nature made him despise his uncle, and lose no opportunity of treating him with contempt and flouting his wishes. He quickly had a chance to learn what one of these was, for on September 30th he travelled from Paris to Orleans with his uncle, and while they were being entertained there Charles seized the occasion to betroth his little daughter, now nearly four, to the young man whom he had taken to calling "our son of Beaujeu".[11] Mary played a considerable part during that visit, for she is said to have offered a banquet to the company. This would seem to have been largely a family affair, for there is no mention of the king's attendance at it, nor indeed at the betrothal ceremony. But he could not fail to have known of this and there is no evidence that he raised any objection to the proposed union, which he must have realised was one of Charles' dearest wishes. Nor did he intervene when, nearly three years later, the betrothal was formally solemnized in the church of Saint-Sauveur in the castle at Blois. But after Charles was dead, Louis, perhaps fearing this linking of the houses of Orleans and Bourbon, set this solemn engagement at naught and had Pierre de Beaujeu married to his own elder daughter Anne.

For the time being, however, the king remained on at least superficially good terms with Charles, and when at last, on June 27th 1462, an event that the duke must long have despaired of took place, and a son was born to him, the king agreed to stand god-father to the child, who was christened Louis. But he managed characteristically to take much of the pleasure out of what should have been, for the child's parents, a deeply happy and memorable occasion, by his irritable temper and awkward behaviour. He happened to be staying at Amboise at the time, so that to cross to Blois was no great matter. But he arrived there only just in time for the christening ceremony and, refusing to enter the castle, demanded to be taken to the church of Saint-Sauveur within the walls. When he had to touch the baby's knees at the moment of baptism it unfortunately made water in his sleeve, an occurrence that most great lords would merely have smiled at, but which made Louis furious. After that it was with difficulty that he was persuaded to visit the room where Mary was still confined, to say a few words to her; but he had better not have gone, for the only words he could find were complaints of her son's uncontrolled behaviour, after which, pleading an urgent engagement, he rushed from the room, increasing his ill-temper still further by catching his foot in the bed-hangings and stumbling as he left.

It may be that part of his ill-humour was due to the fact that Charles had had a son at all, who would in due course inherit his father's dukedom and thus, in the fullness of time, become one of those independent feudatories to whose repression Louis was to devote so much of his energies. It was presumably to counter such a development, by keeping the future duke close to the throne, that Louis soon conceived the idea of marrying the boy to his own second daughter Jane. And having thought of this plan he set the preliminary formalities for the marriage on foot even before the little Louis was two years old, in May 1464.* He characteristically did this in his usual autocratic and ungracious manner, by merely sending an order to his bailiff at Chartres to go and treat with Charles on the matter.[12] However that may be, Charles could hardly have objected to an alliance with the king's daughter for his son. In any case the probability is that by then he had given up such interest as he had ever had in worldly schemes of that kind, and fallen wholly into that state of resignation – 'nonchaloir' – in which he had sought consolation so often during his life. For now his health was beginning to fail and for a year past he had been in the hands of the doctors. Not only his old friend Jean Caillau but another who had tended him in the past, Robert Poitevin, came frequently to see him.[13] And there is a sad proof of how frail he now felt himself to be when, in response to some invitation to join the company he had always so much enjoyed, he wrote:

> Salués moy toute la compaignie
> Ou a present estes a chiere lye,
> Et leur dites que voulentiés seroye
> Avecques eulx, mais estre n'y pourroye,
> Pour Vieillesse qui m'a en sa baillie.

* During 1464 another daughter, Anne, was born to Charles and Mary, but now that they had an heir, little notice seems to have been taken of this event.

In view of the king's plan to bind the child Louis as closely as possible to his own family, it seems strange that he should at the same time have taken steps to deprive the boy of a part of his future inheritance—the County of Asti and the claim to the Duchy of Milan—by doing everything in his power to hand these territories over to the usurping duke, Francesco Sforza, again without reference to Charles. That he did so is yet another proof of his desire to humiliate his uncle, a desire greater than his political wisdom on this occasion, and which comes out strongly in the mocking and contemptuous manner in which he referred to him in his correspondence with the usurper.[14] At one point, for instance, he counselled Sforza to offer to buy Asti from Charles, an insulting proposition in its implication that Charles would sell his devoted Astesans for cash. At the same time he encouraged Sforza by saying that, once Charles was dead, he should have these territories anyway. And one can almost feel Louis' eagerness for his uncle's end in a letter which Maletta, Sforza's ambassador in France, wrote to his master, in which he said: "It seems to his Majesty that this lord is now in feeble health."

Another reason for the king's eagerness to deprive Charles of these Italian possessions and claims may have been a fear that, because Francis of Brittany had signed that letter asking the Duke of Modena and the Venetians to help Charles and his brother to drive the usurper out, he was plotting something with his uncle Charles. And Francis had now become in Louis' eyes his arch-enemy among the great dukes, chiefly because he happened to be on terms of close friendship and alliance with Philip of Burgundy's son and heir, the Count of Charolois. Louis now obviously considered the latter the main threat from Burgundy, although he lost no opportunity of flouting all Philip's wishes also. So intense was his fear and dislike of Brittany that at the end of 1464 he summoned the princes, Charles of Orleans among them, to an assembly at Tours and there harangued them very much in the manner of a new headmaster uncertain of his position with the older boys, one of whom had, he thought, shown signs of rebellion. He told them of all the efforts he was making to put the kingdom on a sounder footing, having inherited it, he said, in a deplorable condition. He relied on them to help him in this and in resisting any who were working against him. But he must be able to count on their loyalty and that was why the conduct of the Duke of Brittany pained him so much. He wished the duke himself no harm. Even if he had him in his power, he would do nothing against him, as long as he begged for grace and pity.[15]

The reply made by René of Anjou on behalf of his peers reveals how puzzled they all were at this revelation of the king's twisted nature and the suspicions which he was apt to nurture—suspicions that as time went on so increased that the princes were forced to do the very thing he feared and combine against him. In the present instance René was able sincerely to protest their loyalty and obedience, reminding the king bluntly that "We have been, some of us, prisoners in order to preserve our loyalty to the crown, and in that suffered many injuries and losses (as everyone knows)"—a plain reference to Charles and himself. He begged the king to put out of his head these imaginary things that he had chosen to see in the Duke of Brittany's letters. He stoutly defended him and in conclusion made something of a mockery of the king's charges against him by suggesting that they should all go in a body to speak to Brittany about them—a suggestion that Louis hastily refused.[16]

Although René was presumably acting as spokesman because Charles was too frail to do so, according to one report[17] Charles did all the same speak on that occasion. It was so plain to him that, by sowing discord among them all, Louis had been doing his best to create havoc in the kingdom that, as the senior prince present, he could not refrain from remonstrating with his nephew, which in view of his age and reputation he had every right to do. At this reproach from a quarter whence he least expected it, all Louis' dislike and contempt for his uncle welled up in him and he turned furiously on Charles and heaped abuse upon him. If this story is true, it is understandable that such infamous and humiliating treatment in the presence of his peers should have been a terrible shock to one who, even as a prisoner in England had always been treated with the deference due to his rank; and that it was more than his failing health could stand. In any case death was already waiting for him and this painful scene could only have hastened its approach by very little.

When the assembly was ended, Charles set out to return to Blois. But he never got there because his health obliged him to break his journey at Amboise. What the actual cause of his death was we do not know, but it must at the end have been something sudden, for a strange surgeon was called, and handsomely paid for looking after him "during the illness of which he died".[18] But he obviously was not able to do anything to save the ebbing life of this man of seventy-one, and on the night of January 4th to 5th Charles of Orleans died.

His wife Mary, who had recently given birth to her other daughter, Anne, hurried at once to Amboise on hearing of his illness. But whether she arrived in time to say farewell to her lord is not known. His body was transported back to Blois on a black-covered cart drawn by four horses caparisoned in black, led by four carters, in black too, and followed by three pages.[19] At Blois, mourning robes had been made for the whole household, over two hundred persons, beginning with those members of it, the great officers and the young esquires, whose names have become so familiar, down to the youngest scullions in the kitchen, and there were included too the barbers, painters, upholsterers and apothecaries who had served the duke and his house, and the tailors who made the funeral garments. Even the guardian of a bear that Francis of Brittany had recently sent to his uncle was given a black outfit to enable him to take part in the procession. The three children were of course in mourning too, Monseigneur de Valois, as Louis was called, Mary and Anne, as well as their nurses, nursemaids and lesser staff. But there was no display; all the garments were made of the most sober materials.

The funeral procession was led by Pierre de Beaujeu and there is no mention that any of the great peers were present. Eight bands of leather lowered the coffin into the grave prepared for it in the Church of Saint-Sauveur.[20] On the tomb was planted a great standard, of blue silk; and nearby there was a hanging of grey-gold material with a cross of white silk on it, which had been cut out of one of Charles' robes. And so he died and was buried as he had lived, without fuss or ostentation.

Two of his familiar friends,[21] of modest estate, had written poems to him in his lifetime, full of those praises which it was customary to address to a great prince. But these two are so personal, and contain so many lines that ring true, that it is clear they came from the hearts of their authors, and there could be no better epitaph for Charles of Orleans. One of them says of him:

> En si hault sang parfonde humilité,
> Clemence grant et magnanimité.
> Cela avez; mais vous passez sans fable
> Ung droit Cesar en liberalité.
>
> En vostre bouche tousjours a verité
> En cueur amour et ardant charité,
> Et loyaulté non jamais variable.

343

And the other apostrophizes him as:

> Vous l'ung des plus nobles du monde,
> Prince, redoubté seigneur,

and goes on to thank him because

> Par vostre humilité parfonde,

unworthy though the writer was,

> J'ai peu science, moins faconde,
> Et encor prudence mineur,
> Et vous me clamez serviteur
> Digne pour estre en table ronde,
> Vous, l'ung des plus nobles du monde,
> Prince, tres redoubté seigneur.

Profound humility, clemency and magnanimity, truth, loyalty and charity, readiness to welcome simple persons although himself of such high blood: these are rare virtues. Yet all that we know of the events of his life do certainly prove that they were his.

Epilogue

THE kings of France are so sharply differentiated from each other, not only in face but in temperament, that it is as a rule difficult to see in any one of them characteristics that he might appear to have inherited from his forerunners, in so far as heredity counts for anything. This is true even in the case of those who descended directly from each other, like the three—Charles VI, Charles VII and Louis XI—in whose reigns Charles of Orleans had lived. And it was true also of Charles VIII, who followed them.

It is therefore the more striking that when, against all expectation, the late-born son of Charles of Orleans succeeded to the throne as Louis XII, thirty-three years after the death of his father, who had spent the greater part of his own life so far from it, one should be able to see in him, as his reign progressed, at least something of that father. He was not, certainly, a passionate lover of peace, as Charles had been, and his ambition, natural enough in a king anxious to extend his kingdom, drove him to fight for the kind of Italian claims that his father had not thought worth an armed struggle. But at least his wars were fought abroad, and Louis was careful not to let them bring on his own subjects the misery that they had for so long endured. It was in his desire not to let them suffer in this way that he resembled his father. He does indeed seem genuinely to have cared for their well-being, so much so that he was given the sobriquet of 'Father of the People'.

Such titles were often conferred in flattery for no very good reasons, but that in Louis' case it was deserved seems to be proved by an incident related by an anonymous chronicler of the time. He tells how, when the king was visiting the town of Troyes in 1510, a large concourse of peasants and other humble people journeyed there from the country just to see him. Such a proceeding was so unusual at that time that a stranger, who happened to be there, asked a labouring man the reason for it. The peasant answered: 'He is so wise, he maintains justice and causes us to live in peace. He has put an end to the pillaging of the soldiers, and governs better than any king ever has before.'[1]

The ordinary people may well have been surprised at this unwonted clemency and care for them, and could hardly have guessed whence their king drew his kindly impulses that none of his predecessors, as far as they knew, had felt. But posterity, able to see the past as they could not, can hardly doubt that it was his father's influence that made Louis the father of his people. Not his immediate, personal influence of course, since Louis was only two when Charles of Orleans died. But the child was brought up in that quiet and civilized court that his father had created at Blois, and where something of his spirit must have lingered. And throughout Louis' childhood and youth there were still many there, from his mother Mary down to many of the courtiers, young and old, who would have been able to tell him of his father: of his youthful struggles to rid the kingdom of the tyrannical John the Fearless; of the patience with which he had borne his long captivity; of the great ode on France, and that other, 'Priés pour paix' that he had written in England, in which he told the nobles that it was their duty to support the people, and the people that it was because of the constant wars that the nobles could not help them in their great distress; and of how, when they welcomed him on his return from captivity, the people seemed instinctively to know that he would bring them peace, as indeed he did.

If the influence of Charles had thus been strong enough to make of his son the kindly king that he undoubtedly was, then Charles had indeed deserved well of his country, both for that body of exquisite poetry which he bequeathed to it and, as a prince, for that humanitarianism, so far in advance of his time, which cast a long shadow even into the century after his death.

APPENDIX I

*The Manuscripts of Prayers; and the possible
meetings of Charles and his brother John in England*

THE claim that MS. lat. 1203 in the Bibliothèque Nationale is the "livret en
papier escript de la main de mondit Seigneur" (Laborde 6547, see p. 166
above) which Pierre Champion, on p. xxxi of the Introduction to his *La
Librairie de Charles d'Orléans*, says has been lost, is made by M. Gilbert Ouy
in his 'Recherche sur la Librairie de Charles d'Orléans et de Jean
d'Angoulême pendant leur captivité en Angleterre, et études de deux
manuscrits autographes de Charles identifiés', *Compte Rendu de l'Académie
des Inscriptions et Belles-Lettres*, 1955, pp. 273–288. This claim may well be
justified and, if so, the identification is valuable. But the theories to which it
leads M. Ouy, and some of those which he developed in the course of his
researches, are such that they cannot go unanswered.

An example of them occurs in his description of MS. lat. 1196, the finer
of the two manuscripts of prayers which Charles had made for him in
England (see p. 166 above), an examination of which was the first step which
led M. Ouy to his discovery. In a miniature on one page of this "nous
croyons", he says, "reconnaître un portrait de Charles d'Orléans lui-même:
c'est le petit personnage représenté en buste a côté de la grande lettrine
ornée des armoiries d'Orléans qui marque, au folio 25, le véritable début du
livre; il apparaît vêtu d'une façon semi-monacale d'une sorte de grand
manteau bleu à capuchon, et portant sur la tête une calotte grise; son visage
émacié est marqué par la captivité, la tribulation et les mortifications que,
sans doute, il s'imposait. Bien qu'il n'existe aucune preuve certaine de
l'identité du personnage . . . tout nous entraîne à penser que c'est bien le duc
poète qui a été ainsi peint en méditation." Pleasant though it would be if a
portrait of Charles had thus at last been discovered, it must be admitted that
this tiny miniature would give us little idea of his looks; for the bust in
question is only half-an-inch high and the face, about the size of a pin's head,
shows little trace of features, let alone of emaciation. There is, incidentally,
no evidence that he endured conditions likely to produce emaciation, or that
he was accustomed to mortify himself.

M. Ouy next discovered, from the 1939 *Catalogue général des Mss. latins
de la Bibliothèque Nationale*, that the 600-line poem *Canticum Amoris* in
MS. 1196 also occurs in MS. 1203. He was in any case already familiar
with MS. 1203 because, in his researches into the library of John of
Angoulême, he had found that it is listed as No. 158 in the inventory
of John's books, made in 1467 after his death, which Dupont Ferrier,
John's biographer, had published in his 'Jean d'Angoulême d'après sa

bibliothèque', *Bibliothèque de la Faculté des Lettres de Paris*, 1897, pp. 39–92. Dupont Ferrier, who had studied John's writing closely, there gives it as his opinion that a little treatise on Hippiatrie, or horse medicine, occupying fol. 24 r⁰ to fol. 39 v⁰ in this MS. is in John's handwriting, as also are some of the prayers, although the contemporary inventory does not mention this, and Dupont Ferrier himself feels obliged to remark that, even in this one MS., "l'on sera surpris des changements dont était susceptible l'écriture du comte".

The question then arose of who was the scribe of those parts of this little MS. not in the hand of John: the *Canticum Amoris* and some of the prayers— in fact the greater part of it. As Dupont Ferrier was not familiar with the handwriting of Charles he thought it was that of some obscure copyist. M. Ouy, on the contrary, is convinced that it is in what he calls the 'easily recognisable' hand of Charles; and this leads him to his conclusion: that MS. 1203 is in fact the "livret en papier escript de la main de mondit Seigneur", which had been thought lost. He considers, moreover, that if Champion had thought of consulting Dupont Ferrier's edition of the 1467 inventory of John's books, and had thus been led to MS. 1203, he too, who knew Charles' hand so well, would have realised that this was the missing manuscript. He makes no attempt to explain why the compilers of the inventory of Charles' books in 1440 should have described this manuscript as being in his hand, when one third of it is, in his view, in the hand of John.

Having decided that the little manuscript was in the hands of the two brothers, M. Ouy then turned to consider what was the origin of it. The compiler of the 1939 catalogue of the Latin manuscripts in the Bibliothèque Nationale thought that it was copied from MS. lat. 1196, at least as far as the *Canticum Amoris* is concerned. But M. Ouy took the reverse and more realistic view, that 1203 was a rough draft for 1196. This may well be so, except for the treatise on horse medicine, which does not appear in MS. 1196; and certainly the whole aspect of the manuscript bears this out. It is a shabby little book of some 60 odd pages, and in its present ugly cardboard cover (replacing the black leather cover described in the 1467 inventory) it looks like some modern student's notebook. Both the oddly assorted contents— some prayers, the *Canticum Amoris* and the treatise on horse medicine—and the handwritings of the different parts, covering the pages often with no margins, sometimes beginning carefully and then tailing off and getting careless, with erasures and occasional quoting of first lines only of prayers, give the impression that it was a kind of commonplace book, filled with odd jottings and abbreviated indications for the guidance of some professional scribe elsewhere. M. Ouy's discovery that still another manuscript in the Bibliothèque Nationale, MS. lat. 3638, which he says is almost entirely in the hand of John, contains rough drafts of other texts later retranscribed in MS. 1196, supported him in this view.

As for the manner in which the brothers compiled the notebook MS. 1203, M. Ouy thinks that they could only have produced it if they were together when they were working on it. He therefore considers that it furnishes "de fortes présomptions en faveur de la thèse selon laquelle, pendant une partie de leur captivité, les deux frères auraient vécu ensemble et travaillé en commun à l'élaboration de ces beaux recueils de piété [i.e. MSS. 1196, 1201 and 1203] conservés aujourd'hui à la Bibliothèque Nationale." "Or", he admits, "cela ruine la thèse, longtemps admise pour vraie, selon laquelle Charles et Jean n'auraient eu aucun contact pendant toute la durée de leur détention outre-Manche." This he thinks so far from the truth that he believes they lived near each other for "une bonne partie de leur long exil", and not only collaborated on such things as this little book, but together built up "une bibliothèque dans laquelle ils avaient travaillé en commun". One of the chief aims of his study was, in fact, to prove that the library of the one cannot be studied without that of the other, so intermingled are they. Six years later these "fortes présomptions" have become definite convictions and M. Ouy, in another essay, states "Nous sommes donc en droit d'affirmer que les deux frères étaient réunis au moment où ils écrivirent ce petit livre". (See his article 'Les Bibliothèques' in the Pléiade vol. *L'Histoire et ses méthodes*, 1961, p. 1091.)

Only someone who had not studied the lives of the brothers closely could have made this affirmation, since the documents mentioned in the present volume show that Charles and John, so far from living with or near each other, were never even in the same county, except for possibly a few months in 1421 when Charles was at Fotheringhay in Northamptonshire while John was transferred, after the battle of Baugé, to the Duchess of Clarence's house at Maxey in that county. The only reference to any meeting between them is in a minute of the Privy Council which records that in 1437 it was agreed that "therle of Angoulesme in Waller's keeping may go to the Duc of Orleans to speke with him in both their keepers sight and hearing". Such a meeting, even if it were often repeated, can hardly have afforded the right opportunity for the joint leisurely compiling of a commonplace book. On the other hand, there is no reason whatever why they should not occasionally have sent the little book to each other, for they were certainly kept in touch by their French servitors, and Charles was always well aware of his brother's circumstances. The fact that this little book, of which John was part-author, was found among his own books at the time of his death, two years after that of Charles, proves that it did in fact go from one to the other of them, at least after their return to France.

Although in the title of this study of his, M. Ouy speaks of two autograph manuscripts of Charles which he has recently identified, his text does not make clear which is the second of these, unless he is perhaps referring to some annotations in Charles' hand in another beautiful manuscript, MS. lat.

1201 (Laborde 6520), which was already known to Champion. M. Ouy's particular interest in this MS. is that it contains two poems, *Philomena* and *Cythara*, by the English 13th century poet John of Hovendene, which Charles' autograph instructions to the copyist seem to prove were transcribed by his orders. This evidence of Charles' interest in the works of Hovendene inclines M. Ouy to think that the duke himself may have been the author of the poem *Canticum Amoris*, which is not known outside of the two manuscripts where it occurs, 1203 and 1196, and which he considers shows the Franciscan influence of Hovendene. M. Ouy analyses this Latin poem in detail, giving reasons which merit attention for attributing it to Charles. One of these is that much of the poem is a kind of hymn celebrating the beauty of the world and of the return of the seasons, beauties to which Charles' later poems show him to have been particularly sensitive. A more positive proof is perhaps the fact that in MS. 1203, where it first occurs, there are some erasures and alterations which might well be those of an author rather than a copyist. Interesting though it would be to think that we have in it a Latin poem by Charles, such an attribution can only be guesswork until further evidence to support it is discovered.

Another contribution to the theory that Charles and John sometimes met while prisoners has more recently been made by Miss Lucy de Angulo in a paper entitled 'Charles and Jean d'Orléans: an attempt to trace the contacts between them during their captivity in England', *Miscellanea di Studi e ricerche sul Quattrocento francese*, pp. 59–92, Turin, 1966.

Miss de Angulo rests her case chiefly on her belief that Sir John Cornwall, whom she regards as a much kindlier man than the evidence seems to show, had charge of John of Angoulême for considerable stretches of time, during which he allowed the brothers to see much of each other. These periods, according to her, were: the time when Charles was in London on his first arrival, before he was sent to Pontefract; a period of indefinite length, beginning in 1428 and covering the years when he had charge of Charles (1429–1432), so that, she says "Charles and Jean were at last together, in the care of the same man, living under the same roof, for the first time in England"; the summer of 1440, during the months prior to the release of Charles.

Unfortunately the documents she quotes by no means support these assumptions, so that unless further evidence should come to light we must continue to believe that, inhuman and unnecessary as it was to keep the brothers apart, the only occasion when they saw each other was in 1437 when it was officially agreed that they might speak to each other "in both their keepers sight and hearing".

APPENDIX II

The Subject of the Love Poems

As I have attempted to show in Chapters IX and X, every allusion in the poems there quoted supports the assumption that their constant theme was Bonne, the young French wife, the 'nompareille de France', from whom the poet had long been separated by the cruel enemy, 'Dangier', and whom he so craves to see again that sometimes he teases himself with the possiblity that she may be coming to visit him; who writes to assure him of her love, to whom he swears lasting fidelity, begging her not to forget him, the news of whose illness fills him with dread, and that of her death with a bitter sense of loss and loneliness. Pierre Champion, still the main French authority on Charles of Orleans, shares this assumption.

But several other writers have refused to accept it. Among these are two of the nineteenth-century editors of Charles' poetry, Charles d'Héricault and J.-M. Guichard. The chief reason for their attitude was a belief, to which both of them subscribed although neither gives any authority for it, that Bonne died in November 1415, at the time of Agincourt. This belief causes Héricault to say (p. xiv of his short biography prefacing the poems) that it is 'pure fantasy' to suppose that Charles would have addressed these poems to her, knowing her to be dead; and he further remarks, very curiously, that there is nothing to prove that they were not addressed to the poet's first wife, Isabella; nothing, one might add, except the fact that she had been much longer dead than Bonne. Guichard (p. vi of his Introduction) considers that to suppose the dead Bonne to be the subject of the poems is to render two-thirds of them inexplicable, but he offers no alternative name.

English writers, perhaps because her name was more familiar to them than that of Bonne, always tend to think that the poems were written to Isabella. Hilaire Belloc (*Avril*, p. 18), although he makes no general pronouncement, is quite certain that the beautiful poem beginning 'Las! Mort qui t'a fait si hardie' (see p. 182 above) was addressed to Isabella, chiefly because the words that she was 'en droitte fleur de jeunesse' fit her premature death so well. But this is a proof of how essential a detailed knowledge of the poet's life is to any analysis of his poetry; for Belloc was one of those who thought that Charles was born in 1391, and so would have been eighteen at the time of Isabella's death, whereas in fact he was only fifteen and thus unlikely to have been capable of writing so mature a poem at that time.

Much stranger than these views, however, is that of R. R. Steele, who considered that the poems were all addressed to an Englishwoman. He developed this idea in the course of his enquiry into the authorship of a collection of some 650 anonymous English poems, which exist in a single manuscript in the British Museum (Harleian 682). Many of these appear to be adaptations of the *ballades* and *chansons* which Charles wrote in England, and of his poems the *Retenue d'Amours* and the *Songe en Complainte*; but there are also many others for which no French equivalent exists. Steele was not the first to suggest that Charles was the author of these English poems;[1] but he was the first to put forward the suggestion, in his *The English Poems of Charles d'Orléans*, that they were the originals, inspired by an Englishwoman, and that the French poems were merely versions which Charles himself subsequently made of some of them—translations, Steele maintains, which were merely 'a work of art, re-written and polished and carefully purged of all personal indications', while the English originals convey 'primarily a sentiment of real feeling'. Anyone who reads the English poems in the manuscript must find it as difficult to subscribe to this view as to agree that, for example, the French *ballades* in which Charles laments the illness and death of his mistress are mere works of art.[2]

Having put forward his theory of an Englishwoman as the sole subject of the English and French love poems, Steele then had to find someone who could so have inspired Charles. His choice fell on a certain Maud, Countess of Arundel, for the following curious reasons. Lord Arundel's first wife was a daughter of Sir John Cornwall, and Steele thinks it possible that Maud may therefore have visited her predecessor's father at Ampthill in 1430, when Charles was there and fell in love with her. Lord Arundel was Governor of Rouen in 1432 and it was therefore likely that his wife was with him there, which would account for Charles' references in his *ballades* to his lady's being in France. Lord Arundel was known to have an irascible temper, and therefore it may well be he who is meant by 'Dangier', the cruel enemy who keeps such a close watch on the lovers. Finally, Maud died in 1436 or 1437, so that the laments written at that time were obviously addressed to her.

The awkward result of his theory is that it forces Steele to conclude that this large body of verse—the 650 English poems and the French versions of a great number of them—was all written between 1430 and 1436 or 7. Apart from the unlikelihood that Charles could have produced them at a time when he was preoccupied with political matters and the increasing hope of his release, this theory presupposes that this man, to whom the writing of poetry was always a solace for his feelings, wrote none at all during the first fifteen years of his captivity.

The many objections to Steele's case, however, have not prevented others from subscribing to it, and Dr. Ethel Seaton, in her *Charles d'Orléans and Two English Ladies* (one of three essays in her *Studies in Villon, Vaillant and Charles d'Orléans*) not only supports part of it but develops it further. She begins by putting forward her view that the French *ballades* (which were written first) were addressed to both Bonne and an English lady, Bonne being celebrated for her 'bonté' while the English lady is 'Beauty'. As for the identity of the latter, although she admits that Steele's suggestion of Maud Arundel is merely "an inspired guess", based on "nothing more than the suitability of dates", she finds it justified by means of acrostics, which reveal her name in literally dozens of the French poems. She further maintains that the *Songe en Complainte*, self-dated November 1437, was solely dedicated to Maud Arundel " and written a year and a half after her death, after months of wretchedness and gloom."

But Dr. Seaton also accepts the theory (which we saw on pp. 208 *et seq.* above was indeed likely) that Charles had a love affair with Anne Moleyns, supporting her belief in it not only by Miss Hammond's discovery but by her own game of acrostics, which revealed to her the name of Anne in nearly all the English poems of Harleian 682, whose authorship by Charles she also accepts. This created a difficulty, since it could hardly be supposed that the affair with Anne started before the death of Maud. Dr. Seaton overcomes this by presuming that, in order to please Anne, who may not have known French well, and inspired by his new passion for her, Charles set to work and, between 1438 and 1440, not only translated his French poems, "ruthlessly adapted and re-dedicated to Anne", but also wrote in English all the poems which have no French equivalent. She ignores the fact that by 1438 he had long since left Wingfield, which was the only place where he could have seen Anne, and that he was then involved in all the intrigues and frustrations preceding his return to France, and reaches her conclusion that "the whole of this line-for-line translation from his verse, together with two long English poems and several ballades and brief lyrics for which no corresponding French is known (6,530 lines all) must have been the work of two-and-a half years." No wonder she considers that this affords "striking proof of Charles' industry and of his facility in a foreign language".

Whatever the reader of the present volume may think of Steele's and Dr. Seaton's theses concerning the amorous life of Charles during his time in England, they obviously have power to make important converts. For Dr. Jacobs, on page 484 of *The Fifteenth Century* (Vol. VI of the Oxford History of England), gives a short summary of them (quoting only Dr. Seaton as reference) as if they were now an accepted part of history.

APPENDIX III

The Library of Charles of Orleans

THE history of the library of Charles of Orleans, partly inherited from his parents and largely added to by himself, is of interest because, together with some of the magnificent manuscripts collected by his grandfather Charles V and some of those of his uncle the Duke of Berry, it later formed the nucleus of what is to-day the Bibliothèque Nationale.

Although Gilles Malet, who had inventoried the great library of Charles V in the Touli du Louvre, later looked after the books of Louis of Orleans, he never catalogued them. Greatly though Charles prized the books he inherited, the circumstances of his life during his adolescence left him neither the time nor the means to add much to the collection, so that we may assume that, at the time of his capture at Agincourt, the library in the castle at Blois was much as it had been six years previously. In the second year of his captivity, presumably because of the need to realise his assets at Blois, Charles had, as we know, ordered an inventory of his books and other possessions to be made (see p. 143 above).

Accordingly in May 1417 an inventory was drawn up by one of his secretaries, P. Renoul. This document, which is now in the Archives Nationales, K.534, was published for the first time by L. Delisle, *Cabinet des manuscrits*, I, 98–112. It contains 91 items, which may not now sound a very large collection but was in fact a considerable library at a time when, apart from the relatively few texts then available, the physical making of a book, especially when it was also illustrated and illuminated, richly bound and often ornamented with fine clasps and other metal work, was a long and painstaking work of art. Renoul frequently describes the bindings of Charles' books, which are generally either of red, green, or sometimes white, leather, and at other times of black or vermilion velvet, or silk damask.

An examination of the inventory reveals that the library contained a good collection of works by the classical writers then known (see p. 22 above): Aristotle, Ovid, Virgil, Horace, Juvenal, Statius, Josephus etc.; a certain amount of theology and some works of the Fathers—Ambrose and Jerome—as well as lives of the Virgin, psalters, gospels etc., together with the inevitable Boethius and *The Golden Legend*. But some omissions deserve mention, as do also some individual entries. For instance, although Valentina's precious copies of the books given her by Christine de Pisan and Honoré Bonet are there, and also the story of King Arthur and the Holy Grail, neither her Sir John Mandeville nor her favourite romances, *Giron le Courtois* and *Perceval le Gallois*, are in the list. Perhaps by then her children had read them to bits. Stranger still, there is no copy of *Le Roman de la Rose*, although an illustrated copy of it is listed in one inventory of her personal books made after her death (see Champion, *La Librairie de Charles d'Orléans*, pp. lxxi–lxxiii of *Pièces justificatives*). Nor does this famous poem appear in later lists of Charles' books. Another surprising omission is the poetry of that familiar of the Orleans household, Eustache Deschamps, although Froissart's *Le Dit Royal* is there. *Les Cents Ballades*, which Louis and his friends had written, does not figure either, but that may have been because it had been sent to Charles in England, for he certainly had it there later (Laborde 6553).

Some of Renoul's notes vividly evoke how much the library meant not only to Charles himself but to the other members of the household at Blois. The duke's young sister and daughter, for instance, always referred to as "mes demoiselles d'Orléans", were great borrowers, and their catholic choice ran from a book on "prouffitable théologie" to a mixed volume of stories. Another volume which was obviously in great demand was called *L'Information des Princes*, for Renoul notes against it: "Mons. de Vertus l'avoit. Mons. de Soisy l'a."

They obviously returned this book so that it could be sent to Charles in England, for we find it in a later list of those he had there. But in general Charles was obviously concerned to keep the library at Blois intact rather than to borrow from it himself for, apart from *Les Cents Ballades* and *L'Information des Princes*, the only volume that Renoul notes as having been sent to him was Boccaccio's *De Casibus* which, he says, was removed by the Chancellor, Guillaume Cousinot, 'pour porter à M. le duc en Angleterre'. This did not of course mean that Charles had no books in captivity, for as a later inventory shows, he managed, by different means, to get together a considerable collection during his imprisonment.

But having thus left the precious library at Blois untouched, at any rate by himself, for twelve years, it is a proof of his desperate need for money that Charles should have decided in 1427 to hand it over to Jean de Rochechouart, Lord of Mortemart, to dispose of (see p. 164 above). The titles of the 85 volumes for which Mortemart subsequently gave Charles his receipt are quoted by Laborde (6323–6408). All but four or five of them appear in the 1417 inventory. Those which do not had perhaps been more recently added to the library, for there is proof that such additions were occasionally made in the fact that in October 1427, after the transfer of the books to Mortemart, Charles' officers managed to buy back for their master a precious book formerly belonging to him, which through the fortune of war had fallen into the hands of the enemy but subsequently passed from owner to owner until it came to one who was willing to sell it (Laborde 6435).

Rochechouart, as we know (see p. 280 above) only sold five of the books and kept the rest safe in his house at La Rochelle. When, after his death in

1435, his brother Guy, Bishop of Saintes, returned them, it is possible that he gave an inventory of them to two of Charles' counsellors, Hugues Perrier and Hue de Saint-Mars, at La Rochelle, and that they handed this to another of Charles' officers, Pierre Sauvage. For a declaration of the papers of Pierre Sauvage, made in 1444, speaks of "Ung inventaire contenant XIII fueillets . . . laissié par maistre Hugues Perrier a moy Pierre Sauvage des biens de Mons. le duc ramene à La Rochelle par Hue de Saint Mars et lui, et a eulx delivrey par feu Mons. de Mortemart dudit lieu de la Rochelle un peu devant que ledit Me. Hugues Perrier partist de Blois pour aller en Avignon et a Venise, qui fu le XIII jour de juing mil ccccxxxvii" (AN, K. 64, No. 8.). Whether the word "biens" included the books as well as the other goods which Rochechouart, the lord of Mortemart, had kept for Charles we cannot tell as this list has unfortunately disappeared.

Its loss however is compensated by the fact that the list of returned books appears in another inventory which was drawn up at Blois about the year 1442. This was divided into three sections. In the first, headed *Copie de la librarye de monseigneur le duc d'Orléans*, 57 manuscripts are listed (Laborde 6447–6503). Of these, 53 can be checked as having been among the 85 that Mortemart had taken. The remaining 4 may well be among them too, but are difficult to check because of a lack of precision in their description. The third section, headed *Livres à recouvrer*, lists 28 manuscripts. Five of these are the 5 that Mortemart sold (bringing his number up to 62) and it must have been due to an oversight that they were listed here again. Of the remaining 23, all but one were on his list, thus accounting for all but one of the original 85 which he took.

The heading *Livres à recouvrer* did not of course imply that these books were finally lost, for *à recouvrer* certainly suggests that there was an expectation of their recovery; so presumably they must have been borrowed by members of the household at Blois, or somehow mislaid there, some time between 1435 and 1442. It is to be hoped that they did in the end turn up, for among them were Valentina's *Histoires du roy Artus*, described as *moult viel* and lacking its beginning, and also, much more precious, the copy of Christine de Pisan's *Description de la preudomé de l'Ome*, which Christine had had made for her.

By Christine, too, was the one manuscript *à recouvrer* (Laborde 6609) which appears neither in the 1417 inventory nor in Mortemart's list. This was her *Chemin de Longue Estude*, which we know was finally recovered, for it is now in the Bibliothèque Nationale (*Mss. fr.* 1643). The identity of that copy with the one in the 1442 inventory was a happy discovery made not long ago in a curious way. The inventory described the book as being bound in red leather, but the copy in the Bibliothèque Nationale had a blue velvet cover, which also appeared to be fifteenth-century work. At the risk of destroying this it was decided to remove it and underneath it was found, in a perfect state of preservation, the original leather binding which is, however, more brown than red (see G. Ouy, 'Les Bibliothèques' in the Pléiade vol. *L'Histoire et ses méthodes*, 1961, p. 1101).

The second section of the 1442 inventory, headed *Autres livres apportés d'Angleterre*, lists 103 books, and is presumably a copy of an inventory said to have been drawn up at Saint-Omer, soon after Charles landed in November 1440 (see p. 252 above). Champion, *Vie*, 329, note 1, refers to this document as if it still existed, but he would appear to be confusing it with that in the second section of the 1442 inventory, for the Saint-Omer document has in fact disappeared.

Of the books that Charles subsequently acquired after he finally settled down at Blois to enjoy the last ten years of his life, there is no inventory. Champion attempted to fill this gap by his very interesting *Essai d'un catalogue* in which he lists all the books known to have been in the duke's possession at one time or another, or that other references to them make it almost inevitable that he should have possessed.[1] But even if these books did in the lifetime of Charles find a place in the library at Blois, it is of course by no means certain that they were among those that eventually found their way into the Bibliothèque Nationale, any more than we can be certain that those which we know had miraculously remained in his library through so many vicissitudes were all eventually handed on by his successors. Moreover the fact that there existed many copies of certain popular books and that their owners did not always inscribe their names in them, makes identification an almost impossible task. But that it can happen the discovery of Charles' copy of *Le Chemin de Longue Estude* is an excellent proof; and that further such discoveries are possible is an exciting possibility.

NOTES

Primary Sources

The *Chambre des Comptes* of Blois. This vast collection of documents which, after the chroniclers, are the second main source for the life of Charles of Orleans, has had a chequered and interesting history.

(a) During the 18th century they were transferred from the castle of Blois to the municipality, which sent a few to the Archives Nationales, but took no care of the rest, storing them in a shop until their condition greatly deteriorated. In 1792, when such archives all over France were threatened with destruction, the municipality sold them *en bloc* to the Baron de Joursanvault, who had for some years been travelling throughout the country to save such documents from the fury of the Revolutionary authorities, and had thus amassed a collection of 80,000.

(b) After Joursanvault's death in 1832 his heirs offered this collection to the State for a very modest sum. The offer was declined and in 1838 the collection was sent to Blois for sale by auction. The two-volume *Catalogue analytique des archives de M. le Baron de Joursanvault* was prepared for the sale, at which only three-quarters of the documents were sold. The copy of the catalogue on which the names of purchasers had been marked was subsequently mislaid. The unsold quarter of the documents were later disposed of piecemeal by a Paris bookseller, who also kept inadequate records of his sales.

(c) At this stage the Conte de Laborde entered the scene and, with the help of a copy of the catalogue, and of another manuscript catalogue that Joursanvault himself had previously made of his collection, Laborde first noted on cards all the documents that seemed to him the most interesting. He then by diligent enquiries at Blois and elsewhere discovered as far as he could the names of the purchasers, whether private persons or institutions. Armed with his cards, he next visited all the purchasers he could to see the documents themselves, either copying the text of each or making a brief summary of it with quotations. These researches took him not only to private persons in France and to the Bibliothèque Nationale and the Archives Nationales in Paris, but to Belgium and England too. In London he found that the British Museum, thanks to its keepers whom he describes as "vigilants, perspicaces et habilement généreux", had acquired the greater part of the documents from the *Chambre des Comptes* of Blois: no less than 4500 documents, almost half of them concerning the affairs of Charles of Orleans while he was a captive in England (and for that reason, says Laborde, as much in place in London as in Paris). All these, and similar documents which they had bought prior to 1838 from other collectors including Joursanvault himself, as well as some from the Paris bookseller in 1839, were classified under *Additional Charters*.

(d) Finally Laborde published his descriptive lists of the manuscripts from the *Chambre des Comptes* of Blois, giving the present whereabouts of each, together with those from several *chambres des comptes* of the Dukes of Burgundy, where he had conducted similar researches, under the rather misleading title of *Les Ducs de Bourgogne etc.* This work is in two Parts, and comprises three "Tomes". The Blois entries, from the Introduction to which the above account is taken, are in Part II, Tome III, which appeared in 1852.

(e) Another collection of manuscripts, many of them from the *Chambre des Comptes* of the Dukes of Orleans, was acquired in 1830 by M. Bastard d'Estang, who bought it from an employé of the Cabinet du Roi, who had himself managed to save the documents from destruction. On the death of Bastard d'Estang his widow gave the collection, in 10 volumes, to the Bibliothèque Nationale where Léopold Delisle, then its administrator, published his *Les Collections de Bastard d'Estang . . . Catalogue analytique* in 1885.

In the following notes I have wherever possible, for greater ease of reference, quoted the numbers in Laborde (Tome III always understood), giving those in the Joursanvault catalogue (Vol. I except where otherwise stated) or those of the *Additional Charters* themselves only for documents which Laborde omits. The Bastard d'Estang references of course do not overlap with any of the others.

The other main published collections of manuscript sources used are:

	ABBREVIATED TO
Choix de pièces inédites, ed. Douët d'Arcq	*Choix*
Lettres de rois, reines etc., ed. Champollion-Figeac	*Lettres*
Les Ordonnances des roys de France	*Ordonnances*
Proceedings of the Privy Council, ed. Nicolas	*PPC*
Foedera, ed. Rymer	Rymer
Letters and Papers Illustrative of the Wars of the English in France, ed. Stevenson	Stevenson
Calendar of the French Rolls, 48th Report of the Deputy Keeper	*Fr. Rolls*
Rotuli Parliamentorum	*Rot. Parl.*

The manuscripts quoted are in the following:

British Museum, Additional Charters	BM, *Add. Ch.*
Bibliothèque Nationale, Paris, Manuscrits français	BN, *Mss. fr.*

Bibliothèque Nationale, Paris, Manuscrits latins   BN, *Mss. lat.*
Pièces originales   BN, *P.O.*
Nouvelles Acquisitions   BN, *Nouv. Acq.*
Archives Nationales   AN

For full titles of books mentioned above and referred to in the notes, see Bibliography.

N.B. Roman figures indicate volume numbers and Arabic figures page numbers, except in the cases of Laborde, Joursanvault and Bastard d'Estang, where they stand for the number of the document quoted.

NOTES

Prologue

1 *Le Livre des faits et bonnes meurs du sage Roy Charles*, 26, 29.

2 *Œuvres*, IV, 269.

3 This palace has of course long since disappeared and even the contemporary documents concerning it were destroyed by fire in 1737. Fortunately Sauval saw them before this and was able to describe the palace in his *Histoire et recherches des antiquités de la ville de Paris*, 1724, II, 273–4, 277, 283.

CHAPTER ONE

1 Le Religieux, II, 17–19.

2 *Choix*, I, 98.

3 *Ordonnances*, VII, 457.

4 See Notes, *Primary Sources*.

5 Le Religieux, I, 705–7, and *Ordonnances*, VII, 467.

6 Le Religieux, II, 246 and Juvenal des Ursins, 398, give the right date for Charles' birth. This was confirmed in 1448 by Charles' secretary, Antonio Astesano, who had it from the duke himself, in his *Traité sur l'origine et le gouvernement de la cité de Milan* (BN, *Mss. lat.* 6166, fol. 62). Finally Charles himself, in a poem which he wrote in 1439, presumably on the occasion of his birthday, says "J'ay quarante cinq" (*Poésies*, I, 144). In spite of these positive statements, Champollion-Figeac, in his *Louis et Charles d'Orléans*, 62 (2nd ed. 1844) quoted an unauthenticated contemporary document giving the date as May 1391. Some later editors of the poetry repeated this error, one of them, Héricault, on p. xl of his Preface, going so far as to say "Cette date qui n'est mise en doute par personne", and concluding that both Le Religieux and Juvenal must have been confusing the date of the birth with that of the baptism which, according to him, took place over two years later. Other perpetrators of this erroneous date are Saintsbury in his article on Charles of Orleans in the *Encyclopaedia Britannica*, and the French P.T.T., in the commemorative stamp issued on the fifth centenary of Charles' death in January 1965.

CHAPTER TWO

1 Le Religieux, II, 407 and Juvenal, 394. The former hotly defends Valentina. "Their accusations were without foundation", he says, and

"That so noble a lady had committed so great a crime is a fact that has never been proved, and no one has the right to accuse her of it."

2 J. Pichon published the text of Bonet's poem, with facsimiles of the illustrations in Valentina's copy.

3 *Œuvres*, IV, 269.

4 J. Romain, *Inventaires et documents*, 74–92, quotes a document listing items for Charles' wardrobe from February 1st, 1396 to January 31st, 1397.

5 Joursanvault, 602.

6 BM, *Add. Ch.* 2157.

7 BN, *Mss. fr.* 10431: 1828, 1829.

8 BM, *Add. Ch.* 2408. Other garments bought for Charles and Philip– quantities of fine linen, coloured boots and shoes, and satin and damask for cloaks and surcoats–are mentioned in *Add. Ch.* 2190–92, 2290, 2301, 2308.

9 *Ordonnances*, VIII, 382, and IX, 696.

10 Laborde, 5993. For Valentina at Asnières, Coucy, Villers-Cotterêts and Châteauneuf BM, *Add. Ch.* 2981, 3095, 3001 and 4269.

11 Laborde, 5786 bis.

12 BM, *Add. Ch.* 2181.

13 Joursanvault, 79 and BM, *Add. Ch.* 4260.

14 For her saddles etc. BM, *Add. Ch.* 2583, 2590, 2599, 2603, covering the years 1397 to 1403, and for the harness and the equipment for the falcons, Laborde III, 5773 and 5865.

15 BM, *Add. Ch.* 2191.

16 BN, *Mss. fr.* 10431, fol. 405, and 10432, fol. 220, also *P.O.* 2154 Orléans, 134.

17 Joursanvault, 545.

18 Laborde, 5941.

19 Delisle, *Le Cabinet des manuscrits*, I, 98–104.

20 Laborde III, 6017, and BN, *P.O.* 1277 Garbet 3.

21 BN, *Mss. lat.* 5747. On this ms. see Champion, *La Librairie de Charles d'Orléans*, 95.

22 Laborde, 5946.

23 Champion, *La Librairie de Charles d'Orléans*, *Pièces justificatives*, lxix–lxxiii, publishes various inventories of Valentina's books made after her death.

24 *Œuvres*, VII, 227.

25 BN, *Mss. lat.* 9684. fols. 1–15.

26 On fol. 92 of the *Livre des bonnes mœurs* by Jacques Le Grand BN, *Mss. fr.* 1798, John wrote in his own hand a poem called *Oratio ad Crucifixum*.

27 This argument, which might be thought conclusive, has escaped the attention both of the principal champion of John's authorship, Dupont Ferrier, in his *Jean d'Angoulême d'après sa bibliothèque*, 51–2, and of those who support the claim of Charles. For other contributions to the subject see Champollion-Figeac, *Les Poésies du duc Charles d'Orléans*, 410–14, Antoine Thomas, *Les Premiers Vers de Charles d'Orléans*, 128–44, and Champion, *Charles d'Orléans, Poésies* II, 604–5. Champion says that one can easily see the name Charles beneath the erasure. This is quite impossible.

28 Laborde, 5813. Later, Charles had a harpist of his own, Jean Petit-Gay, Joursanvault, II, 3541.

29 Bastard d'Estang, 456, and *Ordonnances*, VIII, 405.

30 BM, *Add. Ch.* 4292, 4293.

31 Laborde, 5824.

32 For these gifts, BM, *Add. Ch.* 3061, 2987, 2774, 2739, 2784, 2740.

33 On the first will see Jarry, *La Vie politique de Louis d'Orléans*, pp. 298 *et seq.* The full text of the second (a copy of the ms. of which is AN, K. 534) is quoted by D. Godefroy, on pp. 631–46 of his *Annotations* to his 1653 edition of Juvenal des Ursins' *Histoire de Charles VI* and other chronicles.

34 Juvenal, 449.

35 *Choix*, I, 140–2.

36 For the clothes ordered for this occasion, BM, *Add. Ch.* 2267, 2269, 2262, 2260, 2286, 2271 and 2263.

37 *Choix*, I, 260.

38 Olivier de la Marche, I, 83, and Le Fèvre, I, 6.

39 *Choix*, I, 283–4.

40 For this and the following facts in this paragraph see Joursanvault, 82; Bastard d'Estang, 493; Laborde, 6056; Joursanvault, 619.

41 AN, K. 55, Nos. 27 bis and 28.

42 On the raising of the Valois title to a dukedom and the transfer of it there is no actual document, but from the date of the marriage onwards the title disappears from those used by Louis, and Charles is always referred to as Duke of Valois.

43 The fly-leaf is fol. 42^r of BN, *Mss. lat.* 9684. It is curious that Garbet dates the poem July and not June 29th, but perhaps it was written some time later and this is a slip. On Garbet's presence at the wedding and his poem see Champion, *La Vie de Charles d'Orléans*, 37.

44 AN, K. 55, No. 29.

CHAPTER THREE

1 See P. Raymond, *Enquête du Prévôt de Paris sur l'assassinat de Louis, duc d'Orléans*, 215–49. This is obviously the most authentic account of the murder, but the many chroniclers who also relate it give some details not in the official report. Of these Monstrelet's account is the most vivid, I, 154–61, and gives the impression that, although he was only seventeen at the time, he saw some things for himself and was genuinely horrified by what he heard.

2 Nicolas de Baye, *Journal*, I, 208.

3 Laborde, 6062.

4 Bastard d'Estang, 511.

5 D. Lottin, *Recherches historiques sur la ville d'Orléans*, I, 177 refers to the document describing this, formerly in the Archives du Loiret, *Arch. Com. d'Orléans*, CC 646.

6 Cousinot's *Geste des Nobles*, 94 *et seq.* is the most personal account of events concerning Valentina and Charles at this time, but Monstrelet also describes them vividly, I, 167 *et seq.*

7 Le Religieux, III, 743.

8 *Journal*, I, 212.

9 *Ordonnances*, IX, 261.

10 *Ordonnances*, IX, 696.

11 Le Religieux, III, 753.

12 For this and the following transactions in this paragraph see Laborde, *Glossaire français du Moyen-Age* under *rubis*, 488; BM, *Add. Ch.* 3117 and 3118; AN, K. 56, 18 bis.

13 AN, K. 57, Nos. 1 a² and BN, *Mss. fr. Nouv. Acq.* 6525. The former, a mere scrap of parchment, has John of Brittany's signature on it, while the latter has that of Charles. The text is quoted in *Choix*, I, 309–10.

14 See the report of the occasion, made at Burgundy's command, in Douët d'Arcq, *Document inédit sur l'assassinat de Louis duc d'Orléans*, 6–25.

15 Monstrelet, I, 178–244 quotes the speech in full.

16 Juvenal, 445.

17 AN, K. 56, No. 17².

18 BM, *Add. Ch.* 4298.

19 BN, *P.O.* 2156 *Orléans*, No. 394.

20 Juvenal, 448.

21 Quoted by Monstrelet, I, 269–336.

22 Juvenal, 448.

23 Monstrelet, I, 347–8.

24 AN, K. 56, No. 17².

25 Monstrelet, I, 389.

26 Laborde, 6169.

27 Le Religieux, I, 389, Monstrelet, I, 393–4 and Juvenal, 449, all say she died of grief, anger and despair, but Juvenal is the only authority for her remark about the Bastard.

28 On her emblems and devices see François le Maire, *Histoire et antiquités de la ville et duché d'Orléans*, (2nd ed. 1648) 96, and Claude Paradin, *Devises héroïques et emblèmes*, 1622, 120–1.

29 Monstrelet, I, 394.

CHAPTER FOUR

1 *Ordonnances*, VI, 26–32.

2 Laborde, 6063–6168.

3 Laborde, 6066.

4 Many of the chroniclers describe the meeting at Chartres, but Monstrelet's account, I, 390–401, from which this and the following quotations are taken, is the fullest.

5 *Journal*, I, 260.

6 *Chroniques*, 46.

7 Monstrelet, I, 400.

8 *Cartulaire de Sainct-Lomer*, quoted in N. Mars, *Histoire du royal monastère de Sainct-Lomer*, 232.

9 Monstrelet, II, 45.

10 This and other agreements with Armagnac are AN, K. 56, Nos. 254-8.

11 AN, K. 56, Nos. 20, and 20 bis-quater. See also BM, *Add. Ch.* 7926.

12 AN, K. 534, No. 20 is a contemporary copy of this alliance.

13 For this and the following gifts mentioned in this paragraph, Laborde, 6177, 6189, 6190.

14 AN, K. 534, No. 21 is a contemporary copy of the relevant document.

15 Joursanvault, 91.

16 Juvenal, 446–7, quotes one of these addressed to the Bishop of Beauvais.

17 *Choix*, I, 327–9.

18 Bastard d'Estang, 562, and Joursanvault, 622.

19 Laborde, 6194–9.

20 Bastard d'Estang, 571.

21 *Choix*, I, 329–35.

22 Monstrelet, II, 102.

23 Joursanvault, 127.

CHAPTER FIVE

1 BM, *Add. Ch.* 2604, 4303, 4304, 4307.

2 Laborde, 6201–6, 6214, 6216.

3 Monstrelet, II, 116–21 gives the text of it.

4 AN, K. 56, No. 18. Monstrelet, who quotes it in full, II, 124–49, dates it July 9th, perhaps according to the copy he was using. But the ms. has July 14th.

5 Le Religieux, IV, 435, goes out of his way to say that he had heard many learned and experienced persons praise the justice of all its demands.

6 *Choix*, I, 341–3 gives the text of it.

7 Champion, *Vie*, 89, refers to this version in the Archives du Nord (then B. 1406 now B. 657) and takes it to be the final letter, in spite of the

unlikelihood that Charles would have sent one off before hearing from the king. But E. Castaigne, in *Bulletin de la Société Archéologique et Historique de la Charente*, III, 18, note (1), points out that Battheney, in *L'Archiviste François*, reproduces a facsimile of the final letter, dated July 24th, on *Planche* 47, no. 2, and gives a transcript on p. 44. Battheney unfortunately does not state the whereabouts of the document he reproduces, but there can be no doubt that it was the letter finally sent by the herald, who was paid for taking it "as early as the last day of July" (Bastard d'Estang, 631). (For Castaigne, see Bibliography, under Du Port.)

8 Le Religieux, IV, 437–9.

9 Fenin, 576.

10 For these despatches see Joursanvault, 93 and 95, and Bastard d'Estang, 617, 620, 624.

11 Laborde, 6208.

12 Joursanvault, 100.

13 Joursanvault, 92 and 96.

14 BM, *Add. Ch.* 3125.

15 BM, *Add. Ch.* 4308.

16 For this and the order concerning John of Angoulême see Bastard d'Estang, 626, and Laborde, 6209.

17 Laborde, 6220.

18 *Choix*, I, 346, gives the text of Register XIII of the Council.

19 *Ordonnances*, IX, 635.

20 *Choix*, I, 344–6.

21 Monstrelet, II, 209.

22 For this and the following transactions, *Ordonnances*, IX, 648; AN, K. No. 14; *Ordonnances*, IX, 675.

23 AN, K. 535, No. 27 fol. 18^v.

24 Laborde, 6221.

25 Rymer, VIII, 715–6.

26 BM, *Add. Ch.* 3411, 3412 and 3431–3. For the present of the horse, 3410.

27 For all the arrangements made at this time see Rymer, VIII, 745–50.

28 Monstrelet, II, 339–342.

29 There are two different versions of this letter, one quoted in Rymer, VIII, 737, and the other in *PPC*, II, 28. In the latter the king says that the allies have offered to surrender to him the lands they hold in the Duchy of Guienne and to aid him in recovering the rest of it. He therefore intends to proceed into his duchy in person, and begs them not to help the King of France and the Duke of Burgundy. The version given in Rymer seems more likely to be the authentic, or at any rate the final, one, since it says nothing of the king's intention to go himself which Henry, who fully understood the whole situation, clearly had no intention of doing.

30 Joursanvault, 99.

31 It is Le Religieux who thus describes the king's reaction, IV, 627–9. The story of how copies of the letters to England came into the king's hands is a confusing one. Monstrelet (II, 236–7) says that "letters" in a leather bag with seals were seized by the bailiff of Caen and sent to Paris where they were read in Council. Both Le Religieux, IV, 627–8, and Juvenal, 475, say that the papers were seized from an Augustinian monk, whom the allies had chosen as an emissary to England because of his eloquence. These statements suggest that it was the originals which were seized, but it obviously could not have been since they reached England safely. As it appears to have been customary to make many copies of every document, perhaps these were some that had been prepared for the information of Charles' allies. *Choix*, I, 348–9, quotes two documents describing how old country people brought copies of Charles' letters to the Council, hoping to gain some advantage from acting as messengers, so there seems to have been a fairly active spy system covering his movements and deeds.

32 Monstrelet, II, 282.

33 Monstrelet, II, 284. Juvenal, 474, gives a different version of Berry's remark: "Fair nephew, I have done ill and you even worse. Let us now strive to keep the kingdom in peace and tranquillity."

34 See note 38 below.

35 AN, K. 57, Nos. 21–5.

36 *Choix*, I, 352–2.

37 *Choix*, I, 354–8.

38 The texts of Berry's letter and of Clarence's reply (of which the mss. are BM, Harleian No. 431) are printed in Champollion-Figeac, *Lettres de rois*, II, 328–32. At the end of Berry's letter is written "Item, le duc d'Orliens, en mesme la maniere", and similarly for Bourbon, Brittany and Burgundy. The puzzling reference to Burgundy perhaps indicates that Clarence had also been sent a copy of the document that both Burgundy and Charles had been forced to sign at Auxerre. The letter from Charles was no doubt that which the king had commanded him to write from Auxerre on August 23rd.

39 BM, *Add. Ch.* 3422–4, 237–9.

40 The original of this treaty is lost, but there is a contemporary copy of it in AN, K. 59, No. 4.

41 BM, *Add. Ch.* 1399, an original document of the same date as the treaty, November 14th, gives these details, as does AN, K. 59, No. 3, a single sheet signed "Thomas", of the same date.

42 Dupont Ferrier, in 'La Captivité de Jean d'Orléans', states (p. 44) that the original demand was for 150,000 *écus*, and that Clarence arbitrarily added 60,000 to this for himself, thus making the sum up to 210,000, and he quotes BM, *Add. Ch.* 1399 as his authority for this. But there is no mention of any such thing in this document; and there exist two others expressly referring to the sum of 50,000 *écus* accorded to Clarence personally by the treaty: BM, *Add. Ch.* 1405, and AN, K. 59, No 14. The latter bears the autograph signature "Thomas". In spite of these things the erroneous figures given by Dupont Ferrier are frequently repeated by later historians, including Champion.

43 BM, *Add. Ch.* 1400.

44 For this and the following facts in this paragraph BM, *Add. Ch.* 244, 245; Bastard d'Estang, 661; Joursanvault, 552; Bastard d'Estang, 663; BM, *Add. Ch.* 1403 and 3451.

45 For this and the following facts in this paragraph BM, *Add. Ch.* 3415, 3416, 3418 and 240; *Add. Ch.* 3419–21; *Add. Ch.* 237–9, 3422–4, 3434–6; 3429 and 3430; 3440, 3441.

46 BM, *Add. Ch.* 3131.

47 BM, *Add. Ch.* 234, 3437, 3457.

48 BM, *Add. Ch.* 251.

CHAPTER SIX

1 Le Religieux, IV, 747–67, and Monstrelet, II, 308–32, quote passages from this report. On the original ms. of it see Moranvillé, *Remontrances de l'université de la ville de Paris*, who analyses the text.

2 Monstrelet, II, 345–6. He dates the event as taking place on April 28th as does also Nicolas de Baye, *Journal*, II, 108–9.

3 For this and the two following facts in this paragraph see Joursanvault, 109, 110 and 116.

4 Joursanvault, 114.

5 de Cagny, the Alençon chronicler, is the authority for this, 80–1.

6 Juvenal, 484.

7 AN, K. 57, No. 1f.

8 Laborde, 6227.

9 BM, *Add. Ch.* 2422, 2423.

10 BM, *Add. Ch.* 2424–6.

11 Joursanvault, 111.

12 There were 108 of them. *Choix*, I, 367–9, gives the text of the ms. on which their names were recorded.

13 But apparently only after a struggle, for Joursanvault, 108, quotes a document recording that Waleran de Saint-Pol opposed the dauphin's forces sent to take possession of Coucy in the name of the king on behalf of Charles, who paid for the expedition. The royal forces won.

14 For this and the following facts in this paragraph, BM, *Add. Ch.* 2427; Laborde, 6230; Laborde, 6232; Laborde, 6233.

15 AN, K. 60, No. 5, quoted by Champion, *Vie*, 123, note 1.

16 Monstrelet, II, 466.

17 Juvenal, 498–9.

18 Rymer, IX, 34.

19 Monstrelet, III, 40–1, records this episode and quotes the remarks.

20 Laborde, 6236.

21 For this and the following facts in this paragraph, BM, *Add. Ch.* 64 & 1403; 65; 64 & 1402; 3448; 60.

22 BM, *Add. Ch.* 3459, 1405, 1406.

23 Laborde, 6238.

24 For this and the following facts in this paragraph, Bastard d' Estang, 681; BM, *Add. Ch.* 61 and 62; Bastard d'Estang, 684.

25 Le Religieux, V, 399.

26 Juvenal, 502.

27 *Choix*, I, 370–4.

28 Laborde, 6234.

29 Laborde, 6241.

30 André Favyn, *Le Théâtre d'Honneur et de Chevalerie* (1620), I, 730–3, says he found this information in a lost chronicle by a herald of Orleans called Hannotin de Cleriaux.

31 A small and not very official-looking document, AN, K. 1731, No. 46 bis, adds a puzzling factor to this matter of the Order of the Camail. It is a list, drawn up by Charles himself, dated London March 8th, 1438, of the 25 lords whom he authorised to wear his order. But the names of many to whom we know he had previously given it do not appear on the list. Did he perhaps intend to establish a more formal Order when he was able to return to France, giving full membership only to those of noble birth? There is no explanation of this mystery.

32 Laborde, 6240.

CHAPTER SEVEN

1 Rymer, IX, 56–60, 68–71.

2 Ibid. 91–103.

3 Ibid 103–4.

4 Ibid. 137–8.

5 Ibid. 131–3.

6 Ibid. 151–2.

7 *PPC*, II, 140. This particular minute of the Council's meeting is undated, but presumably refers to the one at this time.

8 Monstrelet, III, 60.

9 Rymer, IX, 208–15.

10 de Cagny, 92.

11 Monstrelet, III, 76.

12 Le Religieux, V, 501–5.

13 Le Religieux, V, 507–11.

14 Juvenal, 504.

15 Juvenal, 505.

16 Le Religieux, V, 527–31.

17 Le Religieux, V, 531.

18 Juvenal alone mentions these letters, which he quotes in full, 510–18.

19 Champion, *La Librairie de Charles d'Orléans, Pièces justificatives*, p. lxxvi.

20 In February he had ordered the payment of what was apparently an annual sum of 6,000 *écus*, backdated to the year beginning in the previous October, for the expenses of John and his fellow hostages, BM, *Add. Ch.* 257, 258. For the March and May payments, BM, *Add. Ch.* 1407, 1408. A long list of Norman towns had had to contribute to these payments.

21 Laborde, 6245.

22 BM, *Add. Ch.* 2607, 4321, 4322.

23 BM, *Add. Ch.* 3466.

24 Laborde, 6244.

25 Sir Harris Nicholas, whose *History of the Battle of Agincourt* is still the best, quotes the statements of contemporary chroniclers, both French and English, concerning the size of both armies and the numbers killed. See 2nd ed. 1832, pp. 75, 76, 109, 258, 266.

26 Le Fèvre de Saint-Rémy, whose contemporaries nearly always called him Toison d'Or, as he was the king-of-arms of that order, says, p. 239, that he himself heard Philip say this at the age of 67.

27 There is some uncertainty as to whether it was Gloucester or York whom Alençon wounded, but it is more likely to have been the former as York was killed in another part of the field. See Nicholas, *op. cit.* 126.

28 Nicholas, *op. cit.* 289, quotes and translates this from the account of the battle by Thomas Elmham, the king's chaplain, who was with him there, in his *Gesta Henrici Quinti.*

29 Le Fèvre, who was present at the battle with the English, reports this conversation, 261.

30 Le Fèvre, 263.

31 BM, *Add. Ch.* 252, 263.

32 BM, *Add. Ch.* 3468, 3469.

CHAPTER EIGHT

1 Rymer, IX, 334.

2 Ibid, 337.

3 BN, *Mss. fr.* 5699 (formerly 10297).

4 Gauluet sold his governorship in April 1418 to André Marchant, a chamberlain of the king, for "une forte somme", Lottin, *op. cit.* I, 186.

5 Bastard d'Estang, 691.

6 BM, *Add. Ch.* 3467.

7 BM, *Add. Ch.* 266, 267.

8 AN, K. 68, No. 10.

9 BM, *Add. Ch.* 4326.

10 AN, K. 68, No. 10.

11 For this and the following two items in this paragraph, see BM, *Add. Ch.* 3157; Joursanvault, 558; Laborde, 6250.

12 BM, *Add. Ch.* 261, 3462.

13 *Geste des Nobles*, 157.

14 Rymer, IX, 362–3.

15 Ibid, 377–82.

16 Ibid, 423.

17 Ibid, 427–40.

18 BM, *Add. Ch.* 70, 71.

19 BM, *Add. Mss.* 21359.

20 For the inventory of the books see Appendix III. Laborde, 6251–6, lists some of the items other than books.

21 BM, *Add. Ch.* 3161.

22 BM, *Add. Ch.* 268–70.

23 Dupont Ferrier, 'La Captivité de Jean d'Orléans', 46 *et seq.*

24. See Bastard d'Estang, 694, AN, K. 68, No. 10, and BM, *Add. Ch.* 4326.

25 BM, *Add. Ch.* 3481.

26 Rymer, IX, 456.

27 Stevenson, I, 392 and III, 523–4. Also Rymer, X, 290.

28 Rymer, IX, 456.

29 Laborde, 6259, 6260.

30 BM, *Add. Ch.* 72.

31 Laborde, 6257, 6258 and (for the quotation) 6261.

32 For this and the other statements in this sentence, Bastard d'Estang, 717; 713; 706, 708, and BM, *Add. Ch.* 3489, 3490.

33 Bastard d'Estang, 720.

34 For this and the following facts in this paragraph, BM, *Add. Ch.* 4338; 3503; Joursanvault, 453.

35 *PPC*, II, 350–8, and Rymer, IX, 626–7.

36 Monstrelet, III, 287.

37 Juvenal, 554.

38 Ellis, *Original Lettres*, I, 1.

39 Rymer, IX, 801.

40 *PPC*, II, 268–70.

41 *PPC*, II, 271.

42 *PPC*, III, 118–20. Arthur of Richemont had been sent there on August 27th, 1419, see *Calendar of the Close Rolls*, Vol. Henry V 1419–22.

43 BN, *Mss. fr.* 12765, fol. 3. Champollion-Figeac, *Poésies*, 416–19, quotes the text, and Champion, *Vie*, 176, has a photograph of the ms.

44 Ellis, *Original Letters*, I, 6–7

45 *PPC*, II, 271.

46 Rymer, X, 438–45.

47 Ibid. IX, 884, and X, 4.

48 For Philip's activities at this time see BM, *Add. Ch.* 284, 286, 290, 292, 3528–30, 3533–7.

49 BM, *Add. Ch.* 2616–19.

50 Laborde, 6301.

51 Laborde, 6302.

52 Laborde, 6305.

53 For this and the following facts, Laborde, 6306; 6265–82; 6308.

54 Laborde, 6283, 6284, 6286.

55 Joursanvault, 558.

56 Joursanvault, 126.

57 Laborde, 6309.

58 Laborde, 6303.

59 For this and the following facts, see BM, *Add. Ch.* 297; 3550; Joursanvault, 3386. See also Joubert, *Documents inédits sur la guerre de cent ans: Négotiations relatives à l'échange de Charles Duc d'Orléans et de Jean, Comte d'Angoulême*. On Thomas Beaufort, see Chapter X, note 5.

60 *Geste des Nobles*, 184.

61 Laborde, 6313. On this manuscript see Porcher, *Chefs-d'œuvre de l'enluminure français du 15ᵉ siècle*, Plate X.

62 Monstrelet, IV, 110–1. See also *Rot. Parl.* IV, 399.

63 This will, which was obviously well-known to Henry VI and his Council (see pp. 237, 238 above) has now disappeared, or at any rate not yet come to light. See *PPC*, III, Preface ix-xii.

CHAPTER NINE

1 *PPC*, III, 10.

2 Rymer, X, 262.

3 Monstrelet, VI, 497.

4 Rymer, X, 288.

5 Ibid. 280–1.

6 *PPC*, III, 79.

7 Ibid. 133.

8 Ibid. 134. *The History of the King's Works*, 572, says that "extensive repairs were carried out between 1421 and 1425".

9 Monstrelet, V, 434.

10 *Fr. Rolls*, 229, 232, 235.

11 *Fr. Rolls*, 238.

12 *Rot. Parl.* IV, 247a, 284a, 300b.

13 *Geste des Nobles*, 198.

14 BM, *Add. Ch.* 336.

15 BM, *Add. Ch.* 337.

16 *Fr. Rolls*, 243.

17 Laborde, 6420.

18 Bastard d'Estang, 764.

19 Laborde, 6322 (the receipt), 6323–6400 for the books, and 6409–33 for the inventory.

20 Ibid. 6436.

21 Ibid. 6400.

22 Ibid. 6504–6617.

23 Ibid. 6524. The ms. is BN, *Mss. lat.* 1196.

24 Laborde, 6520. The ms. is BN, *Mss. lat.* 1201. On both of these see Champion, *La Libraire de Charles d'Orléans*, 79–81 and xxx. See also Appendix I.

25 Laborde, 6547, 6569. Champion, *op. cit.* xxxi, and Appendix I.

26 Laborde, 6545. On the contemporary mss. which may possibly be this one see Champion, *Poésies*, I, ix, x, and *Vie*, 505, note 3.

27 This and the following statements in this paragraph are Joan's replies of February 22nd, March 10th and March 13th to the questions put to her during her trial. See O'Reilly, *Les Deux Procès de Jeanne d'Arc*, II, 56, 110, 121.

28 For these two gifts, see Laborde, 6438, 6439.

29 Lottin, *op. cit.* I, 204, who took his information from the Archives du Loir-et-Cher. There is also a document of 1430 (Joursanvault, 2886) which refers to 'Jean, bâtard de Dunois'. In spite of these things there is a tendency among later historians to state that Charles of Orleans conferred the title on his brother in 1439 during the conference at Gravelines. Champollion-Figeac, *Les Poésies*, ix, says that Charles gave the Bastard the County of Dunois "par lettre patente du 21 juillet 1439", and states that the original of this document is in the Bibliothèque du Roi. Unfortunately he gives no number for it. See also Caffin de Merouville, *Le Beau Dunois et son temps*, 270. Why the Dauphin should have been able to give away a title deriving from land belonging to Charles of Orleans is made clear by two letters from Charles, dated surprisingly 1445–6, stating that he gave to "the bastard of Orleans" his brother, the county of Dunois, accompanying which is the king's confirmation of the gift of this county which depended on the king "à cause de son château du Louvre" (Joursanvault, 3003).

30 Cagny, 148.

31 For Alençon's testimony at the rehabilitation of Joan of Arc, see O'Reilly, *op. cit.* I, 206–14.

32 Chastellain, II, 164.

33 Laborde, 6441.

34 We have Suffolk's own word for this. *Rot. Parl.* Vol. V, 176a & b.

CHAPTER TEN

1 *PPC*, IV, 44. Miss L. de Angulo, on p. 62 of her paper, discussed in Appendix I, makes the interesting suggestion that this transfer of

Charles from royal strongholds to private dwellings indicates a relaxing in the severity of his guardianship. But he still remained under the control of the Council.

2 *PPC*, IV, 44.

3 Rymer, X, 461.

4 BM, *Add. Ch.* 374.

5 Of the three legitimate sons of the Duchess of Clarence and her first husband John Beaufort, Earl of Somerset, none was called Thomas. Yet one of the vain promises made by the Duke of Bourbon in 1427 to obtain his release was that he would free at his own expense "the two brothers John and Thomas, sons of the late Count of Somerset" who were prisoners (Rymer, X, 438–55). In another document concerning this offer the king himself speaks of "our two cousins John and Thomas, brothers, sons of our very dear and very beloved great uncle the Earl of Somerset" (Rymer, X, 478–81). It may therefore be supposed that this Thomas was a bastard of the earl's and thus a half-brother of his fellow prisoner John, who had succeeded his father as earl. There is however another supposition, and that is that he was a bastard of the Duchess's. This rests a) on the eagerness she appears to have shown to obtain his release offered by Bourbon (Rymer, X, 467–8), and b) on a remark in a document dated May 23rd, 1421, i.e. two months after the battle of Baugé, recording an attempt made by Charles of Orleans' officers to exchange John of Angoulême for "messire Thomas Beaufort, son of the Duchess of Clarence", BM, *Add. Ch.* 3552 (see p. 156 above).

6 BM, *Add. Ch.* 3659, 3660.

7 Joursanvault, 132.

8 Bastard d'Estang, 1284.

9 O'Reilly, *op. cit.* I, 214–22 (Dunois). 206–14 (Alençon), and 222–4 (Gaucourt).

10 The date of Bonne's death is nowhere recorded, but the general opinion is that of Champion, *Vie*, 271, that it must have been about this time. Some of the 19th century editors of Charles of Orleans' poetry (Champollion-Figeac, *Notice historique*, p. vii, Guichard, *Introduction*, p. vi, Héricault, *Préface*, p. xiv) assert that she died in 1415, probably in November, but give no authority for such statements, for which in fact none exists. See Appendix II.

CHAPTER ELEVEN

1 Rymer, X, 520.

2 *PPC*, IV, 123.

3 Rymer, X, 564, and *PPC*, IV, 182.

4 See H. N. MacCracken, 'An English Friend of Charles d'Orléans', 142–180.

5 *PPC*, IV, 182 and Rymer, X, 564.

6 BM, *Add. Ch.* 402.

7 *PPC*, IV, 255–9.

8 Stevenson, I, 397.

9 Rymer, X, 438–45 and 478–81. See also my Chapter X, note 5.

10 Rymer, X, 478–81 and *Fr. Rolls*, 279. For the following facts in this paragraph, *Rot. Parl.* IV, 284; Rymer, X, 388; *Rot. Parl.* IV, 339a.

11 Stevenson, II, part 1, 255.

12 Rymer, X, 602.

13 *PPC*, IV, 201.

14 Stevenson, II, part 1, 255.

15 Stevenson, II, part 1, 218–49 translates and quotes this document in full.

16 Rymer, X, 556–61.

17 See for example Samaran, *La Maison d'Armagnac au XVe siècle*, 76, and Dufresne de Beaucourt, *Histoire de Charles VII*, II, 464.

18 Rymer, X, 561–3.

19 Samaran, *op. cit.* quotes it, 370–1.

20 Quoted by Dufresne de Beaucourt, *op. cit.* II, 464.

21 *PPC*, IV, 255–9.

22 Dufresne de Beaucourt, *op. cit.* II, 520.

23 Un Bourgeois de Paris, 305.

24 Dufresne de Beaucourt, *op. cit.* II, 520.

25 *PPC*, IV, 255–9.

26 Rymer, X, 611–13.

27 For a detailed account of this meeting see Stevenson, I, 51–64, which gives the text of the first and second offers made by the French ambassadors.

28 *PPC*, IV, 225.

29 Ibid. 259–61.

30 For the text of the interchange of letters between Philip of Burgundy and Henry VI see Dickinson, *The Congress of Arras*, Appendix A, 213–16. Champollion-Figeac, *Les Poésies*, vii, says that Burgundy's letter is in BN, Collection Colbert, Vol. 64. For the London Chronicle, Kingsford, *The Chronicles of London*, 139. A reference in a manuscript in the BN, Gaignières 20379 (formerly 894) p. 616 to a "Pouvoir donné au Cardinal d'Angleterre pour aller à Calais pour communiquer avec le Duc d'Orléans au sujet de la paix avec la France" which is dated July 8th, 1435, also gives the impression that the visit of Charles was arranged at the last minute.

31 For the visit of the envoys see Gruel, *Chronique d'Arthur de Richemont* (*1393–1458*), 103, (he is the only chronicler who mentions the presence of Charles at Calais). The newsletter from Arras was discovered by Miss Dickinson, in her researches for her *Congress of Arras*, quoted in L. Caillet, *Les Préliminaires du Congrès d'Arras*, Paris 1909. Charles' letter to the Duke of Savoy is Turin, Archivio di Stato, *Negoziazioni con la Francia*, mazzo 52, 1º fascicolo, carta a 3ʳ.

32 See Champion, 'La Dame Anglaise de Charles d'Orléans', 580–2. It was Champion who discovered that this quotation applied to Charles of Orleans and not to Charles V of France, as the text in one manuscript of the poem made it appear to. See also Appendix II and page 321 below.

33 This discovery was made by Miss Eleanor Hammond, in her 'Charles of Orleans and Anne Molyneux', *Modern Philology*, Vol. XXII, Nov. 1924. See also Appendix II.

34 These seven poems, which are on a separate quire in Charles' personal manuscript of his poems, (pp. 310–13 of the ms. and *Poésies*, II, 569–72) are not in Charles's own hand according to MacCracken, in his 'An English Friend of Charles d'Orléans'. He thinks they were included in the volume at the duke's request and suggests that the author of them was the Earl of Suffolk. His reasons are: that the earl was a poet, if we accept the attribution to him of a small collection of *ballades* and *rondeaux* in French, in the manner of Charles of Orleans, in MS. Trin. Coll. Camb. R. 3.20; and that he thinks Suffolk was the author of twenty English poems in a manuscript in the Bodleian, Fairfax 16, one of which "O thow Fortune, which hast the governaunce" is also one of the seven in Charles' manuscript. R. R. Steele, in *The English Poems of Charles of Orleans*, pp. xxii–xxiv, does not accept these attributions to Suffolk and is in general a strong advocate of Charles as the author of any debateable poems. See Appendix II. The fact that they are written in an English hand, if this is so, proves nothing, since Charles could easily have got a scribe able to write English to transcribe them for him, even if he were himself the author. Apart from these seven poems, there are two other English poems in a

different part of the personal manuscript (*Poésies*, I, 256–7), both written in his hand. But Champion, who expresses no view on the authorship of the seven, thinks Charles merely copied these because he liked them.

CHAPTER TWELVE

1 *PPC*, V, 44, and Rymer, X, 663.

2 Bastard d'Estang, 1283, and BM, *Add. Ch.* 638.

3 BM, *Add. Ch.* 3793, 3795–8.

4 *PPC*, V, 52–4.

5 BM, *Add. Ch.* 3818, 3820, 3829, 3864, 4407, 4410–12.

6 Joursanvault, 135.

7 BM, *Add. Ch.* 4403, and Laborde, 6442.

8 For this and the following facts in this paragraph see Joursanvault, 548, and BM, *Add. Ch.* 3816, 6332; Joursanvault, 135 and Bastard d'Estang, 134, 793; BM, *Add. Ch.* 428.

9 Rymer, X, 663.

10 *PPC*, V, 20–2.

11 *PPC*, V, 51.

12 *PPC*, V, 44.

13 For this and the following three facts, BM, *Add. Ch.* 3818; 3819; 3822; 3821.

14 *PPC*, V, 64–6.

15 *PPC*, V, 67.

16 Rymer, X, 679.

17 For this and the next two facts, BM, *Add. Ch.* 3831, 3832 and 4415; 3833; 4418.

18 *PPC*, V, 82.

19 *PPC*, V, 86.

20 Rymer, X, 683–4.

21 Stevenson, II, part 1, pp. lxxv–lxxx.

22 Rymer, X, 707–8.

23 *PPC*, V, 101.

24 Stevenson, I, 432–4.

25 Rymer, X, 707–8.

26 Stevenson, II, part 1, p. lxxx, and Rymer, X, 708–9.

27 Rymer, X, 718–19.

28 Rymer, X, 720–2.

29 Rymer, X, 724–8.

30 BM, *Add. Ch.* 2450.

31 The account of this conference is taken from the *Journal of the Ambassadors*, by the King's secretary, Thomas Bekington, or Beckington, who reported it in great detail. *PPC*, V, quotes the Latin text of the report, 334–402, and gives a summary, pp. xiii–xxx.

32 Rymer, X, 728–9.

33 Stevenson, II, part 11, 446.

34 Stevenson, I, 433.

35 Rymer, X, 728–9.

36 *Lettres de rois* etc., II, 456–60.

37 Bastard d'Estang, 785. A very similar circular letter, dated July 24th, 1439, is BN, *Mss. fr. Nouv. Acq.* 3642.

38 This and the letter to the Bastard are AN, K. 65, Nos. 15⁵, 15⁶, 15¹.

39 Champion, *Vie*, 297 *et seq.* refers to Charles' letters to his town of Orleans as being in the Archives Communales d'Orléans CC. 655, and another addressed to the Bastard, asking him to put some of his castles–Beaugency, Janville and Châteauneuf–in order, as being in the Archives du Loiret, A. 2171. *The Inventaires sommaires* of the documents in these two archives, that for Orleans compiled by Veyrier du Muraud etc., and that for the Loiret by Maupré et Doinel, confirm this. Upon enquiry, however, it appears that these documents are no longer there. They may have been destroyed as a result of the bombardment during the war, but nothing definite appears to be known.

40 All these letters are in AN, K. 65.

41 Stevenson, II, part 11, 440–51.

42 Rymer, X, 764–7.

43 See pp. 158 and 237 above.

44 Rymer, X, 767–8, and *Fr. Rolls*, 336–7.

45 *Fr. Rolls*, 224.

46 Rymer, X, 763–4.

47 Stevenson, I, 432–4.

48 Rymer, X, 763–4.

49 For this and the three following facts, BM, *Add. Ch.* 451; 3904; 3897; Rymer, X, 771, and *Fr. Rolls*, 334.

50 Stevenson, II, part II, 451–64.

51 Rymer, X, 776–82.

52 Rymer, X, 782–6.

53 Rymer, X, 798–800.

54 AN, K. 66, No. 11.

55 Rymer, X, 812–15.

56 Rymer, X, 815–16.

57 AN, K. 66, Nos. 7–10 are all records of sales of Coucy, Soissons, Chauny, Limoges and other properties, mostly in October.

58 Rymer, X, 826.

59 *Paston Lettres*, I, 40.

60 Rymer, X, 826.

61 For this and the following four facts in this paragraph, Rymer, X, 817; 821–3; 824–6; 826–7; 828.

62 *Paston Letters*, I, 40.

CHAPTER THIRTEEN

1 BN, *P.O.* 678 Chardon (personal letter which Charles wrote that day).

2 Monstrelet, V, 437 *et seq.* from which the following account and the quotations are taken.

3 Rymer, X, 830.

4 Rymer, X, 829.

5 Monstrelet gives the text of it, V, 155–83.

6 Olivier de la Marche, I, 250.

7 AN, K. 535, No. 10. Why this was necessary is not clear, as the relationship between them was not close.

8 See Dufresne de Beaucourt, *op. cit.* III, 161.

9 BM, *Add. Ch.* 12074. This sounds as if it were part of the 21,375 *écus* he exacted at Buzançais, with the condition that he should receive it in full before any of the hostages were released. Charles and Berry had soon paid him more than half (see p. 102 above) but apparently not the whole of the remainder, for this condition was still being repeated in 1433 when, at a meeting of the Privy Council on May 25th, there was a question of releasing the hostage Guillaume Bouteiller in exchange for an Englishman who had long been "in harde prison" in France, see *PPC*, IV, 164, where there is also a reference to the fact that "not long ago" Charles had repeated at the Friar Preachers of London (whose library he enjoyed visiting on his rare visits to London), in the presence of the Duke of Gloucester and some of the lords of the Council, that neither his brother John nor any of the other hostages should leave England until Lord Fanhope was "resonably satisfied" as to the promises and sums agreed with him as "by lawe or reson due in eny wise". This repetition is curious in view of the fact that one of the most important of the hostages, Jean de Saveuses, was certainly released before 1433, when de Lannoy met him in France. And at that Council meeting in May 1433, Fanhope agreed to the release of Bouteiller too, but only on condition that Charles paid him an extra 2000 gold crowns. See also *Patent Rolls*, Henry VI, 1429–36, p. 270.

10 Joursanvault, 564.

11 Joursanvault, 563.

12 AN, K. 66, No. 12ᵃ. This is the original document.

13 See Un Bourgeois de Paris, 289, and Jean Maupoint, IV, 26.

14 D. Lottin, *op. cit.* I, 289–90, extracted his account of the reception in Orleans from the municipal archives, on which see Chapter XI, note 39, above.

15 Unfortunately this painting was subsequently destroyed.

16 AN, K. 66, Nos. 15 and 17.

17 For Burgundy's part in all this see Dufresne de Beaucourt, III, 174–5 and 200–1, who quotes the relevant Burgundian documents.

18 *PPC*, V, 139–40, and *Fr. Rolls*, 347.

19 Monstrelet, VI, 30.

20 Rymer, X, 844–6.

21 Rymer, X, 846–7, and *Fr. Rolls*, 347.

22 *PPC*, V, 132.

23 *PPC*, V, 139.

24 BN, *P.O.* Nos. 548–51 Orléans.

25 Stevenson, II, part II, 569.

26 Stevenson, I, 189–94.

27 Quoted by Dufresne de Beaucourt, III, 205, who gives no source.

28 *PPC*, V, 153.

29 *PPC*, V, 167.

30 *PPC*, V, 175–6.

31 This letter, beautifully written and still very black, is BN, *Mss. fr.* 10238, fol. 76.

32 BN, *Mss. fr.* 26069, No. 4387.

33 Joursanvault, 145, and BN, *P.O.* 2158 Orléans.

34 AN, K. 68, Nos. 11 and 11 bis.

35 AN, K. 549, No. 9.

36 AN, K. 68, Nos. 11 and 11 bis—a huge document, listing the contribution demanded of each town. The much-taxed Orléans had to find 4000 *livres*.

37 Joursanvault, 146.

38 Lottin, *op. cit.* I, 298.

39 Rymer, XI, 13–14.

40 *PPC*, V, 210.

41 BM, *Add. Ch.* 4435.

42 AN, K. 67, No. 24.

43 Rymer, XI, 49–51.

44 *PPC*, VI, 32–5.

45 Rymer, XI, 60–3.

46 Rymer, XI, 53, and *Fr. Rolls*, 361.

47 Stevenson, II, 67–76.

48 Stevenson, I, 77–8.

49 Rymer, XI, 63–7. The best known text of the truce is in Monstrelet, VI, 97–107.

CHAPTER FOURTEEN

1 Laborde, 6647.

2 See Chapter XIII note 10 above. Of the other hostages, it is thought that Archambaud de Villars died in captivity. In 1448 a certain Jean Davy was

made captain of Chambord (Joursanvault, 3237 and 3238), so if he is the same man as the hostage, he obviously had been liberated too. Of the fate of Macé le Borgne and Hector de Pontbriant nothing is known.

3 AN, K. 66, No. 11.

4 *Fr. Rolls.* 321, and Monstrelet, V, 346.

5 AN, K. 64, No. 37[17]. On this letter see Delisle, *Deux Lettres, de Bertrand du Guesclin et de Jean le Bon, Comte d'Angoulême.* E. Charavay published the text of it and of the following letters on this whole matter, in *Revue des Documents Historiques,* IV, 21 *et seq.,* but omitted to say where the originals were, with the exception of that of June 11th, which is AN, K. 64, No. 37[20].

6 AN, K. 72, No. 65[5].

7 AN, K. 72, No. 56[9,10,11]. Dupont-Ferrier, 'La Captivité de Jean d'Or-léans', 71–2, accuses the English of unpardonable rapacity in this matter, as he asserts that the original indemnity had already been paid twice over. But this was certainly not so, for in July 1445 Charles gave the Duchess of Somerset his promissory note for what was still outstanding (without mentioning figures), see BM, *Add. Ch.* 3997. Dupont-Ferrier gives no authority for the figures he quotes.

8 BM, *Add. Ch.* 475 and 3980.

9 The contract, the letter and the withdrawal of Jane are all BN, *Mss. fr.* 22340, fols. 121–2. The messages to Rohan, BM, *Add. Ch.* 186–7.

10 Turin, Archivio di Stato, Negoziazioni con la Francia.

11 AN, K. 535, No. 8.

12 For this and the following, see BM, *Add. Ch.* 479; 3998; 4010.

13 See the Itinerary in Champion's *Vie.*

14 Jean de Maupoint, IV, 32, seems to be the only chronicler who mentions this. Dufresne de Beaucourt, *op. cit.* IV, 92–4, says that Suffolk, accom-panied by many English nobles, whom he names, went to Nancy to fetch Margaret, that the king accompanied her for two leagues when she left, and that her father went with her as far as Bar-le-Duc. He quotes as authorities for this a document printed by Stevenson, I, 448, and Mathieu d'Escouchy, *Chronique,* I, 86–7. But the document in Stevenson is merely an account of the expenses of Margaret's journey and subsequently established in London, and Mathieu d'Escouchy makes no reference to any such events at Nancy.

15 Mathieu d'Escouchy, I, 40 *et seq.* is the main authority for all the following events at Nancy.

16 *Le Livres des Faits de Jacques de Lalain*, in Chastellain, VIII, 38–64.

17 BN, *Mss. fr.* 5699 (formerly 10297). See also de Viriville's edition of the *Geste des Nobles*, 99–100.

18 AN, K. 553¹², 719.

19 Antonio Astesano's account of Blois is printed in *Paris et ses historiens* (ed. Le Roux de Lincy etc.), 567–9.

20 Laborde, 6663.

21 Olivier de la Marche, II, 83–104, is the main contemporary authority for the events in this chapter, together with Chastellain.

22 This letter is quoted in Bergé, *Les Ducs d'Orléans et le Conté d'Asti, Catalogue des documents conservés à Asti, Milan, Turin*, 21. Its present whereabouts is not given. Other documents, similarly unreferenced, are given in M. Faucon, 'La Domination française dans le Milanais de 1387 à 1450', which is the main authority for the events of this period.

23 BN, *Mss. fr. Nouv. Acq.* No. 20810. Delisle, *Les Collections de Bastard d'Estang*, quotes it, pp. 135–40.

24 Archives du Loiret CC 656, see p. 144 of the *Inventaire sommaire des archives communales antérieures à 1790*, ed. Veyrier du Muraud etc. (But see Chapter XII, note 39 above.)

25 Joursanvault, 568.

26 In May 1447 Charles had sent Cousinot and others to England to settle with the Duchess of Somerset how much of the original debt had been paid and what was still owing. Unfortunately the figures are not given in the document recording this, AN, K. 72, No. 56¹³. In August considerable sums were sent over to her (BM, *Add. Ch.* 4032, 4033, 12347). In January 1448 even the king came to the help of Charles and John, ordering an impost to be levied to find the money still owing (BM, *Add. Ch.* 4041, 4042). For all that, Margaret had to keep on asking and there are demands from her in 1451 and 1455 (AN, K. 72, No. 56¹⁶,²⁰⁻²³.

27 Olivier de la Marche, II, 115.

28 Archives du Loiret, CC 661, quoted in *Inventaire sommaire*, 146, and Lottin, *op. cit.* I, 300.

29 Faucon, *op. cit.* 76.

30 Laborde, 6660.

31 Laborde, 6652.

32 Lottin, *op. cit.* I, 300.

33 Faucon, *op. cit.* gives the complete text of them, 71–3. He says their authenticity has been questioned, but he himself does not doubt it. Unfortunately he does not say where the originals are.

34 See Champion, *Itinéraire* in his *Vie*.

35 Laborde, 6671.

36 BM, *Add. Ch.* 497, 4059.

37 *Fr. Rolls*, 380–1.

38 Laborde, 6674, and BN, *P.O.* 2158 Orléans, No. 588 (quoted by Champion, *Vie*, 373).

39 Olivier de la Marche, II, 170 and note 2.

40 Laborde, 6685.

41 BM, *Add. Ch.* 4062.

42 Laborde, 6709.

43 Laborde, 7007–11.

44 BN, *P.O.* 2159, Orléans, No. 603.

45 Laborde, 6698.

46 Laborde, 6699, 6700.

CHAPTER FIFTEEN

1 For this and the following items in this paragraph, Laborde, 6727; 6945; 6947; 6949; 6954; 6722; 6732.

2 Laborde, 6735, 6959.

3 Laborde, 6971. On this manuscript, which is Bibliothèque de Carpentras, No. 375, see Champion, *Poésies*, I, Introduction, xvi–xviii.

4 BN, *Mss. fr.* 20026.

5 For this and the following gifts mentioned in this paragraph, see BM, *Add. Ch.* 2624, 2625, 2634–7; AN, KK. 271, fol. 59ᵛ; Laborde, 6751, 6761; AN, KK. 271, fol. 56ᵛ, and BN, *P.O.* 2159 Orléans, No. 663; Bastard d'Estang, 844; AN, KK. 271, fol. 64; Laborde, 6778; BN, *P.O.* Orléans, 570.

6 For this and the following items mentioned in this paragraph, see Laborde, 6805; 6729; 6970; 6958.

7 Laborde, 6776, 6780, 6772.

8 Laborde, 6773, 6739.

9 Laborde, 6765.

10 On this manuscript, and its discovery or rather identification by Champion, see his *Le Manuscrit autographe des poésies de Charles d'Orléans*, and also his *Poésies*, I, Introduction, xviii–xix.

11 See Champion, *Vie*, 491–2.

12 Joursanvault, 570–84.

13 Laborde, 6795, 6800, 6804.

14 Champion, *Vie*, 454 quotes BN, *P.O.* 2846, Tiranti, Nos. 3, 4.

15 Champion, *Vie*, 505–6, quotes BN, *P.O.* 1251, Fricon, No. 6.

16 This quotation is given in La Mure, *Histoire des ducs de Bourbon*, II, 200, note (2), but it is not in the Chronicle itself.

17 BN, *Add. Ch.* 2632, 2634, 2637–40.

18 Laborde, 6771.

19 Laborde, 6934–41.

20 On this poem, of which the manuscript is BN, *Mss. fr.* 12476, fol. 73, see G. Paris, 'Un poème inédit de Martin le Franc', in *Romania*, XVI, 418 *et seq.* Also Doutrepont, *La Littérature française à la cour des ducs de Bourgogne*, 303.

21 See Champion, *Poésies*, I, Introduction, xii–xv.

22 Laborde, 6812–6941, where their wages are listed.

23 See Champion, *Poésies*, II, where, in his *Index des Noms*, 609–30, he gives what little is known of them.

24 See Champion, *François Villon*, II, 92–8; J. M. Bernard, *François Villon*, 26–9; and C. Mackworth, *François Villon*, 90–9.

25 BN, *Mss. lat.* 10286. On this manuscript see Champion, *Charles d'Orléans, joueur d'échecs*, and pp. 166–7 above.

26 Laborde, 6983–6.

27 Ibid. 6977, 6980.

28 Ibid. 6994.

29 Ibid. 6701, 6711.

30 The inventory is Laborde, 6943–67; the chain 6953.

31 Laborde, 6949.

CHAPTER SIXTEEN

1 *Rot. Parl.* V, 176–83.

2 Olivier de la Marche, II, 396.

3 Chastellain, III, 6–29, relates this whole episode, as does also Mathieu d'Escouchy, II, 264–70.

4 BN, *Mss. fr.* 5041, fol. 18 (see Dufresne de Beaucourt, *op. cit.* V, 401).

5 Louis XI, *Lettres*, I, 73–5. The earlier letter, of 1446, is 31.

6 Chastellain, III, 163–4, and Escouchy, II, 318–24, both give a good account of the events leading up to the arrest of Alençon. On the arrest itself see Chastellain, III, 100–1.

7 The text of Charles' speech at the trial is in three manuscripts. One of these, BN, *Mss. fr.* 1104 (where it is on fol. 49) is one of the manuscripts of Charles' poems (on which see Champion, *Poésies*, II, viii–xxi). The others, BN, *Mss. fr.* 5738 (fol. 17) and 5934 (fol. 33ᵛ) are accounts of the *lit de justice*; Champion, *Vie*, 542, prints the text.
Mathieu d'Escouchy, who reports the trial at length, II, 357–61, does not mention the speech, while Chastellain, III, 417–88, does not even say that Charles was present.

8 Mathieu d'Escouchy recounts the Montbazon episode and quotes the remarks of the ambassadors and the king, II, 395–416.

9 Lottin, *op. cit.* 316.

10 Lobineau, *Histoire de Bretagne*, II, cols. 1221–2.

11 Bastard d'Estang, 876.

12 Ibid. 894.

13 Laborde, 7020.

14 Louis XI, *Lettres*, II, 159–60 and 170–1. In this second letter the king clearly indicates his intention to hand over Asti to Sforza, but remarks that as it is at present "en main tierce" the matter cannot be concluded as soon as he would like.

15 Lobineau, *op. cit.* II, col. 1270.

16 Ibid. II, col. 1272.

17 Lottin, *op. cit.* 316.

18 Laborde, 7037.

19 Ibid. 7039–40.

20 J. Roman, 'Compte des obsèques et du deuil de Charles, duc d'Orléans-Valois', in *Annuaire-Bulletin de la Société de l'Histoire de France*, XXII, 225–47, published for the first time the text of a manuscript, BN, *P.O.* 2161 Orléans, in which all the funeral arrangements, and those for the construction of the tomb were described. Later, Louis XII had the body of his father, together with those of Valentina, Philip of Vertus, Mary of Cleves and Charles' first wife, Isabelle, all transferred to the chapel of the Celestines in Paris, which was destroyed at the Revolution.

21 Jean Robertet, the author of the first poem, was secretary to the Duke of Bourbon, and Guillaume Cadier, the author of the second, was also a member of the Bourbon household where his father, Jean Cadier, had been clerk-secretary to John Duke of Bourbon and had been employed on many missions to England while the duke was a prisoner there. For more details of both of them see Champion, *Poesies*, II, 627.

EPILOGUE

1 Lavisse, *Histoire de France*, Vol. V, part 1, 143.

APPENDIX TWO

1 A selection of these poems was first published in 1827 by George Watson Taylor in a limited edition for the Roxburghe Club, under the title *Poems written in English by Charles Duke of Orleans during his captivity in England after the Battle of Agincourt*. In the ensuing twenty years scholars on both sides of the channel either challenged or supported the case for the authorship of Charles. But it was left for Steele, nearly a century later, to take it up again in 1941.

2 It is tempting, because easy, to refute Steele's argument in support of his theory, but this is not the place to do so, because the subject belongs rather to the realm of poetic criticism than to biography. But it may be said that H. MacCracken, in his 'An English Friend of Charles of Orleans', makes out a far more convincing case for his own theory that the author of the English poems was the Earl of Suffolk, who had some reputation as a poet, and who might understandably have beguiled some of the hours when Charles was in his keeping at Wingfield, by making adaptations of the French poems that the duke had with him.

APPENDIX THREE

1 See *La Librairie de Charles d'Orléans*, pp. 5–114.

BIBLIOGRAPHY

The whereabouts and reference numbers of the manuscripts quoted in the text are all given in the Notes referring to them, and are therefore not repeated in this bibliography, which lists only the published sources and authorities I have consulted.

Aldwell, S. W. H., *Wingfield, its church, castle and college*, Ipswich, 1925.

Angulo, L. de, 'Charles and Jean d'Orléans: an attempt to trace the contacts between them during their captivity in England', *Miscellanea di studi e ricerche sul quattrocento francese*, Turin, 1966.

Armstrong Hall, Rev. H., 'Some notes on the personal and family history of Robert Waterton of Methley and Waterton', *Thoresby Society Publications*, 15, Leeds, 1909.

L'Art de vérifier les dates des faits historiques, etc. compiled by the Benedictines of Saint-Maur, re-issued by M. de Saint-Allais, 18 vols. Paris, 1818, 1819. (A useful authority for the lives of French nobles.)

Batteney, (?) *L'Archiviste françois*, Paris, 1775.

Baye, Nicolas de, Greffier du Parlement de Paris 1400–17, *Le Journal*, ed. A. Tuetey, for the Société de l'Histoire de France, 2 vols., Paris, 1885.

Beaufils, C., *Étude sur la vie et les poésies de Charles d'Orléans*, Coutances, 1861.

Belloc, Hilaire, *Avril, being essays on the poetry of the French Renaissance*, London, 1904.

Bernard, J.-M., *François Villon, sa vie, son œuvre, 1431–63*, Paris, 1918.

Bernier, J., *Histoire de Blois, contenant les antiquitez et singularitez du comté de Blois etc.*, Paris, 1682.

Betgé, A., *Les Ducs d'Orléans et le Comté d'Asti. Catalogue de documents conservés à Asti, Milan et Turin*, ed. for the Archives Départementales de Loir-et-Cher, Blois, 1933.

Beurrier, L., *Histoire du monastère et couvent des . . . Célestins de Paris . . . avec le testament de Louys duc d'Orléans*, Paris, 1634.

Bonamy, P. N., 'Mémoire sur le lieu, les circonstances et les suites de l'assassinat de Louis, duc d'Orléans', *Collection des meilleures dissertations relatives à l'histoire de France*, Vol. 17, Paris, 1830.

Bonet, Honoré, *L'Apparicion de Jehan de Meun*, ed. J. Pichon for the Société des Bibliophiles français, Paris, 1846.

Bourgeois de Paris, *Journal d'un bourgeois de Paris sous le règne de Charles VII*, ed. MM. Michaud et Poujoulat in *Nouvelle Collection des mémoires pour servir à l'histoire de France*, sér. 1. Vols. II & III, Paris, 1836.

Bournon, F., 'L'Hôtel Royal de Saint-Pol', *Mémoires de la Société de l'Histoire de Paris et de l'Ile-de-France*, Vol. VI, Paris, 1879.

Bruneau, C. G. E. M., *Charles d'Orléans et la poésie aristocratique*, Lyon, 1924.

Burne, A. H., *The Agincourt War*, London, 1956.

Caffin de Merouville, M., *Le Beau Dunois et son temps*, Paris, 1961.

Cagny, Perceval de, *Chroniques des ducs d'Alençon*, ed. H. Moranvillé for the Société de l'Histoire de France, Paris, 1902.

Calmette, J., *Les Grands Ducs de Bourgogne*, Paris, 1949.

Catalogue analytique des archives de M. le Baron de Joursanvault, 2 vols., Paris, 1838.

Chalvet, P. V., *Poésies de Charles d'Orléans, père de Louis XII et oncle de François Ier, rois de France*, Grenoble, 1803.

Champion, Pierre, *Le Manuscrit autographe des poésies de Charles d'Orléans*, Paris, 1907.
> *Charles d'Orléans, joueur d'échecs*, Paris, 1908.
> *La Librairie de Charles d'Orléans avec un album de fac-similés*, Paris, 1910.
> *Vie de Charles d'Orléans*, Paris, 1911.
> *François Villon*, 2 vols., Paris, 1913.
> *Les Poésies de Charles d'Orléans*, 2 vols., Paris, 1923, 1924, reprinted 1956. (References are to the reprint.)
> *Histoire poétique du XVe siècle*, 2 vols. Paris, 1923
> 'La Dame anglaise de Charles d'Orléans', *Romania*, Vol. XLIX, Paris, 1923.
> *Splendeurs et misères de Paris, XIV–XV siècles*, Paris, 1934.

Champollion-Figeac, A., *Les Poésies du duc Charles d'Orléans*, Paris, 1842.
> *Louis et Charles, ducs d'Orléans, leur influence sur les arts, la littérature et l'esprit de leur siècle*, Paris, 1844.

Champollion-Figeac, J. J., see *Lettres de rois, etc.*

Charavay E., 'Jean d'Orléans, comte d'Angoulême,' *Revue des Documents Historiques, suite de pièces curieuses et inédites*, ed. with notes and commentaries by E. Charavay, Paris, 1877.

Charpier, J., *Charles d'Orléans*, Paris, 1958.

Chastellain, Georges, *Œuvres*, ed. Kervyn de Lettenhove, 8 vols., Brussels, 1863–6.

Chevillard, J., *Généalogie de Messeigneurs les Princes, Ducs de Bourgogne, Anjou et Berry*, Paris, 1700.

Choix de pièces inédites relatives au règne de Charles VI, ed. L. Douët d'Arcq, 2 vols., Paris, 1863–4.

Collas, E., *Valentine de Milan*, Paris, 1911.

Cook, J. Travis, *The Story of the De la Poles*, Hull, 1888.

Copinger, W. A., *County of Suffolk. Its history as disclosed by existing records and other documents*, 5 vols., London, 1904, 1905. (Vol. V on Wingfield.)

Cosneau, E., *Le Connétable de Richemont*, Paris, 1886.

Cousinot, Guillaume, *Fragments de la Geste des Nobles François*, ed. A. Vallet de Viriville, Paris, 1859.

Croy, J. de, *Nouveaux Documents pour l'histoire de la création des résidences royales des bords de la Loire*, Blois, 1894.
'Notes sur l'emplacement de la Chambre des Comptes du Château de Blois', *Revue du Loir-et-Cher*, mai-juin, Blois, 1906.
'Notices biographiques' in 'Cartulaire de la Ville de Blois', ed. J. Soyer and G. Trouillard, *Mémoires de la Société des Sciences et des Lettres de Loir-et-Cher*, Vol. XVII, Blois, 1903–7.
'Un Portrait de Charles d'Orléans', *Mémoires de la Société des Sciences et des Lettres de Loir-et-Cher*, Vol. XIX, Blois, 1909.

Crump, W. B., 'Methley Hall and its builders', *Thoresby Society Publications*, 37, Leeds, 1945.

Davies, J. G. G., *Henry V*, London, 1935.

Delisle, Léopold, *Le Cabinet des Manuscrits de la Bibliothèque Impériale*, 3 vols., Paris, 1868–81.
Deux Lettres, de Bertrand du Guesclin et de Jean le bon, comte d'Angoulême, 1369 et 1444, Paris, 1884.
Les Collections de Bastard d'Estang à la Bibliothèque Nationale, Nogent-le-Rotrou, 1885.

Deschamps, Eustache, *Œuvres complètes*, ed. by Le Marquis de Queux de Saint-Hilaire and M. G. Raynaud, 10 vols., Paris, 1878–1903.

Dickinson, J. G., *The Congress of Arras, 1435*, Oxford, 1955.

Douët d'Arcq, L., 'Document inédit sur l'assassinat de Louis duc d'Orléans', *Annuaire-bulletin de la Société de l'Histoire de France*, Paris, 1864.
Comptes de l'Hôtel des rois de France au 14e et 15e siècles, ed. for the Société de l'Histoire de France, Paris, 1865.
See also *Choix de pièces, etc.*

Doutrepont, G., *La Littérature française à la cour des ducs de Bourgogne*, Paris, 1906.

Dufresne de Beaucourt, G. (Marquis), *Histoire de Charles VII*, 6 vols., Paris, 1885, etc.

Dupont-Ferrier, G., 'La Date de la naissance de Jean d'Orléans, comte d'Angoulême', *Bibliothèque de l'École des Chartes*, Vol. LVI, Paris, 1895.
'La Captivité de Jean d'Orléans, comte d'Angoulême (1412–45)', *Revue Historique*, vol. LXII, Paris, 1896.
'Jean d'Angoulême d'après sa bibliothèque (1467)' *Bibliothèque de la Faculté des Lettres de Paris*, 1897.

Du Port, Jean, sieur des Rosiers, 'La Vie de Jean d'Orléans, dit le bon', ed. E. Castaigne, *Bulletin de la Société archéologique et historique de la Charente*, 1847, printed Angoulême, 1862. (Du Port's book first appeared in 1589.)

Durrieu, P., (Count), *Le Boccace de Munich*, Paris, 1909.

Ellis, Sir Henry, *Original Letters Illustrative of English History*, London, 1824.

Escouchy, Mathieu d', *Chronique*, ed. G. Dufresne de Beaucourt for the Société de l'Histoire de France, 3 vols., Paris, 1863.

Estancelin, L., *Histoire des Comtes d'Eu*, Dieppe and Paris, 1828.

Faucon, M., 'La Domination française dans le Milanais de 1387 à 1450', ext. from *Archives des missions scientifiques et littéraires*, 3e sér., Vol. VIII, Paris, 1882.

Favyn, A., *Le Théâtre d'Honneur et de Chevalerie*, 2 vols., Paris, 1620.

Fenin, Pierre de, *Mémoires*, ed. Mlle Dupont for the Société de l'Histoire de France, Paris, 1837.

French Rolls, Calendar of, 48th Report of the Deputy Keeper of the Public Records, London, 1887.

Froissart, Sir J., *Chroniques*, ed. T. Johnes, London, 1805.

Godefroy, Denys, ed. and annotator of Juvenal des Ursins' *Histoire de Charles VI*, Paris, 1653. (See under Juvenal des Ursins for another edition of his history.)

Goodrich, Norma Lorre, *Charles Duke of Orleans: A literary biography*, New York, 1963.

Gruel, Guillaume, *Chronique d'Arthur de Richemont*, ed. Le Vavasseur for the Société de l'Histoire de France, Paris, 1883.

Guessard, F., 'Gauluet, Pierre de Mornay, c. 1360–1423', *Bibliothèque de l'École des Chartes*, 2e sér. Vol. IV, Paris, 1847–8.

Guichard, J.-M., *Les Poésies de Charles d'Orléans*, 2nd ed., Paris, 1857. (The first edition appeared in 1842, the same year as that of Champollion-Figeac.)

Hammond, E., 'Charles of Orleans and Anne Molyneux', *Modern Philology*, Vol. XXII, Chicago, 1924.

Héricault, Charles d', *Poésies complètes de Charles d'Orléans*, 2 vols., Paris, 1874.

Hibbert, C., *Agincourt*, London, 1964.

History of the King's Works, The, Vol. II (for Bolingbroke Castle), London, 1963.

Huillard-Bréholles, J. L. A., *La Rançon du duc de Bourbon, Jean I, 1415–36*, Paris, 1869.

Jacobs, E. F., *Henry V and the invasion of France*, London, 1948.
The Fifteenth Century 1399–1485 (Vol. VI of the *Oxford History of England*), Oxford, 1961.

Jarry, E., *La Vie politique de Louis de France, duc d'Orléans, 1372–1407*, Paris, Orléans, 1889.
'Le Mariage de Louis d'Orléans et de Valentine Visconti', *Bibliothèque de l'École des Chartes*, Vol. LXII, Paris, 1901.

Joubert, A., *Documents inédits sur la Guerre de Cent Ans, Négociations relatives à l'échange de Charles, duc d'Orléans, et de Jean, comte d'Angoulême . . . contre les seigneurs anglais . . .* Angers, 1890.

Juvenal des Ursins, Jean, *Histoire de Charles VI Roy de France etc.*, ed. MM. Michaud et Poujoulat in *Nouvelle Collection des Mémoires pour servir à l'histoire de France*, sér. 1. Vol. II, Paris, 1836.

Kingsford, C. L., *Henry V, the typical medieval hero*, London, 1901.
Chronicles of London, Oxford, 1905.
English historical literature in the fifteenth century, Oxford, 1913.

Laborde, L. de, (Comte), *Les Ducs de Bourgogne: études sur les lettres, les arts et l'industrie pendant le XVe siècle*, Paris, 1849–52.
Glossaire français du moyen-âge, Paris, 1872.

La Marche, Olivier de, *Mémoires*, ed. H. Beaune and J. d'Arbaumont for the Société de l'Histoire de France, 2 vols., Paris, 1883–8.

La Mure, J. M. de, *Histoire des ducs de Bourbon*, 4 vols., Paris, Lyon, 1860–97.

Lecocq, G., *Étude historique sur Valentine de Milan*, Saint-Quentin, 1875.
Étude historique sur Marie de Clèves, Saint-Quentin, 1875.

Le Fèvre, Jean, Seigneur de Saint-Rémy, *Chronique*, ed. F. Morand for the Société de l'Histoire de France, 2 vols., Paris, 1876–81.

le Maire, François, *Histoire et antiquitez de la ville et duché d'Orléans*, 2 vols., Orléans, 1648.

Le Religieux de Saint Denys, *Chronique*, ed. in Latin and trans. L. Bellaguet, 6 vols., Paris, 1839–52.

Le Roux de Lincy, A. and Tisserand, L. M., *Paris et ses historiens aux XIVe et XVe siècles*, Paris, 1866.

Lettres de rois, reines et autres personnages des cours de France et Angleterre . . . tirées des archives de Londres par Bréquigny, ed. J. J. Champollion-Figeac, 2 vols., Paris, 1866.

Lobineau, G. A., *Histoire de Bretagne*, 2 vols., Paris, 1702.

Lottin, D. (Père), *Recherches historiques sur la ville d'Orléans*, 4 Parts, Orléans, 1836–42. (Part I only for 14th and 15th centuries.)

Louis XI, roi de France, *Lettres*, 11 vols., ed. J. Vaesen for the Société de l'Histoire de France, Paris, 1883–1909.

MacCracken, H. N., 'An English friend of Charles of Orleans', *Publications of the Modern Language Association of America*, Vol. XXVI, New Series, Vol. XIX, Baltimore, 1911.

Mackworth, C., *François Villon*, London, 1947.

Mars, N. (Dom), *Histoire du royal monastère de Sainct-Lomer de Blois*, Blois, 1869. (1st pub. 1646.)

Maupoint, Jean, *Journal parisien*, ed. G. Fagniez for the Société de l'Histoire de Paris, Vol. IV, Paris, 1877, printed 1878.

Maupré, F. and Doinel, J., *Département du Loiret, Inventaire sommaire des archives départementales antérieures à 1790*, Loiret, 1878.

Mazas, A., *Vies des grands capitaines français du moyen-âge*, 7 vols., Paris, 1828, 1829.

Merlet, Lucien, 'Biographie de Jean de Montagu, Grand Maître de France (1350–1409)', *Bibliothèque de l'École des Chartes*, 3e sér. Vol. III, Sept.-Oct. Paris, 1851.

Mirot, L., 'Isabelle de France, reine d'Angleterre, duchesse d'Orléans', *Revue d'Histoire diplomatique*, Paris, 1904, 1905.

Monstrelet, Enguerrand de, *Chronique*, ed. L. Douët d'Arcq for the Société de l'Histoire de France, 6 vols., Paris, 1857–62.

Moranvillé, E., 'Remontrances de l'université de la ville de Paris à Charles VI sur le gouvernement du royaume', *Bibliothèque de l'École des Chartes*, Vol. LI, Paris, 1890.

Mowat, R. B., *Henry the fifth*, London, 1919.

Nicolas, Sir Nicholas H., *History of the Battle of Agincourt and of the Expedition of Henry the fifth into France in 1415*, London, 1827 (2nd. ed. 1852).
See also *Proceedings and Ordinances, etc.*

Oman, Sir C., *The Political History of England*, Vol. IV, London, 1906.

Ordonnances des roys de France de la troisième race, 23 vols., Paris, 1733–1847. Vols. VIII & IX for *ordonnances* of Charles VI, 1404–11, 1751.

O'Reilly, E., *Les Deux Procès de Jeanne d'Arc*, 2 vols., Paris, 1868.

Ouy, G., 'Recherches sur la librairie de Charles d'Orléans et de Jean d'Angoulême pendant leur captivité en Angleterre, et études de deux manuscrits autographes de Charles identifiés', *Compte Rendu de l'Académie des Inscriptions et Belles-Lettres*, Paris, 1955.

Paradin, C., *Devises héroïques et emblèmes*, Paris, 1622.

Paris, G., 'Un Poème inédit de Martin le Franc', *Romania*, Vol. XVI, 17e année, Paris, 1887.

Paston Letters, ed. James Gairdner, 4 vols. London, Exeter, 1904.

Patent Rolls, Calendar of, Henry VI, 1429–36 and 1436–41, London, 1905–7.

Perroy, E., *La Guerre de Cent Ans*, Paris, 1945.

Pisan, Christine de, *Le livre des fais et bonnes meurs du sage Roy Charles V*, ed. MM. Michaud et Poujoulat, *Nouvelle Collection des Mémoires pour servir à l'histoire de France*, Ie. sér., Vol. II, Paris, 1836.

Plancher, U., *Histoire de Bourgogne*, 4 vols., Dijon, 1739–87.

Porcher, J., *Chefs-d'œuvre de l'enluminure française du 15e siècle*, Paris, 1951

Proceedings and Ordinances of the Privy Council of England, 1386–1542, ed. Sir N. Harris Nicolas, 7 vols., London, 1834–7.

Ramsay, Sir J. H., *Lancaster and York, 1399–1485*, 2 vols., Oxford, 1892. (His bibliography contains useful notes on the chroniclers.)

Raymond, P., 'Enquête du Prévôt de Paris sur l'assassinat de Louis, duc d'Orléans', *Bibliothèque de l'École des Chartes*, 6e sér. Vol. I, Paris, 1865.

Reynaud, G., *Les Cent Ballades*, Paris, 1905.

Renan, J. E., *Valentine de Milan, Christine de Suède, deux énigmes*, Abbeville, 1923.

Roman, J., 'Compte des obsèques et du deuil de Charles duc d'Orléans-Valois', *Annuaire-bulletin de la Société de l'Histoire de France*, Paris, 1885.
Inventaire et documents relatifs aux joyaux et tapisseries des Princes d'Orléans-Valois, 1389–1481, Paris, 1894.

Rotuli Parliamentorum, Henry IV–Henry VI, 6 vols, London, 1767–77.

Rymer, Thomas, *Foedera, Conventiones et Litterae*, 20 vols., London, 1705, etc.

Sallier, l'abbé, *Mémoires de l'Académie Royale des Inscriptions et Belles-Lettres*, Vol. XIII, Paris, 1740.

Samaran, C., 'La Maison d'Armagnac au XVe siècle', *Mémoires et documents publiés par la Société de l'École des Chartes*, VII, Paris, 1907.

Sauval, H., *Histoire et recherches des antiquités de la ville de Paris*, 3 vols., Paris, 1724.

Seaton, Dr. M. E., *Studies in Villon, Vaillant and Charles d'Orléans*, Oxford, 1957.

Sellier, C., *Le Quartier Barbette, Monographie historique d'une région de Paris*, Paris, 1899.

Soyer, J., *Étude sur la communauté des habitants de Blois en l'an 1404,* Blois 1894.

Steele, R. R., 'The English Poems of Charles d'Orléans', *Early English Text Society,* Orig. series, Nos. 215 and 220, Oxford, 1941.

Stevenson, J., *Letters and Papers illustrative of the wars of the English in France,* 3 vols., London, 1861–4.

Stevenson, R. L., *Familiar Studies of Men and Books,* London, 1882.

Taylor, G. W., *Poems written in English by Charles Duke of Orleans,* published for the Roxburghe Club, London, 1827.

Thibault, M., *Isabeau de Bavière,* Paris, 1903.

Thomas, A., 'Les Premiers Vers de Charles d'Orléans', *Romania,* Vol. XXII, Paris, 1893.

Vallet de Viriville, A., *Histoire de Charles VII, 1405–61,* 3 vols., Paris, 1862–1865.

Vaughan, R., *Philip the Bold,* London, 1962.

Veyrier du Muraud, Bonnardot et autres, *Département du Loiret, Ville d'Orléans, Inventaire sommaire des archives communales antérieures à 1790,* Orléans, 1907.

Vitry, P., 'Un Portrait de Dunois', *Revue de l'art ancien et moderne,* Paris, 1903.

Wallis, C., *Charles d'Orléans: A selection of poems,* (trans.), London, 1951.

Waurin, Jean de, Seigneur du Forestel, *Recueil des Croniques et anchiennes istories de la Grant Bretainge a présent nommé engleterre,* ed. W. and E. L. C. P. Hardy, 5 vols., 1864–91.

Williams, R. Carleton, *My Lord of Bedford, 1389–1435,* London, 1963.

INDEX

Page references are only given for the most significant events in the lives of the main characters mentioned. Men are listed under their titles or surnames, with one or two exceptions, e.g. the Dukes of Burgundy, better known by their Christian names and sobriquets. Women are listed under their Christian names. Persons of minor importance are not listed. Names mentioned in the Appendices are not listed.

AGINCOURT, battle of, 125–9

ALBRET, Charles, Count of, 45, 53, 75; killed at Agincourt, 129

ALENÇON, John (I), first Count, then Duke of: leads Valentina to Charles VI, 40; signs treaty with Charles at Gien, 60; signs alliance with Henry IV, 78; goes to meet Clarence and the English, 83; pays expenses of embassy to Charles VI, 91; created duke, 102–3; killed at Agincourt, 127–8

ALENÇON, John (II), Duke of: recruited (aged 14) by Philip of Vertus to fight for dauphin, 147; betrothed to Jane of Orleans, 157; taken prisoner at Verneuil, 162; released and helps Joan of Arc, 174; sells Fougères to Duke of Brittany, 174; made member of Order of Golden Fleece, 252; first suspicions of treason, 260–1; present at Treaty of Tours meeting, 269; gives evidence at Joan of Arc's rehabilitation, 324; his treason and trial at Vendôme, 330–4

AMPTHILL, 177

ANGOULÊME, John, Count of: born, 21; possible author of a poem, 25; accompanies Valentina to plead for justice, 40; given as hostage to Clarence, 86; *Geste des Nobles* written for, 135; transferred to Duchess of Clarence, 163; Dunois' attempt to free him, 179; given permission to visit his brother Charles, 224; transferred to keeping of Somerset and taken to Cherbourg, 272; his letters to Charles and Dunois, 272–5; liberated, 275; visits court at Nancy, 278–9; marries Margaret of Rohan, 288; fights in Gironde, 326; accompanies Charles in funeral rites of Charles VII, 338

ANJOU, Louis (II), Duke of: hears John the Fearless confess to murder, 35; restrains fellow princes from pursuing him, 36; agrees to go on mission to him, 40; dies, 142

ANJOU, Louis (III), Duke of: recruited (aged 15) by Philip of Vertus to fight for dauphin, 147; his death, footnote, 199

ANJOU, René, Duke of: vouches for Charles' knowledge of English, 209; first meeting with Charles, 167; exchanges poems at Blois, 269; at Treaty of Tours meeting, 269; visited by Charles at Tarascon, 285; at Blois again, 321–2; speaks for assembled princes at Tours, 342

ANNE, sister of Philip the Good of Burgundy: marries the Duke of Bedford, 160; dies, 188

ANNE MOLINS, 213–16

ARGUEIL, Guillaume de Châlons, lord of: husband of Catherine of Étampes, helps Charles with troops in Italy, 285

ARMAGNAC, Bernard, Count of: signs treaty with Charles and his brothers, 59–60; fights in Orleanist cause, 72–5; not at Agincourt, 126; defends Paris against John the Fearless, 137–8; blockades Harfleur, 139; made Constable, 146; killed in Paris, 146

ARRAS: siege and surrender of, and peace made between Burgundians and royalist allies, 97–100; peace conference between English and French fails, 204–5; Treaty of, between Philip the Good and Charles VII, 248–9; Charles of Orleans swears to it, 249

ARUNDEL, Earl of: sent to help John the Fearless, 73

ASTESANO, Antonio: describes Blois, 279; meets Charles in Asti, 286; travels and acts as secretary to him, 287; at court of Blois, 298

ASTI: part of Valentina's dowry, 4; developments at, 281–90

AUXERRE: Peace of, 81–2

BARBETTE, Hôtel de, 33

BASTARD OF ORLEANS, THE. See Dunois

BAUGÉ, battle of, 156

BAVARIA, Louis, Duke of: brother of Queen Isabeau, 5; taken prisoner by the butchers, 90; released, 92

BAYE, Nicolas de: clerk of the Parlement, 35; records cold winter, 41; comments on Peace of Chartres, 55–6

BEAUFORT, Cardinal: at Calais for Gravelines conference, 227–30

BEAUFORT, Edmund: captured at Baugé, 156

BEAUFORT, Thomas: 156, 178–9

BEAUJEU, Pierre de: adopted by Charles, 296–7; betrothed to his daughter Mary, 339; leads funeral procession of Charles, 343

BEDFORD, John, Duke of: made Governor of Normandy and Regent of France, 157; chief and only mourner at funeral of Charles VI, 159; marries Anne of Burgundy, 160; dies, 205

BERRY, John, Duke of: character, 6; hears John the Fearless confess to murder, 35; goes on a mission to him, 40; signs treaty with Charles and fellow princes at Gien, 60; signs alliance with Henry IV, 78; cancels it, 80; asked by the people to govern Paris, 90–1; receives Henry V's ambassadors, 115; dies, 142

BOLINGBROKE, castle of: 159 and Chapter IX, passim

BONET, Honoré, 16, 17

BONNE, of Armagnac: betrothed to Charles, 61; marriage contract, 61; married, 74; receives a gold ring from him, 87; probable subject of his poetry, 107–9; her whereabouts, 109; probable subject of Charles' poems, 167–71; dies, 180; probable subject of more poems, 180

BOUCICAUT, Marshal: friend of Louis of Orleans, 23; taken prisoner at Agincourt, 128; in keeping of Waterton, 145; at Fotheringhay, 151; dies, 161

BOURBON, Louis (II), Duke of: brings up nephews Charles VI and Louis of Orleans, 5; refuses mission to John the Fearless, 40; grief-stricken at death of Jean de Montagu, 59; dies, 62

BOURBON, John (I), Duke of (previously Count of Clermont); joins allies of Charles, 72; signs their alliance with Henry IV, 78; creates an order of knighthood for lovers of women, 104; taken prisoner at Agincourt, 129; falconers sent him, 134; secret attempt to persuade Henry V to let him return to France, on conditions, 140–1; allowed to go to Dieppe, 153; returns to England, ill, 161; sent with Charles to Dover, 189–92; Charles' poems to him, 190–2; dies, 192

BOURBON, Charles, Duke of: as Count of Clermont, aged 15, joins Vertus to fight for dauphin, 147; leads the Praguerie, 238; as Duke meets Philip the Good at Nevers meeting, 203; retires from public life with gout, 296; dies, 296

BOURBON, John (II), Duke of: as Count of Clermont (Clermondois) favourite of Charles of Orleans, 303; aged 17 made member of King's Council, 303; marries king's daughter Jane, 304; made lieutenant-governor of Gironde, and exchanges poems with Charles, 304; leading part in final French victories of Hundred Years War, 326

BRABANT, Anthony, Duke of: brother of John the Fearless, 65; helps negotiate Peace of Arras, 98; and again in Paris, 117; killed at Agincourt, 128

BRITTANY, John (V), Duke of: signs treaty with Valentina and Charles, 43–4; shows disgust with John the Fearless, 44; signs treaty with Charles and allies at Gien, 60; arrives at Agincourt too late for battle, 126; signs treaty with dauphin at Sablé, 156; but also Treaty of Troyes with Philip the Good, 157; intermediary in release of Charles, 219, 225; made member of Order of Golden Fleece, 251; dies, 263, 267

BRITTANY, Francis (I), Duke of: present at Treaty of Tours meeting, 269

BURTON, Thomas: warden of Fotheringhay, given charge of Charles, 151; brings him to London, 153

BUZANÇAIS, Treaty of, 85

CABOCHE, and cabochiens: lead riots in Paris, 89–91; imprisoned or flee, 94; their pardon agreed by Peace of Arras, 117

CAILLAU, Dr. Jean: gives Charles books, 165; in Asti with him, 286; called to Charles in his last illness, 340

CAMAIL, Order of the: 105; that of Dunois, 155; given to Philip the Good, 251

CATHERINE, daughter of Margaret Countess of Étampes: wife to Guillaume of Argueil, 285; copy of Charles' poems made for her, 296

CELESTINES, Convent of: Louis of Orleans builds a chapel there, 13; is buried there, 35; Valentina's heart taken there, 49

CHARLES VI: organises coronation procession for Isabeau, 3; first attack of madness, 10; forgives John the Fearless, 45; leads army to Bourges, 78–9; forces Charles and his allies to cancel English alliance, 80; leads army to siege of Arras, 97; seized by Burgundians in Paris, 146; dies and is buried, 159

CHARLES VII: when known as dauphin is rescued from massacre in Paris by Tanguy du Châtel, 147; crowned in Rheims, 175; begins to resent power of nobles, 258, 263; benevolent and generous to Charles, 264; dies at Méhun-sur-Yèvre, 337; his funeral procession and burial, 338–9

CHARLES, Count of Charolois, son of Philip the Good: marriage to Isabella of Bourbon, 327–8

CHARTRES, Peace of, 53–6

CHÂTEL, Tanguy du: appointed Provost of Paris, 92; saves dauphin, 147

CLARENCE, Thomas, Duke of: sent to France to negotiate alliance with Charles and allies, 77, 78; leads expedition to France, 83; negotiates Treaty of Buzançais, 85; taken ill at Harfleur, 121; killed at battle of Baugé, 156

CLARENCE, Duchess of: refuses to exchange prisoners, 156; John of Angoulême transferred to her keeping, 163; connection with Thomas Beaufort, 178, 179

COBHAM, Sir Reynold: Charles in his keeping, 218

COMBERWORTH, Sir Thomas: given charge of Charles at Bolingbroke, 159, 161; takes him to Ampthill, 177

CORNWALL, Sir John: goes with Clarence's expedition to France, 83; exacts a payment at Treaty of Buzançais, 85; Charles transferred to his care, 177; created Lord Fanhope, 186; accompanies Charles on his return to France, 244; again exacts money, 252

COUSINOT, Guillaume, Chancellor of Duchy of Orleans: helps Valentina plead her case, 41, 47; head of Charles' Council, 135; author of Geste des Nobles, 135; for his most important acts, 151–2, 155, 156, 182, 282

DESCHAMPS, Eustache: praises Valentina, 5; member of her household, 23–4

DOUGLAS, Earl of: brings reinforcements for dauphin, 162; killed at battle of Verneuil, 162

DUNOIS, John, Count of: brought up by Valentina, 28; her view of him, 49; taken prisoner in Paris by Burgundians, 155; joins dauphin's army on release, 155; with Joan of Arc at siege of Orleans, 175; takes Suffolk prisoner at Jargeau, 175; releases him, 179; meets Charles at Calais, 228; his efforts to free John of Angoulême, 274–6; as captain of king's army captures Le Mans, 286, and Rouen, 289; gives evidence at Joan of Arc's rehabilitation, 324; victor at battle of Formigny, 326; obliged to arrest Alençon and attend *lit de justice*, 331–2

ESSARTS, Pierre des: appointed Provost of Paris, 45; arrests Montagu, 58; removed from his post, 65; reappointed, 73; beheaded by Parisians, 90
ÉTAMPES, Richard of: marries Margaret, sister of Charles of Orleans, 156; dies, 252
EU, Charles, Count of: signs pact with Charles of Orleans, 92; prisoner at Agincourt, 129; Henry V in will forbids his release, 158; is exchanged for Somerset and freed, 226
EXETER, Thomas Beaufort, Duke of: as Earl of Dorset and Admiral of England goes with Clarence to France, 83, 85; made Governor of Paris, 167

FOTHERINGHAY, Castle of: Charles, Eu, Richemont and Boucicaut kept there, 151
FOUGÈRES, town and castle of: Duke of Alençon sells to Brittany, 174
FRANCIS OF ÉTAMPES, son of Richard and Margaret: pensioned by Charles, 296; at Blois, 298, 303; becomes Duke of Brittany, 335; supports Charles of Orleans and John of Angoulême against Sforza of Milan, 337; arouses enmity of Louis XI, 341–2

GARBET, Nicolas: Schoolmaster of Charles and Philip, 21 and 24; writes a poem at wedding of Charles, 32
GARENCIÈRES, Jean, Marquis of: Chamberlain of Louis of Orleans, 23; exchanges poems with Charles, 103
GAUCOURT, Raoul, Lord of: negotiates and signs Treaty of Buzançais with the English, 84–5; Governor of Harfleur, 121; sent to England as a prisoner, 131; Henry V's deathbed refusal to release him, 158; is exchanged with Earl of Huntingdon and freed, 163; with Joan of Arc, 174
GAULUET (Pierre de Mornay): Chancellor of Duchy of Orleans, 38; receives queen and princes there, 49; recruits troops for Charles, 91; goes with Charles to Agincourt, 122; made Marshal, 135
GERSON, Jean: Chancellor of University of Paris: condemns Jean Petit and defends reputation of Louis of Orleans, 101
GLOUCESTER, Humphrey, Duke of: wounded by Alençon at Agincourt, 128; appointed Lord Protector, 160; causes breakdown of Gravelines conference, 230; protests against liberation of Charles, 236–8, 243
GOWER, Thomas: keeper of John of Angoulême, 272, 275
GROOMBRIDGE: John of Angoulême at, 271

HAINAULT, Count of: arranges Chartres meeting, 53; at Agincourt, 125; visits London with Sigismund, 139

HENRY IV: sends Arundel to help John the Fearless, 73; makes alliance with Charles and fellow princes, 77

HENRY V: his conversations with Charles after Agincourt, 130–1; chapters seven and eight, *passim*

HENRY VI: born, 158; crowned in Westminster, 176; and in Paris, 180; gives reasons for liberating Charles, 240–1

HOSTAGES, names of, 86

HUNTINGDON, Earl of: captured at Baugé, 156; freed in exchange for Gaucourt, 163

ISABEAU OF BAVARIA, Queen: her coronation procession, 3–9; sides with Louis of Orleans against John the Fearless, 30; and with latter against her son Charles VII, 146

ISABELLA OF PORTUGAL: passes through London on way to marry Philip the Good, 176; assures Parisians of her desire for peace, 203–4; arranges and presides peace conference at Château d'Oye, 227–31; greets Charles on his return to France, 247

ISABELLE OF FRANCE: born, 9; Queen of England, 29; marries Charles, 30–2; accompanies Valentina to plead for justice, 40; gives birth to Jane, 56; dies, 56

JANE OF BOULOGNE, Duchess of Berry: saves life of Charles VI, 13

JANE OF ORLEANS, Duchess of Alençon: born, 57; betrothed to John (II) of Alençon, 156; meets Joan of Arc, 174; dies, 180

JOAN OF ARC: 172–5; given robe by Orleans Council, 175; captured, 178; tried and burnt, 178–9; her mother, 256; rehabilitation begun, 324

JOHN THE FEARLESS, Duke of Burgundy: character, 29; marries daughter Margaret to dauphin Louis, 29; confesses to murder of Louis of Orleans, 35; justifies it, 44–5; forces Charles to accept Peace of Chartres, 53–5; given authority over dauphin, 60; obtains help from Henry IV, 73; at siege of Bourges, 79; and Arras, 99–100; absent from Agincourt, 121; besieges Paris, 137–8; assassinated, 149

LALAIN, Jacques: at Nancy, 278; at Ghent, 281

LANNOY, Hue de: his despatch from London, 194–8; welcomes Charles to Order of Golden Fleece, 251; they meet again at Ghent, 281

LIVRE CONTRE TOUT PÉCHÉ, LE, 24–5

LOUIS, dauphin: marries Margaret of Burgundy, 29; presides at hearing of Jean Petit, 44; put under authority of John the Fearless, 60; asked by butchers to rule, 73; flouts Burgundy at Bourges, 79; and in Paris, 90; forces Charles to agree Peace of Arras, 99–100; his character, 117–18, 138; tries to defend Paris, 137; dies, 138

LOUIS XI: when dauphin sides with Praguerie, 238; crowned, 338; his dislike of Charles, 339–342

LOUIS XII, son of Charles: born, 339; christened, 339. See also Epilogue

LYS, Pierre du, brother of Joan of Arc, 290

MARGARET OF ANJOU: betrothed to Henry VI, 270; married (Suffolk proxy), 277

MARGARET, COUNTESS OF HAINAULT: present at double wedding of Charles and of her daughter Jacqueline, 30–1; helps make Peace of Arras, 98; and in Paris, 117; see Charles again, 254

MARGARET OF ORLEANS, sister of Charles: born, 31; marries Richard of Étampes, 156

MARGARET OF ROHAN: marries John of Angoulême, 295

MARGARET OF SAVOY, widow of Louis III, Duke of Anjou: possible marriage to Charles of Orleans or John of Angoulême, 276

MARIETTE D'ENGHIEN, wife of Albert de Cany: probable mother of Dunois, 28

MARY OF CLEVES: marries Charles, 250; at Nevers conference, 263; at Nancy, 278; adopts Valentina's emblems, 291–2; her tastes and treasures, 292–3

MARY OF ORLEANS, daughter of Charles: born, 322; received in Orleans, 336; Villon's poem to, 336

MAXEY: John of Angoulême sent there, 163

MONTAGU, Jean de: Grand Master of Household, 57; executed, 58, body taken down, 83

MONTGOMERY, Sir Nicolas: given custody of Charles, 151, and Bourbon, 151, 153

MORTEMART, see Rochechouart

NEVERS, important meetings at, 203, 261–4, 328–9

NEVERS, Philip, Count of, brother of John the Fearless: made Great Chamberlain, 63; marries sister of Count of Eu, 92; killed at Agincourt, 129

Nevers, Charles, Count of, son of Philip: at Blois, 301–2

ORDONNANCE CABOCHIENNE, 89

ORLEANS, Louis, Duke of: as Duke of Touraine marries Valentina, 3; his houses, in Paris, 11; exchanges Duchy of Touraine for that of Orleans, 12; his library, 22; his wills, 27; father of John, later Count of Dunois, 30; at marriage of Charles, 31; murdered, 33; buried in chapel of Celestines, 35; obsequies celebrated and character cleared, 100–1

PARIS, Peace of, 66; state entry of Charles and allies, 94

PETIT, Jean: defends John the Fearless, 44–5; defence examined and burnt, 95, 96, 101

PHILIP THE BOLD, Duke of Burgundy: seizes power, 11, dies 29

PHILIP THE GOOD, Duke of Burgundy: when Count of Charolois kept from Agincourt, 125; succeeds to dukedom, 150; allows his wife Isabella to organise and preside peace conference at Château d'Oye, 227–31; exchanges *ballades* with Charles, 232–5, 239; receives him on his return to France, 247–53; organises conference of princes at Nevers, 261–4; helps Charles during his Italian visits, 284, 285, 287, 288; asks Charles for help 328–9; protests to Charles VII at Montbazon, 335; at coronation of Louis XI, 338

POETS AT COURT OF BLOIS, 299–303

POITEVIN, Robert, the queen's doctor: attends Charles, 286, 340

PONTEFRACT, castle, 145

PONTOISE, Peace of, 92

RANSOM FOR CHARLES, first mention of, 204–5

RETENUE D'AMOURS, LA, 105–8

RICHEMONT, Arthur, Count of: joins Charles' army, 64; prisoner at Agincourt, 129; in keeping of Waterton, 145, and Burton, 151; released to try and secure loyalty of brother the Duke of Brittany, 153; marries Margaret, sister of Philip the Good, 160; but joins dauphin, 163; made Constable and succeeds to Dukedom of Brittany, 332; at Vendôme in 1458, but not at *lit de justice,* 332; pleads for Alençon's wife and children, 334; to Fontevrault with Charles, 334–5; dies, 335

ROCHECHOUART, John of, Lord of Mortemart: agrees to store and sell Charles' books and other goods, 164; his brother returns the books, 280

SABLÉ, Treaty of, 156

SIGISMUND, Emperor: visits London to try and make peace, 138; signs alliance with Henry V, and leaves, 139; Henry writes secret letter to, 140

SOMERSET, Earl of: captured at Baugé, 156; exchanged with Eu and freed, 225; John of Angoulême transferred to his keeping, 272; appointed lieutenant-general for France, 272; dies, 273

LE SONGE EN COMPLAINTE, 221–4

STERBOROUGH CASTLE, 218–19

STEWART, Sir John, Earl of Buchan: 97; helps Vertus and dauphin with Scottish archers, 148; killed at battle of Verneuil, 162

STOURTON, Sir John: Charles transferred to, 225; takes him to Calais, 227

SUFFOLK, William, Earl of: taken prisoner by Dunois at Jargeau, 175; released, 179; takes charge of Charles, 186; marries Alice Chaucer, 187; allows Charles to see de Lannoy, 195–7; leads English embassy to France and makes Treaty of Tours, 267–70; created Marquess and acts proxy at marriage of Margaret of Anjou, 277; impeached and murdered, 324–5

INDEX

TIGNONVILLE, Guillaume de: Provost of Paris, 34; removed from post, 45
TOURAINE, John, Duke of: marries Jacqueline of Hainault, 30; becomes
    dauphin, 138; dies, 142
TOURS, Treaty of, signed, 270
TROYES, Treaty of, 153

VALENTINA VISCONTI, Duchess of Orleans: marries Louis, then Duke of
    Touraine, 3; her first children, 14; gives birth to Charles, 15; banished
    from Paris, 16; pleads for justice for Louis' murder, 40, 47–8; dies, 49; her
    devices and emblems, 50
VAULX, Pierre de: physician to Valentina, 20; lends Charles silver cups, 77;
    prescribes for him in Blois, 93; is paid for cups, 122
VENDÔME, the *Lit de Justice*, 332–4
VENDÔME, Louis, Count of: prisoner at Agincourt, 129; helps Charles, 152
VERNEUIL, battle of, 162
VERTUS, Philip, Count of: born, 22; present at Peace of Chartres, 54–6; and
    Auxerre, 81; escapes from Paris during Cabochien riots, 91; leads
    dauphin's faction, 147–54; dies, 154; his will, 155
VILLON, at Blois, 301, and Orleans, 336

WATERTON, Robert; Constable of Pontefract: has charge of different prisoners,
    144–5, 151; Henry V's suspicions of, 150–1
WINGFIELD, Castle of, 187

YOLANDA OF ARAGON, Duchess of Anjou: brings up dauphin Charles, 199;
    invited by Charles of Orleans to peace conference, 199; her children, 199